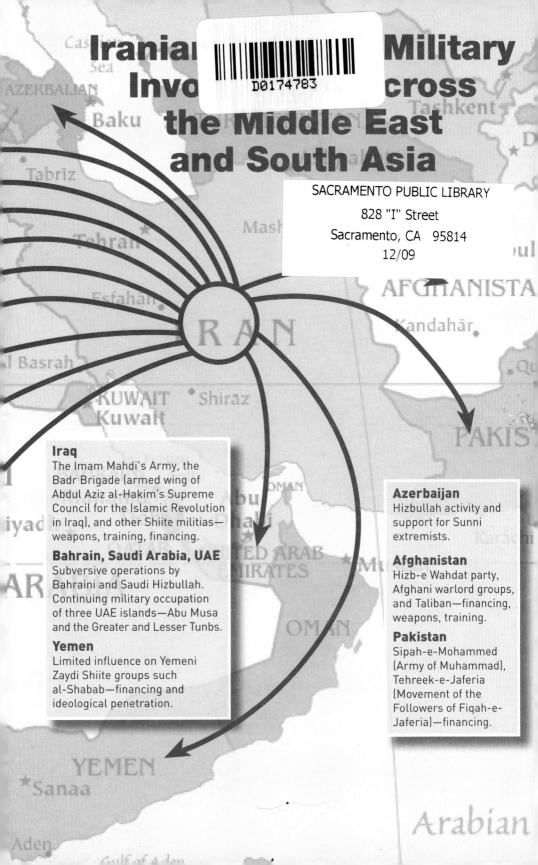

Iranian Military Involvement Across the Middle East and South Asia

Iraq
The Imam Mahdi's Army, the Badr Brigade (armed wing of Abdul Aziz al-Hakim's Supreme Council for the Islamic Revolution in Iraq), and other Shiite militias—weapons, training, financing.

Bahrain, Saudi Arabia, UAE
Subversive operations by Bahraini and Saudi Hizbullah. Continuing military occupation of three UAE islands—Abu Musa and the Greater and Lesser Tunbs.

Yemen
Limited influence on Yemeni Zaydi Shiite groups such al-Shabab—financing and ideological penetration.

Azerbaijan
Hizbullah activity and support for Sunni extremists.

Afghanistan
Hizb-e Wahdat party, Afghani warlord groups, and Taliban—financing, weapons, training.

Pakistan
Sipah-e-Mohammed (Army of Muhammad), Tehreek-e-Jaferia (Movement of the Followers of Fiqah-e-Jaferia)—financing.

THE RISE OF NUCLEAR IRAN

HOW TEHRAN DEFIES THE WEST

THE RISE OF NUCLEAR IRAN

HOW TEHRAN DEFIES THE WEST

DORE GOLD

Since 1947
REGNERY
PUBLISHING, INC.
An Eagle Publishing Company • Washington, DC

Library of Congress Cataloging-in-Publication Data

    Gold, Dore.
     The rise of nuclear Iran : how Tehran defies the West / Dore Gold.
       p. cm.
     Includes bibliographical references and index.
     ISBN 978-1-59698-571-1 (alk. paper)
     1. Nuclear weapons—Iran. 2. Nuclear energy—Government policy—
Iran. 3. Nuclear arms control—Iran. 4. Iran—Foreign relations—1997- I.
Title.
     UA853.I7G65 2009
     355.02'170955—dc22

                          2009029556

Published in the United States by
Regnery Publishing, Inc.
One Massachusetts Avenue, NW
Washington, DC 20001
www.regnery.com

Manufactured in the United States of America

10 9 8 7 6 5 4 3 2 1

Books are available in quantity for promotional or premium use. Write to
Director of Special Sales, Regnery Publishing, Inc., One Massachusetts
Avenue NW, Washington, DC 20001, for information on discounts and
terms or call (202) 216-0600.

Distributed to the trade by:
Perseus Distribution
387 Park Avenue South
New York, NY 10016

To my father, Isadore Glasband,
whose untimely death affected my whole life.

Contents

PART 3: WHY WESTERN DIALOGUE WITH IRAN FAILED

A Note on Terms

In order to assist the English-speaking reader, the spelling of Arabic and Farsi terms throughout this book has been based on common usage in the United States and the United Kingdom (i.e., spellings commonly used by major newspapers and government agencies), and not on formal transliteration.

Glossary

Ayatollah—The "Sign of Allah." The highest level of authority for a Shiite cleric.

Basij—Literally, "Mobilization." Paramilitary force serving along side of the Revolutionary Guards as a reserve force. Formally merged with the Revolutionary Guards in 2007.

Faqih—A theologian or jurisprudent.

Fatwa—A formal legal opinion on Islamic law.

GIA—French Acronym for "Armed Islamic Group." GIA seeks to overthrow the Algerian government and establish an Islamic state. Receives Iranian aid. GIA has been designated as an international terrorist organization by the U.S. Department of State.

Hamas—Arabic acronym for "Islamic Resistance Movement." Founded in 1987, Hamas serves as the Palestinian branch of the Muslim Brotherhood. Hamas has been designated by the U.S. Department of State as an international terrorist organization.

Hojatieh—A secret Shiite society in Iran, founded in 1954, that supported violent measures against memebers of the Bahai faith. It also sought to spread the belief among its adherents that they had to prepare for the return of the Hidden Imam. Ahmadinejad was likely influenced by the Hojatieh.

Hizbullah—Literally, "Party of God." Formed in 1982, Hizbullah is a pro-Iranian Lebanese Shiite Militia. Iran created Hizbullah offshoots in the Arabian Peninsula. Designated as an international terrorist organization by the U.S. Department of State.

Hojat al-Islam—Proof of Islam. The title of middle-ranking mullahs just one level below ayatollah.

Imam—Prayer leader. In Twelver Shiite Islam, the Imam is one of the twelve descendents of Ali. The Twelfth Imam is currently the Hidden Imam, but will be revealed as the *Mahdi*.

Jihad—Literally, struggle. Originally a holy war waged by Muslims against hostile non-Muslims or for conquest of territory for Islam.

Jahaliyah—The period of ignorance or darkness in pre-Islamic Arabia before the Prophet Muhammad spread Islam in the seventh century.

Kafir—Infidel. All mankind except the Muslims and the *ahl-e-kitab* (the people of the book).

Khod'eh—Tricking the enemy into misjudging his position.

Mahdi—Literally, "The Guided One." A figure who will appear just before the "end of days," who is also the Twelfth Imam.

Majlis—Iranian Parliament.

Maktab—Religious elementary school.

Mujtahid—Cleric who may interpret the Koran.

Mullah—Derived from the Arabic word *mawla* meaning "master." Used as a title for a religious scholar in Iran.

Rahbar—Supreme Leader.

Sayyed—A descendant of the Prophet and as such entitled to special honors and monetary benefits from charitable donations. (Literally, gentleman).

Tahdiya—Literally, a calm. A temporary lull in the fighting between Israel and Hamas, which they negotiated indirectly through the Egyptians. A tahdiya is far less formal than a cease-fire agreement between two parties.

Taqiya—Dissimulation. Hiding one's true faith and beliefs when in a position of weakness.

Ulama—The religious leadership. Singular: alim.

Velayat-e faqih—Rule by the jurisprudent.

Introduction:

Diplomacy or Democracy

THE RISE OF A NUCLEAR IRAN appeared to be a forgone conclusion on the eve of the Iranian presidential elections of June 12, 2009. The election did not look like it was going to change that direction. Indeed, all four candidates supported continuation of the Iranian nuclear program. Each came from the heart of the Iranian establishment and their very candidacies had to be pre-approved by Iran's powerful Guardian Council, half of whose members were directly appointed by Iran's Supreme Leader Ayatollah Ali Khamenei. In any case, while the Iranian president had a voice in nuclear matters, it was the un-elected Supreme Leader who had the ultimate authority in deciding Iranian nuclear policy and the direction of any future negotiations with the West as a whole.

In fact, the leading challenger to President Mahmoud Ahmadinejad, former Prime Minister Mir Hossein Mousavi, had been significantly involved in launching the Iranian effort to procure black market centrifuges for the enrichment of uranium in 1987,[1] as classified documents obtained by the International Atomic Energy Agency [IAEA] prove.[2] Moreover, former Iranian President Hashemi Rafsanjani, who emerged as a key Mousavi ally, had been one of the most important sponsors of the Iranian nuclear program throughout the late 1980s and early 1990s.

Though Mousavi was leading the reformist wave in the streets of Tehran against the Iranian regime in 2009, at the time of the 1979 Islamic Revolution he was known as an ideological hard-liner who participated in the interrogation of U.S. diplomats who had been taken hostage in the U.S. Embassy in Tehran. He additionally called for putting them on trial in the editorials that he wrote for the official newspaper of the Islamic Republican Party. Mousavi served as prime minister under Ayatollah Ruhollah Khomeini (Iran's first Supreme Leader) from 1981 to 1989. His government was known for its purges of the Iranian bureaucracy and advancing strict Islamic laws.[3] He was thrust into his new role as a symbol of real democratic change more by circumstances than by his past career.

What ignited the streets of Tehran was not Mousavi's popularity but rather the sense that the Iranian elections had been rigged. The Iranian regime argued that Ahmadinejad won in every one of Iran's thirty provinces and received nearly 63 percent of the votes that had been cast—twice as many as Mousavi. Most observers expected a close race. Yet it was claimed that Ahmadinejad received not only a massive majority but also an unprecedented mandate, given that voter turnout reached roughly 85 percent. In 2009, the Supreme Leader declared Ahmadinejad the winner even before the publication of the official results.

Moreover, further undermining the credibility of the results was the Iranian government's announcing the results of the presidential elections within two hours of the polls closing, an incredibly short amount of time considering the 40 million paper ballots which were cast.[4]

Adding to the general suspicion was the memory that there had been serious questions about the election returns when Ahmadinejad was first elected to the presidency in 2005. After gaining only 19.5 percent of the vote during the first round of voting, he unexpectedly won the second round with 64 percent of the vote. These results caused many at the time to suspect that the results of Iranian elections had been arranged in advance.[5]

In both elections, the direct involvement of the Islamic Revolutionary Guard Corps helped advance Ahmadinejad. The Revolutionary Guards and especially their large paramilitary mobilization units—known as the Basij—served as campaign activists for Ahmadinejad in his 2005 election. Ahmadinejad, who himself had been an officer in an engineering unit connected to the Revolutionary Guards during the Iran-Iraq War,[6] reciprocated by appointing fellow veterans of the Revolutionary Guards to more than half the positions in his cabinet.[7] In 2009, the election process was under the control of another handpicked Revolutionary Guards general who controlled the Interior Ministry.[8]

The Revolutionary Guards are best known as the loyal protectors of the Islamic Republic. They have the most sensitive security assignments, including responsibility for the military side of the Iranian nuclear program. Yet, the overall power of the Revolutionary Guards within Iran's political system has been steadily growing in recent years. By 2007, the Revolutionary Guards were estimated to control about one third of the Iranian economy through subsidiary companies and trusts.[9] Their corporations won lucrative infrastructure contracts, which only built up their wealth and internal power. They also began to run candidates in Iranian elections in order to block Iranian reformists, giving the impression that they were engaged in a "creeping" takeover of Iranian political life.[10] At the same time, other centers of power, like Iran's clerics, had been declining in influence. They constituted the majority in the first Majlis, or Parliament, of the Islamic Republic in the early 1980s, but by the time of the last parliamentary elections on March 2008, the clerics had only 30 representatives out of a total of 290.[11] As the power of the military grew, even the Islamic Republic's clerical leadership held less sway.

Ahmadinejad's electoral victory was the latest development in a long-term process that had been underway for years. Some serious analysts have concluded that the 2009 elections amounted to nothing less than a military coup by the Revolutionary Guards and the conversion of Iran from a theocratic state with partially democratic institutions to an outright military dictatorship.[12] Symbolically, the street clashes of June 2009 pitted the Revolutionary Guards and their Basij units—backing up the riot police—against reformist demonstrators seeking to prevent the corruption of what remained of Iran's limited electoral system.

Since he came to power in 1989, the Supreme Leader Ayatollah Ali Khamenei enjoyed political legitimacy that emanated from the religious status associated with his position that had been created by his predecessor, Ayatollah Khomeini, in the aftermath of the 1979 Islamic Revolution. The coercive measures employed by the regime have eroded that legitimacy and made the Iranian leader more reliant on military force and on an alliance with the Revolutionary Guards.

There were earlier demonstrations against the ruling elite of the Islamic Republic. For example, in July 1999, thousands of students in Tehran University revolted shouting "Down with the Dictator" as they called for greater freedom in Iran.[13] The student movement spread to other Iranian provinces, mobilizing more than a million young people. The regime crushed the demonstrators and arrested thousands. With the events of June 2009, Iranian protestors openly challenged the legitimacy of the ruling military elite who were busy using the new political atmosphere to consolidate their power and control over the Iranian state. The emerging triumvirate of power consisted of Ayatollah Khamenei, President Ahmadinejad, and the Revolutionary Guards.

The Iranian clerics were split over this new shape of Iran. Indeed, on June 19, 2009, when Khamenei addressed his supporters at Tehran University, during the height of the street riots, many mullahs stayed away. Nonetheless, Khamenei was not left standing alone; the powerful Assembly of Experts, an elected body of 86 religious leaders, which has the authority to replace the Supreme Leader, came out the following day with a statement expressing its "strong support" for his Tehran speech.[14]

These developments in Iran posed a series of difficult dilemmas for the Obama administration. President Barack Obama had come to power only six months earlier, dedicated to the idea that his foreign policy team, unlike that of the Bush administration, would undertake a high-level political dialogue with Iran. Through this new policy of "engagement," Obama hoped that Iran could be persuaded to halt its drive for nuclear weapons, before it actually acquires an atomic bomb. As an early first step, Obama issued a statement in March, on the occasion of the Iranian holiday of Nowruz, in which he said that the United States wants the Islamic Republic of Iran to take its rightful place in the community of nations."[15] To make engagement work, Iran could not be categorized as an enemy.

For this reason, in reacting to the events in Iran during June 2009, Obama did not want to be perceived as tilting to the side of the Iranian regime or to the demonstrators in the streets. He sympathized with the Iranian protestors, but did not want to kill the chances of success of one of the central pillars of his Middle East policy: diplomatically engaging with the Iranian regime in the future over its nuclear program and its support for terrorism.[16] Obama's neutrality on developments in Iran reached its height when he declared: "It's important to understand that although there is some ferment taking place in Iran, that the difference between Ahmadinejad and Moussavi in terms of their actual policies may not be as great as advertised."[17]

Obama's statement was intellectually correct and even appropriate if it had been made in a closed meeting in the White House,
but as a public declaration it made him seem indifferent to the
tremendous sacrifices being made daily by brave Iranians standing
up to Khamenei's security forces in the name of democracy. For a
regime whose political legitimacy had eroded as it came to rely
increasingly on the instruments of repression, the stand of the
United States toward Iran could be important for the opposition.
If the opposition forces expect that the United States and the West
are about to reach an accommodation with the Iranian regime that
will improve Iran's economic and global standing, then they will
have much less incentive to continue a struggle that they will perceive to be hopeless.

Obama's reaction to events in Iran sparked an intense debate in
the United States. Reportedly, the administration had been split on
the issue with Vice President Joseph Biden and Secretary of State
Hillary Clinton privately calling for a harder line against the Iranian government than that advocated by Obama. His Republican
opposition was sharply critical of his Iran policy. The House
Minority Whip, Representative Eric Cantor (R-Virginia) insisted
that Obama jettison his "equivocal" posture and issue a statement
with "moral clarity" that backed the Iranian people.[18] Obama's
opponent in the 2008 presidential race, Senator John McCain (R-
Arizona) concluded that as a consequence of Obama's stance, the
European heads of state had provided the Iranian demonstrators
with more support than the United States had offered.[19]

A little over ten days after the Iranian elections, Obama finally
hardened his tone toward Iran and condemned the government's
crackdown against the demonstrators. He said he was "appalled
and outraged by the threats, beatings and imprisonments of the
past few days." But beyond his adoption of tougher language,
Obama did not propose a new line of policy to replace his hope of
reaching out to the Iranian government with a new diplomatic
overture.

As events in Iran develop over time, it is clear that the Obama administration is not about to quickly abandon its policy of engagement with Iran. At some point, high-level U.S. negotiators might very well sit opposite their Iranian counterparts seeking to persuade them to comply with the repeated demands of the international community to verifiably halt their determined drive to obtain nuclear weapons. The ongoing backing of the Islamic Republic of international terrorism, regional subversion, and the undermining of human rights are also likely to be raised. But the nuclear question will be the main issue the two sides will need to address if a negotiation between them begins.

With engagement at the center of U.S. Iran policy, it is imperative to understand how Iran managed to defy the efforts of the West to halt its nuclear program for at least a decade or more. For engagement is not a new idea or policy. Indeed, it can be shown that virtually every U.S. administration has sought to diplomatically engage with Iran since the Islamic Revolution in 1979— including the administration of President George W. Bush. More importantly, the Europeans actually engaged with Iran on the nuclear issue in order to halt its uranium enrichment efforts, resulting in agreements that were subsequently violated by the Iranians.

In order to avert the failures of the past, it is critical to examine what happened during these past efforts at engagement and establish what exactly went wrong. This inquiry might also answer a more fundamental question of whether diplomacy with the Islamic Republic is the best line of policy to stop its march to nuclear weapons or alternatively, whether the demonstrators who seek democracy and political freedom should be backed. It just might be that freedom is not only an objective value that should be protected, but a source of global security as well.

Part 1:

THE ANATOMY OF DIPLOMATIC FAILURE

Chapter 1:

The Art of Diplomatic Deception

FROM 2003 TO 2005, Iran's chief nuclear negotiator was Hassan Rowhani. He represented Iran in the key negotiations that resulted in a temporary suspension of its uranium enrichment activities in 2003. Despite being replaced in August 2005, anything he might utter about Iran's nuclear program was extremely sensitive, even after he no longer had the job. This did not hold Rowhani back from making a staggering disclosure in a speech delivered in a closed-door meeting in Tehran as he was leaving his post, when he bragged that he had successfully outmaneuvered—and essentially deceived—the western powers, led by the European Union, with whom he had negotiated: "When we were negotiating with the Europeans in Tehran, we were installing equipment in parts of the facility in Isfahan."[1]

Isfahan was known by western intelligence agencies to be precisely where the Iranians had erected a facility for completing the second important stage in the production of fuel for their clandestine nuclear weapons program: the conversion of uranium "yellowcake," partly processed uranium ore, to a uranium gas, known as uranium hexafluoride, or UF_6. Then UF_6 gas could be inserted into thousands of gas centrifuges at another Iranian nuclear plant and

---

IRAN'S CLANDESTINE NUCLEAR FUEL PRODUCTION PROCESS

Description of Nuclear Activity	Nuclear Product		Nuclear Facility
Stage 1 Uranium mining and processing	"Yellow Cake"		Saghand, Gachin
Stage 2 Uranium conversion	UF_6 (Uranium Hexafluoride)		Isfahan
Stage 3 Uranium enrichment	5% U-235 Uranium Fuel for nuclear reactors	90% U-235 Uranium Fuel for atomic bombs	Natantz

The only difference between Uranium fuel for civilian purposes and atomic bombs is how enriched it becomes.

---

spun at high speed to yield exactly the kind of highly enriched uranium needed to produce nuclear weapons.

Rowhani was proud of Iran's technological success in completing this second critical stage of uranium fuel production. He explained that Iranian diplomacy had succeeded in providing Tehran with the time it urgently needed so that, in his words, "...we were able to complete the work on Isfahan."[2] He boasted that as a result of what his diplomacy had accomplished, "the world would face a fait accompli" which "would change the entire equation."[3] In another interview, he detailed the real magnitude of Iran's success by relying on the diplomatic process with Europe: "The day we started the process, there was no such thing as the Isfahan project."[4] Thus, while Rowhani sat at the negotiating table, participating in the first trial run of the West's engagement with it over the nuclear question, Iran quietly moved from having no uranium conversion capability whatsoever to actually completing its clandestine conversion plant.

In fact, during the period of its nuclear talks with the Europeans, Iran began actually converting 37 tons of yellowcake into UF_6 at Isfahan. According to western assessments, that amount was sufficient to generate enough nuclear fuel for building five atomic bombs.[5] Iran also had 164 centrifuges for uranium enrichment when negotiations with the Europeans began. But by the time Rowhani left his position in 2005, the number of Iranian centrifuges went up to nearly 1,000.[6] The more centrifuges they had, the sooner they would be able to produce enough material for a single nuclear device. Once the Iranians reached 3,000 centrifuges, they would be able to produce enough material in one year for a single nuclear bomb. In short, Rowhani's diplomacy had moved the Iranian nuclear program much closer to reaching this military goal.

Though the Iranians argued with their western counterparts that their entire uranium enrichment effort was intended to fuel a peaceful civilian program, there was a huge hole in their argument. Tehran had kept its nuclear program a complete secret for almost two decades. Rowhani only began to negotiate with the Europeans when Iran's nuclear infrastructure was disclosed in 2002. If the Iranian nuclear program was a legitimate civilian effort to produce electricity, then why was it hidden from the world?[7]

It was significant that Iran did not have a single nuclear reactor operating for the generation of electricity, undercutting its argument that its nuclear program was for civilian purposes. Tehran also had special arrangements with Russia for fueling its still incomplete Bushehr reactor, on the shores of the Persian Gulf, that was declared to be for civilian use.

In any case, most countries that had nuclear reactors for electricity did not seek to build up a uranium enrichment capability, largely because it was uneconomical[8]—countries like South Korea, Finland, and Sweden, which imported nuclear fuel rather than going to great expense to manufacture it domestically.[9] This should have been all the more true for a country with vast oil and natural gas resources. Iran clearly had other priorities.

Hassan Rowhani knew the details of what he was talking about. He served as chief nuclear negotiator by virtue of his position as the Secretary of the Supreme National Security Council of Iran, a consultative body that brought together the heads of Iran's intelligence and military services with its political leadership. He had been in that position for sixteen years.[10] Therefore, he had been exposed to some of the most sensitive decisions Iran had made in defense and foreign affairs since 1989. Rowhani was not trained as a professional diplomat or as a nuclear physicist; rather, he had been a theology student in Qom. Nevertheless, he had been an insider among Iran's clerical rulers, and for many years had been a political ally of the Supreme Leader, Ayatollah Ali Khamenei.

Rowhani had his own ulterior motives for speaking so openly about his successful manipulation of the West. He had served as chief nuclear negotiator during the presidency of Mohammad Khatami, who was regarded in the West as a pragmatic reformer. After the 2005 presidential elections brought Mohammad Ahmadinejad to power, Rowhani was dismissed from his position as Secretary of the Supreme National Security Council. It is likely that he wanted to impress more hard-line circles in Tehran with what he had accomplished during his term. But regardless of his motivation, his disclosures were a shocking glimpse into Iranian motivations.

Rowhani's startling remarks that the Iranian nuclear program was steadily progressing despite western diplomatic efforts were circulated in an internal regime journal read by Iran's ruling elite, called *Rahbord*, that was published in late 2005. Reporting on Rowhani's speech on April 3, 2006, Britain's *Daily Telegraph* ran a headline that tersely captured the significance of what he had said: "How We Duped the West, by Iran's Nuclear Negotiator."[11]

Rowhani also boasted successfully driving a wedge between the United States and the Europeans, who remained determined to engage Tehran despite all the warnings they had received from Washington: "From the outset, the Americans kept telling the Europeans, 'The Iranians are lying and deceiving you and they have not told you everything.'" Rowhani then derisively noted: "The Europeans used to respond, 'We trust them.'"[12]

Rowhani's confession was not a fluke, for he was not alone in characterizing Iranian diplomacy this way. His deputy, Hossein Musavian, made the very same point several months earlier on Iranian Channel 2 television: "Thanks to the negotiations with Europe we gained another year, in which we completed (the uranium conversion facility) in Isfahan."[13] A third Iranian negotiator also admitted that the Iranian authorities simply "needed to gain time to see certain projects through unimpeded."[14]

Then there was the admission of Abdollah Ramezanzadeh, government spokesman under President Khatami, who looked back on this entire period and summarized Iranian negotiating strategy succinctly: "We had an overt policy, which was one of negotiation and confidence building, and a covert policy, which was a continuation of the activities."[15]

This policy of diplomatic deception had another element. He explained how important it was for Iran "to prove to the entire world" that it needed nuclear power plants for electricity. He then added rather ominously: "Afterwards, we can proceed with *other activities*" (emphasis added).[16] Outwardly, Iran wanted the peaceful use of nuclear energy, but its hidden intention, according to Ramezanzadeh, was to engage in "other activities," which it preferred to hide.

From the statements of these former officials, it became clear that the purpose of Iranian diplomacy was not to reach the kind of new agreements with the Europeans who hoped for signing ceremonies with great fanfare in front of dozens of network television cameras. Iran's former deputy foreign minister, Mohammad Javad Larijani, proposed a very different logic for Iran's diplomatic engagement with the West: "Diplomacy must be used to lessen pressure on Iran for its nuclear program."[17] He added that diplomacy was, for him, a "tool for allowing us to attain our goals."

Mohammad Javad Larijani's insights were especially important to consider since his brother, Ali Larijani, had replaced Hassan Rowhani as the head Iranian nuclear negotiator after Ahmadinejad came to power. Ali Larijani did not sound much different than Rowhani in his understanding of Iranian diplomatic strategy. He told Iran's Network 2 in November 2006 that as the nuclear talks with the West dragged on, Iran continued to record successes in nuclear technology.[18] When their statements in Farsi—the Persian language—were examined, as opposed to what they said for external consumption, the Iranians were remarkably candid about their intentions, despite their efforts to hide them from western negotiators.

Thus, while the European Union was hoping that through its diplomacy with Iran it could achieve an agreed suspension of Tehran's nuclear activities, Iran was using diplomacy to accelerate its nuclear work. As Mohammad Javad Larijani openly stated, "Iran should expand its nuclear program and use diplomacy to realize this goal."[19] For Rowhani and his colleagues, negotiations were not a means for resolving a difficult international problem or producing what in the West would be called a win-win situation. The nuclear talks were a "contest of wills" for Tehran and not an opportunity to reach some kind of "common ground" through compromise.[20] In their view, what gave an international agreement value was not the idea that a more peaceful outcome had been reached, but that Iranian interests had been advanced.

Ultimately, Rowhani's statements unveiled a fundamental belief that negotiations were an opportunity to protect Iran's national power, by advancing its nuclear program, as well as a means to defeat the efforts of its opponents to curtail it.[21] Diplomatic duplicity—saying one thing at the negotiating table while doing the exact opposite—was not something of which to be ashamed, but rather could be a source of national pride. For that reason, former Iranian officials from across Tehran's foreign policy establishment spoke about it so openly.

What Rowhani's admission also demonstrated was that Europe's efforts at diplomatic engagement with Iran over its nuclear program had indeed been tried and had utterly failed. The Europeans' commitment to diplomatic engagement had been completely exploited by Iran. By coming to the negotiating table, Iran not only went forward with developing its uranium enrichment work, but also succeeded in fending off the pressures the West was considering to get it to stop. Iran delayed referral of its file to the UN Security Council, its allies watered down UN resolutions as they were drafted, and it saw to it that the very threat of a military option was removed, even while the United States and its allies tried to argue that all the options for a western response were still on the table.

If the West tries diplomatic engagement again with the Islamic Republic, it would have to be formulated very differently. It is essential to understand why engagement has never worked. And even if the errors of the Europeans' engagement with Tehran are averted in the future through newly designed diplomatic initiatives by the United States and its allies, it is far from clear whether they would obtain any positive results. And yet preventing Iran from obtaining nuclear weapons is becoming imperative.

Chapter 2:

Could the Islamic Republic of Iran Be Deterred?

W HAT ROWHANI DID NOT DARE SAY in public was that the western world would shortly face an Islamic Republic of Iran armed with operational nuclear weapons. The full significance of this development had often been overlooked in the West. Few viewed Iran as a state that already had all the attributes of what diplomats used to call "a great power" despite the fact that its population numbered nearly seventy million (three times the population of Iraq). Yet Iran's vast land area, stretching from Turkey in the west to Afghanistan in the east, was greater than France, Germany, and Great Britain combined.

During the twentieth century, the United States and its western allies had to confront and deter great powers seeking to dominate the whole of the European continent. That had been the impetus for American intervention in two world wars—and in the Cold War as well. The emergence of a single hegemonic state subjugating all of Europe, it was feared, could alter the entire global balance of power. In contrast, with the exception of the 1990 Iraqi invasion of Kuwait, Middle Eastern states seeking military domination of their neighbors were rarely judged as posing a threat great enough to warrant an assertive military response.

But an Iran with nuclear weapons would not be just another Middle Eastern country whose leadership was seeking merely to guarantee its political survival or intimidate its neighbors. Since 1979, the Islamic Republic had openly exhibited its aspirations for regional supremacy, which would only be magnified by its crossing the nuclear threshold. This would pose a similar challenge to what the West had encountered in Europe decades earlier.

Ever since ancient times, Iranians had called their territory Iran, though until 1935 the world referred to it as Persia. And given its long history, Iran possessed the ambition to have its true weight as a great power felt beyond its borders on a global scale. Iranians recall the central role played by the pre-Islamic Persian Empire in the ancient world. Iran is not an Arab state; Iranians are distinguishable from their Arab neighbors by virtue of their language, ethnicity, and their historical memory. In fact, to refer to an Iranian as an "Arab" is considered an insult.

While the pre-Islamic period known as the *jahaliyah,* or "period of ignorance," is typically not a source of historical pride in most of the Arab states, among Iranian leaders a very different perspective has prevailed. Past presidents of the modern-day Islamic Republic, like Mohammad Khatami, would speak with pride about "Iran's glorious civilization" which, in his words, was "concurrent with the Greek city states and the Roman Empire."[1]

Iran also had a more recent imperial past than the Greeks or Romans under the Safavid Empire (1501–1722), whose founder, Shah Ismail, instituted the largest branch of Shiite Islam—known as Twelver Shiism—as Iran's state religion. Despite the campaign he launched to convert the Iranian population to Shiism, there remained important pockets in Iran where Sunni Islam was practiced, especially among ethnic minorities that included Arabs, Baluchis, Kurds, and Turkmen.

For centuries, Shiites had essentially been a persecuted minority sect in Islam that initially differed from mainstream adherents of Sunni Islam over the question of who was the successor of the Prophet Muhammad: those who supported Muhammad's son-in-law, Ali, as opposed to the Sunni Caliphs, came to be known as the "Party of Ali" (*shi 'at 'ali*). These differences over the succession evolved into theological differences, particularly over the special spiritual status of the eleven descendents of Ali, who were known by Twelver Shiites as Imams.

Moreover, the martyrdom of the Third Imam, Hussein, in a war with the Ummayad Caliphate, became a defining historical event, which for many Shiites served as a model to be emulated. With the rise of the Safavids, the largest of the Shiite traditions with its own cult of martyrdom, became grafted onto the Iranian state, along with its long-term struggle with the majority Sunni world. Indeed, in the sixteenth century, the Safavid Shahs waged wars against the Sunni Sultans of the Ottoman Empire.

For this purpose, Shah Abbas brilliantly manipulated the European powers, unveiling the Iranians' extraordinary skill in international power politics. He deceived the Portuguese, leading them to believe that he was considering converting to Christianity in order to win their support and to cement an alliance against the Ottomans. At the same time, he built a relationship with the British, who ultimately helped him assault Portuguese garrisons in the Persian Gulf and evict their forces from the area. Abbas fused diplomacy and military power in order to realize his imperial ambitions and to advance the cause of Shiite Islam.[2]

At its zenith, the Safavid Empire extended its rule well beyond Iran's present borders into Central Asia in the north as well as into parts of western Afghanistan and Pakistan in the east. Even today, the language used in much of Afghanistan, Dari, is a Persian dialect. To the west, the Safavid Empire covered half of Iraq, where Iran had deep historical influence. Indeed the name Baghdad, which literally means "God given," is derived from a combination of two Persian words, indicating the long Iranian connections to this territory.

The Safavid Empire itself, moreover, reached southward to the Persian Gulf, where it even extended to the shores of parts of the Arabian side of the coast.[3] The Arab states along the western shores of the Persian Gulf are fully aware of this history. In fact, given his concern that the Iraq War in 2003 was going to lead to Iraq coming under Iranian domination, Saudi Arabia's King Abdullah once berated a high-level U.S. official: "You have allowed the Persians, the Safavids, to take over Iraq."[4] The large pockets of Shiite populations that still were a part of these Arab states were a constant reminder that they contained areas which Iran once governed or influenced.

At a minimum, these areas continued to be seen as part of modern Iran's sphere of influence, and some, like Bahrain, have been proclaimed at times to be part of Iran itself. Indeed, in a major news conference after his election victory in 2005, President Mahmoud Ahmadinejad declared that his government would "give priority to the establishment of relations" not only with Iran's neighbors, but specifically "with countries that once fell within the zone of Iran's civilization."[5]

Given this background, it can be reasonably asserted that Iran perceives itself as a natural hegemonic power in its region.[6] With roughly one tenth of the world's supply of oil and natural gas, Iran had the financial capacity to acquire the military strength it needed to realize many of its historical ambitions.

But Iran is not just any other influential state which is about to cross the nuclear threshold; there are serious reasons to doubt whether the concept of deterrence, which had been used effectively during the Cold War to prevent nuclear attacks by the Soviet Union on the United States and its NATO allies, could be relevant

Modern Iran Compared to the Territorial Extent of the 16th Century Safavid Empire

to an Islamic theocracy that so idealizes the cult of martyrdom. Given that the Islamic Republic was the first to systematically employ suicide bombing attacks in the present era, it could very well be immune to deterrence and the threat of full scale retaliation should it employ nuclear weapons.

Since Ayatollah Ruhollah Khomeini came to power in 1979, establishing the Islamic Republic, Iran has not acted like the typical state, carefully calibrating its national interests, but rather as the vanguard of a revolutionary movement. Its Constitution openly calls for the "continuation of the Revolution at home and abroad." Just after the Revolution, Khomeini, in one of his most controversial comments, said, "We do not worship Iran, we worship Allah. For patriotism is another name for paganism. I say let this land burn. I say let this land go up in smoke, provided Islam emerges triumphant in the rest of the world."[7]

Iran indeed defied the kind of rational behavior that might have been expected of a state in its identical situation. In its early years, it did not appear to fully weigh the balance of power and limit its own actions accordingly. For example, even during its long and difficult eight-year war with Iraq from 1980 through 1988, when it badly needed spare parts for its embattled armed forces, Iran was fully prepared to wage asymmetric warfare against the United States through organizations it created, like Hizbullah, which launched suicide bombing attacks on multiple U.S. targets, including the U.S. Marine Corps Barracks in Beirut, where 241 American servicemen were killed on October 23, 1983.[8]

Though Iran operated through front organizations that took credit for the Beirut operation, Tehran left no doubt about its own pivotal role in that assault, having dispatched its Revolutionary Guards to train the perpetrators in Lebanon's Bekaa Valley. They made no effort to hide their involvement; their presence was very much out in the open. According to U.S. intelligence intercepts of Iranian communications, Iran even used their ambassador to Damascus (and "godfather" of Hizbullah) Hojat al-Islam Ali Akbar Mohtashemi-Pour (hereafter, Mohtashemi) to orchestrate the bombing itself.[9]

Rather than a one-time event, this was an outright campaign against America. Earlier in the year, Hizbullah bombed the U.S. Embassy in Beirut, and a little less than two months after the Marine barracks attack, Iranian-sponsored attacks were launched on the U.S. and French embassies in Kuwait, which, like Lebanon, also had a substantial Shiite population which Iran sought to penetrate and recruit.[10] In the years that followed, Hizbullah seized western hostages in Lebanon; American citizens, but also British, French, and German nationals, as well.

But it was Iran's behavior on the battlefield with Iraq in the 1980s that most seriously raised doubts about whether it could be deterred like most states. Motivated by powerful revolutionary zeal, Iran persisted during the conflict in launching human wave attacks against a better-equipped Iraqi Army, including whole formations of twelve- to fifteen-year-old children, recruited by the Revolutionary Guards to clear minefields for the Iranian Army.[11]

Emulating the martyrdom of the Third Imam, Hussein, was translated in the 1980s into acts of self-sacrifice by Iranian troops against the Iraqis and into suicide bombing operations by Iranian-supported groups, like Hizbullah.

At the height of the Iran-Iraq War, the child volunteers of Iran were part of the Revolutionary Guards' mobilization force, known as the *Basij*. They reached a total strength of 400,000 soldiers.[12] The commanders of the *Basij* not only provided Iran with an ideological vanguard for suicide operations in the 1980s, but also a battle-hardened background for many men who acquired positions of power two decades later, as the Iranian nuclear program reached completion.

The Iran-Iraq War could have been over after its first two years, when Iran recovered the territories it lost from the initial assault that had been launched by the armies of Saddam Hussein in 1980. But Iran kept the war going for another six long years, despite losing hundreds of thousands of its people and facing repeated Iraqi chemical weapons attacks on it troops. Iran could not be deterred. The Islamic Republic continued to fight on, even as Tehran itself absorbed hundreds of Iraqi missile attacks towards the war's end. Furthermore, its naval units were prepared to harass and even attack the superior forces of the U.S. Navy in the Persian Gulf at the same time.

At the time of the Islamic Revolution, a leading religious leader who was close to Khomeini, Dr. Hadi Modaressi, provided some insight into this military behavior that would become a trademark of Tehran's policies in the coming years: "We welcome military aggression against us because it strengthens the revolution and rallies the masses around it."[13]

When Ayatollah Khomeini died in 1989, the critical question of whether Iran would respond to the same calculations of deterrence as other states remained. Khomeini was replaced by Ayatollah Ali Khamenei, who became Iran's new Supreme Leader. Iran did not become a *status quo* power. As Hossein Shariatmadari, one of

Khamenei's key spokesmen, and his hand-picked editor-in-chief of the daily *Kayhan*, explained, "We uphold the worldwide Islamic movement. We believe the world order should change."[14]

Khamenei himself was even more direct in a statement quoted in the Iranian daily *Ressalat* on July 7, 1991:

> Where do we look in drawing up the National Security strategy of the Islamic Republic of Iran? Do we look to preserve the integrity of our land, or do we look to its expansion? Do we look to *bast* (expansion) or to *hefz* (preservation)? We must definitely look to expansion. The Islamic Republic's survival depends on the support of a global Islamic force.[15]

Despite acquiring two relatively pragmatic presidents in domestic affairs from 1989 to 2005, Ali Akbar Rafsanjani and then Mohammad Khatami, foreign and defense policy was still mostly dominated by the hard-line Khamenei, who eventually called himself "Supreme Leader of Muslims" and not just "Supreme Leader of Iran."[16] The Iranian leadership clearly saw itself exercising its jurisdiction well beyond Iran's national boundaries.

Iran thus retained its ambitious self-image as a vanguard for the whole Islamic world. Iranian presidents did not really provide a countervailing rational leadership to offset the ideological rigidity of the Supreme Leader. After all, it was the supposedly moderate Rafsanjani who actually declared on December 14, 2001: "The use of an atomic bomb against Israel would totally destroy Israel, while the same against the Islamic world would only cause damage." Then Rafsanjani hauntingly added: "Such a scenario is not inconceivable."[17]

During those years, Iran continued to defy the world and directly threatened the United States, using Hizbullah branches in the Persian Gulf and projecting its power in the region. In 1995, Bahrain became the headquarters of the newly created U.S. Fifth Fleet, but it was struck by waves of rioting by its Shiite population.

Bahraini officials produced evidence in Washington that the Bahraini branch of Hizbullah had been involved in an effort to overthrow their pro-American government with the assistance of an Iranian intelligence officer tied directly to Khamenei.[18]

A year later Saudi Hizbullah bombed the Khobar Towers housing complex in eastern Saudi Arabia, killing another nineteen U.S. servicemen. FBI Director Louis J. Freeh, who investigated the attack, reached the conclusion that it had been "sanctioned, funded and directed by senior officials of the government of Iran."[19] The Iranian embassy in Damascus issued passports to the perpetrators of the attack, who were trained by Iran in Lebanon's Bekaa Valley.[20]

In short, Iran left its fingerprints all over a bombing that Freeh would call "an act of war against the United States of America."[21] Moreover, Iranian subversion spread globally during these same years as far as Singapore in the east, where Hizbullah recruited cells to attack western shipping by using explosive boats, and reaching Argentina, in the west, where it directly ordered bombing attacks on Israeli and local Jewish community targets in 1992 and 1994 that left hundreds dead.[22] A Hizbullah presence was built up over the years in the Lebanese Shiite communities that resided in the remote tri-border area between Paraguay, Brazil, and Argentina. Iran was ready to defy the United States near some if its most vital military facilities and in its own backyard in South America.

Iran's long southern coastline dominated the 34-mile wide Strait of Hormuz, through which 40 percent of the world's oil supply regularly flowed. During the 1990s, the Iranians built up their military power in this sensitive waterway. It was the Shah of Iran who claimed the strategically-situated island of Abu Musa from the Emirate of Sharjah (United Arab Emirates) just inside the entrance of the Persian Gulf back in the early 1970s, arguing that he wished to pre-empt Arab revolutionaries from threatening shipping in the area.[23] But at the time, the Shah also agreed that the island came under joint Iranian-UAE administration.

In the 1990s the Islamic Republic evicted the UAE and asserted full control of the strategic island. Iran also militarized its presence there with Chinese anti-ship missiles.[24] By 1997, Iranian officials spoke openly about closing off the Strait of Hormuz. Iran continued to control two other UAE islands, known as the Greater and Lesser Tunbs, which it also seized during the Shah's reign from Ras al-Khaimah, another UAE emirate. These islands were immediately adjacent to the Persian Gulf's inbound shipping lanes, used by oil tankers. Iran also conducted large-scale military maneuvers in the waters of the Persian Gulf. Together, these actions were a daring provocation against the interests of the entire industrial world.

Finally, after the September 11 attacks, Iran seemed completely oblivious to what the United States might do when it offered sanctuary to part of the al-Qaeda leadership fleeing from U.S. forces who had vanquished the Taliban in nearby Afghanistan; they were not incarcerated, but were in direct communication with al-Qaeda operatives abroad, like the cell that launched a May 12, 2003, multiple truck bombing attack on western housing complexes in Riyadh, Saudi Arabia.[25] It seemed that Iran had no fear about letting al-Qaeda direct operations from its soil. The more the West let Iran launch terror attacks with impunity, the more its self-confidence grew and its image of western weakness deepened. This was an extremely inauspicious beginning for starting a stable relationship of deterrence of any sort.

In 2005, a new wrinkle in the problem of deterring Iran was added when Mahmoud Ahmadinejad was elected president of Iran. He openly spoke during his first address at the United Nations about hastening the re-appearance of the Hidden Imam from the tenth century, a messianic figure known in the Shiite religious tradition as the Mahdi. His arrival could actually be accelerated, according to secret religious societies to which Ahmadinejad belonged, under conditions of global chaos.[26] Wars could accelerate the arrival of this Shiite version of the "end of days."

Ahmadinejad himself explicitly linked the spread of chaos to the arrival of a new era of divine revelation. In a meeting with French Foreign Minister Philippe Douste-Blazy and two other EU foreign ministers in New York on September 15, 2005, Ahmadinejad shifted the focus of their conversation unexpectedly and asked the European diplomats: "Do you know why we should wish for chaos at any price?" He then answered his own rhetorical question: "Because after chaos, we can see the greatness of Allah."[27]

Moreover, according to Ahmadinejad, the return of the Hidden Imam was not an event for the distant future: "Those who are not versed [in the doctrine of Mahdism] believe the return [of the Hidden Imam] will only occur in a very long time, but according to the divine promise, [his return] is imminent."[28] The threat of massive retaliation against Iran for using nuclear weapons would not necessarily deter adherents of these secret groups, known as *Mahdaviat*, who hoped war would deliver their spiritual leader. The prospect of numerous civilian losses would play into the regime's obsession with martyrdom and death.

Ahmadinejad himself had been attached to an engineering unit of the Revolutionary Guards, many of whose commanders fought in the front lines of the Iran-Iraq War. He had adopted Mahdist doctrines two decades earlier when they were in active combat. Ahmadinejad relied on his fellow Revolutionary Guards, who had since come of age, to fill key positions in the ministries of his new government, including his defense and foreign ministers and his chief nuclear negotiator.

Under such conditions, to rely on western defense doctrines that presumed the rationality of one's adversary appeared to be highly risky in the Iranian case. From 1979 to 2009, Iran was consistently prepared to take incredible risks to confront the United States. The last Iranian clashes with America occurred on the soil of Iraq, while the U.S. armed forces sat along two of Iran's borders, in Afghanistan and in Iraq. Iran had not been deterred by this massive American presence in any way. Indeed, the Director of the

CIA, Michael V. Hayden, concluded in late May 2008: "It is the policy of the Iranian government, approved at the highest levels of that government, to facilitate the killing of American and other coalition forces in Iraq. Period."[29]

Iran was clearly a difficult country to deter, given the firm commitment of its political-military elites to continue to export the Islamic Revolution and to challenge the West directly. What western governments needed to consider was how these activities would change in the event Iran was protected by a nuclear umbrella. In tearing down the Taliban regime in Afghanistan at the end of 2001, as a response to the September 11 attacks, Washington demonstrated the consequences for regimes that harbor international terrorist groups, threatening the United States and its citizens.

But would the West have invaded Afghanistan if the Taliban had been armed with nuclear-tipped missiles that could reach London or even New York? Would al-Qaeda's Afghan camps have remained intact and continued to launch global terror attacks with impunity? Could the United States and its allies deter a new wave of international terrorism on the scale of September 11, if it was sponsored by a nuclear Iran?

In recent years, the United States and its allies have vociferously expressed their opposition to Iran acquiring nuclear weapons and insisted that it suspend the enrichment of uranium. As French President Nicolas Sarkozy stated in Israel during a July 2008 visit: "I reiterate here in the clearest manner: As far as France is concerned, a nuclear Iran is totally unacceptable."[30] And yet, despite these kinds of declarations, which other nations have also made, Iran has steadily progressed with its nuclear program, defying all: France, the European Union, and the entire UN Security Council.

Iran is unlikely to take seriously any western efforts in the future to deter its nuclear capability, given the fact that the United States and its allies have repeatedly made threats, yet ultimately failed to do enough to halt the Iranian drive for nuclear weapons.

Consequently, the starting point for any policy seeking to halt Iran's drive for atomic weapons is an understanding of how it has defied western powers from their very first diplomatic forays into the world of nuclear negotiations with Tehran.

Chapter 3:

The Revelation of the Iranian Nuclear Program and the Western Response

HASSAN ROWHANI'S CANDID DISCLOSURES on how he had duped the West occurred amidst a fierce international debate that had been raging between the United States and the European Union for a number of years. At issue was how to contend with Iran in light of what was becoming known about its nuclear program and its continuing quest for regional hegemony across the Middle East.

In 2002, an exiled Iranian dissident group known as the National Council for Resistance in Iran (NCRI) began revealing details of a nuclear program, previously unknown to the world, being pursued by Tehran in defiance of international agreements it had previously signed, such as the 1968 Nuclear Non-proliferation Treaty and the 1974 Safeguards Agreement mandating reporting any processing and use of nuclear material.

Of greatest concern to the international community was the news that Tehran was working on a secret uranium enrichment complex at Natanz, where two centrifuge enrichment plants were under construction. The world also learned that Iran was building a heavy water production plant and reactor at Arak. By reprocessing its spent fuel, Iran would be able to produce plutonium. Iran immediately asserted that it had an "inalienable" right to pursue nuclear technology and that its program was for "peaceful" civilian uses.

The world was less certain. Iran could easily pursue enrichment technology for "peaceful" purposes without affecting its option to produce nuclear weapons. Lengthening the spin cycle of the uranium gas in the centrifuges (thereby increasing the level of enrichment) by another 25 percent was all the difference between producing nuclear fuel for a civilian reactor and moving up to highly enriched weapons-grade fuel for an atomic bomb.[1] It was an additional effort that Iran could easily make.

Furthermore, as the Iranians had no plans for constructing any plutonium-fueled electrical power plants, their pursuit of plutonium production clearly had more sinister implications. If Iran was indeed pursuing a peaceful nuclear program, as it argued, why had it kept its work secret until it was uncovered by the Iranian opposition? As the West evaluated the revelations in 2002 of the nuclear facilities at Natanz and Arak, it could not come up with a satisfactory answer.

The facts of the matter were that uranium enrichment and plutonium production were the two main routes used by countries like Pakistan and North Korea to obtain fuel for an atomic bomb—and Iran appeared to be developing both.

Within months of the first disclosures, U.S. intelligence sources confirmed their veracity.[2] State Department spokesman Richard Boucher gave the American assessment in 2003 without mincing any words: "We believe Iran's true intent is to develop the capability to produce fissile material for nuclear weapons."[3] On November 17, 2004, Secretary of State Colin Powell also verified that the Iranian opposition disclosures were, for the most part, correct. He then added further information about the growing capabilities of the Iranian missile force.

Powell, who had led the Bush administration's diplomatic drive at the UN Security Council in 2002 to make the case for disarming Saddam Hussein's Iraq, might have been expected to be extremely leery about expressing himself again on intelligence concerning weapons of mass destruction in the Middle East, especially after U.S. inspectors determined in January 2004 that Iraq had none. He certainly would not want to be burned again by presenting data before the world community that would later be doubted by the very same U.S. security agencies that had provided it in the first place.

Therefore, Powell must have been convinced that the Iranian case was very different from the Iraqi file and much more urgent. Additionally, he must also have been confident of the intelligence he had seen. For Powell was surprisingly willing to speak out and disclose new U.S. intelligence data indicating that Iran was also working on a nuclear warhead that could be fitted on its ballistic missiles:

> I have seen some information that would suggest they have been actively working on delivery systems.... You don't have a weapon until you can put it on something that can deliver a weapon. I'm talking about what one does with a warhead. We are talking about information that they not only have missiles, but information that suggests they are working hard about how to put the two together.[4]

Western intelligence agencies had known since the latter part of the 1990's that Iran had obtained rocket propulsion systems previously used in the former Soviet Union's space program.[5] A multistage Iranian space lift vehicle would have the same components as an intercontinental range ballistic missile, and could eventually be capable of striking North America. In 1997, it was reported that the Iranian military indeed had successfully test-fired rocket engines based on the Soviet designs.[6] U.S. reconnaissance satellites were able to detect these engine tests from space and even identify the propulsion system that was being used.[7]

But Powell had even newer intelligence about Iranian nuclear warheads. Several months earlier the CIA took possession of the laptop computer of a senior Iranian technician that contained thousands of pages of information in *Farsi*—as well as actual blue-prints—of how to construct a warhead.[8] One document tracked the fight path of a missile, but also had some notations explaining how to detonate a warhead 2,000 feet above target.[9] Mention of that specific height was extremely revealing; for while exploding conventional warheads at such an altitude would have no effect on the ground, nuclear-tipped missiles detonated at that height would have a devastating impact on a ground target.

The laptop also had sketches of a spherical device that could be detonated by a system of high explosives; a professional analysis would conclude years later that it was the design of a "nuclear trigger."[10] There were also sketches of how to place the same spherical device into the nose-cone of an Iranian 1,300-kilometer Shahab-3 missile—which could put at risk both Saudi Arabia and Israel.

Thus the three main elements of Iran's drive to be a nuclear power—enriched uranium and plutonium production, long-range ballistic missiles, and weaponization (the design and production of nuclear warheads)—spoke to purposes other than the peaceful pursuit for civilian use that Iran espoused. The intelligence picture that seemed to be emerging in 2003 and 2004 was that Iran was advancing in all three areas. Together, they constituted a full-blown nuclear weapons program.

U.S. intelligence agencies were not the only authority confirming what the Iranian opposition had disclosed. The International Atomic Energy Agency (IAEA), the UN watchdog, which inspected the nuclear facilities of signatories to the 1968 Nuclear

Non-Proliferation Treaty (NPT), entered the picture. The Shah's Iran had signed the NPT on July 1, 1968, and six years thereafter it completed a Safeguards Agreement with the IAEA governing, among other things, the control of nuclear materials and the provision of information to the agency. Iran did not acknowledge the existence of its centrifuge enrichment plants at Natanz until February 2003. For the IAEA, Tehran's concealment of its nuclear activities was a "breach" of its treaty obligations.[11] The IAEA thus requested and gained access to the Natanz facility and took samples for analysis.

Significantly, IAEA inspectors found traces of weapons-grade uranium in the samples that had no function in purely civilian nuclear programs. While the IAEA sought to avoid being confrontational with Iran in its conclusions about the implications of the data it was accumulating, it did not conceal incriminating evidence. For example, IAEA found that some Iranian nuclear activities were taking place on Iranian military bases, belying Tehran's claim that its nuclear program was for peaceful purposes. Confronted with these details, Iran's defense minister, Ali Shamkhani, admitted that the Iranian military was involved in the production of centrifuge equipment for uranium enrichment.[12]

The Iranians tried to conceal the role of the Iranian military; when IAEA requested from Tehran purchase orders for spare parts used in developing centrifuges, the Iranian team preparing the material made certain that the portions of the purchase orders that were prepared by the Iranian Ministry of Defense be crossed out in black ink.[13]

When the information on Iran's clandestine nuclear activities first came out, Tehran found itself in a tight spot. If it admitted the truth of what it had been secretly doing, it faced immediate international sanctions. It had concealed nuclear activities that it was legally obligated to report to the IAEA and deliberately deceived the international community on an extremely sensitive issue. But equally, if Iran refused to cooperate with the western powers, it also faced tough international sanctions. For that reason, the Iranian regime adopted a sophisticated policy of admitting much of what it had done in the nuclear field and granting the IAEA selective access to some Iranian facilities, while offering to negotiate with European powers over the future of its nuclear activities.

Containment or Engagement: The Western Debate over Iran

When the news of the Iranian program first broke, the Bush administration recognized the evidence as deadly serious. They wanted to refer Iran immediately to the UN Security Council where harsh economic measures might be taken to induce them to halt all nuclear activities. In the American view, the West had to move quickly and decisively to diplomatically confront the Iranians before Tehran fully mastered the production of the entire nuclear fuel cycle, as Hassan Rowhani plainly stated was their goal. Once that happened, most specialists agreed that attempts to freeze the Iranian nuclear program would simply come too late.

In contrast, the Europeans thought that this action was premature, preferring a diplomatic dialogue with Iran over any diplomatic showdown. The EU countries were almost as concerned about Washington's intentions in handling the Iran crisis as they were about Tehran's. British Foreign Secretary Jack Straw told German Foreign Minister Joschka Fischer that London did not want the western alliance split again over Iran as they had been on Iraq. They decided together to propose that Europe work to avert a new crisis over the Iranian nuclear program by leading, along with the French, a new diplomatic effort to get the Iranians to stop uranium enrichment altogether.

Also fueling the United States–European clash were divergent perspectives of the situation. European statesmen viewed Iran less as a potential strategic threat and more as an enormous business opportunity. The EU was Iran's largest trading partner. Foreign trade made up a far larger proportion of the GNP of European economies than the American economy. UN sanctions on Iran in 2003 would simply cut into business that several European states were determined to expand.

For example, in late March 2003—only seven months after the initial revelations—British Foreign Secretary Jack Straw approached Secretary of State Colin Powell requesting U.S. permission to license aircraft parts needed for a sale European aerospace giant, Airbus, sought to make to Iran.[14] The British wanted to push the sale of Rolls-Royce engines for the Airbus aircraft. Powell turned Straw down but could not hold back the Europeans from trying a new diplomatic dialogue with Iran. The British foreign secretary was enthusiastic about talking to Iran; he described Rowhani as "a man we could do business with."[15] Straw's critics even called him "Tehran Jack."[16]

European officials had other considerations, as well. Wanting to avert another western coalition from going to war against Iran, they recalled that the 2003 Iraq War began with a series of UN Security Council resolutions imposing economic sanctions on Saddam Hussein in order to force him to disclose and dismantle his weapons of mass destruction. When Baghdad failed to comply with those resolutions, the United States went to war. European leaders did not want to help Washington set the diplomatic stage for a military option against Iran. Generally, they objected to the use of force even being mentioned as a last resort against Iran.

Given these considerations, the Europeans decided to embrace the Iranians' offer for diplomatic engagement. The EU-3—Britain, France, and Germany—dispatched their foreign ministers to Tehran to negotiate with the Iranians. They came as individual European states, although the EU foreign policy head, Javier Solana, would join them. The EU-3 struck an agreement with the Iranians on October 21, 2003, by which the Iranians consented "to suspend all uranium enrichment activities and reprocessing activities," as well as accept more intrusive inspections by the

IAEA, whose monitors placed seals on all the centrifuges at Natanz.[17] The European envoys hoped that suspension of Iran's uranium enrichment would become a permanent cessation over time.

But very quickly, the Iranians and Europeans found they had differences over the question of how narrowly—or broadly—they wanted to define the word "suspension." The Iranians wanted it defined as their agreeing to refrain from putting radioactive material into the centrifuges. The Iranians could argue that uranium conversion was not specifically mentioned in the agreement. (Indeed, conversion became an issue in later negotiations.) The Iranian interpretation of "suspension" would also allow Iran to continue to build more centrifuges and be ready to vastly expand their production of uranium in the future. In contrast, the Europeans sought to define suspension as freezing all enrichment-related activities.

Rowhani and his team did not want any precise legal definitions appearing in the text, preferring to leave the issue vague. As a result, the Tehran Agreement called for suspending enrichment and reprocessing activities "as defined by the IAEA." The IAEA ultimately backed the broad European definition of the enrichment suspension, but the Iranians still felt that they had some room to maneuver, given that no definition actually appeared in the text of the agreement, which they jointly released with the EU-3.

Nonetheless, the EU negotiators were almost euphoric about their success. In late 2003, the Iranians also signed an Additional Protocol to their 1974 Safeguards Agreement with the IAEA, which would allow inspectors much greater access to Iranian nuclear sites, though they ultimately dragged their feet in ratifying the new Protocol.

As they concluded new agreements with Tehran, European diplomats felt they had demonstrated their alternative approach to U.S. policy that worked. Indeed, the following month the EU foreign policy chief, Javier Solana, was upbeat and even complimented the Iranians: "They have been honest. Let's see if they continue all the way to the end."[18] Solana insisted that Iran should not be made to appear before the UN Security Council as a result.

But Tehran proved to be far from honest as it became clear that Europe's policy of diplomatic engagement did not alter Iran's strategy of diplomatic deception. For despite its October commitments, Iran soon declared in June 2004 that it would continue to manufacture centrifuges for uranium enrichment and experiment with the UF_6 gas that went into them. These were prohibited activities which Iranian diplomats had argued during previous negotiations were not within the scope of the 2003 Tehran Agreement. Iran had been overruled by the IAEA and they had agreed to accept the IAEA's judgment in these matters. But now, the Iranians were reversing themselves by retreating from what they had previously agreed, and in doing so were trying to establish a *fait accompli*.

Even more significantly, Iran did not grant IAEA's inspectors the immediate access they requested to the Lavizan Technological Research Center where nuclear weaponization work had been done; Tehran sought to delay the inspections and used the time to not only demolish the six buildings at the facility but also remove several meters deep of the top soil where it once existed, in order to prevent IAEA from taking incriminating soil samples. The Iranians similarly concealed potentially incriminating material at its Kalaya Electric Facility, where they retiled several rooms before inspectors arrived so that their swipes would not show that radioactive materials had once been present.[19] The Kalaya Electric Facility was where western experts believed Iran tested its centrifuges for enriching uranium between 1999 and 2002, using undeclared nuclear materials that it imported in 1991.[20]

Nevertheless, rather than press for immediate U.S. Security Council action, as Washington continued to suggest, the EU-3 still sought to resuscitate the EU-Iranian agreement from 2003. They wanted to give diplomacy another chance. European leaders still believed that their policy of engagement could get Iran to halt its nuclear activities, by offering Tehran economic inducements, like membership in the World Trade Organization. The new package for Iran was to include spare parts for their commercial aircraft as well as new aircraft.

A second agreement was hammered out in Paris on November 15, 2004. It laid out in far greater detail than the earlier Tehran agreement what activities Iran was supposed to suspend. It was characteristic of the European side to feel that the West had to be still more forthcoming to Tehran. A European diplomat speaking anonymously to the *New York Times* gave his assessment that more goodwill gestures towards Iran were needed: "We will succeed only if we can provide a lot of carrots."[21] And the "biggest carrot" the EU could give was the involvement of the U.S. But the Bush administration had serious reservations about Europe's entire diplomatic strategy. The agreements with Tehran, it was argued in Washington, were lulling the West into "a false sense of security."[22]

Moreover, new evidence about the Iranian nuclear program was surfacing which only further aroused suspicions about Tehran's true intent. The IAEA sought to inspect the Parchin Military Complex in late 2004 to investigate intelligence suggesting Iran was testing conventional high explosives used in the detonation of nuclear weapons.[23] This could have been the Iranian "smoking gun," for there was no way even the most skilled diplomat could talk his way out of this kind of discovery and argue that the work done at a military facility was for nuclear medicine or some other civilian use.

The Parchin story was not confined to the world of nuclear experts; it had already been reported by ABC News in September 2004.[24] Iran should have felt compelled to cooperate on Parchin in order to avoid any further bad publicity in the West about what it was up to at a suspected nuclear site. Yet despite Parchin being an open secret, the Iranians repeatedly turned down the IAEA's requests to freely inspect the site.[25] In January 2005, when the IAEA was finally allowed to make an inspection of Parchin, the Iranians narrowly restricted the visit. The IAEA was given access to only one of the four areas in Parchin that it sought to inspect, and in that one area, the IAEA was allowed to investigate only a limited number of buildings. Additionally, the IAEA could not take environmental samples where it wanted.[26] In short, Iran managed to protect its most highly sensitive nuclear weapons sites from inspection.

Not surprisingly, the new European–Iranian agreement did not last long. The Iranians tried to amend the agreement right after signing it. Though they had undertaken to shut down every centrifuge in their possession, a few days later, they sought an exemption for nuclear research from the British, who turned them down.

Moreover, other parts of the Iranian nuclear program moved forward. The EU–Iran Agreement left Iran completely free to produce the products that could be used to manufacture weapons-grade plutonium. This was not an unintended oversight. European diplomats set aside the issue of plutonium production by means of the Arak heavy-water reactor as a concession to Tehran in order to nail down agreement on uranium enrichment.[27]

Iran exploited every opening it was given. Pierre Goldschmidt, the IAEA Deputy Director, reported on March 1, 2005, that work on Iran's heavy-water reactor was steadily progressing even as Iranian–European negotiations over the implementation of their past understandings continued. Satellite imagery of the Arak site showed the extensive construction work the Iranians were doing from February 2004 to February 2005, while Europe and Tehran were talking.[28] Clearly, precious time for halting the Iranians was lost.

One of the critical questions for ascertaining how close Iran was to making nuclear weapons was whether they had mastered the technology of taking the spent fuel from a heavy-water reactor and reprocessing it to extract weapons-grade plutonium. Iran tried to disguise the extent of its activity in this sensitive area. It told the IAEA that it had halted this work in the early 1990s, but IAEA tests showed that Iran was engaging in plutonium research much later than that.

The U.S. ambassador to the IAEA, Jackie Sanders, blasted Tehran for trying to deceive the international community: "Iran has been caught, yet again, misleading the IAEA about its past plutonium separation experiments, claiming until confronted with scientific proof to the contrary that it stopped its undeclared reprocessing experiments in 1993."[29]

The Europeans did not give up trying to halt Iran's construction of a heavy-water reactor entirely. On several occasions in 2005, they proposed the idea to Tehran of European support for Iran's acquisition of light-water reactors, instead of the heavy-water reactor that Iran was planning. These would be more "proliferation resistant," especially if fuel-supply arrangements for the light water reactor were put in place that required the Iranians to give up any spent fuel after it was used.[30] In contrast, the spent fuel from Iran's planned heavy-water reactor would be able to produce enough plutonium for manufacturing two atomic bombs a year.[31]

The Iranians argued that they needed the Arak facility to produce isotopes for peaceful purposes in medicine, agriculture, and industry. However, a light-water reactor would have the same civilian applications with none of the risk of generating weapons-grade plutonium bi-products. Was it fair to say that a heavy-water reactor was needed for medical isotopes? In the words of Robert Einhorn, the U.S. Assistant Secretary of State for Non-proliferation between 1999 and 2001, relying on the heavy-water reactor Iran was building for these limited civilian needs was completely inappropriate: "A 12-inch hunting knife also could be used to spread jam on your toast in the morning."[32]

Less than nine months after agreeing to suspend all enrichment activities, Iran announced its intention to break the seals that the

IAEA had put on its uranium conversion equipment on August 1, 2005. Conversion was resumed shortly thereafter.

On August 5, 2005, the EU formally proposed light-water reactors for Iran and provided assurances for the long-term supply of fuel for them. The Iranians came back with a terse response: "The proposal by the E3/EU on August 5, 2005 is a clear violation of international law and the Charter of the United Nations.... " The Iranian reply concluded that what the Europeans offered "... amounts to an insult on the Iranian nation, for which the E3 must apologize."[33]

Astoundingly, despite the Iranian statement, France's Foreign Minister Philippe Douste-Blazy told *Paris Match* later in the month: "Our hand is still extended." He then added: "France remains convinced that it is through dialogue that we'll find a solution to the problem we face in Iran."[34] British Foreign Secretary Jack Straw declared that the threat of a military option against Iran was off the table as he spoke at a conference of the British Labor party shortly thereafter: "There is no question of us going to war against Iran." He insisted: "This can only be resolved by diplomatic means."[35] German Chancellor Gerhard Schroeder, during his election campaign, said bluntly, "Let's take the military option off the table. We have seen it doesn't work."

In the meantime the Iranians could take pride in their diplomatic accomplishments against the Europeans: prior to August 2005, the EU-3 had insisted that Iran close its uranium-conversion facility as part of any new agreement. But since the Iranians unilaterally restarted their conversion plant, the Europeans dropped this demand.[36]

Less than a year later, the IAEA Director General, Dr. Mohamed ElBaradei, reported to the IAEA Board that amidst the materials that the agency had seen from the Iranians was a 15-page document describing the procedures for forming uranium metal and casting uranium hemispheres for "the fabrication of nuclear weapon components." The Iranians lamely argued that they themselves did not actually ask for the weaponization document, but rather it had been provided at the initiative of the nuclear network of A. Q. Khan, the Pakistani nuclear scientist who had clandestinely sold nuclear technology to Libya and Iran. There was no way to confirm that this was indeed the case. When IAEA inspectors went back to Iran in early 2006 and requested to examine the document again, suspiciously, Tehran turned them down.[37]

The mounting concerns about the Iranian nuclear program were sometimes inadvertently helped by Iranian negotiating errors. Amir Zamaninia was the Iranian Foreign Ministry's director general for international political affairs; he had to make a statement to the IAEA Board of Governors on March 13, 2004, explaining how Iran had dutifully met its international obligations under the Nuclear Non-Proliferation Treaty. He was trying to explain why the Iranians were experimenting with Polonium-210, a specialized material used as an initiator for neutrons in the beginning of a nuclear explosion.

The Iranian diplomat argued that polonium research did not have to be reported under various NPT agreements, adding that in any case it had civilian applications for the oil and gas industry. In order to reassure his international audience about polonium, he stated that Iran had never procured beryllium, which he defined as "an indispensible item in research geared into a military program." Yet in 2005, IAEA received evidence that Iran had indeed attempted to acquire the very beryllium metal which the Iranian statement from the previous year had openly admitted was for military purposes.[38] The argument that Iran was engaging in civilian research alone was falling apart.

In early December 2005, the IAEA secretariat repeated a request for a meeting with the Iranians to discuss yet another alarming discovery. The IAEA had information about Iranian tests of "high explosives and the design of a missile re-entry vehicle, all of which could have a military nuclear dimension,"[39] some of which it had gotten from sensitive intelligence shared by the

United States. This new information pointed to an Iranian interest in the design of nuclear warheads which completely contradicted Tehran's constant assertion that it was only engaging in a civilian nuclear program. There was no way that this research could be explained away as yet another civilian program. Red warning lights should have been going off in western capitals.

However, undaunted by the disturbing implications of this mounting data, the EU still extended a hand to Iran and held "exploratory talks" with Tehran in Vienna during December 2005 to see how they could get out of the diplomatic impasse that had been created. But Tehran did not extend a hand back to Europe. President Mahmoud Ahmadinejad, elected in June 2005, was forming his new government at this time. Despite the talks in December, Iran finished removing all remaining IAEA seals from its enrichment equipment by January 10, 2006.

The EU-3 needed to respond. It released a statement in less than a week that finally admitted "Iran's documented record of concealment and deception."[40] The Europeans proposed for the first time that the Security Council become involved.[41] On February 4, 2006, the IAEA Board voted to refer the case of Iran to the UN Security Council.

Getting to the point of referring Iran to the Security Council had taken several years of the Iranians and the Europeans apparently speaking right past one another at the negotiating table. During this time, the Iranians were engaged in an almost transparent effort of diplomatic deception, which was finally fully unveiled, while the Europeans kept offering more diplomatic carrots in return.

Movement on Iran at the UN Security Council was slow, serving the Iranian interest of playing for time. First, despite the severity of the issue, the Security Council members did not go directly to adopting a resolution. They drafted a less-binding "Presidential Statement" which was read out by the rotating president of the Security Council, who, for the month of March 2006, was the Argentinean ambassador to the UN. The March 29 statement emphasized the importance of Iran reestablishing a "full and sustained suspension of all enrichment-related and reprocessing activities." It set out a thirty-day deadline, at which point it expected the IAEA to report back whether Iran had complied.

Iran rejected the Presidential Statement within 24 hours. But rather than move immediately to a binding resolution, the UN Security Council members let four months pass until they adopted their first actual resolution on the Iranian nuclear program, choosing instead to try offering other "carrots" to the unreceptive regime.

Despite everything that had occurred, the European Union seemed to be rigidly glued to its policy of engagement. In May 2006, it offered Iran yet another package of positive inducements, including economic assistance, to halt its nuclear enrichment programs. Europe must have felt bolstered when Secretary of State Condoleezza Rice revised the Bush administration's policy by expressing Washington's willingness for the first time to come to the negotiating table with Tehran, "as soon as Iran fully and verifiably suspends its enrichment and reprocessing activities."[42] It was only a conditional offer for a dialogue, but it was an effort to reach out to Iran, nonetheless.

In the face of all these new western gestures, Ahmadinejad's rhetoric only became more combative: "Your incentives are definitely not more valuable than nuclear technology." He then added: "How dare you tell our people to give up gold in return for chocolate?" And in another disdainful rejection of Europe's efforts at engagement, he said: "I declare that our people do not need your assistance for development." [43]

The European policy of engagement and dialogue with Iran had patently collapsed. Indeed, Germany's former foreign minister, Joschka Fischer, who had been a part of the EU-3 talks with Tehran, had to frankly admit in May 2006 that Europe's negotiating effort with Iran had "failed."[44] He had no illusions about what Iran was ultimately seeking: "There can no longer be any reasonable doubt that Iran's ambition is to obtain nuclear weapons capability."[45] This was not Washington's assessment, but the conclusion of the foreign minister of a German government that had been hostile to U.S. policies during the Iraq War.

Europe had not completely jettisoned its old policy. It now pressed Washington to begin direct talks with Tehran, but Undersecretary of State Nicholas Burns, Rice's point man on Iran, still stressed that diplomatic isolation of Iran—and not diplomatic engagement—was the only acceptable approach for dealing with the Iranian nuclear challenge.[46] Prime Minister Tony Blair demoted Straw from his position as foreign secretary; most political observers tied his dismissal to his failed handling of the Iran portfolio. And yet the EU foreign policy chief, Javier Solana, was still declaring in October 2006 that the European diplomatic dialogue with Iran had to continue even if the nuclear talks failed.

The Bush administration clearly did not buy into this thinking and was extremely leery of the EU approach. Whatever European leaders concluded about the merits of their policy of engagement, Rowhani's admission in Tehran about the success of Iran's nuclear diplomacy had backhandedly proven how ineffective their diplomatic engagement of Iran had been, given the continuing progress the Iranians made in exploiting the time they had been given to advance with their nuclear program.

The time invested in the EU's diplomatic initiatives with Iran was not cost-free. From the time the Iranian nuclear program was first revealed in 2002 until the UN finally acted in 2006, four years went by. Iran had bought the time it needed and clearly was not shy about telling the world of its achievement. UN Security Council Resolution 1696 was adopted on July 31, 2006, and required Iran to suspend its enrichment and reprocessing efforts. Like the March Presidential Statement, it sought a report on Iranian compliance within thirty days.

When nothing happened, it would take another five months for the UN Security Council to follow up with Resolution 1737 on December 23, 2006. These resolutions were explicitly adopted with references to Chapter VII of the UN Charter, which deals with cases of aggression and threats to international peace. Chapter VII resolutions were binding under international law. Yet Iran was not moved. Ultimately, over the next two years the UN would adopt a total of five Security Council resolutions on Iran that would not deter Tehran from proceeding with its program.

For those who still believed that uranium conversion and enrichment were for civilian purposes alone, there was a harsh reminder from the Supreme Leader Khamenei's close advisor and spokesman, Hossein Shariatmadari, the editor of *Kayhan*. He reminded an audience at Babol University, in the city of Mazandaran, that "a country that has attained the knowledge of nuclear enrichment is only one step away from producing nuclear weapons." He described this as a "political decision," rather than a further technical step, adding the ritual assurance that Iran would not produce nuclear weapons.[47] Western diplomacy had brought Iran one step away from crossing that Rubicon.

The unsuccessful efforts of the Europeans to diplomatically engage Iran were actually not new. What will emerge in the chapters that follow is that the West has in fact sought to undertake a diplomatic dialogue with the Islamic Republic for decades. Indeed, virtually every U.S. administration tried to reach out one way or another to Tehran. It is really impossible to understand the limits of any engagement policy with Iran today without appreciating why these past efforts didn't work out.

It is especially important to look at how the United States and its allies systematically misread Iran's real intentions. This becomes possible because of an abundance of declassified materials that have come to light. Many details have emerged that were probably not known to policymakers at the time concerning some of the most volatile incidents that took place. Looking back at these critical junctures in Iran's interaction with the West is a vital exercise to undertake in order to avoid repeating past errors that were made when engagement was previously tried, but many times backfired, producing the very opposite of what was hoped for.

Part 2:

THE HISTORY OF
MISREADING IRAN

Chapter 4:

Underestimating Enmity: President Jimmy Carter and the New Islamic Republic

PROFESSOR BERNARD LEWIS is one of the greatest experts on the Islamic world in the West. He began his career during the Second World War with British intelligence, and by the 1970s received an appointment at the Institute of Advanced Studies at Princeton University. He is fluent in Arabic, Persian, and Turkish. His analysis of the Middle East is frequently based on his understanding of original texts in Middle Eastern languages, taken from state archives and libraries from around the world. In early 1979, an assistant of his was looking through the Arabic and Persian book collection of the Princeton University library and found a text that Lewis had not seen before.

The text in question was an Arabic book containing the lectures from 1970 given by an Iranian Shiite leader, who had been exiled in 1964 by the Shah of Iran first to Turkey and then to Iraq, where he preached in the holy city of Najaf, an important center of Shiite scholarship. Najaf was revered as the burial place of Ali, the fourth caliph, whom Shiites felt should have been the true successor of Muhammad, and whose eleven descendents were each regarded as an Imam of the Twelver Shiite community. The author of the obscure text in Lewis's hands, entitled *Islamic Government*, was Ruhollah Khomeini. (After the book was adapted from his lectures, Khomeini had been given one of the highest honorific titles in Shiite Islam, Ayatollah, which meant in Arabic "the Sign of God" [ayat Allah].)

Little was known about Khomeini in the outside world. He was born in 1902 to a religiously distinguished family of Shiite scholars. He was a *sayyed*, which literally meant "gentleman" but referred to his coming from a family that claimed direct descent from the Prophet Muhammad through Ali, and in Khomeini's case, through Musa ibn Jaafar, the Seventh Imam.[1] Those who became mullahs often distinguished themselves by wearing a black turban, which Khomeini made into one of his trademarks.

In the eighteenth century, Khomeini's family actually lived in Kashmir, India, where his great-grandfather had set up a theological school. His grandfather, Sayyed Ahmad, who was sent to study Shiite traditions in Najaf, eventually settled back in the village of Khomein in Iran. Khomeini became well known for his incendiary sermons that attacked the Shah for his 1964 military agreement with the United States (known as the Status of Forces Agreement) which granted immunity from local prosecution to American forces serving in Iran. In November 1964, he was sent to Turkey but later settled in Iraq.

From his exile in Najaf, Khomeini had become one of the fiercest opponents of the Shah's regime. In January 1978, in order to discredit Khomeini, perhaps through the instigation of the Shah's security apparatus, a semi-official Iranian newspaper called Khomeini "the Indian Sayyed," asserting that, given his background, he had close ties with the British from whom he received funding.[2] His importance in the internal politics of Iran was clearly rising.

Lewis's discovery of Khomeini's book was extremely important. The Ayatollah was responsible for a revolution that was unfolding in Iran, yet few individuals in Washington knew much about his ideology or what policies he might advocate should he sweep into power. The Shah of Iran had been an unshakable pillar of U.S. policy in the oil-rich Persian Gulf ever since the United States helped restore him to power in 1953. During a state visit to Tehran in 1977, President Jimmy Carter was still toasting the Shah as "an island of stability in a turbulent corner of the world."

Knowledge about the Shah's opposition was limited. By January 1979, he was forced to leave Iran in the wake of mounting anti-government rioting over the previous eight months. Within weeks, Ayatollah Khomeini returned to Iran after fourteen years of exile, replaced the monarchial regime, and put in place the foundations of what was to become an Islamic republic.

Even the CIA did not have a copy of the book that Professor Lewis had discovered.[3] The *Washington Post* and two other U.S. newspapers took a strong interest in Lewis's discovery, and ran several pieces quoting the book, but the text Lewis had uncovered seemed to contradict the upbeat conventional wisdom in the Carter administration at the time about the new Iranian leader. Carter's ambassador to the UN, Andrew Young, took this to an extreme when he said that he was willing to bet "that in another year or so" Khomeini would be seen as "some kind of saint when we finally get over the panic of what is happening there."[4]

Islamic Government showed that Khomeini was fiercely anti-American—and anti-Semitic, even suggesting that Jews were seeking "to rule over the entire planet."[5] It also unveiled Khomeini's extremist ideology that advocated violence, calling for "an armed *jihad*" against ruling governments "that do not bow to the wishes of an oppositional movement by returning to the straight path of Islam."[6] Reading Khomeini, it was clear that he envisioned this movement going beyond the boundaries of Iran: "We must take the lead over other Muslims in embarking on this sacred *jihad*, this heavy undertaking; because of our rank and position, we must be in the forefront."[7]

Yet, in February 1979, just as Khomeini was returning to Tehran, Henry Precht, the head of the Iran desk in the U.S. Department of State, addressed an audience of two hundred at the State Department and raised serious doubts about the veracity of the Khomeini excerpts appearing in American newspapers. Precht had been arguing in internal meetings in Washington that with Khomeini's takeover from the Shah, Iran might be more stable than in the past. [8] Gary Sick of the National Security Council concluded that this was fast becoming "the new conventional wisdom."[9]

Responding to the newspaper stories about Khomeini's writings, Precht contended that they were a collection of students' notes, at best, or even a forgery.[10] Professor Thomas Ricks, an academic insider who had access to key officials in the U.S. Department of State, wrote in the *Washington Post* that the excerpts from *Islamic Government* appearing in the press were taken "out of context."[11]

Why were leading officials in the U.S. Department of State in denial about the true intentions of Khomeini? Since the Carter administration took office in 1977, many official organs of the U.S. government were having difficulty making an accurate evaluation of what was going on in Iran. In 1978, the CIA was working on a new National Intelligence Estimate (NIE) on Iran, entitled "Iran: Prospects Through 1985." An interim report of the study concluded that the "shah will be an active participant in Iranian life well into the 1980s." It added, "There is no threat to the stability of the shah's rule."[12]

French and Israeli officials disputed this kind of analysis, arguing that the Shah's regime could collapse within a year. Israel's ambassador to Iran, Uri Lubrani, prepared a report to this effect for the Israeli cabinet, which was shared with the CIA, but it was dismissed in Washington as too alarmist. The Israeli government was also reluctant to accept Lubrani's analysis. Few western governments wanted to hear that the pivotal western ally was in real trouble.

Lubrani had seen the warning signs of a disintegrating monarchy before, when he was ambassador to Ethiopia during the last days of Halie Salassie. Despite Lubrani's warning, CIA Director Admiral Stansfield Turner would later admit that the Islamic Revolution in Iran had caught the United States by surprise.[13] Though some U.S. officials dissented from the NIE's optimistic conclusions about the Shah of Iran, it nevertheless indicated how out of touch a significant part of the U.S. bureaucracy was at the time.

How the United States was to handle the rapidly deteriorating situation in Iran during 1978 as Iranians demonstrated against the Shah was at the heart of an enormous controversy within the Carter administration, which it ultimately failed to resolve. The State Department, represented by Henry Precht, initially sought to dilute the powers of the Shah of Iran, advocating a broader-based regime to replace him. The U.S. had a special status in Iran and was able to make recommendations on internal Iranian affairs to the Shah. But once the Shah was gone, the policy shifted to creating a new relationship with Khomeini.

The National Security Council looked down upon the State Department's approach, having a much keener sense of the dangers emanating from Iran. Thus the U.S. National Security Advisor, Zbigniew Brzezinski, concluded: "I simply had no faith in the quaint notion—favored by American lawyers of a liberal bent—that the remedy to a revolutionary situation is to paste together a coalition of the contending parties, who—unlike domestic American politicians—are not motivated by a spirit of compromise but (demonstrably in the Iranian case) by homicidal hatred."[14]

The Carter administration was indecisive about which of the two approaches should be adopted. This indecision was even reflected in embarrassing ways. On December 27, 1978, President Carter directed the *USS Constellation* to sail toward Iran from the western Pacific Ocean, in support of the Shah. Six days later, he issued a contradictory order for the *USS Constellation* to remain where it was in the South China Sea and not enter the Indian Ocean.

On the surface, Carter did not seem to be aligning with either side in his administration. If anything, he appeared to be partial to keeping the Shah, by resisting recommendations that floated up from the bureaucracy envisioning his departure. Yet policy not only entails the formal statements of an American president but also how his bureaucracy and U.S. allies abroad understand his approach. For example, the Shah and his generals became convinced that it was Carter who stood behind his ouster. The United States, as one Iranian general observed, "took the Shah by the tail, and threw him into exile like a dead rat."[15]

General Toufanian, the Shah's de-facto minister of war in early 1979, expressed his own bewilderment that the United States could do nothing about the broadcasts of the BBC's Persian Service from Masirah Island in Oman, which regularly carried Khomeini's speeches and were listened to by millions of young Iranians with transistor radios. These broadcasts could be interpreted as signals that the British Government no longer backed the rule of the Shah.[16] He asked straight out "Cannot the U.S. silence the British Broadcasting Corporation Farsi broadcasts?"[17] Since the United States and Great Britain were known to be the closest of allies, the continuing BBC broadcasts must have raised the question among the Shah's generals whether Washington had acquiesced to their transmission.

It was also possible to conclude that United States' support for the Shah had become tepid. Earlier in December 1979, Carter was asked during a breakfast meeting with reporters if he thought the Shah would survive. His mixed answer could only be interpreted as a vote of no confidence in the Shah: "I don't know. I hope so." He then added: "We have never had any intention and don't have any intention to intercede in the internal political affairs of Iran."[18] A statement of neutrality by the U.S. president when the Shah was fighting for his political life could not be interpreted as any kind of public support.

To make matters worse for the Shah, the U.S. ambassador to Iran, William Sullivan, in a cable he wrote to Washington on November 9, 1978, concluded that the United States had to start preparing for a completely new political situation whereby the Shah and his senior military officers would have to leave the country.[19] He argued that Khomeini might reach an accommodation with younger officers in the armed forces.[20] As Sullivan felt that the new religious leadership in Iran, including Khomeini, would still contribute to blocking the Soviet domination of the Persian Gulf region, he presented Khomeini as a man with whom Washington could ultimately do business.

Sullivan was not alone in this naïve misinterpretation of Khomeini. In fact, U.S. diplomats heard similar ideas from leading Iranians. Shapour Bakhtiar, the Shah's prime minister, stated to two political officers from the U.S. Embassy in October 1978 that Khomeini was becoming more flexible, and that his move to France had broadened his horizons because he was meeting with Iranians who had studied in the West, including in the United States.[21] When even a high-level Iranian source gave such an upbeat reading of Khomeini, it is understandable that the U.S. ambassador might reach a similar conclusion.

By early 1979, Sullivan was advising that Washington should work with Mehdi Bazagan, who was positioned to become Khomeini's first prime minister.[22] Carter recalled in his own memoirs that he utterly rejected Sullivan's approach. He still hoped that the United States could rely on the interim government set up by Shapour Bakhtiar, with the help of the Shah. "Ambassador Sullivan," Carter explained, "was recommending that we oppose the plans of the Shah, insist on his immediate departure, and try to form some kind of alliance with Khomeini."[23]

At the very same time that Sullivan was advocating that Washington work with Khomeini and his people, President Carter dispatched General Robert E. Huyser, the deputy commander of U.S.

forces in Europe, to Tehran in order to reinforce Iranian military chiefs supporting the Bakhtiar government, and prepare a military takeover of Iran as a last resort. Sullivan, who took his orders from the Department of State, continued to have a much more benign view of Khomeini's future leadership than did General Huyser and those giving him orders.

The main reason for the misinterpretation of what was going on in Iran was the brilliant manipulation of the United States and its western allies by Khomeini and his entourage. As noted earlier, Khomeini had been in exile in Iraq. But the Shah became concerned that his stature had grown precisely because of the location of his exile. Since Iraq's strongman, Saddam Hussein, reached an accord in Algiers with the Shah in 1975 over their outstanding territorial disputes, Najaf had become open to thousands of Iranian religious pilgrims, who could come to Iraq and hear Khomeini; many brought back tapes of his lectures to Iran.[24] In 1978, the Shah sent a message to Saddam Hussein that it would be better if Khomeini left Iraq.

Anticipating Khomeini

Khomeini accepted the French offer of sanctuary outside of Paris, in a suburb known as Neauphle-le-Chateau, where he held meetings with visitors and gave numerous interviews to the western media from October 1978 until February 1979. French security services opposed the idea of granting Khomeini political asylum, but they were overruled by President Valery Giscard d'Estaing. Western diplomats stationed in Tehran hoped that Khomeini would fade from the public consciousness once he was in France.

French officials even told Khomeini not to get involved in politics while he was on their soil. Nonetheless, Khomeini was able to exploit western freedoms to get his revolutionary message out to the Iranian people far more effectively. His recorded cassettes continued to reach Iran. Khomeini's son, Sayyed Ahmad, headed a committee of advisors at Neauphle-le-Chateau which developed the messages that were to go out to the western audiences. These included Abol-Hassan Bani Sadr, the first president of the eventual Islamic Republic, and Ibrahim Yazdi, a naturalized U.S. citizen who would become Iran's foreign minister.

Khomeini was advised by the committee to stop or at least limit his attacks on the United States. Also, he was to avoid talking about his view of the issue of women's rights. He turned out to be a good student, faithfully implementing the advice he was given. He generally stuck to vague formulae when he addressed journalists about the future.[25] At one point, he even spoke about starting on a "clean slate" with the United States once the Shah was removed.[26] The French security services remained concerned about the radicalizing effects in Iran of Khomeini's continuing presence; they even proposed sending him from France to Algeria, but they were again overruled by the political echelon in Paris who considered him as a kind of pope.

As a result, Khomeini came across to many as a moderate who only sought to bring an end to the tyrannical regime of the Shah.[27] These impressions were further reinforced by Yazdi, who toured the United States and reassured the Carter administration as well as influential academics of Khomeini's ultimate intentions. The State Department's Henry Precht seemed to have become a true believer in the possibility of a positive relationship between Khomeini and the United States; he apparently called the Washington bureau chief of the *New York Times* in mid-December 1978 to give a heads-up to its correspondent in Paris to cover Khomeini's press conference the next day, where the ayatollah was supposed to make positive references to the United States. [28]

The U.S. bureaucracy began preparing to open a new relationship with Khomeini. Some of the earliest messages from Washington came through the French government. Two weeks before Khomeini left France for Iran, the Carter administration authorized its first direct contacts with the ayatollah's entourage; Warren Zimmerman, the political counselor at the U.S. Embassy in Paris, met with Yazdi, from whom he undoubtedly heard the same messages of reassurance about Khomeini.[29] But much of this diplomatic soft stroking turned out to be completely unreliable. In retrospect, it is difficult to understand how the role of Iran's future leader was so fundamentally misread. Where did all the positive interpretations of Khomeini's future role originate?

Years later, Khomeini admitted that he had employed traditional techniques of deception employed by Shiite leaders in the past in the lead up to his return to Iran. He specifically referred to the tactic of *khod'eh*, "tricking one's enemy into a misjudgment of one's true position."[30] He practiced *khod'eh* in the selection of Morteza Motahari, who was to coordinate the Islamic Revolution from Tehran while Khomeini was in exile. In order to accelerate the Shah's departure, he took part in the formation of a new Regency Council that would take over. But Motahtari had no intention of recognizing the new body. His real position was that it was necessary to shape the council so that he could secure the votes for its immediate dissolution after the Shah was gone. The Shah's people figured out that Khomeini's man on the ground in Iran was not really cooperating; Motahari's action was a classic case of *khod'eh*.[31]

Given Washington's need to quickly find Iran specialists so that it could cope with a rapidly changing situation in Tehran, academics from American universities were brought in to a greater extent than in the past to consult with different arms of the U.S. government.

The sentiment sweeping U.S. college campuses at the time was the Shah's regime had been a brutal tyranny that regularly tortured its citizens through its secret service, known as the SAVAK. Khomeini's revolution, this line of thinking went, had to be better than that of the hated Shah, regardless of the paucity of information that existed about the Ayatollah's true intentions. Thus, academics consulted by the government tended to be supportive of Khomeini.

Professor Richard Cottam of the University of Pittsburgh, who had been a former State Department official, gave upbeat assessments about the readiness of the people in Khomeini's circles to work with the United States.[32] He had met Khomeini in Iraq in 1978 before his move to France. Cottam was also in direct contact with Yazdi and was able to maintain regular contacts with the Iranian opposition to the Shah, well before the U.S. government initiated such channels itself. A cable from the Department of State to the U.S. Embassy in Tehran conveyed one of Cottam's reports.

On the one hand, he stressed that the "groups around Khomeini and oppositionist [to the Shah] in Tehran were fearful of a military coup which would lead to bloody repression." He said that he had been in Tehran on January 2–3, 1979, and the "oppositionists were quite definite in their information about a coup." They even had the names of six Iranian generals. On the other hand, Cottam indicated that while the opposition "feared the U.S. would back such a coup," Khomeini's circles were "ready to think in sophisticated terms about future relations with [the] U.S." He raised the theme that they were afraid of the Soviet Union and were "desirous of relying on the U.S. for Iran's defense."[33]

Professor James Bill foresaw the deterioration of the Shah's regime in early 1978, but once Khomeini came to power he described the ayatollah as a "man of impeccable integrity and honesty."[34] He did not envision Khomeini remaining in Tehran and exercising power directly.

Khomeini himself fed this kind of incorrect speculation, skillfully using the Shiite doctrine of *taqiya*—displaying one intention while harboring another—with western reporters while he was still in France. He told the British daily *The Guardian* on November 16, 1978: "I don't want to have the power of government in my hand; I am not interested in personal power."[35] Perhaps for that reason a number of analyses were published in late 1978 that envisioned Khomeini's future rise to power as a relatively innocuous development. Thus the *Washington Post* was willing to consider the possibility in December 1978 that a future "Islamic democracy" under Khomeini might look like a "parliamentary democracy along western lines."[36]

Professor Richard Falk of Princeton University, a specialist in international law who had been an anti-war activist during the Vietnam War, went to visit with Khomeini while he was still living outside of Paris. Upon returning to the U.S., he wrote an op-ed in the *New York Times* published February 16, 1979, entitled "Trusting Khomeini." In the article, Falk argued that the people around Khomeini were "uniformly" individuals who were "moderate" and "progressive." It seemed he took the reassurances he was given about Khomeini's intentions at face value. Falk asserted that they had "a notable record of concern for human rights." Falk concluded that Iran might become a "desperately-needed model of humane government."[37]

The predictions about a moderate Iran that would respect human rights that were heard both inside and outside the U.S. government as the revolution played out turned out to be completely wrong. Revolutionary Iran was not a paragon of human rights. Many of the experts who voiced optimistic scenarios for the future of Iran completely underestimated the intense ideological fervor of the Islamic Revolution and that of its leader. Like many of their counterparts in the Department of State, they could not fathom the depth of anti-American enmity that lay at the very core of the new Iranian leadership.

The Reality of Khomeini's Rule

Formally, the regime that Khomeini established after he arrived in Tehran on February 1, 1979, was a provisional government headed by Prime Minister Mehdi Bazagan. Ibrahim Yazdi emerged as his deputy. But in fact, Iran was being run by the clandestine Revolutionary Council. Its rule was brutal. Sheikh Sadeq Khalkhali, who had been a close aide to Khomeini going back to the 1960s, was appointed as a judge who was supposed to deal with drug trafficking. He acquired the title "Judge Blood" as he sent hundreds of people before firing squads on a variety of offenses.[38] A virtual bloodbath followed.[39] Not only were the Shah's generals executed, but also his prime minister, minister of education (who was a leader in the Iranian women's movement), and the governor of Iran's National Bank.

Ironically, though the Shah's regime had been associated with massive abuses of human rights, in 1977 it had opened up his prisons to the International Committee of the Red Cross (ICRC), which established an office in Tehran during the same year. The Shah ordered a halt to the use of torture in his prisons, and ICRC reports that were issued at this time indicated an improvement in the human rights situation in Iran's prisons. After Khomeini came to power, whatever liberalization had begun was completely reversed, and torture was re-introduced into Iranian prisons. The offices of the ICRC in Tehran were shut down.[40]

Khomeini set the tone for much of what eventually happened in the area of human rights in the Islamic Republic. Across Iran, revolutionary courts that were based on local mosques sprang up called *komitehs*. They helped purge the universities and shut them down for several years.[41] They also arrested, tried, and executed anyone suspected of anti-Islamic or anti-revolutionary activity.[42] Secret trials were held that led to summary executions.[43] Those charged with crimes by the *komitehs* were not entitled to the presence of any defense lawyer. Khalkhali once remarked on this point: "There is no room in the Revolutionary Courts for defense lawyers because they keep quoting laws to play for time, and this tries the patience of the people."[44]

With the brutality of the revolutionary regime in Iran an established fact, it might have been anticipated that a marked shift in attitudes would transpire in official circles about the dangers emanating from Khomeini's rule. The first warning sign for the United States of the new situation came on February 14, 1979, when the

U.S. Embassy in Tehran came under heavy machine gun fire from the roofs of surrounding buildings. A ground assault by irregular guerrilla forces followed.

Many of the attackers on the U.S. Embassy compound wore the scarves of Palestinian terrorist groups, leading Ambassador Sullivan to conclude that they had been trained in Lebanon in Palestine Liberation Organization (PLO) camps, run by a Marxist group.[45] Indeed the attackers came from a Marxist fedayeen militia that was one of many irregular forces that were circulating freely in Tehran right after the fall of the Shah.

A poorly armed Iranian rescue force eventually arrived and brought the first assault on the U.S. Embassy to a halt. Deputy Prime Minister Ibrahim Yazdi soon arrived on behalf of the provisional government. He was apologetic about the attack, explaining that it had been carried out by "undisciplined elements of the revolution." He assured the U.S. diplomats that in the future they would be given full protection. Yazdi added that the new Iranian government was not against the United States, but now there would be a different relationship between Washington and Tehran than there had been in the era of the Shah.[46]

Yazdi left behind a local Iranian force which remained on the embassy grounds for the following months. Sullivan had little faith in Yazdi's guarantees. As it turned out, the group of bodyguards assigned to the U.S. Embassy from a "student militant organization" had been previously assigned as a "hit squad" to assassinate the Americans.[47] The Marxist fedayeen were essentially replaced by radical Islamist mujahideen.

After what he went through in February 1979, it is not surprising that Sullivan concluded years later that the Carter administration's acceptance of the "casual assurances that the embassy was safe was rather reckless."[48] He thought that the U.S. embassy in Tehran should have been closed down, or at least should have adopted more protective measures. The risks to Americans from the new regime were completely underestimated.

It quickly became clear that Khomeini was not going to become an Iranian Gandhi, having built up a military network for himself to support his takeover of Iran via the Islamic revolution. In his youth in the 1940s, he was connected to the "Fedayeen of Islam," an Iranian militant organization whose "holy killers" engaged in assassination.[49] Even while he was in Iraq, he had maintained a secret network of loyalists in Iranian cities,[50] including Ayatollah Montezari, Ayatollah Mottaheri, Akbar Hashemi Rafsanjani (a future president of Iran), and Ali Khamenei, his eventual successor as Supreme Leader of Iran.

In the 1970s, Khomeini saw to it that many of his loyalists underwent military training in Lebanon, Libya, and South Yemen. His two sons, Mostafa and Ahmad, were enrolled in PLO courses near Beirut. Ahmad even became an honorary member of al-Fatah, the PLO's largest constituent organization.[51] The leader of the PLO, Yasser Arafat, built up an alliance with Khomeini during the period of his exile in Iraq, and visited him in Najaf. As a result of this alliance, Khomeini took over Iran in 1979 with a substantial force of trained guerrillas at his disposal.

Hani al-Hassan, the PLO's first ambassador to Tehran, boasted on Tehran Radio in 1979 that more than 10,000 anti-Shah guerillas went through the PLO camps.[52] The PLO training camps played a pivotal role in Khomeini's emerging organization as well. Hadi Ghaffari and Jalal ad-Din Farsi, founders of the Islamic Revolutionary Guards, were both trained in the PLO camps.[53] The eventual commander of the Revolutionary Guards, Mohsen Rezai, was also a graduate of a PLO camp near Beirut.[54]

While the PLO worked closely with Khomeini to provide him with the necessary military capabilities to carry out the Islamic Revolution, the Carter administration was eagerly seeking a formula for obtaining PLO attendance at a planned Arab–Israeli peace conference that was to be held in 1977 in Geneva, under joint Soviet–American auspices. Had President Carter and Secretary of State Cyrus Vance been fully cognizant of the centrality of the PLO role in the subversion of the regime of the Shah of Iran, it is doubtful that Washington would have invested political capital in Arafat's organization.[55]

The Carter Team Reaches Out to Engage Khomeini's Iran

Despite the mounting risks to American and western interests in Tehran, there were rising hopes in official U.S. circles that Washington could do business with the new Iranian regime. An unsigned letter dated September 2, 1979, from a U.S. official in the U.S. Embassy in Tehran to L. Paul Bremmer, who served as deputy executive secretary in the Department of State, conveyed this view: "Things are quite exciting in Tehran. Not surprisingly, I am spending about 85% of my time helping American businessmen distinguish between revolutionary rhetorical form and back-to-business substance."[56]

The letter assumed that the Iranian leadership was becoming more pragmatic: "The Khomeini crowd really seem to want to get people back to work and they are willing to take the necessary steps (and to make the necessary compromises in revolutionary terms) to do it if Americans will modify contracts to reflect the changes wrought by the revolution." The analysis implied that Iran's revolutionary zeal had already ebbed.

Sitting in Washington, Henry Precht was reaching similar conclusions after consulting with U.S. diplomats coming from Tehran. In September he wrote a "secret" analysis to the U.S. Charge d'Affairs, L. Bruce Laingen, stating that he understood there was "a deep sense of inadequacy governing among the leadership" in Iran. In fact, he suggested that there was also "a desire for U.S. help, but an inability to ask for it or even accept it." Implicit in this description was the assumption that Washington might obtain some leverage from the emerging situation, which could improve the standing of the United States in Iran.[57]

There was a general understanding in the diplomatic community that some degree of normalcy was returning to Iran, but also that the position of the Khomeini regime was not that stable. Laingen called upon the French ambassador in Tehran, Raoul Delaye, in late October 1979, who was convinced that "Khomeini will inevitably fail and that the immediate gain will be by the left."[58] In the meantime, the French had signed a contract to build a new power plant for the Iranian city of Tabriz, and as a result the number of French workers in Iran was expected to grow.

Laingen himself prepared an analysis of political trends in Iran that was more subtle than that of the French. It was possible to discern a "recent outspokenness of the moderates," which Laingen attributed to "disillusion with some aspects of the revolution—especially trends toward authoritarian clerical rule." As a result, he wrote to the Department of State that the moderates were "once again finding their voice and beginning to speak out."[59]

During the nine months between the February attack on the U.S. Embassy and the seizure of the U.S. Embassy personnel as hostages in November, the "governing attitude" in Washington, according to Gary Sick of the National Security Council, was to encourage the normalization of relations between Iran and the United States.[60] For example, Khomeini's army needed spare parts in order to wage their military campaign against a growing separatist movement in Iranian Kurdistan. The Carter White House supported the supply of U.S. weapons to Khomeini's forces, helping the Islamic Republic crush the Kurds. In August 1979, U.S. spare parts were being supplied to Iran, despite the criticism that had been voiced in the U.S. Senate about the widespread human rights violations that were being reported from the Islamic Republic.[61]

As a result, the size of the U.S. staff stationed in Tehran, after being initially cut, actually grew. Undoubtedly, this environment must have contributed to a certain amount of complacency in the U.S. Embassy, despite the February attack. For example, many classified files were not destroyed or shipped back to Washington, but rather were retained in the embassy compound. These files were eventually seized when the U.S. Embassy was captured. Their contents were subsequently published in dozens of volumes.

The United States made every effort to engage diplomatically with the new Iranian regime. In early October 1979, Secretary of State Cyrus Vance met with Ibrahim Yazdi, who had become Iran's foreign minister, at the opening of the UN General Assembly in New York. According to the U.S. record of the conversation, Vance said that Washington "wished Iran's leaders well and had set in motion certain forms of cooperation."[62] Vance tried to be as forthcoming as possible: "We were prepared to go further if Iran wished. We wanted to join the Iranians in combating the mistrust that existed...."[63] The United States plainly wanted to engage Iran.

Yazdi did not reciprocate. He dismissively said that "these views had been conveyed to him in the past" by the U.S. Charges D'Affaires in Tehran. Yazdi felt that the United States "did not understand and accept the reality of the new Iran." He complained that the United States was still engaging in "unwarranted interference in Iran's internal affairs." Yazdi demanded that the United States accept the Islamic Revolution: "Your acceptance of the Revolution must be translated in some tangible actions."[64] He was suspicious of the U.S. role in organizing the Gulf states into new security initiatives. He also asked whether U.S. plans for a Rapid Deployment Force in the area was directly connected with Iran's revolution. The Vance–Yazdi discussions clearly show that the Carter administration was anxious to reach out to Iran, but Iran was not ready for the embrace.

The U.S. side seemed to misread Iran completely, and came away with optimistic conclusions about the future of U.S.-Iranian relations. Assistant Secretary of State Harold Newsom, who attended the Vance meeting with Yazdi, reflected that "the Iranian suspicions of us were only natural in the post-revolutionary situation but that after a transition period common interests could provide a basis for future cooperation." He qualified his assessment, adding that the new U.S.–Iranian relationship would not be "on the scale of before but sufficient to demonstrate that Iran has not been lost to us and to the West."[65]

Another sign of Washington's desire to advance normalization was the decision of Zbigniew Brzezinski to meet Prime Minister Barzagan, Foreign Minister Yazdi, and Defense Minister Chamran in Algiers on November 1, 1979, during celebrations for the 25th anniversary of Algeria's independence. The Iranians recall that the meeting was at Brezezinski's request, which those involved on the U.S. side denied.[66] It was held in Barzagan's hotel room, rather than in a neutral location, which is somewhat indicative of the strong U.S. interest in holding the meeting and not standing on ceremony.

There were urgent matters to discuss. A few days earlier, on October 22, President Carter had given permission for the Shah of Iran to come to New York for medical treatment for malignant lymphoma and severe jaundice, once it became clear that the hospitals in Mexico, where he had been staying, were inadequate for the treatment he needed. He was no longer responding to chemotherapy. An American doctor who visited the Shah determined that he would need to undergo further diagnostic testing at Sloan Kettering Hospital in New York.[67]

Yazdi warned Brzezinski that the Iranian government was disturbed by the arrival of the Shah in the United States. Brzezinski tried to find common ground with the Iranians, stressing the idea that Iran and the United States shared common strategic interests—presumably against Soviet expansionism in the Middle East.

Within three days of the Brzezinski–Yazdi meeting, Iranian militants stormed the U.S. Embassy in Tehran and took its staff hostage. Initially sixty-two U.S. citizens were held. The attack on the U.S. Embassy had been organized by five students who called their student coalition "Strengthen the Unity." But for the operation, they called themselves the "Muslim Students Following the Imam's Line," in order to firmly establish that they were loyal to Khomeini and not to any of the Marxist militias that still existed.[68] Several days prior to the attack, Ayatollah Khomeini released a Friday message to Iranian students urging them to "expand your attacks against America and Israel with full force, and to compel the U.S. into extraditing this criminal, deposed Shah."[69]

Besides its leader, Ibrahim Asgharzadeh, one of the original members of the group, by his own public admission was Mahmoud Ahmadinejad, who would eventually serve as president of Iran (though he would later argue that he did not actually enter the embassy compound, contrary to the claim of several hostages, who remembered his face).[70] The student committee directing the attack notified a member of the Assembly of Experts, the body of clerics drafting the Islamic Republic's new constitution, ahead of time, as well as the Revolutionary Guards.

The takeover of the U.S. Embassy appeared to involve the collusion of the highest levels of the Iranian government. The Revolutionary Guards who were assigned to protect the U.S. Embassy had withdrawn.[71] Indeed, the students thanked the Revolutionary Guards for not preventing the takeover.[72] A Top Secret U.S. intelligence assessment dated December 29, 1979, analyzed the captors of the Americans: "Although the label 'students' is used in the media and in this report when referring to the principal captives the label is not correct." The document said they were members of a "mojahedin [sic] faction." The analysis added that "the leadership of the collective group (which is called the committee) receives counsel on propaganda and security matters from PLO and fedayeen advisors."[73]

The students appeared to be well-trained or were reinforced by other Iranian revolutionary personnel. There was Hossein Sheikhol-eslam, the notorious "Gap Tooth," who took charge of some of the most important interrogations, like that of the CIA station chief, Tom Ahern.[74] He had been a student at the University of

California at Berkeley in the early 1970s and hence spoke perfect English. Physically, he had a missing front tooth, which gave him a memorable face with the American hostages.

Years later "Gap Tooth" would become involved in the export of the Iranian revolution abroad through a position he was given in the Iranian foreign ministry as an undersecretary. He placed Revolutionary Guard agents in Iranian embassies abroad.[75] He was later spotted in Damascus on October 22, 1983, a day before an attack on the U.S. Marine Barracks in Beirut, when he unexpectedly checked out of his hotel and headed into Lebanon.[76] Years later, he would greet a high-power U.S. delegation headed by Robert McFarlane that visited Tehran in the context of what came to be known as the Iran-Contra scandal.[77]

The ideology of the "students" involved in the U.S. Embassy takeover was imbued with strong anti-American expressions that reflected those of the Islamic Revolution. In a statement they released which was broadcast on Iranian radio on February 26, 1980, it became clear that they directed their message beyond Iran, first to the surrounding regimes: "All the oppressed must join together and remove the roots of corruption from their countries." But their call for action extended to the West, as well: "World peace and safety depend on the extinction of the oppressors; the oppressed will not reach the heritage granted to them by Almighty God so long as these ignorant hegemonists are alive in the world."[78]

The United States was the focus of their rage: "The world of Islam is now in combat with the world of blasphemy, and the noble nation of Iran, after providing thousands of martyrs and numerous casualties, is still faced with satanic plots from all directions, especially from America." According to the students, the United States was the root cause of all the setbacks that the Muslim world suffered: "The criminal America . . . as the Immam [sic.] says, is the cause of all misfortunes of the Muslims and is plotting against us overtly and covertly."[79]

The Carter administration was very careful about making any threatening moves against Iran in the immediate aftermath of the seizure of the U.S. Embassy. Vance called it a "strategy of restraint."[80] Carter's policy was summarized as follows: "The United States would pursue a campaign of political, diplomatic and economic initiatives to convince the revolutionary leadership in Iran—by persuasion if possible and by pressure if necessary—that it was in their interest to release the hostages promptly and safely."[81] Any military contingency planning was kept secret.[82]

For example, on November 6, 1979, a day after the embassy fell, U.S. National Security Council officials apparently leaked to the *Washington Post* that there would not be any change in the status quo—"no military alert, no movement of forces, no resort to military contingency plans."[83] President Carter thought about diverting the U.S. Navy's aircraft carrier, *USS Midway*, from the Indian Ocean to the Persian Gulf. But he asked his military advisors if the movement of the carrier could be kept off the front page of the *New York Times*. Carter was concerned about being too provocative.

Ultimately, Carter decided against moving in with more naval airpower as changing the carrier's deployment would be detected. The United States had two choices: threatening the use of force to demonstrate American power in order to provide muscle to U.S. diplomatic efforts, or relying on pure diplomacy, setting aside any hint of a military option, for now. President Carter chose the latter option.

Ayatollah Khomeini initially neither supported nor denounced the seizure of the U.S. Embassy, but rather sought to gauge how Washington would react. He let 36 hours go by before publicly backing the assault on the U.S. Embassy and the seizure of its diplomats.[84] His son, Ahmad Khomeini, recorded in his memoirs years later that prior to clarifying his position, the ayatollah was concerned that the United States might take offensive military action that could topple his regime.[85] Having received no ultimatum from Washington, Khomeini became more assertive as he addressed the Students Following the Imam's Line: "The Americans can't do a damn thing.... The speculation about American military intervention is nonsense."[86]

The United States prepared a diplomatic offensive instead. The Department of State reached out to Ayatollah Beheshti, who served on the Revolutionary Council, informing him that the United States was ready to send an emissary to meet with the Iranian leadership to resolve the crisis. Two envoys were chosen, Ramsey Clark, a former attorney general who knew Khomeini and supported Third World causes, and William Miller, a former foreign service official who spoke Farsi.

After meeting with Carter and Vance, the two envoys were flown to Turkey, where they waited for word of their meeting with Khomeini. But the Iranian leader denied them permission to enter Iranian airspace. Moreover, Khomeini issued a decree that no Iranian official was permitted to meet with a representative of the U.S. government.[87] The Iranian pre-condition for any negotiations was the return of the Shah to Iran to stand trial. The Carter administration's first effort to use diplomacy to free the American hostages failed.

The United States did not immediately slam sanctions on Iran in order to ratchet up diplomatic pressures. The State Department managed to limit the first American measures against Iran to only prohibiting the supply of spare parts for the Iranian armed forces that had been ordered during the era of the Shah.[88] After this limited step, the Carter administration took further measures only when it learned that the Iranians were about to act.

Thus, once it became clear on November 12, 1979, that Iran would no longer sell any oil to the United States, Washington preempted Tehran by announcing that it was prohibiting American citizens from buying Iranian oil. Subsequently, on November 14, the United States learned that the Iranian government planned to withdraw its assets from American banks, so the Carter administration quickly froze all Iranian assets in the United States.

Carter tried unconventional diplomacy as well. He opened a channel with the PLO. Three days after the U.S. Embassy was overrun, a two-man PLO delegation arrived in Tehran to negotiate, including Khalil al-Wazir (Abu Jihad), who orchestrated PLO attacks on Israel, and Saad Sayel (Abu Walid), the chief of PLO military operations.[89] The identities of the envoys revealed the extent to which Iranian-PLO ties had been rooted in military cooperation.

The PLO channel was only partly successful. The Iranians wanted to use the hostage issue to drive a wedge between different sectors of American society, so after the PLO's intervention, they decided to release thirteen African-American and female hostages.

There was an effort to use the UN as a diplomatic instrument to help the captured U.S. diplomats. A month after the assault on the U.S. Embassy, the UN Security Council adopted Resolution 457 calling on Iran to release the hostages and requesting the UN secretary-general to mediate between the parties. Iran rejected the resolution. The Carter administration also turned to the International Court of Justice (ICJ) in The Hague in order to help it build an international consensus against Iran on the basis of international legality.

The ICJ ruled that the hostages must be released immediately. Iran was not moved. By the end of December 1979, when the United States sought to move to active economic sanctions against Iran at the UN, it found Japan and the Europeans reluctant to go beyond their past condemnations of Iranian behavior and actually give up their oil and business links with Iran.[90] When finally a sanctions resolution came up for a vote on January 13, 1980, it was not adopted because of a Soviet veto, though 10 out of 15 Security Council members supported sanctions.[91] Iran completely ignored all this diplomatic activity in the UN and in other international institutions.

By relying on conventional diplomacy that might be used to resolve a territorial dispute between two European states, the

Carter administration badly misread Iran and its revolutionary regime. As the National Security Council's Iran expert, Gary Sick, described, the "fatal flaw of U.S. policy" was the assumption that the United States could bring sufficient pressure on Iran to accelerate Tehran's decision to free the hostages. This grew out of "the tendency *to underestimate Khomeini's willingness and ability to absorb external economic and political punishment in the pursuit of his revolutionary objectives*" (emphasis added).[92]

And America's western allies did not make the diplomatic option any easier. Even after the Soviet veto in the UN Security Council, the Carter administration declared that it was going to proceed with organizing international sanctions, nonetheless. Deputy Secretary of State Warren Christopher was dispatched to Europe for this very purpose. The United States seemed to have a strong hand: the seizure of American diplomats from their embassy was an indisputable violation of their diplomatic immunity and of international law.

In this regard, Christopher was backed up by a ruling of the ICJ and the initial resolution of the UN Security Council. However, it soon became clear to him that European commercial interests were blocking the adoption of any sanctions against Iran. Despite the fact that American diplomats were languishing in captivity as a result of a completely illegal act, Christopher was turned down. The European refusal to cooperate with the United States in implementing sanctions was universal. European diplomats tried to argue that new sanctions against Iran would only drive Tehran into the arms of the Soviet Union.[93]

It would take until September 1980 for the Iranians to signal that they wanted to end the hostage crisis. The death of the Shah of Iran on July 27, 1980, made the original demand for his extradition a moot point. The Iraqi attack on Iran in late September also gave Tehran new motivation to resolve the hostage issue. Iran's highest priority then became stopping the invasion of the forces of Saddam Hussein, rather than its previous focus on the

United States. But there was no real forward movement until President Carter lost the U.S. presidential elections to Ronald Reagan in November 1980.

The White House dispatched Deputy Secretary of State Warren Christopher to Algeria, which proved willing to serve as an intermediary with Iran. For thirteen days in January 1981, Christopher negotiated the release of the American hostages. Christopher used Reagan's imminent inauguration for negotiating leverage, arguing that the Iranians were better off cutting a deal with "the devil they knew," rather than with the new administration, which might be much tougher.[94]

The agreement was reached on January 18, 1981. But the hostages were not released until Inauguration Day. At the lunch following his being sworn in, President Reagan announced: "Some thirty minutes ago the planes bearing our prisoners left Iranian airspace." The Iranian nightmare that began with the fall of the Shah appeared to be over.

But even the Reagan administration, which entered office with the return of American hostages, would soon be confounded by the Iranian challenge. It, too, underestimated and in many cases was outmaneuvered by Iran. As a result, the United States failed to halt Iran's determination to become a hegemonic power in the oil-rich Persian Gulf and across the Middle East. And to reach this status, the Iranians would conclude, they needed nuclear weapons.

Chapter 5:

Iran Attacks America in Beirut, but the Secretary of Defense Is in Denial

THE U.S. MARINE CORPS' 24th Marine Amphibious Unit deployed to Beirut in May 1983 to join a multinational peacekeeping force in Lebanon, which also included British, French, and Italian troops. Lebanon had been in a state of chaos since the outbreak of the Lebanese Civil War in 1975. With the eviction of Palestinian terrorist groups from Jordan by King Hussein in 1970, Lebanon emerged as the main front against Israel. The Palestinians had also become a party in the civil war itself by joining the Sunni Muslims and fighting against Lebanon's Christian militias. Syria intervened militarily in 1976 but soon clashed with its own Lebanese allies, who had sought its involvement in the first place. Israel entered Lebanon in 1982 in order to uproot the strongholds of the Palestine Liberation Organization (PLO). At the end of that operation, the multinational peacekeeping force was deployed to oversee the PLO's evacuation of Beirut.

After the Israel Defense Forces (IDF) withdrew from Beirut, the multinational forces returned to the Lebanese capital to provide a stabilizing presence for Lebanon's internal situation and strengthen its fragile government. The Reagan administration was seeking the withdrawal of both Israel and Syria from Lebanon, but only the Israelis were starting to pull back. In the meantime, national reconciliation talks between Lebanese factions were scheduled for the end of October 1983, with preliminary talks on October 24 at Beirut's International Airport.[1] The United States had historical ties with Lebanon, where American missionaries and educators had been active since the mid-nineteenth century. President Dwight D. Eisenhower had used the U.S. Marines in 1958 to bolster the embattled Lebanese government, which was facing increasing threats from pan-Arab groups loyal to Egypt's president Abdel Nasser.

Early in the morning on Sunday, October 23, 1983, Lebanese Shiite militiamen ambushed a water delivery truck en route to the Marines with its daily delivery, and replaced it with a fake water truck, outfitted with about 12,000 pounds of high explosives combined with canisters of compressed gas. An Iranian citizen, Ismalal Ascari, drove the enormous truck-bomb along the airport service road next to the Marine barracks, which was established with their headquarters immediately next to Beirut International Airport.[2]

At 6:22 a.m., while most of the troops were still asleep, the truck plowed through the outer barbed wire fence and a wall of sandbags and crashed into the rear wall of the four story concrete barracks, heading for the center of the building. When the speeding truck reached the lobby, it exploded, causing the deaths of 241 U.S. servicemen. Several minutes later, another suicide bomber struck the headquarters of France's Third Company of the 1st Parachute Infantry Regiment in West Beirut, killing 58 French soldiers. On November 4, less than two weeks later, a third suicide truck bomb was detonated at Israel's military headquarters in the southern Lebanese port of Tyre, killing 60 people, including 29 Israeli soldiers.

The commanding officer of the Marine forces in Beirut, Colonel Timothy J. Geraghty, would later recall that the attack on the Marines' base constituted the highest loss of life in a single day for the U.S. Marine Corps since D-Day or Iwo Jima in World War II.[3] Over half a mile away, all the windows in the control tower of the Beirut International Airport were shattered. The explosion left an eight-foot deep crater. Expert opinion would characterize the blast as the largest non-nuclear explosion that had ever been detonated on the face of the Earth.

In Washington, President Ronald Reagan convened the National Security Council to prepare the United States response to the attack. The truck bombing was extremely similar to the suicide bombing attack on the U.S. Embassy in Beirut on April 18, a little over six months previously, that had killed over 60 people; at the time, a shadowy pro-Iranian group had taken credit. Reagan wrote in his daily diary: "We all believe Iranians did this bombing just as they did with our embassy last April."[4]

Nevertheless, in a meeting with the NSC, Secretary of Defense Caspar Weinberger was adamant: the United States did not have specific knowledge of who actually attacked the Marine barracks, and therefore he was not prepared to authorize air strikes on any suspected targets.[5] On November 14, President Reagan approved an attack on Lebanese targets that was to be carried out two days later.

Weinberger apparently aborted the planned air strike. Reagan deferred to Weinberger's judgment; he would note in his diary on November 16 that Israel by itself destroyed one of the Iranian camps that the United States had targeted, but ultimately decided not to move against. It was called An Nabi Shit: "That was one of the targets we were looking at but didn't have enough information yet."[6]

Years later, during an interview on PBS in September 2001, Weinberger reiterated this position: "We still do not have actual knowledge of who did the bombing of the Marine barracks at the

Beirut Airport, and we certainly didn't then."[7] Weinberger complained that the United States lacked proper intelligence, especially adequate human intelligence to get into terrorist organizations. He explained that made finding out who was responsible for the attacks more difficult.[8]

But the evidence at the time of the attacks completely contradicted Weinberger's argument. First, Iran had been operating within Lebanon since June 1982, when it exploited Israel's invasion of Lebanon to dispatch its Islamic Revolutionary Guard Corps to the Bekaa Valley in Eastern Lebanon in order to come to Lebanon's defense. The first elements of a large contingent of Iran's Revolutionary Guards arrived in Damascus on June 12, 1982, to deploy in the Bekaa Valley. Over time it would become a force of 1,500 men. The Lebanese Shiite leader, Hussein Musawi, began organizing the militia of the new pro-Iranian group, which would eventually call itself Hizbullah.

Second, while Washington had doubts about the identity of the perpetrators of the October 1983 attacks, the French had no doubt the Iranians were to blame. Information available at the time appeared to be sufficiently damning for President Reagan to initially authorize a joint U.S.-French air assault in retaliation for the terrorist attacks on both countries' military contingents in Beirut.[9] But the French ultimately acted alone, launching an air strike against the barracks housing the Revolutionary Guards in Baalbek in Lebanon. Weinberger recalled that he told the French Minister of Defense, Charles Hernu, "Unfortunately it is a bit too late for us to join you in this one."[10] Thus both Israel and France had independently reached the conclusion that the Iranians were behind the escalation of attacks occurring in Lebanon.

Third, and most importantly, Weinberger did not need to receive French intelligence reports to determine who attacked in Beirut, for the identity of those who stood behind the bombing of the Marine barracks was available within the U.S. intelligence community. Around September 26, 1983—less than a month before the attack—Iran's Ministry of Foreign Affairs sent a cable to the Iranian ambassador to Damascus, Ali Akbar Mohtashemi, directing him to contact Hussein Musawi and instruct him "to take a spectacular action against the United States Marines."[11]

The message had been intercepted by the United States National Security Agency (NSA), but was not passed along until two days after the bombing to Admiral James A. Lyons, the Deputy Chief of Naval Operations for Plans, Policy and Operations. According to other intercepted cables, the Iranians transferred $25,000 to their Damascus embassy to help fund this operation.[12] The NSA had also intercepted a subsequent telephone conversation from the Revolutionary Guards in Baalbek to the Iranian Embassy in Damascus in which they requested permission to carry out the planned attack.[13]

The upshot of all this evidence was summarized years later by Colonel Timothy J. Geraghty, the local Marine Commander in Beirut: "Members of the intelligence community compiled an all-sources damage assessment after the Marine barracks bombing. In it, they studied signals, overhead, and human intelligence and concluded *the evidence was overpowering that Iran had been behind it* (emphasis added). An intelligence expert close to the final assessment stated he did not know anyone who studied the information and drew any other conclusion." [14]

Other striking events could have tied Iran to the operation against the United States. For example, the very morning of the bombing of the Marine barracks, the Iranians suspiciously evacuated their Beirut embassy; its personnel quickly fled the building. Like the French, the Lebanese government had no doubt about who perpetrated the attacks in Beirut. A few weeks after the bombings, Lebanon cut off diplomatic relations with Iran. The director-general of the Lebanese Foreign Ministry went to the Iranian Charge d'Affaires and gave him and his embassy staff three days to leave Lebanon. It is probable that the Lebanese government took these steps out of consideration for the United

States—the Lebanese president-Amin Gemayel was on the eve of visiting Washington—yet the highest levels of the U.S. government inexplicably were still not prepared to finger Tehran.[15]

The United States itself found further incriminating evidence against Iran. FBI explosives experts concluded from their forensic analysis that the explosive material used was pentaerythritol tetranitrate, known as PETN. This explosive was manufactured commercially, but it was primarily used by the United States military. When commercially manufactured PETN was detonated, normally it was completely consumed. In the case of the Marine barracks in Beirut, the FBI found unconsumed PETN particles, which indicated it was the raw bulk form of the explosive.[16]

The raw bulk form of PETN was not manufactured anywhere in Lebanon; however, it was definitely produced in Iran.[17] Experts analyzing the remnants of the explosion agreed that whoever constructed the truck bomb had to have possessed specialized training in the use of explosives. It was noteworthy years later that the commander of the Revolutionary Guards in Lebanon's Bekaa Valley, Mustafa Mohammad-Najjar, would be promoted in August 2005 to become the Minister of Defense of Iran.

Weinberger was not alone in missing the Iranian connection. A New York Times analysis published nearly a year later on September 21, 1984, disclosed that some experts in the intelligence community believed that the April 1983 attack on the U.S. Embassy in Beirut was planned and organized by Palestinians, despite the fact that an Iranian group had taken credit.[18] They considered the October attacks even more mysterious: "Details about who was responsible for the attacks on the French and American garrisons in Beirut are even hazier."[19] But the broader Middle Eastern context for what was happening in Lebanon should have given observers more than sufficient evidence of Iranian involvement.

Since the 1979 overthrow of the Shah, Ayatollah Khomeini had sought to export the Islamic Revolution, chiefly through Shiite communities in the Arab world. The Iranians supported Shiite uprisings in the Eastern Province of Saudi Arabia in 1979 and in 1980, while in 1981 there was a pro-Shiite coup attempt in Bahrain, located in the Persian Gulf—Shiites made up 70 percent of its population.[20]

In Kuwait, 17 percent of the population was Shiite, including a significant Iranian expatriate community. Iran's neighbor, Iraq, which in the late 1970s had a Shiite majority of 55 percent (a quarter million of which had Iranian ancestry), was another target for Iranian revolutionary activity. In this context, Tehran sought to dispatch 600 Iranian volunteers to Lebanon in 1979 to build up the Iranian presence, but was blocked by Syria at the time.[21]

Lebanon, with only a 30 percent Shiite population, was in some ways the most ideal site in the Middle East for exporting Iran's Islamic Revolution. Because it had been immersed in a civil war since 1975, unlike Saddam Hussein's Iraq, its central government was weak and could not resist the growth of a new Shiite autonomous area. This permitted the Iranians to set up state-like Islamic institutions within Lebanon. As Iran's ambassador to Lebanon noted, "The biggest obstacle to starting Islamic movements in the world is the people's attachment to governments, but since the republic of Lebanon does not have much power, there is no serious obstacle in the way of the people of Lebanon."[22]

Iranians had special attachments to Lebanon, as well. When the sixteenth century rulers of Iran, the Safavids, decided to adopt Shiite Islam, instead of Sunni Islam, as the religion of their empire, they imported Shiite clerics from Lebanon for that very purpose. Khomeini's revolutionaries knew Lebanon well, from their days training in PLO camps in Lebanon. Many of Lebanon's Shiite scholars had studied in the seminaries of Najaf, Iraq, where Khomeini had given lectures during his years in exile.

Iran had new motivations to dispatch a contingent to Lebanon when it became clear that the local Shiite movement in Lebanon, *Amal* (Hope), did not accept the principle of *velayat-e faqih* (the rule of the jurisprudent), by acknowledging Khomeini's supremacy.[23]

Amal also opposed the dispatch of the Islamic Revolutionary Guards to Lebanon when it was proposed in early 1980.[24] In Tehran's judgment, a new Shiite organization was needed to show greater loyalty.

The Birth of Hizbullah

Part of the difficulty in pinning down who was targeting the West in Lebanon was the nature of the Shiite militias that were forming at the time. They operated around closely connected families and were extremely difficult for intelligence agencies to penetrate. The Shiites' use of *taqiya*, the religiously approved doctrine of deception to protect themselves in the Sunni dominated Middle East, further complicated what information intelligence managed to gather.[25]

While Iran's presence in Lebanon was no secret, the Lebanese Shiite groups expended tremendous energies trying to obfuscate Iran's critical role in promoting the wave of terrorist attacks that were transpiring. For example, while Palestinian terrorist groups would phone in to western wire services to take credit for attacks they conducted (and therefore build up their stature with potential recruits in Lebanon), Shiite militias repeatedly used the names of front organizations to hide the real culprits behind the attacks. Years later, one of Hizbullah's founders, Naim Qassem, who is now the organization's deputy secretary-general, explained that Hizbullah delayed announcing its responsibility for different attacks "... for the purpose of confusing the enemy as to the identity of the faction undertaking operations."[26]

But there was little reason to doubt that Hizbullah was behind the Beirut bombings—and behind Hizbullah was the hand of Iran. Hizbullah was secretly founded in 1982 by Ali Akbar Mohtashemi, the same Iranian ambassador to Damascus who had received secret instructions from Tehran to attack the Marines and other western forces in Beirut. During Hizbullah's early years, he personally chaired the Lebanese *Majlis al-Shura* or Consultative Council—Hizbullah's initial seven-man ruling body—and served as Khomeini's personal representative at the council's meetings.

Indeed, in subsequent years the Secretary-General (the head) of Hizbullah acquired a second title: the Personal Representative of the Supreme Leader (of Iran) in Lebanon. Moreover, over the years, the Consultative Council of Hizbullah contained two permanent representatives from Iran—including a high-ranking member of the Revolutionary Guards.[27]

Given this background, and Mohatshemi's role in particular, Hizbullah is indisputably a thoroughly Iranian product. In its early days, its Consultative Council met on a monthly basis within the Iranian Embassy in Syria. Recently, Naim Qassem revealed on an Iranian Arabic television channel, *al-Kawathar*, that when Hizbullah "commenced its activities in 1982, it did so according to the opinion and religious ruling of Imam Khomeini, may Allah bless his secret. . . . "[28] But Hizbullah did not come to be known by that name until 1985, when it declared its existence in an open letter. Deception was an essential part of Hizbullah strategy which its leaders effectively mastered. Naim Qassem confirmed their use of front organizations; he disclosed that Hizbullah's early operations "were undertaken under different banners."[29]

One front organization was known as the "Islamic Jihad Organization" and another was called the "Revolutionary Justice Organization."[30] Heading Islamic Jihad was Imad Mughniyeh, a Lebanese Shiite who was born in 1962 and recruited by Fatah's Force-17 in the mid-1970s to protect Yasser Arafat. After the PLO's security networks in Beirut were dismantled as a result of Israel's incursion in Lebanon, Mughniyeh sought a new paymaster. He turned to the Iranian Embassy in Beirut, recognizing that Tehran was emerging as the rising power in Lebanon. Mughniyeh came to the attention of Ali Akbar Mohtashemi, who was effectively Hizbullah's chairman in its early years.[31]

Mughniyeh's family would play a critical role in Shiite networks during Hizbullah's formative years. Imad Mughniyeh was initially responsible for the personal security of Sheikh Muhammad Hussein Fadlallah, the most noted spiritual leader of the Lebanese Shiites. His brother, Jihad Mughniyeh, replaced him when he took command of Islamic Jihad. Hizbullah denied it had any connection with Mughniyeh, an argument that came to be parroted by western academics, but after his 2008 assassination, the Hizbullah leadership went out of its way to eulogize him, even describing him as one of the organization's greatest martyrs.[32]

The cover name Islamic Jihad confused many observers as it was intended to, for it gave Hizbullah deniability regarding its involvement in specific operations. It was yet another case of the effective use of *taqiya*. The deception resulted in conflicting assessments within the CIA. Less than a year after the attack on the Marine barracks in Beirut, a top secret document belonging to the CIA's Directorate of Intelligence indicated that the U.S. intelligence community did not fully accept the argument that Hizbullah had nothing to do with the front groups that had taken credit for various attacks. Even before Hizbullah had formally identified itself, the CIA paper, which was dated September 27, 1984, had identified it as "the pro-Iranian radical Shia movement in Lebanon," and specifically called Islamic Jihad the "terrorist component" of Hizbullah.[33]

In contrast, Robert Baer, who during the 1980s was a field officer for CIA Operations on the ground in Lebanon, wrote years later that he was convinced that Islamic Jihad was "a distinct organization" from Hizbullah.[34] It stands to reason that he formulated this position in the period in which he served in Lebanon. The hostage-takers of Islamic Jihad, according to Baer, "were taking orders from Iran." But Iran was also using its Revolutionary Guards in Lebanon to give orders to Hizbullah. Whether Islamic Jihad was part of Hizbullah or autonomous from it, the Iranians and their Lebanese supporters managed to obfuscate who exactly was perpetrating the terrorist attacks against western positions.

The second front organization for Hizbullah, the Revolutionary Justice Organization, was under the command of Ahmad Musawi, an Iranian who worked for the Iranian Foreign Ministry. His brother had been Iran's charge d'affaires in Lebanon, but had been kidnapped on July 4, 1982, by Lebanese Christian militias along with his entourage of three Iranians. Within weeks David Dodge, the acting president of the American University in Beirut, was kidnapped and subsequently held captive in Tehran. The seizure of the four Iranian diplomats set off a series of kidnapping initiatives in Lebanon that were intended to help seek their release. Hizbullah did not want to be associated with the kidnapping of western hostages, so having front organizations that took credit instead was extremely useful.

Islamic Jihad claimed responsibility for the bombing of the U.S. Embassy and the subsequent kidnapping of the CIA station chief in Beirut, William Buckley. As late as 1986, the CIA knew almost nothing about Islamic Jihad. Although it understood that Islamic Jihad had some Iranian and Syrian backing, it did not believe these states had substantial influence over the group. As a result, it was the CIA's assessment that Islamic Jihad "operated largely independent of state control."[35] And yet, Iran was deeply involved with both Islamic Jihad and the Revolutionary Justice Organization.

Some of America's best experts on the Middle East failed to see Iran's decisive input in orchestrating terrorism against the West. Gary Sick, who had served on the National Security Council under President Carter with special responsibility for Iran, nonetheless concluded in his 1986 memoirs:

The success of the Iranian revolution against the shah and the extreme religious nationalism of Khomeini's rhetoric made Iran a model for revolutionary groups of almost any stripe. Iran cultivated the image and avoided direct criticism of guerrilla actions, often leaving the impression of closer association with these groups and their operations than have been justified. This sometimes backfired. Iran was occasionally embarrassed—and its interests damaged—by acts of violence over which it probably had little or no influence.[36]

Sick thus concluded, "It would be an error to assume that Iran was the origin or control point for the terrorist plague in the Middle East."

Sick was not alone in seeking to separate Hizbullah from Iran. A variation of his view was offered by Augustus Richard Norton, a former U.S. Army Officer who served as a UN military observer in Southern Lebanon in the early 1980s; while he now admits that Hizbullah was Iran's "stalking horse" in Lebanon during the 1980s, he concludes that by the end of the decade, Iranian support for Hizbullah "wavered." He adds that "Iran did not exercise direct control of the kidnappings" in Lebanon. Instead, he asserts that Iran was only able to "exert strong ideological influence."[37]

Yet recently, Mohtashemi explicitly admitted that Hizbullah was nothing less than a full-blown Iranian security organization, describing it as one of "the institutions of the ruling regime in Tehran and a main element of its military."[38] He disclosed that Hizbullah operatives underwent military training in Iran and even fought alongside the Revolutionary Guards against Saddam Hussein's armies in the Iran-Iraq War.[39] This connection was corroborated by Hizbullah's operatives.

Sheikh Subh al-Tufeili, who served as Hizbullah's first secretary-general in the 1980s, left no doubt about its direct ties to Iran; he plainly admitted years later: "Hizbullah is a tool, and it is an integral part of the Iranian intelligence apparatus."[40] Moreover, Hizbullah's current deputy secretary-general, Naim Qassem, disclosed in 2007 that the authority for Hizbullah suicide operations came from the *velayat-e faqih*—the rule of the jurisprudent: Ayatollah Khomeini and later Ayatollah Khamenei.[41]

Although many in the U.S. security establishment saw the direct Iranian connection with terrorism, they did not always appreciate

Iran's critical role in Hizbullah operations. Many felt that the United States and its allies had to be restrained with Iran, because of the lack of certainty about its precise role in the attacks on the United States. Yet in the absence of a U.S. response to successive Iranian provocations, Iran did not sit back quietly, but exploited what it perceived as western weakness by adopting a policy of continuing escalation.

The Consequences of Western Restraint

A wave of Iranian-backed attacks followed the events in October 1983 in Beirut. The United States was not the only target. France's sole retaliation against the camp at Baalbek was insufficient to deter further Hizbullah attacks against French interests. Hizbullah attacked French soldiers in Southern Lebanon in December 1983, killing ten.[42] The Hizbullah offensive began to spread across the entire Middle East.

On December 12, 1983, six bomb attacks occurred in the Persian Gulf emirate of Kuwait. The United States and French embassies were targeted, as well as the compound of the Raytheon Corporation, a leading U.S. defense contractor. Bombs were also detonated against the control tower of Kuwait International Airport. The group taking credit for the attack used the same cover name—Islamic Jihad—as the Beirut attackers. Kuwaiti security authorities apprehended seventeen suspects, most of whom were connected with the Iraqi Shiite group, al-Dawa. But Lebanese Shiites were also involved, including the brother-in-law of Imad Mughniyeh, Mustafa Yusuf Badr al-Din. They became known as the Dawa-17; and efforts to secure their release from a Kuwaiti prison drove Iranian-sponsored terrorism for several years.

Roughly twenty years later, when Iraqi al-Dawa became a part of the Iraqi government after the fall of Saddam Hussein, its leaders explained that the Kuwaiti attacks were directed by the Islamic Revolutionary Guard Corps using what they claimed was a rogue unit of al-Dawa.[43] Iran was directly involved in the bombings of the U.S. and French embassies in Kuwait, just as it had been in Lebanon.

Iranian-supported terrorism against the West mushroomed in the 1980s. The United States was always a special target. For example, in April 1984, outside the U.S. Air Force Base in Torrejon, Spain, Hizbullah bombed a restaurant, killing eighteen U.S. servicemen and wounding eighty civilians. Back in Beirut, another Hizbullah truck bomb was used to attack the temporary annex of the U.S. Embassy, killing twenty-four people.

Later in the year, Kuwait Airways Flight 221 was hijacked to Tehran. Two U.S. Agency for International Development (USAID) employees were on board.[44] One USAID worker was provided with a bullhorn and was forced to call for the release of the "Dawa-17" on behalf of the hijackers. Iranian television cameras at the airport recorded his plea. It was clear he was trying to save his own life. Despite his efforts, he was shot six times and his body was thrown on the airport tarmac.

The other USAID worker was killed as well. While President Reagan cautiously criticized the Iranians whom he said "have not been as helpful as they could have been in this situation," the director of the State Department's Office of Counterterrorism, Robert Oakley, was far more blunt, accusing the Iranian government of "active collusion" with the hijackers.[45] Though Iranian security forces eventually stormed the aircraft and released the remaining hostages, considering the evidence of Iranian collusion with the hijackers, it is likely that this Iranian action was staged to bring the whole episode to a close. It was revealing that rather than putting the hijackers on trial, Iran let them go free.

France continued to be targeted by Hizbullah and Iranian-backed attacks. In 1985, a wave of thirteen terrorist attacks struck Paris, mostly aimed at the metro system. In March 1987, French authorities uncovered a widespread Hizbullah apparatus in France after the arrest of a Paris-born terrorist operative named Fouad Saleh.[46] It turned out that Saleh was tied to a senior Iranian diplomat in the Iranian embassy in Paris, whom the French ultimately expelled.[47]

That same year a senior Hizbullah operative, Muhammad Hamadeh, was arrested in Germany and under interrogation revealed the existence of Hizbullah arms depots along the French-German border. Following his capture, Hizbullah began carrying out terrorist attacks against German targets. A Hizbullah operative was also arrested in Italy in November 1984, leading to the discovery of a Hizbullah network in Italy that had planned to bomb the U.S. Embassy in Rome.

The Hizbullah terror wave also targeted U.S. commercial airlines, the most famous instance of which was the hijacking of TWA Flight 847 from Athens to London on June 14, 1985. Mughniyeh led the Hizbullah team that was behind the hijacking.[48] The aircraft was diverted to Algiers and to Beirut. The majority of its 153 passengers and crew were U.S. citizens. The hijackers killed a U.S. Navy diver, Robert Dean Stethhem, who was one of the passengers, and threw his body on the Beirut airport tarmac. The hijackers sought the release of the "Dawa-17" as well as the release of 766 Lebanese prisoners held by Israel that were mostly Shiites.

The State Department reported the analysis of the situation heard from Lebanese Shiite leaders. The terrorists were made up of two groups: a main group of hijackers and an inner group of hooded terrorists, neither under the control of Hizbullah or Iran. This inner group was not interested in the Lebanese prisoners held by Israel but only in the "Dawa-17" held by Kuwait.[49] Undoubtedly, these reports strengthened the perception that Mughniyeh was not part of Hizbullah and not controlled by Iran. U.S. diplomacy initially looked to Syria as the key state that could help resolve the hijacking. But after some efforts with Damascus, Secretary of State George Shultz concluded: "We were getting the impression, however, that Iran, not Syria, was in the position to call the shots when it came to the remaining American hostages."[50] Indeed, during the hijacking, Mughniyeh, whose fingerprints were later found on the aircraft, had been spotted near it with an officer from the Revolutionary Guards.[51]

Iran became diplomatically active at the end of the hijacking crisis, when the Speaker of the Majlis (parliament), Ali Akbar Hashemi Rafsanjani, apparently pressed the hijackers to bring the TWA hijacking incident to an end on June 30. Rafsanjani would emerge as a rising star of the Islamic Republic. As a youth he had been sent to a religious seminary in Qom where Khomeini was one of his teachers. In the formative years of the Islamic Republic, Khomeini gave him critical assignments. He helped form the Revolutionary Guards and then was responsible for their coordination with the regular armed forces. He also became Khomeini's handpicked candidate to be parliamentary speaker, a position he assumed from 1980 through 1989 (after which he was elected President of Iran).

In short, within the Iranian leadership, there were few who carried greater weight and could close the TWA affair. For this purpose, Rafsanjani traveled to Damascus to deliver the Iranian position just before the release of the TWA passengers. President Reagan sent Rafsanjani a message of thanks when the ordeal ended. Was Iran beginning a new cooperative path or was this a case of the arsonist helping to put out the fire that he himself had lit? Rafsanjani only said: "We were not involved in the hijacking. If we had known who the hijackers were we would have frustrated their plans."[52] Iran was again obfuscating its real role.

In an internal document prepared by its Directorate of Intelligence earlier in 1985, the CIA fully appreciated Iran's pivotal role in the outburst of terrorism against the United States: "Iranian-sponsored terrorism is the greatest threat to U.S. personnel and facilities in the Middle East." Iranian leaders were seen as aspiring to achieve "the successful export of their revolution," however they had to confront "the presence and influence" of the United States, which they viewed as "major impediments" to the realization of their goals. Tehran was seeking no less than a withdrawal of the United States from the Middle East. Implicitly critiquing the West's restraint in responding to this growing threat, the CIA analysis warned: "Iranian-sponsored terrorism will continue and possibly increase so long as the clerics in Tehran do not perceive any significant costs in launching such operations." [53]

The Search for Iranian Moderates and the Problem of the Western Hostages

Iran's role in terrorism against the West became even more evident as more countries had to contend with Hizbullah hostage-taking during the rest of the 1980s. In mid-1985, six American hostages were held in Lebanon: William Buckley, the CIA station chief in Beirut; Benjamin Weir, a Presbyterian minister; Father Lawrence Martin Jenco, a Catholic priest; Terry Anderson, an AP reporter; David Jacobsen, director of the American University Hospital in Beirut; and Thomas P. Sutherland, a university dean. President Reagan wanted all seven hostages released, but there was a special concern for Buckley, not only because of his CIA association, but because the United States suspected he had been tortured.

By this time, the Reagan administration understood that it needed to appeal to Iran in order to free the U.S. hostages in Lebanon. And from the experience of TWA 847, it was assumed that the key individual in the Iranian system was Ali Akbar Rafsanjani, who became viewed as a pragmatist with whom Washington could do business. With Khomeini aging, and U.S. officials focusing on the future succession of power in Tehran, the Reagan administration sought to open channels to influential Iranians who might lead the Islamic Republic in the years ahead. Moreover, the CIA was reporting a new threat of growing Soviet influence in Iran.[54] These were the essential ingredients of what evolved into the arms for hostages idea that was a key component of the Iran-Contra scandal during Reagan's second term in office.

Indeed, just as Hizbullah prepared to free the last of the hostages from TWA 847, the U.S. National Security Council proposed in a draft directive that the U.S. government work with its allies to supply arms to Iran in order to create new openings within the regime in Tehran.[55] The NSC paper suggested that a future U.S. policy on Iran must "encourage Western allies and friends to help Iran meet its import requirements so as to reduce the attractiveness of Soviet assistance and trade offers, while demonstrating the value of trade relations with the West."[56] The paper then specifically added: "This includes provision of selected military equipment on a case-by-case basis." In this area, clearly Iran had real needs. The Islamic Republic had been at war with Iraq since 1980, and its army badly needed U.S. weapons and spare parts. After all, the Iranian armed forces had been equipped by Americans prior to the fall of the Shah six years earlier in 1979.

The NSC report asserted that Iran was undergoing "dynamic political evolution." The report essentially sought ways in which the United States could exploit the fluid situation that was emerging. Other U.S. assessments also concluded that there was an intensifying struggle between competing factions over the future orientation of the Khomeini regime. The main subject of this competition between Iranian factions was whether Iran should normalize its relations with the outside world. The NSC draft report was vociferously opposed by the Department of State and the Department of Defense, but nonetheless the NSC would operate as though it had been approved and was administration policy.

The CIA was following similar internal trends in Iran. It identified three main groups who sought to influence the future direction of Iranian foreign policy. The first group was Islamic radicals who sought to export the revolution with subversion and terrorism. The second group was made up of conservatives who sought to bolster Iranian power chiefly through the export of the revolution's ideology as opposed to subversion. The third were the pragmatists who were willing to do anything to advance Iran's state interests but also did not rule out terrorism for that purpose. Its report concluded: "We believe there is a better-than-even chance that the pragmatists will emerge as the dominant force after Khomeini and will formulate Iranian foreign policy on the basis of perceived state interests rather than revolutionary aspirations."[57]

These distinctions were very important for evaluating the next generation of Iranian leaders. Unfortunately, many analysts confused pragmatism with moderation. Sometimes the terms were mistakenly used interchangeably. For a pragmatist, according to the CIA's analysis, was flexible about means without conceding ends. Yet while the pragmatists were seeking to diversify Iran's foreign contacts, they were not ready to jettison their reliance on terrorism as a *modus operandi*.

As the United States set out to develop links to this pragmatic camp in Iran, the question of its real political orientation would hover over U.S.-Iranian relations for the next decade with respect to its most noted representative, Rafsanjani: was he truly a moderate who did not share the strategic goals of the Islamic Revolution with his mentor, Ayatollah Khomeini, or was he a cunning pragmatist who was ready to compromise on tactics in order to advance the very same strategy as Khomeini?

The question of whether a moderate faction was indeed emerging in Iran was considered by experts beyond U.S. officialdom. There were reasons to doubt that moderates could exist in what was still a revolutionary situation. Professor Fouad Ajami, a professor of Middle East Studies at Johns Hopkins who himself came from a Lebanese Shiite background, warned in the *New York Times* about the new obsession with finding Iranian moderates: "The Reagan officials have fixed the radical label onto the Ayatollah Ruhollah Khomeini's designated successor, Ayatollah Hussein Ali Montazari. The moderate label has been assigned to the Speaker of the Parliament, Hashemi Rafsanjani. But this is all guesswork."[58]

In the midst of the controversy over Iran's future orientation, an Iranian middle-man, Manuchehr Ghorbanifar, whose reputation was hotly debated in western circles, reached out to high-level Israeli officials with the idea that he could build a relationship with "Iranian moderates," if he could supply to them American-manufactured TOW wire-guided anti-tank missiles. A secret CIA profile on Ghorbanifar, dated July 1984, reported that he had been examined in Frankfurt, Germany, by an agency officer who decided that "he failed [the] exam on significant issues of fabrication." He had "deliberately" provided false information on the Beirut kidnapping. The CIA report concluded that "he was practicing deception on all relevant questions."[59]

Yet Ghorbanifar's value had been validated by both significant Saudi and Israeli contacts, like the famous international financer Adnan Khashoggi and former Mossad deputy-head David Kimche, who had since become the director-general of Israel's Foreign Ministry. Moreover, it was not clear that all parts of the CIA rejected his value outright, particularly its counterterrorism section.[60] What must have made him particularly attractive to the Reagan administration was when he added to his proposal that Iran would free seven U.S. hostages in Lebanon to prove that the deal he was reporting was serious; the hostage offer he raised, however, again underlined Iran's tight link to the seizure of Americans in Lebanon.

What Iran wanted in return, according to Ghorbanifar, was a "dialogue" with the United States.[61] The "moderates" (Ghorbanifar's word choice) with whom he was in contact, he suggested, might even overthrow Khomeini. Indeed, months later during a meeting in Washington between senior officials in the National Security Council and CIA Director Bill Casey and his deputy, it was assumed by those attending that any weapons delivered through the Ghorbanifar channel to Iran would go to a faction in the Iranian military seeking to overthrow Khomeini.[62] Ghorbanifar's proposal to Israel fit neatly into the new policy guidelines that had been recently under consideration within the U.S. government, which sought to encourage U.S. allies, like Israel, to reach out to Iran.

President Reagan authorized the first transfer of U.S. arms to Iran through Israel, which dispatched ninety-six TOW missiles on August 30, 1985, to Ghorbanifar's contact. Who in fact received the weapons? Was it a faction seeking to overthrow the clerical leadership of the Islamic Republic? It turned out to be the Revolutionary Guards—the most loyal military force in Iran to Ayatollah Khomeini. Iranian Prime Minister Mir Hussein Mousavi promised to release one hostage at this point, but not a single American was released. Nonetheless, a second shipment of American arms went out two weeks later so that the United States supplied to Iran, through Israel, a total of 504 missiles.

At this point Reverend Benjamin Weir was released in Lebanon. President Reagan's National Security Advisor, Robert McFarlane, who headed the contacts with Iran on the U.S. side, had requested that Buckley be released first if only one hostage could get out, considering the fact that, as already noted, it was assumed that he probably had undergone torture. Ghorbanifar claimed that Buckley had been too sick to be moved.[63] The following month an Islamic organization announced that Buckley had been executed in retaliation for an Israeli Air Force attack on the headquarters of the PLO in Tunis. The United States later learned, however, that the story was completely fake; Buckley died of torture in captivity months earlier, even before Ghorbanifar made his first offer to the Reagan administration.[64]

The Iranians had outmaneuvered their American counterparts. Reagan himself felt he had been "snookered" by the Iranians into believing that more arms sales would lead to the hostages' freedom—according to the testimony of White House chief of staff Donald Regan.[65] At the beginning of the arms-for-hostages initiative, Ghorbanifar wanted to establish his credibility as an intermediary, so in front of his interlocutors he telephoned Tehran and spoke to Abbas Kangarloo, a deputy prime minister of Iran with responsibility for intelligence operations. It was the same Kangarloo, Ghorbanifar later claimed, who ordered Buckley's capture to begin with.[66] The more the United States got into the arms-for-hostages negotiations, the more it became clear as day that Iran was not the solution to the hostage crisis but its cause. Iran was tightly tied into the seizure of western hostages in Lebanon, regardless of the name of the Islamic organization that took credit.

Rafsanjani himself sent mixed signals over the question of whether he viewed terrorism and hostage-taking as legitimate or unacceptable behavior. He said in early 1987: "The people of Lebanon are so ignored and so oppressed that they have no other defense for themselves other than this." In the late 1980s, Iran persisted in supporting terrorist attacks but carefully sought to hide its role by using surrogate organizations such as the Turkish-based "Islamic Jihad" (TIJ), which shot a Saudi diplomat in Ankara in October 1988 and a Saudi military attaché a year later. TIJ used car-bombs to assassinate a U.S. Air Force serviceman in October 1991 and to injure an Egyptian diplomat in Turkey, as well.[67]

While Iran denied that it supported terrorism or had any responsibility for the ongoing hostage crisis, there was growing evidence in the years that followed that Iran was behind virtually all the cases of hostage-taking. Looking back on this period years later, senior U.S. officials told the *Washington Post*: "Iran had a substantial amount of authority in almost all cases." One official added: "We used to spend endless hours debating here the degree of Iranian control. The evidence now is that control was 99.9 percent."[68] These officials had good reasons for their certainty: the money used to pay the terrorists holding the hostages came from official Iranian sources, though they were Lebanese nationals they used Iranian travel documents, and they regularly conferred with Iranian diplomats.[69]

CIA Director Bill Casey appeared in classified hearings before the House Appropriations Committee in late 1986 after the Iran-Contra scandal was disclosed. He wanted to provide what he described as "the rationale behind the operation." He spoke about the need for the United States "establishing contact with leaders in a future Iran." The outreach to Iran came from the National Security Council; the CIA had a supporting role. Casey explained as the operation got under way that the CIA was following a presidential directive from January 17, 1986, stipulating that the CIA provide support for a program "aimed at...establishing a more moderate government in Iran."[70]

In looking back on the initiative, beyond the financial irregularities connected to the funding of the Contras in Central America, Casey ticked off the National Security Council's main accomplishments: "The NSC was able to establish a new and direct channel to Majlis (the Iranian parliament) Speaker Rafsanjani...once we decided the channel was reliable."[71] It seemed as though Rafsanjani had been identified as the key figure for assuring that a moderate regime would emerge in post-Khomeini Iran.

Ultimately, from the start of the arms for hostages negotiations in August 1985 until November 1986, when the U.S.-Iranian contacts were leaked to a Lebanese weekly, only three out of seven American hostages were released.[72] Between 1987 and 1988, U.S.-Iranian relations severely deteriorated as a result of Iranian escalation in the Iran-Iraq War. Previously, Iranian aircraft had come dangerously close to the oil terminals of the Arab oil producers; in an incident on June 5, 1984, a Royal Saudi Air Force F-15 actually downed an Iranian F-4 Phantom on the Saudi side of the Persian Gulf.

The Iranian Air Force began attacking tankers in the Persian Gulf carrying the oil of Iraq's Arab allies like Kuwait. The United States reflagged individual tankers, regardless of where they were registered, in order to deter the Iranians who would presumably not want to attack a U.S.-flagged ship. In response, the Iranians undertook extensive mining operations that threatened the American-flagged tankers and their U.S. Navy escorts.

During the summer of 1987, after a U.S.-flagged tanker hit a mine, U.S. Navy Seals boarded an Iranian ship in international waters that was caught laying the mines. Less than a year later, an

Iranian mine nearly blew in half the USS Samuel Roberts, a navy frigate. Much of the effort to harass the U.S. Navy was led by a naval contingent of the Revolutionary Guards. Rafsanjani would only comment: "For us it is not difficult to render the whole region insecure. Dropping mines in the Persian Gulf is like sowing wheat in the land."[73] The statement sounded like an admission.

The United States retaliated against the mining operation by striking out against Iran's naval presence. First, American forces attacked two Iranian oil platforms, which had served as forward operating areas for the Revolutionary Guards. In the military exchange with Iran, the United States ultimately destroyed almost half of the Iranian Navy and put an end for the time being to the seaborne presence of the Revolutionary Guards.[74]

Iran's relations with Saudi Arabia, America's key Arab ally in the Persian Gulf, also took a sharp turn for the worse. Tehran sought to politicize the 1987 Pilgrimage to Mecca, demanding that a referendum be held at the Great Mosque over the question of Kuwait's acceptance of U.S. protection for its tankers. What followed was a major clash in Islam's holiest city between the Saudi National Guard and Iranian pilgrims that lead to 402 deaths, most of whom were Iranians. Ayatollah Khomeini called the Saudis "these vile and ungodly Wahhabis," adding that Mecca was in the hands of "a band of heretics."[75]

Rafsanjani joined in, calling the Saudis "Wahhabi hooligans" who had massacred Shiites before in Najaf and Karbala in the early nineteenth century and destroyed the monuments they venerated in the holy city of Medina as well. Iranian rhetoric and acts of subversion fueled the military tensions that were transpiring across the Persian Gulf, which the United States was being increasingly drawn into.

What ended the escalation between the United States and Iran was actually an accident. On July 3, 1988, Iran Air Flight 655 was making a regularly scheduled flight from Bandar Abbas, the main base of the Iranian Navy on the Persian Gulf, to Dubai in the

United Arab Emirates. The U.S. Navy's guided missile cruiser, USS Vincennes, mistook the Iran Air Airbus for an Iranian F-14 Tomcat fighter and shot it down over the Strait of Hormuz, killing its 290 passengers and crew. The Iranian government charged that the USS Vincennes intentionally shot down the plane, and rejected the argument that this was simply a case of misidentification.

The downing of the aircraft appears to have had the unintentional side-effect of deterring further Iranian provocations in the Persian Gulf, although there is evidence that Iran retaliated for the loss of its civilian aircraft. For example, while the 1988 downing of Pan Am Flight 103 over Lockerbie, Scotland, that led to 270 fatalities, was ultimately linked to Libyan terrorists, U.S. officials had some evidence implicating Hizbullah founder Ali Akbar Mohtashemi for supporting the operation. [76] Indeed, there were intelligence reports that Mohtashemi paid $10 million for financing the Lockerbie attack.[77] But these apparently were not conclusive enough for U.S. authorities to take action against Iran, and instead the diplomatic pressures for the downing of Pan Am 103 were concentrated on Libya, alone.

With the downing of its civilian aircraft, Iran feared that it faced the combined military power of Iraq and the United States. As a result, Ayatollah Khomeini agreed to cease-fire proposals put forward by the international community and he ended the Iran-Iraq War. This did not mean that Iran was moving in a more moderate direction. On February 19, 1989, months before his death, Khomeini issued a *fatwa*, or religious opinion, calling for the execution of Salman Rushdie, a British Indian author, whose work, *The Satanic Verses*, Khomeini regarded as blasphemy. The fatwa complicated the normalization of Iran's relations with the West. Britain broke off diplomatic relations with Iran as a result of Khomeini's death sentence.

The reason for this was that the Iranians took the *fatwa* seriously, and Iranian terror attacks escalated. While Rushdi went into hiding, the Japanese translator of the book was stabbed to death in 1991. An Italian translator was also stabbed, but survived. There was also a bomb attack in Central London in an attempt to kill Rushdie. Indeed, in the years that followed, Iran's commitment to Khomeini's fatwa became a measure of whether the regime in Tehran showed any signs of moderation.

Reaching Out to Rafsanjani

After the U.S.-Iranian naval clashes abated, Washington continued to turn to Rafsanjani as the moderate who might help with the release of American hostages in Lebanon, especially once he was elected president of the Islamic Republic in July 1989. With the death of Ayatollah Khomeini on June 3, 1989, there were expectations that Tehran would become more pragmatic. The Iranians fed this speculation; IRNA, their official news agency, reported that they were ready to help with the release of all the western hostages in Lebanon, with the careful caveat that their influence in this matter was only "spiritual."[78] President Rafsanjani himself told the Pakistanis that he was prepared to help with the hostage issue, but in exchange he wanted some act from Washington demonstrating that it was no longer hostile to the Iranian regime.

President George H. W. Bush responded to these Iranian feelers. Already in his inaugural address on January 20, 1989, he hinted that his administration would be prepared to revise its policy toward Iran, and even engage Tehran, under certain conditions: "There are, today, Americans who are held against their will in foreign lands, and Americans who are unaccounted for. Assistance can be shown here and will be long remembered. Goodwill begets goodwill. Good faith can be a spiral that endlessly moves on."[79] Months later, he actually contacted the UN secretary-general, Perez de Cuellar, and told him he was dispatching his national security advisor, General Brent Scowcroft, to meet him with the purpose of reaching out to Rafsanjani.

During the early part of the Bush presidency, the intelligence assessment of Rafsanjani was that he had "subordinated militant Islamic ideology to practical considerations in his conduct of foreign policy."[80] This sounded like the United States assumed that he was not just a pragmatist, but might even be a moderate. In January 1989, Khomeini himself sent an envoy with a personal message to the Soviet leader, Mikhail Gorbachev. Three weeks after Khomeini's death, Rafsanjani visited Moscow, marking an acceleration of the Soviet-Iranian thaw. These developments must have given American analysts the sense that a U.S.-Iranian rapprochement was possible.

Perez de Cuellar did not want to burn Rafsanjani, who might be attacked by rivals for receiving a message from President Bush. As a result, the secretary-general dispatched his trusted Italian-born special envoy, Giandomenico Picco, to carry a message about what de Cuellar assessed to be Bush's position on U.S.-Iranian relations. The 1979 meeting between Khomeini's first prime minister, Mehdi Barzagan, and U.S. National Security advisor Zbigniew Brzezinski, in Algiers, brought down the former and was one of the final steps that led to the seizure of the U.S. Embassy in Tehran. Picco relayed to Rafsanjani the impression the UN had of Bush's policy; "I do know for a certainty President Bush has sought the release of the American hostages...he would react swiftly by taking action on Iranian monetary assets blocked by the United States and other appropriate gestures...."[81]

Rafsanjani responded by saying that he regretted even hearing this message. Then he tried to clarify Iran's connection to the hostage issue: "We have had no relations for some time with those holding the hostages." He further explained that the hostage takers were not the "traditional" Hizbullah. It was the same deception the Iranians had used before, separating themselves from the kidnappers and further separating Hizbullah from the kidnappers as well. Rafsanjani was lying. Picco was probably not aware of the fact that internal documentation of the CIA a year earlier fingered

Imad Mughniyeh as a key figure in determining the fate of U.S. hostages and even concluded that he was in Tehran during 1987.[82]

In fact, years later, after Mughniyeh's death on February 12, 2008, Iran dispatched a high-level delegation to Beirut, led by Iranian Foreign Minister Manouchehr Mottaki, to attend his funeral. Iranian television reported that no less than Iran's president Mahmoud Ahmadinejad commemorated "the assassinated Hizbullah commander."[83] Mughniyeh was regarded as an Iranian hero. For its part, Hizbullah established an exhibit in the Lebanese town of Nabatiye in his memory.[84] The veneration he earned flew in the face of the arguments Rafsanjani made nearly two decades earlier when he claimed to have little knowledge about those who held the hostages—and that they were not regarded as "traditional" Hizbullah. These acts, moreover, firmly established the tight links between Iran, Hizbullah, and Mughniyeh, notwithstanding the repeated arguments of western analysts that Mughniyeh ran a rogue operation, independent of Iran or even Hizbullah.

Iran's direct involvement in the hostage issue was clearly proven yet again by the fate of Lt. Col. William R. Higgins of the U.S. Marine Corps, who served with UNIFIL (United Nations Interim Force in Lebanon), which was deployed in Southern Lebanon. He had been kidnapped in 1987 by a group calling itself "Believers' Resistance," which was essentially another Hizbullah front.[85] On July 28, 1989, Israeli commandos captured Sheikh Abdul-Karim Obeid, a local Hizbullah leader, in order to use him as a bargaining chip to obtain Ron Arad, the Israeli Air Force navigator who had been held in Lebanon since 1986.[86]

Hizbullah threatened to kill Higgins if Israel did not let Sheikh Obeid free. Israeli intelligence believed Hizbullah was bluffing and recommended ignoring its demand. Hizbullah then released a videotape showing Colonel Higgins dangling from a rope by his neck. The Iranians, and their Hizbullah surrogates, undoubtedly felt they could execute an American officer and drive a wedge between Israel and the United States at the same time.

Higgins's execution was shown on U.S. television networks and understandably shocked American viewers; it also led to considerable criticism of Israel. The Israeli military carefully examined the film frame by frame and found that Higgins was wearing winter clothes, even though the execution, according to Hizbullah, had taken place during the heat of summer in the Middle East. Years later when Higgins's body was recovered in 1991, pathologists were able to determine that he had been killed much earlier than July 1989, when Shekh Obeid was captured; his corpse had been kept by Hizbullah for a future occasion. Significantly, a U.S. Federal Court ruled on October 10, 2000, that Iran was behind the kidnapping and murder of Lt. Colonel William R. Higgins; it awarded his widow, Robin Higgins, and her daughter $353 million from Iranian assets.

The Higgins episode showed that even in the post-Khomeini period, Rafsanjani's Iran in 1989 and its client Hizbullah were using hostages for political purposes. It also established that while Lt. Colonel Higgins was seized by a seemingly unknown splinter group, it was "traditional" (using Rafsanjani's language) Hizbullah that would decide his fate. And once Hizbullah was involved, Iran was clearly connected to Higgins's kidnapping and murder. Yet Rafsanjani would still argue that Iran did not have influence with "those holding hostages."

Despite Rafsanjani's transparently false statements about his connections with the hostage issue, the indirect U.S.-Iranian contact through the UN continued. It soon became clear that the Iranians were seeking a diplomatic *quid pro quo* for releasing the hostages, like settling the issue of their frozen assets, or obtaining Washington's support of their territorial claims vis-à-vis Iraq. The latter would require the United States to advocate adherence of the two states to the substance of the 1975 Algiers Agreement between the Shah and Saddam Hussein that Baghdad had discarded when it launched the Iran-Iraq War in 1980. In short, the hostages had diplomatic value for Iran.

The Bush administration also decided in 1989 to speed up action in resolving its differences with Tehran over the question of its frozen assets. However, what ultimately brought the American hostage issue to an end were not these attempts by Washington to engage Iran, but rather developments in the Middle East that were beyond the Bush administration's control.

First, prior to its invasion of Kuwait, Iraq went ahead by itself and recognized its old Algiers Agreement with Iran, resolving their main territorial differences. And more importantly, once Iraqi troops invaded Kuwait, they opened the gates of Kuwait's central prison, which allowed the "Dawa-17" to escape.[87] They soon joined their Hizbullah compatriots in Lebanon. One of the main grievances of Hizbullah, which it voiced with every hijacking during the 1980s, was suddenly removed. It should not have come as a surprise that by December 4, 1991, Terry Anderson, the last American hostage in Lebanon, was set free.

In fact, during the period in which the Bush administration was exploring a dialogue with Rafsanjani's Iran, Tehran's behavior was still extremely disturbing. Bush himself conveyed his concerns to his UN intermediary, Perez de Cuellar, on January 19, 1990, that the United States had in its possession information that Iran and Hizbullah were sending sophisticated weaponry to Europe in order to launch attacks on the United States and other western targets. Some of these shipments had been physically seized by Spain.[88] The CIA was still warning in April 1992: "We believe Iran also is supporting Hizballah's plans to attack U.S. interests."[89]

Under Rafsanjani's presidency, terrorism continued to serve as an essential instrument of the Iranian state. Political assassinations against opponents were still conducted at the same rate as in the Khomeini era.[90] In 1990, during his period in office, Tehran established the Quds Force (Qods, in Farsi), a special branch of the Revolutionary Guards for the export of the revolution through subversion and terrorism beyond the borders of Iran.[91]

Its commander would report directly to the Supreme Leader Ali Khamenei, but given the structure of Iranian decision-making, it is highly likely Rafsanjani was kept informed about its most sensitive operations.

Chapter 6:

Nuclear Expansion under the Robe of Moderation

A T THE OUTSET OF THE ISLAMIC REVOLUTION in 1979, Ayatollah Khomeini closed down much of the activity of the Iranian Atomic Energy Commission.[1] The Iranian government viewed the Shah's nuclear projects as prohibitively expensive to maintain. However, as the Iranians absorbed terrible losses throughout the Iran-Iraq War—ultimately one million casualties—Khomeini began to have serious doubts about his own *fatwa*, or religious ruling, that prohibited the production of nuclear weapons.[2] He may have been persuaded by the arguments of others, like Ayatollah Mohammad Beheshti, a highly influential cleric in the Iranian hierarchy who died in 1981, but already actively promoted the idea of an atomic bomb for the Islamic Republic in 1979.[3]

In a 1988 letter responding to the commander of the Revolutionary Guards, Brigadier General Mohsen Rezai, Ayatollah Khomeini acknowledged Rezai's analysis that if Tehran wanted to continue the war with Baghdad it would need hundreds of new fighter bombers, thousands of tanks, and "a substantial number of laser and atomic weapons...."[4] He did not raise any religious objections to Rezai's list. The sensitive letter was leaked by Ali Akbar Hashemi Rafsanjani in 2006.

Given that Iran had none of the military equipment that the Revolutionary Guards needed, it should have come as no surprise that in 1988 Iran accepted UN Security Council Resolution 598, ending the Iran-Iraq War. Khomeini's acknowledgment of Rezai's list implied that Iran needed the weapons detailed in his letter to protect its security in the future. The Iranian Atomic Energy Commission resumed work that very same year.

Iraq under Saddam Hussein did not trust the self-imposed nuclear restraint implicit in Khomeini's fatwa, and assumed that Iran was seeking to develop its nuclear technology further. Under the Shah, Iran had an ambitious program to construct nuclear reactors across the country. It had contracts with the German company Siemens to build two 1,200 megawatt reactors at Bushehr on the Persian Gulf for the civilian production of electricity. At the time of the Islamic Revolution in 1979, one of the Bushehr reactors was 90 percent complete—and hence about three years from starting—while the other was 50 percent compete.

During the Iran-Iraq War, the Iraqi Air Force bombed the Bushehr nuclear complex on six different occasions between 1984 and 1987. The close connection between an Iranian civilian nuclear program and a nuclear program with military applications must have been foremost in the minds of Iraqi military planners. Israel destroyed the French-supplied Osiraq nuclear reactor in Baghdad in 1981 with the same concerns in mind.

Rafsanjani turned out to be the powerhouse behind the growth of the Iranian nuclear program, although over the years he made completely contradictory statements about Iran's nuclear intentions. Inside Iran he would say one thing and abroad he would say the exact opposite. For example, in an address before the Revolutionary Guards in 1988, Rafsanjani openly stated: "We should fully equip ourselves both in the offensive and defensible use of chemical, bacteriological, and *radiological weapons* (emphasis added)."[5] Yet some years later, appearing on the CBS program *Sixty Minutes*, Rafsanjani replied to a question over whether Iran had a nuclear weapons program by saying: "Definitely not, I hate these weapons...."[6]

Rafsanjani was not alone in using deceptive double-talk about nuclear weapons for Iran. Ali Khamenei, in his capacity as Iran's president, spoke to Iran's Atomic Energy Organization in 1987, explaining: "Regarding atomic energy, we need it now." He argued that it was necessary in order to let Iran's enemies know that the Iranians could defend themselves. In other words, nuclear technology was important because of its military utility. But years later, as Iran's Supreme Leader, Khamenei said the very opposite: "We do not need a nuclear bomb. We do not have any objectives or aspirations for which we will need to use a nuclear bomb."[7] Iran's nuclear diplomacy appeared to be based on the doctrine of *taqiya*: saying one thing and meaning something else.

In 1988, Iran began taking tangible steps to expand its nuclear work. It signed a nuclear agreement with Argentina. It approached Pakistan for help in enriching uranium. Iranian officials had already met in Dubai a year earlier with the representatives of the Pakistani scientist, A. Q. Khan. Iran also received shipments of uranium from South Africa. And in the years that followed, Iran struck a new understanding with Russia to rebuild the Bushehr facility once it became clear that the Germans would not complete the project. It also reached out to India to buy a new nuclear research reactor.[8]

But these efforts were conducted in deep secrecy so the international community was unaware of their nuclear ambitions. At the time, a completely different perception was emerging about Rafsanjani's Iran, shaped by indicators that Rafsanjani's administration represented a break from the revolutionary zeal of the

Khomeini period. For example, one of the greatest backers of the export of the Islamic Revolution, Ayatollah Montazeri, had been ousted as Khomeini's designated successor in 1989, with Rafsanjani's help. Moreover, he forced the fiercely anti-American founder of Hizbullah, Ali Akbar Mohtashemi, to step down as interior minister.[9]

In light of these changes, the *Washington Post* ran a story in 1990 headlined: "Iran's Extremists Seen Losing Power in Government."[10] Iran appeared to be changing. Rafsanjani openly declared that it had never been the goal of Iran "to export the revolution by force," further reinforcing the impression that a new era of Iranian pragmatism had begun.[11]

Constructive Engagement with Tehran

Despite the disappointing experiences of the Reagan team, there was growing support on the American side from some of the most senior levels of George H. W. Bush's administration for engaging in a diplomatic dialogue with Iran. After all, during the Gulf War in 1991, launched in response to the Iraqi invasion of Kuwait in 1990, Iran had not hindered American military operations in any way. Though Iraqis flew many of their front-line Iraqi aircraft to Iranian airfields to escape the U.S. air campaign, Iranians prevented them from using the planes in the Iraqi war effort.

Moreover, Rafsanjani was seeking to normalize relations with Iran's neighbors. Tehran formally reestablished diplomatic relations with Egypt and Saudi Arabia. As Egyptian and Saudi troops had fought side by side with the United States against the armed forces of Saddam Hussein's Iraq, it appeared a convergence of interests between all of Iraq's adversaries might be exploited at the war's end. These developments may have led some to assume that the export of the revolution had ebbed and Iran would no longer threaten its neighbors. The U.S. National Intelligence Estimate on Iran in October 1991 stated that: "Rafsanjani's goals vis-à-vis the

United States are to reduce bilateral tensions and U.S. economic and political pressures on Iran."[12]

Thus, in early 1992, the official responsible for the Middle East in the National Security Council, Richard Haass, decided to launch a formal review of the Bush administration's policy on Iran. He proposed a strategy of "constructive engagement" that would involve lifting some economic sanctions.[13] Though Haass's proposal was not adopted, the idea that Rafsanjani was a moderate had taken off. The *New York Times* ran a front-page Sunday profile on Rafsanjani on April 19, 1992, which tried to portray him in as positive a light as possible. It was entitled: "Rafsanjani Sketches Vision of a Moderate, Modern Iran" and started with:

> Ali Akbar Hashemi Rafsanjani would like to be seen as a thoroughly modern mullah. The Iranian President studies economic issues at least two hours a day, gets CNN in his office and speaks English perhaps even better than his Berkley-educated brother. Although he holds the title of Hojatolislam—one rank lower than Ayatollah—he sprinkles his speeches and sermons with statistics, not quotations from the Koran.[14]

The article concluded that Rafsanjani's government was torn between "impulses of extremism and moderation."[15] In a correction to the article appearing a week later, the *New York Times* reminded its readers that Rafsanjani had "continued the harsh revolutionary policies" of his predecessors. As an example, the correction noted that Rafsanjani "refused to rescind the death sentence imposed on the writer Salman Rushdie."[16]

Despite the convergence of Iranian and American interests in opposing Iraq in the 1991 Gulf War, Iran did not conclude that it should reach a new rapprochement with the United States that, by necessity, would include scaling back its growing nuclear ambitions. In fact, among the Iranian clerics who discussed the lessons of the Gulf War, very different conclusions were reached that in no way resembled what some policymakers in western capitals attributed to the Iranian elites at the time. These Iranians considered that the United States would probably not have come to Kuwait's defense if Saddam Hussein already had an operational nuclear weapons capability.[17] The lesson to be learned was that Iran needed nuclear weapons in order to protect the Islamic Revolution from external intervention. Tehran, after the Gulf War, still saw the United States in adversarial terms, and its basic anti-American hostility had not been ameliorated by the war against their common rival, Iraq.

It should have come as no surprise that Iran intensified its search for nuclear technology. Throughout the 1990s, Iran secretly approached four countries seeking to purchase a heavy water nuclear reactor.[18] These reported attempts set off warning lights with U.S. officials since used fuel rods from a heavy water reactor can be reprocessed to produce high-quality, weapons-grade plutonium.[19] As a result of these Iranian efforts, Washington found itself increasingly involved in efforts to prevent states from Argentina to China from reaching agreements with the Iranians that gave them access to nuclear technology.

Rafsanjani looked to China as a vital source of nuclear technology. During the 1980s and for most of the Iran-Iraq War, the Chinese were Iran's main source of conventional weapons,[20] resulting in strong defense ties between the two countries. As the West discovered twelve years later, in 1991 the Chinese provided Iran with 1,005 kilograms of UF_6 gas, the uranium feedstock that could be enriched in centrifuges to produce weapons-grade uranium fuel for atomic bombs.[21] In 1992, Rafsanjani visited Beijing in order to sign an agreement for the construction of four nuclear power plants.[22] While lacking the details of every deal, the U.S. intelligence community understood that it had to engage in a major effort to identify the nuclear agreements that were being sought between Iran and China, and later with Russia as well.[23]

For example, U.S. satellites reportedly spotted a large number of Chinese technicians at Isfahan, where there also appeared to be a plutonium production plant under construction.[24] In what would become a pivotal nuclear plant for Iran's uranium enrichment efforts years later, the Chinese helped build an industrial scale uranium conversion facility at Isfahan for producing UF_6 gas from processed uranium ore, like yellowcake.

Later in 1997, the United States and China reached an agreement that the Chinese would cancel the uranium conversion plant, but the Chinese nonetheless provided the designs and blueprints to the Iranians who secretly built the facility themselves.[25] In a separate deal, the Iranians purchased an electromagnetic isotope separation unit from China which was necessary for the stage of uranium enrichment after conversion.[26]

Then there was the case of Kazakhstan, the former Soviet republic, which contained nuclear military facilities of the U.S.S.R. Iran formally approached Kazakhstan in 1992, expressing interest in purchasing low-enriched uranium and beryllium from its Ulba Plant. However, it was at Ulba that the Soviet Navy used to fabricate high-enriched uranium for its propulsion reactors. Iranian nuclear experts were known to have visited the plant. The United States purchased Kazakhstan's enriched uranium in 1994. When U.S. officials arrived to pack it up, empty canisters in a room next to one holding a stock of high-enriched uranium bore a Tehran address.[27]

Russia grew into a greater problem in the 1990s. The Iranians engaged in a massive conventional weapons buildup between 1991 and 1997 and shifted increasingly to Russian arms that became available after the Cold War at reduced prices, such as sixty front-line combat aircraft (MiG-29 and Su-24), 300 T-72 tanks, and three Kilo-class diesel submarines. This cooperation extended to non-conventional weapons as well.

For example, the United States knew that the Russian Minister of Atomic Energy, Victor Mikhailov, was making deals with Iran that would accelerate Iranian development of nuclear weapons. He supplied gas centrifuges for the production of weapons-grade uranium, furthering Iran's nuclear infrastructure pursuits.[28]

In March 1992, CIA Director Robert Gates concluded in Congressional testimony that Iran was aspiring to become "the preeminent power in the Persian Gulf." He then specifically detailed that the Iranians were actively pursuing an atomic bomb: "We judge that Tehran is seeking a nuclear weapon capability." He warned that unless the West prevented them from obtaining sensitive nuclear technologies, they could reach their goal by 2000.[29]

However, the Iranian nuclear program was held back by the pressure that Washington was willing to exert in thwarting Tehran's nuclear trade. In an address to a graduating class at an Iranian air force academy, Rafsanjani openly criticized the United States over this effort, saying, "With utter insolence, the United States declares that Iran does not have the right to utilize nuclear technology even for non-military purposes." He then appeared to contradict himself by implying that nuclear technology had another purpose as well.

After speaking about Iraq's weapons of mass destruction during the Iran-Iran War, he added: "We have learned that preserving our independence and survival in this unsuitable international climate is not possible without science, technology, and the necessary tools." He did not specify what technological "tools" would preserve Iran's survival, but he appeared to leave little doubt that he was referring to nuclear weapons.[30]

President Clinton and Renewed Containment

When the Clinton administration came into office in 1993, it appeared to toughen its approach to Iran in comparison with the outgoing Bush team, which had contemplated, at times, a rapprochement with Tehran. Secretary of State Warren Christopher, who as deputy secretary of state under the Carter administration had actually negotiated the release of the American hostages from the U.S. Embassy in Tehran, frequently used more confrontational rhetoric than his predecessors.

Christopher left no doubt about Iran's role in supporting international terrorism: "Iran is one of the principal sources of support for terrorist groups around the world." And he specifically noted the Iranian government's "determination to acquire weapons of mass destruction" which left it as "an international outlaw."[31] After visiting the Middle East and speaking to leaders from around the region he characterized Iran as "a dangerous country."[32] The Clinton administration sought ways of significantly increasing Iran's isolation by persuading American allies to cut back their overall economic ties with its regime, and not just their nuclear sales.[33]

The dangers that Iran posed to the West had become increasingly clear at this point. Anthony Lake, President Clinton's National Security Advisor, was tasked with developing the administration's Iran strategy.[34] He explained the main aspects of the emerging Iranian problem in a major article in *Foreign Affairs*:

> Iran is actively engaged in clandestine efforts to acquire nuclear and other unconventional weapons and long-range missile-delivery systems. It is the foremost sponsor of terrorism and assassination worldwide. It is violently and vitriolically (sic) opposed to the Arab-Israeli peace process. It seeks to subvert friendly governments across the Middle East and in parts of Africa.[35]

That was only part of his list, which included Iran's military threats to its smaller neighbors and its abysmal human rights record.

In a not-so-oblique attack on the former Bush administration, Lake noted: "Previous administrations have tried their hand at building up 'moderates' in Iran." Recalling the historical record of this effort, he said, "What we learned from that experience is that the same 'moderates' are responsible for the very policies we find so objectionable."[36] The highest levels in Washington had finally internalized that Rafsanjani was no moderate.

Lake's new policy for Iran—along with Iraq—would be called "dual containment," an expression coined by Clinton's Middle East advisor on the National Security Council, Martin Indyk, who presented it in a 1993 address in Washington. Regarding Iran, in distinction from Saddam Hussein's Iraq, the new policy asserted that Washington was not seeking to overthrow the leadership of the Islamic Republic. "The Clinton administration was not opposed to the Islamic government in Iran. It only hoped to modify Iranian international behavior."[37] The policy implicitly assumed that within the Iranian regime there were individuals who would argue that Tehran's past behavior had isolated the country, requiring it to be changed. Clinton left the door open for a dialogue with the Islamic Republic the moment more moderate elements in the regime took control.[38]

Of course, the United States could not isolate Iran by itself. It needed allies to make its containment policy toward Iran work. The Clinton team seemed to have a reasonable chance of gaining that support. After all, in 1993 and 1994, Iran was facing an extremely difficult economic situation with 30 percent inflation and a huge international debt. The price of Iranian light crude had dropped from just over $20 per barrel in 1990 to less than $15 per barrel in 1994.[39]

Iran looked susceptible to the pressures that the Clinton administration was putting in place. Its economic woes made it a far less attractive market for its past European trading partners as well. It made sense that Iran would consider forgoing or at least slowing down its ambitious nuclear programs as well as its massive conventional weapons acquisitions. But, despite its difficult financial predicament, Iran was able to spend billions of dollars on building its nuclear infrastructure while maintaining an aggressive posture toward its neighbors. They were facilitated by Europe's adopting a very different policy from that of the United States, known as "critical dialogue."

European Engagement of Iran through "Critical Dialogue"

In May 1992, German Foreign Minister Klaus Kinkel spoke about the need to launch a "critical dialogue" with Iran, through which Bonn would try to use trade and other incentives to modify Iranian behavior. Underlying this proposal was not only a political belief that engagement rather than economic sanctions would change Iran, but hard economic interests as well. As Kinkel later commented: "You cannot reproach us for following our economic interests."[40] If Washington hoped for support of attempts to stop Iran's nascent nuclear program as well as its backing of global terrorism, Europe was proving to be a very difficult partner.

The European Council of Ministers made "critical dialogue" the official policy of the European Union when they met in Edinburgh in September 1992, two months before Clinton's election:

> Given Iran's importance in the region, the European Council reaffirms its belief that a dialogue should be obtained with the Iranian Government. This should be a critical dialogue which reflects concern about Iranian behaviour [sic.] and calls for improvement in a number of areas, particularly human rights, the death sentence pronounced by a *Fatwa* of Ayatollah Khomeini against author Salman Rushdie, which is contrary to international law, and terrorism.[41]

Looking back on the very different approaches of the United States and Europe, the Foreign Minister of the Netherlands, Hans van Mierlo, would quip: "We have a critical dialogue," and then he added, "The United States has no dialogue."[42] France was very direct about its interests in engaging Iran. Its prime minister, Edouard Balladur, confessed in 1995 that while "we French want to respect human rights...we have an economic position to defend in the world." France, he explained, had to "find a good balance."[43]

The Japanese also lent their support to the EU's policy of "critical dialogue." The Japanese Foreign Ministry in this period opined that it was not entirely clear that Iran was connected to international terrorist attacks, announcing, "The United States claims Iran is behind many terrorist bombings around the world, but there is no solid evidence."[44] Japanese Prime Minister Tomiichi Murayama commented on what was, in his opinion, the political utility of engaging Iran: "Iran is not made up only of radicals, and it is necessary to support the moderates."[45] It was not clear which moderates he had in mind.

Europe was committed to its benign view of Iran even in the face of the reports that Iran was purchasing all the necessary components for acquiring nuclear capability. The German government downplayed the danger. According to the official view presented in early 1996 in the German Parliament by Chancellor Helmut Kohl's government, there was no concrete evidence that Iran was engaging in any nuclear activities that ran counter to its obligations under the Nuclear Non-proliferation Treaty.[46] Therefore, maintaining a critical dialogue did not undermine the most sensitive western security interests. The gap between the United States and its European allies on Iran seemed wider than ever.

Another practical question raised by the EU's Iran policy was its debt. Declining oil prices had created a real crisis for Iran, which actually stopped making payments to creditor governments. It owed roughly $30 billion. In 1993, however, Germany led the creditor governments in re-scheduling the Iranian debt at concessionary rates below what was being charged in international financial markets. Italy, Japan, and France followed. The special rates given to Iran by western governments essentially subsidized the Iranian state budget with billions of dollars. Secretary of State Warren Christopher warned subsequently that "concessionary credits... allow Iran to divert scarce resources to military programs and to sponsoring terrorism."[47]

Foreign investment was an additional way for the Iranian economy to obtain more funding from the West. Starting in 1987 with the passing of sanctions against Iran, U.S. oil companies were prohibited from importing Iranian oil for American consumers. However, they were still permitted to sell Iranian oil in their overseas markets. Consequently, by 1994, U.S. oil companies were the largest customers for Iranian crude oil.[48] Approximately $4 billion worth of Iranian oil per year was being traded by American companies outside the United States.[49]

In 1995, Rafsanjani sought to increase U.S. private investment in the Iranian oil sector. He offered Iran's Sirri offshore oil fields to Conoco, one of America's oil giants, which would lead to massive investment in the Iranian oil industry. Ten days after Conoco signed a $1 billion contract with Iran, Clinton issued an Executive Order to stop any U.S. investment in the Iranian oil fields. Within a matter of months, the French petroleum company, Total, came into the picture and signed a contract with Iran to develop the same fields that it had offered to Conoco.

The U.S. Congress responded in 1996 with the Iran and Libya Sanctions Act (ILSA), which gave President Clinton the authority to impose secondary sanctions on European firms investing more than $40 million annually in the oil or gas sector of Iran. ILSA had an important caveat allowing the President to waive its application if doing so would serve U.S. national security interests. However, a loophole in the sanctions legislation exempted foreign subsidiaries of U.S. companies run by non-U.S. nationals from incurring penalties. Consequently, G.E., ConocoPhillips, and Halliburton exploited this loophole for their Iranian operations.[50] Undeterred by the new U.S. law, Total signed a larger, $2 billion contract with Iran in 1997, with other partners, Russia's Gazprom and Malaysia's Petronas. The United States and its European allies were clearly working at cross-purposes.

Critical Dialogue at Work

On September 17, 1992, an Iranian team assassinated Dr. Sadegh Sharafkandi, the secretary general of the Iranian Democratic Party of Kurdistan, and three other party members at the Mykonos Greek Restaurant in Berlin. The Iranian dissidents had been guests of the German Socialist Democratic Party, which was hosting a Congress of the Socialist International. The Iranian attack on German soil transpired three months after Kinkel announced his policy of engaging Iran through "critical dialogue," and during the very same month that the European Union adopted this as a new European-wide policy.

Though Iran was quickly implicated in the attack, Europe's reaction to the slayings was to adopt a "wait and see" stance until the investigation and trial were complete, though the United States urged a more confrontational approach. This became clear in October 1993, shortly before the opening of the Mykonos trial, when Ali Fallahian, the Minister of Intelligence and Security (MOIS) and chief of Iran's foreign intelligence services, was hosted in Bonn by Bernd Schmidbauer, the special advisor on intelligence for Chancellor Helmut Kohl. The official German explanation of the meetings was that they dealt with humanitarian matters. The Iranian ambassador to Germany, Sayed Hussein Musavian, was interviewed by the weekly *Die Zeit* and said that the visit dealt with counter-terrorist training, halting drug trafficking, and weapons of mass destruction.[51]

The United States was outraged by the Fallahian visit to Bonn. Fallahian had boasted about his ministry's success eliminating the heads of the Iranian opposition abroad: "We succeeded in striking fundamental blows to their top members."[52] Secretary of State Warren Christopher sent Richard Holbrooke, his new envoy to

Germany, to protest. The German response was that the visit was part of their effort to moderate Iranian behavior through what they called "constructive engagement."[53] Germany's own Federal Crime Office, however, suspected that Fallahian was connected to the Mykonos attack and wanted to arrest him while he was visiting the German government in Bonn, but this was overruled.

Nonetheless, the connections of Iran to the Mykonos attack came out piece by piece. During his visit, Fallahian himself requested that the suspects held by the Germans be released, thereby creating a tie between the attack and the Iranian government. A June 1993 report by a German federal agency determined that the Mykonos attack had been planned in the Iranian Embassy in Bonn.[54] After examining the evidence, the German federal prosecutor issued an international arrest warrant for Fallahian in March 1996. Finally, when a Berlin court issued its judgment on the Mykonos murders on April 10, 1997, while it didn't identify any Iranian officials by name, it nonetheless determined "Iran's political leadership ordered the crime."[55]

After the German court's ruling, the European Union was still not willing to jettison its policy of "critical dialogue," which was suspended but certainly not revoked. There was some debate about the whole policy of "critical dialogue" inside Germany. The German Green Party even called for Kinkel's resignation. But the European foreign ministers seemed determined to get back to business when they met in late April 1997 to discuss the verdict, even though the Europeans made a show of adopting a few anti-Iranian measures. With the exception of Greece, the European states all recalled their ambassadors from Tehran. Australia, Canada, and New Zealand did the same.

Furthermore, the European Union states announced they would halt bilateral visits to Iran on the ministerial level. They also decided to deny visas to Iranians who had positions in the security or intelligence establishment. They prohibited arms sales to Iran. But they would not accept the Clinton administration's policy of isolating Iran. The Europeans insisted on preserving their economic and trade ties to Iran. France's foreign minister, Hervé de Charette, even tried to limit the European suspension to a six-month period, but his efforts were rejected.[56]

The Iranian reaction to these deliberations about the future of "critical dialogue" was blunt: Iran's Supreme Leader, Ali Khamenei, who was implicated by the German court's findings, stated: "We don't give a damn about your ending the critical dialogue." He also declared: "We never sought such a dialogue."[57] There was no apology to Germany or even any remorse expressed by the Iranian side. As a negotiating tactic, the statement basically clarified that Iran was not going to make any special concessions in order to preserve its special relationship with Europe. It was perhaps predicated on the assumption that the Europeans need Iran more than Iran needed the Europeans.

Fundamentally, European officials still believed that the policy of "critical dialogue" could be used to moderate Iranian behavior. What made their persistence astounding was that the Mykonos attack was not the only Iranian terror strike on European soil that was linked to the highest levels of the Iranian regime. In 1989, the leader of the Iranian Kurds at the time, Abdul-Rahman Qassemlou, came to Vienna, Austria, in order to negotiate a Kurdish autonomy agreement with representatives of President Rafsanjani. The Iranian delegation included an intelligence official who years later would become the president of Iran, Mahmoud Ahmadinejad.[58] But on the second day of the Vienna talks, Qassemlou and two of his associates were shot to death in a Viennese apartment. The autonomy negotiations had been a setup. The Austrians found the Iranian hit squad, but did not indict them. Instead, the authorities let all three go back to Tehran.[59]

Several years later, on August 8, 1991, Shahpur Bakhtiar, the former prime minister of Iran, was found dead in his residence in Paris along with his secretary. They had died of asphyxiation as well as puncture wounds from sharp weapons. The French authorities managed to trace down primary suspects Muhammad Azadi and Ali Vakili Rad, both of whom had obtained false passports in Tehran. The French court handling the case concluded that Ali Vakli Rad was "a key operative in the Ministry of Intelligence." He also worked for the Qods force, the overseas arm of the Revolutionary Guards, and in that capacity reported to Azadi. According to two former members of President Clinton's National Security Council, in 1996–97 alone, more than twenty Iranian dissidents were assassinated beyond the borders of Iran.[60] Iranian operatives were plainly engaging in political assassinations on European soil.

European Engagement and Iranian International Behavior

The European policy of "critical dialogue" did not keep the Iranians from using political assassination abroad to eliminate their opponents. Moreover, an examination of the period in which "critical dialogue" was predominant reveals no corresponding moderation in Tehran's actions toward its neighbors or reduction in international terrorism. It was actively involved in two suicide-bombing attacks in Buenos Aires, with the help of Hizbullah, in 1992 and 1994. In the Middle East, Rafsanjani's Iran, in fact, persisted in undermining the security of its neighbors and backing the use of terrorism as an instrument of state policy, European policy notwithstanding.

Iran was fully prepared to assert its military power against its neighbors in the Arabian Peninsula. On November 30, 1971, the Shah of Iran had sent forces to seize the strategically-situated island from the Emirate of Sharjah, just before it joined the United Arab Emirates (UAE), which became independent a month later. The Greater and Lesser Tunb, two islands that belonged to the UAE emirate of Ras al-Khaima, were also siezed. The Shah agreed at the time that Abu Musa should come under the joint administration of Iran and the UAE.

Nearly twenty years later, Rafsanjani made a high-profile visit to the disputed Persian Gulf island of Abu Musa in early 1992. After Rafsanjani's visit, Iran evicted the UAE from Abu Musa and claimed the island was to be under Iran's exclusive control. When the Arab Gulf states requested that Iran evacuate the three islands, Rafsanjani responded by saying that the UAE would "cross a sea of blood before reaching them."[61]

The struggle over the three islands had broader implications for the West. Abu Musa was situated 160 kilometers from the entrance to the Persian Gulf. Iran deployed ground forces on Abu Musa and equipped them with Chinese HY-2 Silkworm anti-ship missiles.[62] The forces came to include a contingent of the Revolutionary Guards. Iran constructed an airport. There were also reports that Iran stationed 130 kilometer-range C-801 anti-ship missiles on Abu Musa. By 1997, Iranian officials actually spoke

Strait of Hormuz

openly about closing off the Strait of Hormuz, thereby cutting off a good portion to the international oil traffic from the Arabian Peninsula. The Greater and Lesser Tunbs were in an even more sensitive location, immediately adjacent to the Persian Gulf's inbound shipping lanes, used by the world's oil tankers.

The UAE was not the only target of Iranian activism in the Persian Gulf. Bahrain, the formerly oil-rich island country just off the shore of Saudi Arabia, remained a tempting target for the export of the Iranian Revolution. The ruling al-Khalifa family was Sunni and its subjects consisted of a large Shiite majority. In December 1981, the Bahrainis broke up a plot by Bahraini Shiites to overthrow their government. In the spring of 1995, Bahrain faced a new wave of rioting by its Shiite population and a new conspiracy to launch a coup against the al-Khalifa royal family.[63]

The Clinton administration may have been doubtful about the extent of Iranian involvement, so Bahrain presented documentary evidence in Washington in June 1995 linking what was called Bahraini Hizbullah, which was established in the Iranian city of Qom in 1993, and the Quds Force of the Revolutionary Guards. Richard Clarke, the counterterrorism coordinator in the Clinton National Security Council, was given a document by the Bahraini ambassador outlining a plan by the Revolutionary Guards to install a pro-Iranian government in Bahrain.[64] It was learned that Bahraini Hizbullah had been training for over two years in Iran and in Lebanon.

Six of the forty-four conspirators who were arrested made televised confessions that they were trained in Iran and by Hizbullah in Lebanon. One of those captured explained that his instructions were to gather information on the U.S. military presence in Bahrain, which in July 1995, it was announced, was to become the headquarters of the new U.S. Fifth Fleet.[65] New Shiite riots broke out in November 1995; in response, the Bahraini government expelled an Iranian diplomat in early 1996, whom it charged was involved in provoking the rioting.[66]

Another disturbing aspect of Iran's international behavior in the mid-1990s was its successful penetration of the Sunni Muslim world, beyond the Shiite communities of the Middle East. In late 1991, Rafsanjani headed a large delegation to Khartoum, the capital of Sudan, which included Ali Fallahian and Brigadier General Mohsen Rezai, the commander of the Revolutionary Guards. Middle Eastern and western intelligence agencies estimated that Iran stationed up to 2,000 Revolutionary Guards in Sudan to train the Sudanese Army. Sheikh Hassan al-Turabi, the Sudanese strongman who came out of the Sunni Muslim Brotherhood, sought to unify the Islamic world and thus reached out to Shiite Iran. He was also a great admirer of Ayatollah Khomeini.

Al-Turabi's pan-Islamic philosophy brought him to convene what he called the Popular and Islamic Conference in April 1991, in order to unify all the anti-western terrorist organizations across the Middle East and Asia. The conference brought Islamist groups like Hamas, which was the Palestinian branch of the Muslim Brotherhood, and Afghan mujahideen groups headed by Osama bin Laden, together with nationalists like Egyptian Nasserists and Yasser Arafat of the PLO. In a second follow-up conference in 1995, many of the same participants attended (Arafat, in the meantime, had joined the Oslo peace process under the auspices of the Clinton administration); but the 1995 event also included Hizbullah. The Iranians had managed to build an important bridge to the radicals of the Sunni Muslim world.

Several Arab countries were affected at this time. President Hosni Mubarak of Egypt was visiting Addis Ababa, Ethiopia, in June 1995 when an assassination squad opened fire on his limousine. The organization that was behind the attack was the Gamaat Islamiya (the Islamic Associations), an Egyptian militant Islamist organization strongly tied to Sudan. The Iranians were actively training terrorist groups in Sudan. A year later, Mubarak himself charged that Iran was behind the attack on his entourage in Ethiopia.[67]

Furthermore, the Algerian government determined that Iran was assisting the FIS (the Islamic Salvation Front), which was the main Islamic opposition to the regime. There were reports that the even more extreme GIA (Armed Islamic Group) was holding meetings in the Iranian Embassy in Algiers.[68] One GIA leader, Emir Gousmi, held an Iranian passport. As a result of this accumulating evidence against Tehran, Algeria severed diplomatic relations with Iran in March 1993. The Jordanians also had problems with Iran; in December 1995, they declared a first secretary in the Iranian Embassy in Amman as *persona non grata* because of his connections with Hizbullah.[69]

Finally, Hamas opened an office in Tehran in 1994.[70] That same year, Hamas adopted the Hizbullah strategy of suicide bombing attacks against Israeli civilian targets. Previously, suicide bombing had not been used by Sunni Muslims. Between 1994 and early 1996, Hamas and the Palestinian Islamic Jihad, which was even more closely identified with Iran, unleashed dozens of these attacks against Israel. They had adopted this Iranian strategy and with Iranian financial backing used it with deadly effectiveness. In short, Iran was engaged in highly aggressive actions across the Middle East, despite the efforts of the European Union to moderate Iranian behavior.

While the EU embraced "critical dialogue," there was a growing Iranian presence in the heart of Europe itself. Iran had ties with the Bosnian Muslim leadership before the breakup of Yugoslavia in the early 1990s. The CIA was reporting in 1983 that Yugoslav authorities had arrested Bosnian Muslims whom they claimed were involved in "pan-Islamic activities on behalf of the Khomeini regime," after returning from Iran.[71]

But with the outbreak of full-scale war in the Balkans, Tehran fully intervened in the conflict, first through Iranian humanitarian aid organizations and then through massive arms shipments, despite the existence of a UN arms embargo. The Bosnian Muslim leader, Alija Izetbeovic, made repeated visits to Tehran in 1992 and 1993 seeking more assistance. In September 1992, the Croatians seized an Iranian 747 at Zagreb Airport filled with weaponry bound for the Bosnian Muslims, but later dropped their objections to serving as the conduit for Iranian arms.[72]

By 1995, three Iranian arms flights were coming into Croatia every week. That very same year, as a result of the growing intervention, there were 2,000 Iranian Revolutionary Guards serving in Bosnia, which became the center for Iranian intelligence operations in Southern Europe.[73] The West may not have objected to Iran's clandestine involvement in the supply of arms, since until the mid-1990s it had itself failed to come up with a formula to halt the fighting and a way of balancing the military superiority of the Bosnian Serbs. Nonetheless, the growing Iranian presence in Southeastern Europe should have set off warning lights that Rafsanjani's Iran was still seeking opportunities to expand its influence abroad even in Europe's backyard, the EU's "critical dialogue" notwithstanding.

The AMIA Attack: Terrorism and Nuclear Proliferation Rolled into One

Beyond Europe, "critical dialogue" did nothing to modify the worst behavior of the Iranian government toward other continents. For example, on July 18, 1994, a Hizbullah suicide bomber struck at the Jewish Community Center building (AMIA) in Buenos Aires, Argentina, killing 85 people and wounding 151. The truth behind the attack would take years to come out. In fact, the Argentinean authorities investigated the attack for more than a decade; even though considerable time had passed, their findings would have global implications.

Argentina's Attorney General, Dr. Alberto Nisman, issued a detailed 800-page report on October 25, 2006, that concluded: The decision to carry out the attacks was made not by a small splinter group of extremely radical Islamic functionaries, but it was extensively discussed and was ultimately adopted by a consensus of the highest representatives of the Iranian government at the time.[74]

As a result of the attorney general's report, an Argentinian judge issued international arrest warrants for seven Iranians and one senior Hizbullah member on the charge of "crimes against humanity."[75] INTERPOL issued red notices for the arrest of six of the group. The original eight suspects included: Iran's Minister of Intelligence and Security Ali Fallahian, Iran's Foreign Minister Ali Akbar Velayati, the Commander of the Revolutionary Guards Mohsen Rezai, the Commander of the Quds Force (the external operations branch of the Revolutionary Guards) Ahmad Vahidi, two Iranian embassy officials in Buenos Aires, and Imad Moughniyeh, whom the Argentinian investigation identified as the head of Hizbullah's External Security Service. The eighth suspect in the attack for whom the Argentinians issued an international arrest warrant was no less than Ali Akbar Rafsanjani, the President of Iran.

The Buenos Aires attack put to rest a number of questions about Iranian-backed terrorism that had been hotly debated since the bombing of the Marine barracks in Beirut in 1983. It was now clear that Imad Moughniyeh was not part of some breakaway Shiite dissident group that had nothing to do with Hizbullah; he had an official role in Hizbullah, by virtue of his heading its External Security Service.

Moreover, Iran was not just inspiring Hizbullah ideologically, it was working hand in glove with Hizbullah in terrorist operations, through its most senior officials. Finally, despite all the ink that had been spilled trying to establish that Ali Akbar Rafsanjani was a moderate, the Argentina attack proved he was still capable of approving devastating terrorist attacks against innocent civilians, thousands of miles away from Iran, if it served the interests of the Iranian state.

What Iranian interest did the bombing in Argentina serve? It was difficult to explain as part of a retaliatory strike in response to Israel's elimination of Abbas Musawi, the secretary-general of Hizbullah, in February 1992. Such a retaliation had taken place the same year when Hizbullah bombed the Israeli Embassy in Buenos Aires. The Argentinean team investigating the 1994 attack came up with an entirely different motive that had nothing to do with the Arab-Israel conflict. It concluded that the fundamental reason for Iran's action was Argentina's "unilateral decision to terminate the nuclear materials and technology supply agreements that had been concluded some years previously between Argentina and Iran."[76]

Nisman's report contained important details on the Iranian nuclear program. The first contract between Iran and the Argentinean company, INVAP, was signed on May 4, 1987; the contract called for Argentinean assistance in helping the Iranians convert a facility in Tehran, supplied by the United States during the days of the Shah, so that it could use uranium enriched to 20 percent U-235. This was well above the normal enrichment levels for civilian uses. Nisman's report contains the main reason why Argentina decided to cancel the nuclear contract with Iran: "the statements made by President Rafsanjani, who maintained that Iran had a right to make nuclear weapons and that it would never be deterred from this aim."

As a result, Nisman's report continued: "Argentina decided to discontinue relations with Iran in terms of nuclear technology transfer."[77] The 1994 AMIA bombing represented a new chapter in Iran's struggle with the outside world: its drive to acquire nuclear weapons was intimately linked to its employment of terrorism to advance the goals of the Iranian state. It was clear more than ever that the policy of "critical dialogue" between 1992 and 1997 had utterly failed to halt any aspect of Iran's aggressive behavior.

Iran Escalates: Khobar Towers

In Shiite Islam, special reverence is given to the family of the Prophet Muhammad, which is why it is believed by Shiites that the succession to lead the Islamic community in the seventh century should have gone from Muhammad to his son-in-law, Ali. The most important holy sites for Shiites not only include Najaf and Karbala, the Iraqi cities where Ali and his son, Hussein, respectively are buried, but also Damascus, next to which was the burial place of Hussein's sister, Zaynab, and the location of her shrine. It was in the Zaynab Shrine that another Hizbullah branch, known as Hizbullah al-Hijaz or just Saudi Hizbullah, recruited many of its operatives. The shrine was ideally situated, for new Shiite recruits could be transported from Syria to regular Hizbullah training camps in neighboring Lebanon and plan for future operations.

Saudi Arabia is overwhelmingly a Sunni Muslim country, but it has a significant Shiite community concentrated mostly in its oil-rich Eastern Province. Under the Wahhabi school of Sunni Islam that was virtually a state religion in Saudi Arabia, Shiites were oppressed, both socially and economically, and discouraged from engaging in many of their religious rites. This made the Saudi Shiite community a perfect target group for the export of the Iranian Revolution. After the rise of Khomeini in 1979, Iran succeeded in provoking a Shiite uprising in the area of the Saudi coastal town of Qatif, as it had in neighboring Bahrain. Fifteen years later, the Saudi Shiites were still ideally suited for recruitment into Iran's regional terrorist networks in the Arab world, were organized as branches of Hizbullah.

In the early 1990s, Hizbullah was expanding its terrorist capabilities. According to the CIA's assessment in July 1991, Hizbullah was going to "continue to build its international terrorist infrastructure." Moreover, ideologically it maintained "its militant opposition to the West, particularly the United States." As a result, "the group could lash out at the time and place of its choice."[78] Subsequent developments showed that Saudi Hizbullah would become its preferred instrument for carrying out its anti-American agenda. Saudi Hizbullah actually called itself Hizbullah al-Hijaz, named for the Islamic Holy Land where Mecca and Madina were located, rather than using the Saudi name which would acknowl-edge the Saudi royal family. Hizbullah al-Hijaz was established in 1983 by Saudi Shiites who were studying in Qom, Iran's center of Shiite learning.[79]

Ahmad al-Mughassil was a Saudi Shiite from Qatif who served as the military commander of Saudi Hizbullah in the mid-1990s. He actively recruited Saudi Shiites to his organization at the Zaynab Shrine. He recruited a fellow resident of Qatif and then arranged for him to undergo religious training in Qom, Iran. In 1993, he instructed his operatives to conduct surveillance of potential American targets in Saudi Arabia, including the U.S. Embassy in Riyadh. His reports were passed on to officials in Iran.

Al-Mughassil's men identified the Khobar Towers residential complex in Dhahran, which was situated in eastern Saudi Arabia, as a location where the United States and other countries housed military personnel that were assigned to the kingdom. In late 1994, a high-level Iranian government official was in contact with Mughassil, who situated himself for most of this period in Beirut, to inquire about the progress of Saudi Hizbullah surveillance activity.

During the first half of June 1996, Mughassil met with more than a half-dozen members of Saudi Hizbullah at the Zeinab Shrine in Damascus to plan an attack on Khobar Towers. Several months earlier, two of his men had tried to smuggle plastic explo-sives from Lebanon through Syria and Jordan to Saudi Arabia, but were caught at the Saudi border. The Saudi authorities interro-gated the two and learned about Mughassil and his role in Saudi

Hizbullah. They also learned that Mughassil was connected with the Quds Force of the Revolutionary Guards.[80]

Despite their capture, the attack plan against Khobar Towers proceeded. After a truck bomb was assembled in Lebanon's Bekaa Valley, it was successfully driven to Daharan. On June 21, 1996, Mughassil himself drove the truck bomb and parked it next to Building 131 of the Khobar Towers complex. Minutes after he left, the truck exploded with a force of 20,000 pounds of TNT, killing nineteen U.S. servicemen from the U.S. Air Force and wounding 372 other Americans. A detailed staff report prepared by President Clinton's National Security Council one day after the attack blamed the Quds Force and "their front, Saudi Hizbullah."[81] Anthony Lake, the National Security Advisor, agreed with his staff's assessment and so did the CIA.[82]

The Clinton administration felt that it did not have good options. The Joint Chiefs of Staff had contingency plans for going to war against Iran which included bombing coastal military facilities, ports, air force bases, and missile bases. The Clinton national security team considered what would happen if a U.S. retaliatory strike was launched and they were told that Iran would launch a counter-strike and use terrorist cells. They also considered striking at terrorist training camps in Lebanon alone. They finally adopted a secret plan they called an "intelligence operation option." The problem with this idea was that it took the CIA months to put in place the simultaneous intelligence actions that were authorized to send the Iranian leadership a powerful deterrence message.

But in public, the United States did not want to tie Iran too directly to Khobar Towers, probably because that would build public pressure for a major military action against Tehran. State Department spokesman Jamie Rubin explained that while Washington did have "specific information with respect to the involvement of Iranian government officials," nonetheless, the United States had not yet concluded "whether the attack was directed by the government of Iran."[83]

This left open the possibility of a rogue operation. Sandy Berger, who would replace Lake as Clinton's National Security Advisor, also tried to create doubt about the degree of Iranian governmental responsibility for Khobar Towers. He was quoted saying: "We know it was done by Saudi Hizballah. We know that they were trained in Iran by Iranians. We know there was Iranian involvement. What has yet to be established is how substantial the Iranian involvement was."[84]

The main problem for the Clinton administration at the time was that all the details on the Khobar Towers attack were not immediately available. Saudi Arabia was not interested in a full-scale American attack, especially if it would have to absorb the Iranian retaliatory blow; as a result, the Saudis dragged their feet in cooperating with the FBI's investigation of what happened.

By the time the FBI managed to overcome Saudi reluctance and start constructing a fuller picture of the attack, U.S. policy on Iran was changing yet again. In 1997, Warren Christopher was no longer secretary of state, having been replaced by Madeleine Albright, who was becoming frustrated with the U.S. containment policy and was less critical of the Europeans for their past policy of "critical dialogue." On her first trip to Europe, she commented: "Of course, our critical silence doesn't seem to have accomplished that much either."[85] U.S. policy was preparing to change. Foreshadowing Albright's new approach, Assistant Secretary of State for Near Eastern Affairs Robert Pelletreau issued a statement in Dubai expressing hope that a new U.S.-Iran dialogue could begin during the next administration. Washington now wanted to engage with Iran.

In the meantime, the U.S. Congress initiated an entirely different track for handling the Iranian threat. The Speaker of the House of Representatives, Newt Gingrich (R-Georgia), concluded on February 5, 1995, that the only policy that made sense for dealing with Iran's revolutionary regime was one that sought its overthrow.[86]

To further the idea of regime change, Congress proposed $18–20 million in funding authority for covert operations against Iran in the Intelligence Authorization Act for Fiscal Year 1996. The Clinton administration preferred to direct the funds to changing regime behavior, arguing that a policy of regime change violated past U.S. international undertakings. Consequently, Congress was reluctant to earmark funds for a special radio service that would reach out to the Iranian people over the heads of the Iranian government.

Mohammad Khatami and a New Era of Iranian Reform?

Rafsanjani's term ended in May 1997. Mohammad Khatami took office as Iran's president after a landslide election, beating the Parliamentary Speaker, Ali Akbar Nateq-Nouri, who had been the pick of the conservative establishment. The commander of the Revolutionary Guards issued written orders to vote for Nateq-Nouri, who also received far more television and radio exposure than Khatami.[87] Nonetheless, Khatami won 69 percent of the vote.[88] With this overwhelming victory and the mandate it implied, there was a strong belief in the West that Iran might be heading in a new moderate direction. Khatami fed this hope and spoke about the need for a "dialogue of civilizations."

In a CNN interview with Christiane Amanpour in early 1998, Khatami set a new tone for Iran: "We believe the holy Quran that says: slaying an innocent person is tantamount to slaying all humanity." He added: "Terrorism should be condemned in all its forms and manifestations."[89] This was not just a journalistic interview. The Clinton administration had actually been given an opportunity to suggest Amanpour's questions; she was engaged to the State Department spokesman, Jamie Rubin.[90]

On the one hand, clearly the United States wanted to probe Khatami and see if was possible to establish a new relationship with Iran under his presidency. On the other hand, there was the unfinished business of Khobar Towers. Secretary of State Albright sent a message to Khatami in October 1997 through the Swiss Embassy in Tehran. She indicated that Washington was ready for an official dialogue. The Iranians didn't even bother to respond.[91]

Albright continued the effort to reach out to Iran. She gave a major address on Iran in June 1998 endorsing Khatami's "dialogue of civilizations." She explained the reasoning behind her initiative: "We must always be flexible enough to respond to change and seize historic opportunities." Albright spoke about developing with the Iranians "a roadmap leading to normal relations." Again there was no sign from the Iranian side that it appreciated the new U.S. approach.[92] It was as though the Iranians did not want to acknowledge that there had been any American concession that would require them to reciprocate. Indeed, Khatami commented: "We believe there is a change in their tone," then he added, "but we're always looking for action."[93]

Albright appeared to be taking a more accommodating position toward Iran when she announced that the administration was going to exercise its power to waive the imposition of ILSA sanctions against foreign companies doing business with Iran. She announced in May 1998 that the United States would not take any actions against Total, Gazprom, and Petronas, she explained, because Washington needed the cooperation of France, Russia, and Malaysia for other burning international issues from Russian ratification of START II to coordination on the conflicts in Bosnian and Kosovo.[94] These arguments had nothing to do with Iran as such, but the easing of U.S. sanctions could still be seen as a signal to Khatami's government.

But the American outreach to Iran was bound to go nowhere, for no "historic opportunity" really existed. On the ground, Iran remained unreformed. In fact, six months after the election, CIA Director George Tenet admitted before the U.S. Senate's Armed

Services Committee that Khatami's Iran was unreformed in one very significant way: "we have yet to see any significant reduction of Iran's support for terrorism."[95]

The CIA's own internal analysis showed that Hizbullah had hoped that Khatami's opponent, Nateq-Nouri, would have won the Iranian presidential elections. But despite the Khatami victory, Iranian support for Hizbullah remained unchanged. The report concluded: "Even if Khatami wanted to change Tehran's policy toward Hizballah, he probably does not have the authority to make a change without the approval of Khamenei, who has long been one of the group's foremost supporters."[96]

President Clinton directly tackled the dilemma of seeing if U.S. engagement with Khatami's Iran was possible, while at the same time addressing the unfinished business of the Khobar Towers attack. In mid-1999, his White House team drafted a direct message for Khatami.[97] It stated that the United States had evidence that Iran's Revolutionary Guards were directly involved in planning and executing the Khobar Towers attack. Moreover, the Revolutionary Guards were still involved in terrorist activities abroad. In order to improve U.S.-Iranian relations, he wanted a commitment from Khatami that Iranian involvement in terrorism would end, and the individual involved in the Khobar Towers attack would be brought to justice.

The message was delivered directly to Khatami by Oman's foreign minister, Yusuf bin Alawi, a month later. Six weeks later, the Iranian response came. The Iranian message totally rejected Clinton's "allegations" about Khobar Towers as "inaccurate and unacceptable." It saw the repetition of these charges "in the gravest of terms." It accused the United States of helping terrorist elements. This was not the tone of an Iranian leadership that was interested in opening a dialogue with America. The bottom line was that even when the President of the United States was reaching out discreetly to engage Iran, he was unable to establish a channel of communication.

There were increasing reasons to wonder whether it was true that Khatami was a politician ushering in a new era and a more moderate political trend in Iran. He clearly was offering a new agenda for Iran. But his "reformist" allies included Iranian politicians who claimed to be reformists, but were far better known for their involvement in revolutionary violence. For example, no less than Ali Akbar Mohtashemi, the founder of Hizbullah, became a Khatami supporter.[98] Then there was the case of Mohammad Mousavi Khoehina, who had been the mastermind of the 1979 takeover of the U.S. Embassy in Tehran and had encouraged Khomeini to issue the *fatwa* condemning Salman Rushdie to death. He also joined Khatami's reformists, along with Hassan Sanei, who headed the foundation that offered the reward for murdering Rushdie.

Khatami wanted to improve Iran's relations with the West, but that was not necessarily true of his supporters. Many of the reformers were focused on issues of domestic policy. They did not necessarily distinguish themselves in their vision of Iranian foreign and defense policy. There was a real reform movement in Iran, but the question remained whether Khatami and his allies were dedicated members of it or just "window-dressing for the system, both inside and outside the country."[99]

Khamenei had not supported Khatami's presidential candidacy, and saw Khatami's election as a threat to his powers. He challenged Khatami and his reformist supporters, openly criticizing them as being under western influence. He charged that they benefitted from the support of the United States and Britain. Khamenei subsequently created his own consultative body on foreign affairs so that he could pursue an independent foreign policy for Iran in accordance with his own worldview and block any normalization of ties between Iran and the United States.[100]

There was a discernable increase in the involvement of the Revolutionary Guards in the struggle between Khatami and Khamenei. As the guardians of the Islamic Revolution, they backed Khamenei, which was facilitated by his replacing the longtime head of the Revolutionary Guards, Brigadier General Mohsen Rezai, with a new commander, Yahya Rahim Safavi, right after Khatami's election.

Yet, in November 1997, the deputy commander of the Revolutionary Guards, Mohammad Baqar Zogqadr, issued the first of several warnings to Khatami: "The IRGC [the Islamic Revolutionary Guards Corps] will react swifty to anything that would threaten this holy regime."[101] Safavi also lashed out with initially implicit attacks on Khatami's policies: "Can we withstand American threats and domineering attitude with a policy of détente?"[102] In a clear attack on Khatami, Safavi continued by questioning whether Iran could "foil dangers" through a "dialogue of civilizations."

It is important to recall that the Iranian Constitution under the Islamic Republic had language that could be interpreted in a way to justify what the Revolutionary Guards were doing. Article 150 stated: "The Islamic Revolutionary Guards Corps, organized in the early days of the triumph of the Revolution, is to be maintained so that it may continue in its role of guarding the revolution and its achievements." Thus, Safavi and his officers could see themselves as having the authority to protect the Islamic Revolution from any threat—whether external or even internal if a clear threat to the regime was present. Indeed, events during Khatami's presidency gave the Revolutionary Guards the sense that they might have to act.

Safavi and Khatami clashed over how to deal with Iranian students, who were generally sympathetic to the Iranian president's domestic agenda for reform, but were conflicted with the security forces. More specifically, the Revolutionary Guards' paramilitary forces, the Basij, had attacked movie theatres and universities in the latter part of Rafsanjani's presidency. In 1999, they attacked a student dormitory, igniting nationwide student protests.

On July 12, 1999, twenty-four top Revolutionary Guard commanders sent Khatami a letter demanding action against the students: "Our patience has run out. We cannot tolerate this situation anymore." The letter, which they made public, made clear that the Revolutionary Guards would take action if Khatami did not change his policies.[103] Khatami was learning that there was a limit to what he could do in Iran before facing military intervention and being toppled in a coup d'etat.

The pressures on Khatami from the Revolutionary Guards worsened. Khatami called on Safavi to desist from making more political statements. The Revolutionary Guards in response warned Khatami to stop all attacks on their commander. Safavi reminded Khatami that he was operating in accordance with the will of the Supreme Leader and had his political backing: "We do not interfere in politics, but if we see that the foundations of our system of government and our revolution are threatened . . . we get involved." Indeed, in order to clarify under whose authority he was making these statements, Safavi continued: "When I see that a political current has hatched a cultural plot, I consider it my right to defend the revolution against this current. My commander is the exalted leader, and he has not banned me [from doing so]."[104]

During his lifetime, Ayatollah Khomeini sought to keep the Iranian military out of the political arena. After his death, this began to change. During his presidency, Rafsanjani invested heavily in the Revolutionary Guards. His military procurement programs in the early 1990s included weapons for the Revolutionary Guards that would allow them to organize themselves into regular military formations. He promoted the involvement of the Revolutionary Guards in the Iranian economy, so that they began to own companies. Rafsanjani essentially bought their political loyalty to him, even while their commander-in-chief was the Supreme Leader, Ali Khamenei.

But what clearly emerged as a result of the struggle between Khatami and the Revolutionary Guards was that this pivotal Iranian elite force was under the indisputable authority of the Supreme

Leader and not under the Iranian president. That also meant Iran's weapons development programs—from ballistic missiles to uranium enrichment—were also the province of Ali Khamenei and only marginally affected by Mohammad Khatami. Years later, when the UN Security Council blacklisted individuals who were involved in either Iran's ballistic missile or nuclear programs, there was only one mentioned who was engaged in both: Major General Yahya Rahim Safavi, the commander of the Revolutionary Guards.[105] Khatami's ability to influence Safavi in these sensitive areas was virtually nil.

Khatami was powerless to stem the growing influence of the Revolutionary Guards on Iran's political life during his years in office despite the overwhelming support he enjoyed from the Iranian electorate. During his second term in office from 2001 through 2005, for example, a former Revolutionary Guards commander Ezatullah Zarghami, became chief of Iran's national television and radio. The Revolutionary Guards were permitted in this period to field their own list of candidates for the Iranian parliamentary elections. Unhappy about the fact that the contract for operating Tehran's new international airport went to a Turkish consortium, and not to a company with which they had close ties, the Revolutionary Guards closed the airport down in protest.[106]

Despite these developments, Khatami had a very definite role to play for Iran. An important division of responsibility between Khatami and Khamenei had emerged during these years. Khatami's eloquent CNN interviews and visionary UN initiatives succeeded in disarming the West from responding to Iranian provocations from the Mykonos killings to Khobar Towers. The West paid attention to Khatami, but not to the realities of Iranian policies that were being executed by Khamenei and by the Revolutionary Guards. Noone wanted to take strong measures against Iran—and sustain them—for such action might undermine the reformist trend led by Khatami.

Indeed, the Clinton administration felt compelled to give its policy of outreach to Khatami and engagement with his government one more chance. On March 17, 2000, Secretary of State Albright delivered a carefully crafted address at Washington's Omni Shoreham Hotel in which she apologized for the U.S. role in the toppling of Iran's former prime minister, Mohammad Mosaddeq: "In 1953, the United States played a significant role in orchestrating the overthrow of Iran's popular Prime Minister, Mohammad Mosaddeq. The Eisenhower administration believed its actions were justified for strategic reasons; but the coup was clearly a setback for Iran's political development."

Albright then attacked U.S. policy for backing the Shah in subsequent years: "Moreover, during the next quarter century, the United States and the West gave sustained backing to the Shah's regime. Although it did much to develop the country economically, the Shah's government also brutally repressed political dissent." The speech was full of expressions of optimism about Iran: "The democratic winds in Iran are so refreshing, and many of the ideas espoused by its leaders so encouraging."

But Albright also expressed some reservations about Iranian policy. She criticized the persecution of Bahais and converts to Christianity; she pointed out that thirteen Iranian Jews had been detained for more than a year without being charged. Then she added: "Despite the trends towards democracy, control over the military, judiciary, courts and police remains in *unelected hands* (emphasis added)." The speech essentially praised Khatami and directly attacked the Supreme Leader Ali Khamenei, who, unlike Khatami, was not popularly elected.

There were two problems with what Albright did. First, this was the kind of close embrace that Khatami did not need, putting him in the position of doing Washington's bidding. Was this supposed to strengthen Khatami and the reformist political trend he represented? It also made an address, which its State Department drafters undoubtedly felt was magnanimous because of the apologies to Iran it contained, into direct intervention in the internal struggle between the Iranian President and its Supreme Leader.

Second, there was a more fundamental question of what the speech was supposed to accomplish, even if the reference to *unelected hands* had not been put in. Albright was not naïve about Iran and she even said in her address: "To date, the political developments in Iran have not caused its military to cease its determined effort to acquire technology, materials and assistance needed to develop nuclear weapons, nor have these developments caused Iran's Revolutionary Guard Corps or its Ministry of Intelligence and Security to get out of the terrorism business."

While the speech was intended to build up democratic forces in Iran, Washington knew that Khatami and his associates did not have the authority to alter Iranian policy in these highly sensitive areas. Unless Washington was hoping to promote a change in the internal balance of power between Khatami and Khamenei, and thereby alter Iranian behavior, there was no way its policy of engaging Khatami could accomplish anything significant.

When Khamenei responded to Albright ten days later, it was clear he was not impressed with the American apology for 1953: "Just a few days ago an American minister delivered a speech. After half a century, or even over 40 years, the Americans have now confessed that they staged the 28th Mordad [August 19, 1953] coup . . . An admission years after the crime was committed, while they might be committing similar crimes now, will not do the Iranian nation any good."[107]

Albright's speech did not strengthen Khatami's allies. The very next month, the Judiciary, under the control of Supreme Leader Khamenei started arresting leading journalists and putting them in prison.[108] In the meantime, the Iranian nuclear program continued unabated and did not face any real international pressures that would have given Tehran pause about its continuation. Yet it was at this time that Iran made significant progress in some of its most sensitive weapons programs.

Iranian Missile Progress During Khatami's Presidency

In fact, while the Clinton administration sought to engage Khatami's Iran, U.S. intelligence agencies picked up an extremely ominous sign the very same year that Khatami was elected. In late 1997, a U.S. reconnaissance satellite over the Shahid Hermat Industrial Group research facility, situated south of Tehran, observed the heat signature from a static rocket engine test from a new generation of Iranian ballistic missiles.[109] A powerful engine test in Iran with a large infrared signature could be detected from outer space. Assessments estimated that a new Iranian missile, with an 800-mile range, would be ready for flight-testing in either 1998 (CIA estimate) or 1999 (DIA estimate).

It was not the first test of a rocket engine of this size at the Shahid Hermat facility. Earlier in the year, a few months prior to Khatami's election, Vice President Al Gore warned Russian Premier Victor Chernomydrin that the United States knew Moscow had transferred parts and technology to Iran from Soviet SS-4 medium range ballistic missiles.[110] The SS-4 was the missile the Soviet Union deployed in Cuba in 1962 whose range reached just beyond the southern United States, as far as Dallas, Texas in the west and Washington, D.C. in the north. Apparently, the Iranians were studying its engines. There was some speculation in Washington that Khatami's perceived moderation might lead to cutbacks in Iranian programs of this sort and to a cooling of Iranian-Russian relations.[111]

Yet the Iranian weapons programs progressed. On July 22, 1998, Iran tested its new Shahab-3 (Shooting Star) missile which was assessed to have a 1,300 kilometer range—within striking distance of Turkey, Israel, and U.S. forces in the Persian Gulf. At the same time, there were signs of continuing Russian-Iranian cooperation. In mid-1998, customs officials in Azerbaijan, the former Soviet republic that borders Iran, intercepted a shipment from Russia of 22 tons of a specialized steel alloy that was suitable for rocket fuel tanks, but had little use for any other purpose.[112] Russian companies were suspected of supplying navigation and guidance technology to the Iranians as well as material for coating missile warheads.[113]

Under Khatami, with continued Russian assistance, the Iranian missile program was in fact accelerating. Robert Gallucci, who served as a special U.S. envoy on the Iran-Russia technology transfer problem, explained its true dimensions. Russian assistance was contributing to many key aspects of the Iranian missile program: the warhead, the fuselage, and guidance systems.[114] Iranians were also receiving training in Russia, while Russian missile experts were traveling to Iran to work on the development of long-range ballistic missiles. Russia's continuing involvement in Iran was critical, for it was shortening the development time for Iranian ballistic missiles.

Gallucci believed that the Russian assistance programs had not only helped Iran deploy the Shahab-3, but also move on to even longer range systems, including intercontinental range ballistic missiles.[115] That meant that at some point in the future, Iran would not only be able to strike at the heart of Europe, but also at the eastern seaboard of the United States. Iran's growing capabilities had to say something about its intentions; it was not a benign Middle Eastern state that had matured and grown out of its earlier revolutionary impulses, but rather it was positioning itself to be an aggressive power on the world stage. This became all the more evident when the truth behind its involvement in international terrorism came to light.

The Truth behind Khobar Towers Comes to Light

The results of the FBI's further investigation of the Khobar Towers attack were finally made public nearly ten years later, after they were made available to the U.S. Federal District Court Judge in Washington, D.C., Royce C. Lamberth. They revealed that while Saudi Hizbullah was meeting its operatives in the Zeinab Shrine, the real operational commander was Brigadier General Ahmad Sharif of the Revolutionary Guards who worked out of the Iranian Embassy in Damascus. He was assisted in Damascus by another Iranian official from the Ministry of Intelligence and Security. Indeed, its notorious minister, Ali Fallahian, who was linked to the earlier Mykonos and Buenos Aries attacks, was directly involved in providing intelligence support. And the entire operation was approved by Iran's Supreme Leader, Ali Khamenei.[116]

Khobar Towers began to look like a replay of the 1983 attack on the U.S. Marine Corps barracks in Beirut, in which the Iranian Embassy in Damascus played a pivotal role in organizing a Hizbullah strike against the United States. In 1983, the Iranian goal was to force the United States out of Lebanon, where Tehran was just establishing its western Middle East outpost in the Arab world. Sixteen years later, Iran was seeking to push the United States out of the Persian Gulf. In both cases, terrorism served the ambitious Iranian goals of exporting the Islamic Revolution and emerging as the dominant power in the Middle East. Iran was not becoming a more moderate state.

And more disturbingly, while it presented the face of moderation, it was systematically acquiring the means to achieve its aims with non-conventional weaponry and long-range delivery systems. If a relatively weaker Iran had enough inner conviction and confidence to strike at U.S. forces in the Middle East on two occasions in 1983 and 1996, then how would a nuclear-armed Iran behave in another decade? If American military superiority did not give the Iranians pause before these attacks, then how would deterrence work with a nuclear-armed Iran? Amidst a growing optimism of new diplomatic opportunities for engaging Iran in the late 1990s, there was also deeper understanding of how dangerous Iran might become.

Chapter 7:

After 9/11:
A Missed Opportunity for
U.S.-Iranian Engagement?

THE SEPTEMBER 11 ATTACKS ON THE UNITED STATES evoked an uncharacteristic outpouring of sympathy in Iran to America's losses. Candlelight vigils were spontaneously held in Tehran.[1] Even the Iranian government strongly condemned the attacks. For the first time since the Islamic Revolution in 1979, there were no chants of "Death to America" during Friday prayers in mosques around Iran.[2] Diplomats became hopeful of the opportunity to potentially revise the relations of the West with Iran.

In the UN-sponsored "Six-Plus Two" talks on Afghanistan, where U.S. and Iranian diplomats had been meeting since 1999, contact between the two sides seemed to have changed. The Bush administration sent a message through the Swiss government, inviting Iran to join the War on Terror that the United States had launched in response. While most of Afghanistan's immediate neighbors who participated in the "Six-Plus Two" forum objected to the upcoming American war against the Taliban, the Iranians did not voice any opposition in private.[3] Had strategic circumstances put the United States and Iran on the same side?

The Taliban, who had given sanctuary since 1996 to Osama bin Laden and al-Qaeda, also had tense relations with Iran. In 1998, when Taliban military forces were seeking to ethnically cleanse northwestern Afghanistan of its Shiite population, who were known as Hazaras, they forced eleven Iranian diplomats, intelligence officers, and a journalist into the basement of the Iranian consulate in Mazar e-Sharif and shot them to death.[4] During the same campaign, the Taliban massacred roughly 5,000–6,000 Shiites in western Afghanistan.[5]

The Taliban also captured about forty-five Iranian truck drivers who were ferrying arms to the Afghan Shiite forces.[6] Iran decided to signal to the Taliban that they were in danger of triggering a war with the Islamic Republic. Iran massed 70,000 Revolutionary Guards, with tanks and aircraft, on the Iranian-Afghan border, and conducted large-scale military exercises. By October 1998, there were 200,000 troops from the regular Iranian Army deployed in the border area.

Thus, when the United States went to war with the Taliban in 2001, it was fighting a regime that had also been an enemy of Iran. As President Khatami commented, "If they toppled the Taliban, it would serve the interests of Iran."[7] As U.S. troops moved into Afghanistan, it might have seemed that Iran's approach to the United States was really changing. Tehran was prepared to allow U.S. aircraft to use airfields in the western part of Afghanistan.[8] Iran agreed to allow the United States to conduct search-and-rescue operations in the event that U.S. pilots flying missions over Afghanistan had to bail out over Iranian territory.[9]

It seemed that Iran wanted assist the United States in crushing the Taliban. Iran decided to share intelligence with the United States for that purpose. One of the Iranian delegates to the "Six-Plus Two" talks had come from the Iranian military and became a vehicle for reaching out to Washington. The "Six-Plus Two" format was hardly an intimate setting for two adversarial countries to probe each other's views. Besides the United States and Iran, there were also representatives from Pakistan, China, Uzbekistan, Tajikistan, Turkmenistan, and even Russia in attendance. Nonetheless, the Iranians used the New York meeting to communicate directly with the United States.

Hillary Mann, who served at the U.S. Mission to the UN in New York, attended the talks as a U.S. delegate. She distinctly recalled an Iranian official pounding on the table during their meeting and complaining that the discussions in New York were "just nice talk but we're not going get anywhere if this bombing campaign doesn't succeed."[10] He then unfurled a map on the table, pointing to targets the U.S. Air Force needed to focus on in Afghanistan to help the ground troops of the Northern Alliance, Iranian allies and Afghan opposition to the Taliban, break through southward to take the Afghan capital, Kabul.

The American diplomats passed the map along to the U.S. Central Command (US CENTCOM), the regional command for the Middle East responsible for military operations in Afghanistan and Southwest Asia. The significance of the Iranian intelligence is difficult to establish. It is noteworthy that neither the U.S. CENTCOM commander, General Tommy Franks, nor his deputy, Lieutenant General Michael DeLong, discussed any Iranian contribution to the American war effort in Afghanistan in the memoirs they wrote.[11]

Behind the scenes, the Bush administration formed a subgroup within the "Six-Plus Two" states that included the United States, Iran, and two European states to give both sides some political cover. It began to meet monthly in Geneva.[12] The Northern Alliance still controlled a small portion of the country on the eve of the war; consequently, Iran even tried to facilitate U.S. coordination with their Northern Alliance allies.

Symbolically, as the "Six-Plus Two" talks got underway at the UN in New York in November 2001, U.S. Secretary of State Colin

Powell shook hands with Iranian Foreign Minister Kamal Kharrazi. Prior to September 11, when Secretary of State Madeleine Albright attended the identical forum at the UN with Kharrazi in 2000, there was no private conversation or handshake.[13] Iran appeared to be helpful in another diplomatic forum in late 2001: the Bonn Conference for shaping political order in postwar Afghanistan. It appeared that with their shared enmity towards the Taliban, the interests of Iran and the West were converging.

The idea that Washington should seek a rapprochement with Khatami's Iran had been very much alive among U.S. officials who had served in the latter part of the Clinton administration and had been active in the policy debate at the beginning of the Bush presidency.

For example, Puneet Talwar served on the Policy Planning Staff of the U.S. Department of State between 1999 and 2001 and prepared a major analysis of U.S.-Iranian relations for *Foreign Affairs* that came out right before September 11. It called for Washington to adopt a policy of *moderate engagement* with Iran that included ending opposition to World Bank lending to Iran, the fingerprinting of Iranian passport holders entering the United States, and modifying U.S. sanctions to allow American NGO's to become more active in Iranian civil society.[14]

However, there was also new evidence that Iran was not the ally that some in Washington had hoped for. On November 8, 2001, CIA Director George Tenet reported in the Bush administration's Principals' Meeting, with the secretaries of state, defense, and the national security advisor, that he had evidence that "[t]he Iranians may have switched sides and gone to side with the Taliban."[15] He reported there was sensitive intelligence indicating that the Revolutionary Guards were shipping weapons to the Taliban. There were also indications that the Revolutionary Guards were reaching out to al-Qaeda, and that hundreds of its operatives were using Iran as a transit station for escaping Afghanistan to reach countries like Yemen.[16]

The explanation was that Tehran was becoming increasingly worried about the implications of the United States having a strategic foothold in Afghanistan, along Iran's eastern border. As the U.S. war effort progressed, Iran tried to fill the vacuum that had been created in Afghanistan by using its intelligence services to penetrate large parts of the country. It was one thing to have the United States get rid of the Taliban, but it was quite another matter for a massive U.S. force to become ensconced in an adjacent country.

As a result, the emerging picture of the Iranian role in Afghanistan was complex and contradictory. Hussein Ibrahimi, the personal representative to Afghanistan of Supreme Leader Ali Khamenei, was urging Afghan clerics to resist U.S. plans for Afghanistan in early 2002.[17] These new trends were summarized on March 23, 2002, by Zalmay Khalilzad, who served on the U.S. National Security Council and dealt with the Middle East and Southwest Asia. He explained that the Iranian government had sent its Quds Force into Afghanistan as well as Sepah-e Mohammed, an Afghan militia created by the Revolutionary Guards.[18] With these forces, Iran could build up its own levers of power to the detriment of the United States. The reports of Iranian cooperation with residual Taliban forces raised the question of whether Iran was saying one thing through diplomatic channels and doing the exact opposite on the ground.

Iran Remains Unreformed

Though it still seemed to be a pivotal moment in the relations between Iran and the West, both appearing to share common interests over the future of Afghanistan, the fundamental question remained: was Iran prepared to abandon its active support for international terrorism and its aggressive drive for nuclear weapons in the new strategic circumstances that were emerging?

The answer came in another Middle Eastern theater far away from the war with the Taliban. In 2002, Yasser Arafat launched an armed revolt by his Palestinian Authority against Israel, which was known as the Second Intifada. It included the dispatch of suicide bombers from areas under their jurisdiction into the heart of Israeli cities. On January 3, 2002, Israeli Naval Commandos boarded a freighter in the Red Sea called the Karine-A and found 50 tons of Iranian weaponry that were bound for the Gaza Strip. The shipment included anti-tank missiles, mortar shells, sniper rifles, and 122 mm Katyusha rockets that had a 25-kilometer range. These could strike targets far beyond the 7-kilometer range of the Qassam missile, which was domestically manufactured in the Gaza Strip.

There were also two tons of C-4 plastic explosives which were far more powerful than what the Palestinian organizations had been using in their suicide bombing attacks. Many of the weapons that were discovered on the Karine-A had Iranian markings. Had the ship arrived, it would have undoubtedly escalated the violence against Israel, as many more Israeli civilians would have come under the range of Iranian-supplied weaponry.

Israeli intelligence sources stated that they had hard proof that the Revolutionary Guards, with the approval of Supreme Leader Ali Khamenei, were behind the dispatch of the Karine-A.[19] The route of the Karine-A had been carefully reconstructed after its crew had been interrogated. The freighter picked up its cargo along the coast of Iran near Qeshm Island, in the Persian Gulf, right next to the Strait of Hormuz. Qeshm Island was also situated directly opposite from Bandar Abbas, the main port of the Iranian Navy on the Persian Gulf. It was difficult to argue, given its location, that the Iranian government did not know about the shipment. The siezure of Karine-A proved false the claim that Iran was moderating its foreign policy and moving away from supporting terrorism.

Moreover, the Karine-A was part of a larger pattern. On February 1, 2002, Jordan's King Abdullah told President Bush while visiting the White House of seventeen separate Iranian-supported efforts to launch rockets and mortars from Jordanian territory on

Israel. The report, which appeared initially in the London-based Arabic daily, *al-Sharq al-Awsat*, received confirmation from Secretary of State Colin Powell when he appeared in front of the House International Relations Committee days later.[20] Iran was plainly undermining the security of western allies in the Middle East, regardless of its promises in diplomatic channels of cooperation in Afghanistan.

There was also the nuclear question. During 2001–2002, though Ali Akbar Hashemi Rafsanjani was no longer president of Iran, he served as chairman of the powerful Iranian Expediency Council, which had the power to nullify legislation of the Iranian Parliament. Speaking at Tehran University on December 14, 2001, he made a bone-chilling statement which implied that there were scenarios mandating the first use of nuclear weapons. He began by describing Israel as an instrument or method of "global arrogance, led by the U.S. and the U.K. If one day," he continued, "the world of Islam comes to possess the weapons currently in Israel's possession [implying nuclear weapons]—on that day, this method of global arrogance would come to a dead end."[21] He clearly meant that with nuclear weapons on the side of Islam, Israel would cease to exist. He then explained why: "The use of a nuclear bomb in Israel will leave nothing on the ground, whereas it will only damage the world of Islam."[22] In short, the Islamic world could survive an Israeli counterstrike to its nuclear first strike.

What made this hostile statement by Rafsanjani especially disturbing was the fact that, at the very same time, Iran was still aggressively pursuing the very nuclear weapons capability that would allow it to carry its plans out. In January 2002, the CIA issued a report concluding that Iran was "one of the most active countries seeking to acquire (weapons of mass destruction) technology from abroad."[23] The report specifically referred to nuclear weapons "and their delivery systems." There were, at the time, reports surfacing that indicated that Iran was making greater progress on nuclear weapons than was previously thought.[24]

Clearly there were two images of Iran emerging in early 2002. Either it was a state that was willing to cooperate with the United States and the West to defeat the Taliban and turn over a new leaf, or its cooperation was only a short-term tactical shift of an unreformed Iran that continued to support terrorism and pursue nuclear weapons at any cost. The debate over these two questions would rage in the U.S. foreign policy community and among America's European allies for years to come.

With the evidence he had, President George W. Bush decided that Iran was unreformed. His national security advisor Condoleezza Rice noted that "Iran's direct support of regional and global terrorism, and its aggressive efforts to acquire weapons of mass destruction, belie any good intentions it displayed in the days after the world's worst terrorist attacks in history."[25] Thus in his State of the Union address on January 29, 2002, Bush tied Iran, as well as North Korea, to his main focus, which was Saddam Hussein's Iraq. Together these countries, in Bush's words, constituted an "Axis of Evil."

The speech was cleared by the National Security Council and by the State Department; neither Secretary of State Colin Powell nor his deputy, Richard Armitage, had a problem with the phrase "Axis of Evil."[26] For those who still hoped for a new era of U.S.-Iranian reconciliation under the presidency of Mohammad Khatami, Bush's inclusion of Iran was a clear setback. But for those who wanted to put pressure on the regime for its unacceptable behavior, the speech was long over due.

The Iranians reacted to Bush's comments. The Supreme Leader Ali Khamenei replied, "The Islamic Republic is proud to be the target of the hate and anger of the world's greatest evil; we never seek to be praised by American officials."[27] But the Iranians did not cut off their channel of communications with the administration. There had been a meeting between the U.S. Special Afghanistan envoy, James Dobbins, and a senior Iranian diplomat in Tokyo on January 21, 2003. Then, in reaction to Bush's State of the Union speech, the Iranians cancelled their February meeting with the U.S. side.

But a month later, on March 30, 2002, Dobbins again met with senior Iranians. The United States was a major power that could not be boycotted because of a speech. And by October 9, 2002, when British Foreign Secretary Jack Straw arrived in Tehran to gain Iranian support for the upcoming war on Iraq, President Khatami offered to provide intelligence and advice to overthrow Saddam Hussein, the same way Iran initially assisted in the earlier war with the Taliban. The United States was sitting on Iran's eastern border and was about to deploy along its western border; it followed that the Iranians would, under those conditions, seek to be closer to Washington, rhetoric of January 2002 notwithstanding.

Did Iran Offer a Deal to the Bush Administration That It Refused?

Despite Iran's problematic behavior, the belief persisted in many western quarters that there was still an opportunity to diplomatically engage Iran. Tim Guldimann was the Swiss ambassador to Iran who represented U.S. interests in the absence of a U.S. Embassy. On May 4, 2003, he faxed a document to the Swiss Embassy in Washington that was delivered to the Department of State.[28] It contained a "roadmap" for the normalization of U.S.-Iranian relations, proposing direct talks between the United States and Iran.

Guldimann's document purportedly represented an official offer by Iran to reach what amounted to a "grand bargain" with the United States, resolving all its outstanding differences on Iran's nuclear program, its support for terrorism, and its efforts to block all Arab-Israeli peacemaking. For example, the document proposed that Hizbullah become "a peaceful political party."[29] The United States was expected to refrain from supporting regime change in Iran and to abolish all sanctions against the Islamic Republic.

The idea that Iran would reach out to the Bush administration was not far fetched, as the United States had just successfully over-thrown Saddam Hussein in neighboring Iraq, and the insurgency that followed had not fully developed. If it was an authentic pro-posal, the Guldimann fax could have been a revolutionary docu-ment, bringing Iran's war of more than twenty years with the West to an end.

Sadegh Kharrazi, the Iranian ambassador to France, drafted the Iranian offer in consultation with Ambassador Guldimann in Tehran. Kharrazi was a nephew of the Iranian foreign minister, Kamal Kharrazi, and was well-connected to the Iranian establish-ment. His sister had married the son of Ayatollah Khamenei. He argued that Khamenei himself supported the proposals contained in the document.[30] When Washington did not appear to be inter-ested in acting on the offer presented by the Swiss, Sedegh Khar-razi commented that "the American government missed a golden opportunity."[31] But was that really the case?

Flynt Leverett, a former senior director for Middle East affairs at the National Security Council, charged in a *New York Times* op-ed in January 2006 that the Bush administration's failure to act on the Guldimann fax was part of a general pattern it had fol-lowed to turn away "from every opportunity to put relations with Iran on a more positive trajectory."[32] Leverett presented the docu-ment as a detailed proposal from the Iranian Foreign Ministry, which it was not. He also wrote that "it was presented as having the support of all major players in Iran's power structure, includ-ing the supreme leader, Ayatollah Ali Khamenei."[33]

Leverett's analysis unleashed a wave of articles arguing that the West and Iran could resolve their differences, but that inept Amer-ican diplomacy had ensured conflict would continue nonetheless. What emerged from this flurry was the belief that the United States was at fault for the crisis in their relationship, not Iranian actions.

The *Washington Post* picked up the story of the Guldimann fax a year later, reporting that Condoleezza Rice could not recall ever seeing the document in her capacity as National Security Advisor in 2003. It led with a report that the document supplied by the Swiss had been reviewed and approved by no less than Ayatollah Ali Khamenei, President Mohammed Khatami, and Foreign Minister Kamal Kharrazi.[34]

Nicholas D. Kristof wrote in a stinging column in the *New York Times* that the Guldimann fax was part of an "incipient peace process" between the United States and Iran.[35] He summarized other contacts as well. He blasted "the hard-liners in the Bush administration," arguing that the U.S.–Iranian rapprochement that might have resulted from this process "could have saved lives in Iraq, isolated Palestinian terrorists and encouraged civil society groups in Iran." Instead of adopting this peace process with Iran, "U.S. hard-liners chose to hammer plowshares into swords."[36]

The fact of the matter was that while Ayatollah Ali Khamenei had seen the document, according to Guldimann's own cover letter for the fax, the Iranian leader had voiced his own reservations about its contents. Guldimann wrote that on May 2, 2003, Sadeq Kharazzi told him about two long discussions with Khamenei about the document, but that "the Leader uttered some reservations for some points." Guldimann reported that Kharazzi believed "the Leader agreed with 85-90% of the paper." But Guldimann could not determine from his conversation the points with which Khamenei could not agree.[37]

Critics of the Bush administration's handling of the Guldimann fax tried to put the onus on the White House and the Pentagon for nixing what they viewed as a budding relationship between Iran and the United States. But some of the harshest critiques of the Swiss ambassador's initiative came out of the State Department, which, on the whole, had sought to forge new openings with Tehran. Hillary Mann, who headed the State Department's Iran section, read the document and thought "it was incredibly significant and ground breaking."[38] She prepared a memorandum for Secretary of State Colin Powell and her boss, Richard Haass, who headed Policy Planning in the Department of State. Haass was less enthusiastic: "I thought the paper was interesting but I was skeptical." He was not certain that it reflected the thoughts of Iranian power centers.[39]

Deputy Secretary of State Richard Armitage amplified his colleagues' doubts about the memorandum by telling *Newsweek* that it represented creative diplomacy by the Swiss ambassador; but, he added: "We couldn't determine what was the Iranians' and what was the Swiss ambassador's."[40] Armitage admitted in a television interview on PBS's *Frontline* that while Secretary of State Colin Powell, who was his immediate superior, and he were "very interested" in an opening with Iran, they could not relate to Guldimann's fax as a "serious endeavor."[41]

The State Department's best Iran experts also viewed the initiative by the Swiss ambassador the same way. Armitage felt that the Swiss ambassador to Tehran was so intent on improving Iran's ties with the West that he colored the substance of the Iranian message. Finally, its contents did not correlate with the contents of the messages that Washington was receiving at the time through direct channels with high-ranking Iranian intelligence officials. Of course, Guldimann and those who defended his initiative had no idea that such contacts existed between the United States and Iran.

There was also an Iranian side to the controversy. Hossein Shariatmadari was the editor-in chief of *Kayhan*, Iran's major state-run newspaper. Supreme Leader Ali Khamenei personally appointed him to the position. He is viewed in Iran as Khamenei's personal spokesman. When Shariatmadari gave interviews to foreign journalists, he was called "the Supreme Leader's representative." On August 1, 2007, the PBS program *Frontline* interviewed Shariatmadari and asked about the Iranian offer that appeared in "a fax sent by the Swiss ambassador to the State Department." The PBS interviewer wanted to verify the claim that the fax had been approved by "very senior officials here in Iran."[42]

Shariatmadari admitted: "I heard that story too." Then he was rather blunt in his reply to the question: "Whoever wrote that letter was in no position to do so." He further explained: "Such issues are of paramount political importance, and *no such thing was discussed at the highest levels* (emphasis added)."[43] Perhaps Shariatmadari was covering for his boss, Ayatollah Ali Khamenei, and was willing to deny the whole initiative since nothing came of it anyway. That explanation for Shariatmadari's interview would have made sense if it was delivered in Farsi on Iranian television.

But what was to be gained by giving an interview through an English interpreter for an American television network? If the myth that the Bush administration had killed a "grand bargain" with Iran was eroding opposition to Iran within the United States, then it made more sense to let the Guldimann fax story stand, putting the onus on the U.S. government for failing to engage Iran when there was a supposed opening.

Still, it was clear that Khameini saw the material in the Guldimann fax, even if the text was not entirely approved. There is a third possibility that neither the advocates of the Swiss initiative nor its detractors raised. The fax arrived at the Department of State just one day after President Bush landed on the USS Lincoln, on which hung the famous banner "Mission Accomplished." He came to the aircraft carrier to declare America's victory over Saddam Hussein.

At the time, the United States was at the high point of its power, and Iran was understandably nervous that it could be next. The fax might well have been a sophisticated diplomatic probe through which the Iranians hoped to learn more about U.S. intentions. The Iranian government could certainly intentionally misrepresent its own moderation in order to ward off a potential military threat—that was the essence of the doctrine of *taqiya*. By the time Shariatmadari gave his interview to PBS in 2007, the United States was bogged down fighting the Iraqi insurgency, and Tehran was less nervous. Regardless of its real motivations in getting involved with the Swiss channel to the United States, Tehran gave no tangible indication by its actions that its policy was about to change. The Guldimann fax could have been a missed opportunity for U.S.-Iranian engagement.

Iran Hosts al-Qaeda and Strikes at Saudi Arabia

While the debate raged in Washington during May 2003 over the Guldimann fax, in Riyadh, Saudi Arabia, another side of Iran's policy became evident very quickly. On May 12, four vehicles carrying explosives and heavily-armed commando teams moved through the streets of the Saudi capital looking for residential compounds which housed foreigners, especially those who were assisting the Saudi government with internal security like the Vinnel Corporation, a U.S. security firm that had been training the Saudi National Guard for years.

The commando teams shot their way into some of the compounds, and at one of them they managed to detonate two bombs. Twenty-one people were killed and over 160 were wounded. Among the fatalities were seventeen Americans.[44] The Saudi authorities blamed al-Qaeda for the attacks. It was the beginning of a wave of al-Qaeda operations across the Saudi Kingdom, whose purpose Deputy Secretary of State Richard Armitage believed months later was to "take down the royal family and the government of Saudi Arabia."[45]

The United States had been at war with al-Qaeda in Afghanistan for less than two years. New in this attack was the fact that the United States had intercepted communications suggesting that al-Qaeda leaders based in Iran had directed the Riyadh bombings. The intelligence had been sufficiently persuasive to cause Washington to halt its quiet contacts with Iran in Geneva and ask Lakhdar Brahimi from the UN to attend instead. Brahimi was provided with a message from the U.S. government expressing "deep, deep concern that individuals associated with Al Qaeda have planned and directed the attack in Saudi Arabia from inside Iran." Washington conveyed a second strong message to

Tehran through the British government, as well, which still maintained an embassy in the Iranian capital.[46]

The connection beween al-Qaeda and Iran was not new, but it was counterintuitive. After all, the Islamic Republic of Iran was a Shiite theocratic state, and al-Qaeda was a Sunni extremist terrorist organization, which had been under the influence of the strong anti-Shiite orientation of Saudi Arabia's Wahhabi religious establishment. As noted above, al-Qaeda's Taliban allies, who came under the same Saudi influence, had been butchering Afghanistan's Shiites during their takeover of the country. During the Clinton administration, the National Security Council combed through piles of intelligence on the Iran-al-Qaeda link and reportedly concluded that "there was nothing to suggest more than some furtive tapping around in the dark between the Iranian government and al-Qaeda."[47]

But it was the 9/11 Commission Report that revealed that much of the conventional wisdom about Shiites being unable to work with Sunni extremists was wrong. During the mid-1990s, when Osama bin Laden was living in Sudan, al-Qaeda had extensive interaction with Iran and its Lebanese surrogate, Hizbullah:

> While in Sudan, senior managers in al Qaeda maintained contacts with Iran and the Iranian-supported worldwide terrorist organization Hezbollah, which is based in southern Lebanon and Beirut. Al Qaeda members received advice and training from Hezbollah. Intelligence indicates the persistence of contacts between Iranian security officials and senior al Qaeda figures after bin Laden's return to Afghanistan.[48]

Ali Muhammad, the Egyptian-born al-Qaeda trainer, was tried in the Southern District court of New York and testified on October 20, 2000, that he set up a meeting between Osama bin Laden and the head of Hizbullah's international operations, Imad Mughniyeh.[49]

Al-Qaeda operatives, including eight to ten of the nineteen September 11 hijackers, used Iranian territory to transit to other locations.[50] Prior to the September 11 attacks, according to White House Counterterrorism Coordinator Richard Clarke, al-Qaeda's Egyptian branch, Egyptian Islamic Jihad, operated openly in Tehran itself. [51] After U.S. forces entered Afghanistan to topple the Taliban, al-Qaeda essentially split in two.

Part of its senior leadership sought refuge in western Pakistan, along the Afghan border, while many others moved from Afghanistan into Iran. The Iranians sheltered them in hotels and guesthouses located around eastern border cities, like Mashhad and Zabol.[52] These al-Qaeda refugees in Iran were not junior operatives, but some of the most prominent elements in the organization's command structure, including bin-Laden's son, Saad.

For example, there was the case of Abu Musab al-Zarqawi, the Jordanian Islamist who ran a training camp near Herat in western Afghanistan. With the fall of the Taliban, he moved westward into Iranian territory, as well, and took up residence in Mashhad on January 5, 2002.[53] While the information about his period in Iran is fragmentary, there were Arab and European reports that while he was there he visited training camps run by the Revolutionary Guards and received help from the Quds force.

According to one of his deputies, named Omar Bizani, who was apprehended by Iraqi security forces after the fall of Saddam Hussein, Zarqawi also established an overseas network that Iran nurtured.[54] Documents from the German Federal Office of Criminal Investigation apparently revealed that Iran "provided al-Zarqawi with logistical support.... "[55] He did not stay in the remote areas of eastern Iran, but according to German sources he made telephone calls from Tehran.[56] Zarqawi would come to head al-Qaeda in Iraq, which would turn into one of the leading forces in the insurgency against the U.S.-led coalition.[57]

There had been a certain degree of confusion about the exact status of the al-Qaeda operatives in Iran, largely due to the actions of the Iranians themselves. In June 2002, Iran transferred sixteen al-Qaeda operatives to Saudi Arabia, in order to demonstrate solidarity with the U.S.-led war on terrorism. Indeed, al-Qaeda operatives told Arab security services during their interrogations that the Iranians asked them to leave after Bush included Iran as part of the "Axis of Evil" in his January 2002 State of the Union address. This was consistent with CIA reports, noted above, that already in late 2001 Iran was opening itself up to al-Qaeda members that fled Afghanistan. Nonetheless, it became generally assumed that the rest of the al-Qaeda group in Iran, that was not asked to leave, was under some kind of house arrest.

The May 12, 2003, Riyadh attacks made clear that the senior al-Qaeda leadership that was still harbored in Iran was planning and ordering al-Qaeda attacks on Saudi Arabia from their Iranian sanctuary. Two key figures included an Egyptian, Muhammad Ibrahim Makawi, who was also known as Saif Adel, and Mahfouz Ould Walid, also known as Abu Hafs the Mauritanian. Saif Adel was emerging as the military chief of al-Qaeda; with Osama bin Laden and his deputy Ayman al-Zawahiri in hiding, the Iranian-based leadership assumed operational control of al-Qaeda's military committee.

There was also the case of Mustafa Hamid, a senior al-Qaeda operative who had been an instructor in the use of explosives in a camp near the Afghan city of Jalalabad before the fall of the Taliban. He was Saif Adel's father-in-law and became the primary interlocutor between al-Qaeda and the Iranian government. According to the U.S. Treasury, he was harbored by the Revolutionary Guards. In late 2001, he would travel to Tehran delivering messages from the Taliban and negotiate on behalf of al-Qaeda.[58]

Two years later, the Iranian role in giving sanctuary to al-Qaeda continued and would be openly acknowledged by the State Department's third-ranking official, Nicholas Burns, who admitted: "Some Al Qaeda members and those from like-minded extremist groups continue to use Iran as a safe haven and as a hub to facilitate their operations."[59]

Iran and the Iraqi Insurgency

British Foreign Secretary Jack Straw arrived in Tehran in 2003 in order to win Iranian support—or at least acquiescence—for the impending coalition campaign to topple Saddam Hussein. Despite the continuing tensions that existed in U.S.-Iranian relations, President Khatami made Straw an offer that Tehran would provide the West with intelligence and operational advice to defeat Iraq. Moreover, he expressed interest in an Iraqi equivalent of the "Six Plus Two" that would produce coordination for the postwar future of Iraq.

Given Washington's experience with how Iran switched sides in Afghanistan, backing the Taliban and harboring al-Qaeda, the Iranian offer was not very tempting. In any case, the Iranian Foreign Minister pledged to Straw noninterference in the affairs of Iraq. This commitment was repeated by the Iranian ambassador to the UN, Mohammad Javad Zarif, in a conversation with Zalmay Khalilzad, who was then a U.S. envoy to the Iraqi opposition.[60]

Yet, right from the start of the Iraq War in March 2003, Iran, in fact, became directly involved, its international assurances notwithstanding. With the fall of Saddam Hussein, the Revolutionary Guards infiltrated Iraq with 2,000 combat personnel and Quds Force members equipped with radio transmitters, money, propaganda, and supplies.[61] The Quds Force was a critical instrument for this intervention.

An Iraqi intelligence document captured by U.S. forces lays out how the Quds Force, under the overall command of Brigadier General Qassem Suleimani, was divided into four Corps level units. It was the Quds Force First Corps, known as Ramazan Headquarters, that had three camps inside Iran that were adjacent to the Iraqi border.[62] The northern camp was commanded by a

Quds force commander named Mahmoud Farhadi who eventually was captured by U.S. forces in Iraq in September 2007 while he was visiting Iraqi Kurdistan.[63]

Iran was creating for itself military options for the future. U.S.-led coalition forces also uncovered a document issued in Iran for its supporters in Iraq. It urged "holy fighters" in Iraq to get close to the U.S. forces and their allies, calling on them to "maintain good relations with the coalition forces."[64] But simultaneously Iran prepared an opposite strategy, according to the document. It advised its supporters to establish "a secret group that would conduct attacks against American troops."

In a way, the two Iranian directives did not contradict one another, for those who became closer to coalition forces could effectively gather intelligence for the latter group, who were to execute military operations against the U.S. presence in Iraq. Tehran did not have a problem giving a directive to its Shiite allies in Iraq to say the opposite of their intentions and ultimately do the opposite of what they had said.

The United States was already publically criticizing Iran for its intervention only a month after U.S. forces invaded Iraq. At his Wednesday White House Briefing on April 23, 2003, Press Secretary Ari Fleischer began by openly stating:

> We note that some recent reports about Iranian activities and we have made clear to Iran that we would oppose any outside organization's interference in Iraq, interfering with their road to democracy. Infiltration of agents to destabilize the Shia population would clearly fall into that category, and that is a position that we have made clear to the government of Iran.[65]

Fleischer wanted to indicate the extent to which the Bush administration was concerned: "It's important that you understand what is going on, the seriousness of it...." By October 2003, the United States was arresting Iranians in Iraq.[66]

Iran had a two-pronged strategy in Iraq. Even before the U.S.-led invasion of 2003, Tehran had invested in a diverse group of Iraqi parties whom it hoped it could rely upon as surrogates to safeguard Iranian interests. There was the Supreme Council for the Islamic Revolution in Iraq (SCIRI) under Ayatollah Muhammad Baqir al-Hakim, who accepted the doctrine of the *velayat-e faqih*, (the Rule of the Jurisprudent) that held the Iranian Supreme Leader was the ultimate source of political and legal legitimacy—unusual for an Iraqi movement. They created a militia of Iraqi refugees in Iran called the Badr Brigade (later called Badr Corps) that was helped by the Revolutionary Guards.

There was also the Islamic Dawa Party that for two decades supported the creation of an Islamic state in Iraq; it had been involved in the 1983 attacks on the U.S. and French Embassies in Kuwait with Hizbullah and Iran. The Dawa Party's militia had been partly funded by the Revolutionary Guards. Finally there was Moqtada al-Sadr who was a rival of SCIRI and had his own *Jaysh al-Mahdi* which also received Iranian aid.

Some of these groups' members rose in the new post-Saddam political system. Interim Iraqi Prime Minister Ibrahim al-Jafaari and Prime Minister Nuri al-Maliki had their roots in the Dawa Party. Abu Mahdi al-Muhandis started in the Dawa Party and was in fact a member of the cell that attacked the U.S. Embassy in Kuwait. He later rose in the ranks of SCIRI and took command of its Badr Corps in which capacity he worked with the Quds Force. In December 2005, al-Muhandis was elected to the Iraqi Council of Representatives in Iraq; after his past was disclosed, he fled Iraq and sought asylum in Iran.

When Al-Muhandis was heading the Badr Corps, his Chief of Staff was Hadi al-Ameri, who rose to become an important Iraqi parliamentarian in post-Saddam Iraq.[67] Over the years, Iran provided Iraqi Shiite clerics with regular salaries.[68] In short, Iran's long-term work with leading Iraqi politicians set the stage for considerable Iranian political influence in Baghdad, even without any military intervention. But apparently, the Iranian political establishment felt that this investment was necessary since, left to themselves, the Iraqi Shiites would not automatically become pro-Iranian. Iraqi Shiites were ethnically Arab, not Persian, and during the eight year Iran-Iraq War they had remained loyal to Saddam Hussein and the Iraqi state. The new Iraq could only be cemented to Iran by making a considerable effort with the Iraqi political elites, which Tehran was prepared to do.

The Iranian two-pronged strategy also had a military side that became more evident as the Iraq War went on. The main Iranian strategy for influencing the battle for Iraq was through supply of weaponry. By July 19, 2005, the United States protested to Iran that the Revolutionary Guards were funneling weaponry to the Iraqi insurgency, particularly to the Shiite militias. U.S. commanders were focusing on a new generation of Improvised Explosive Devices (IED's) which were increasingly being used as roadside bombs.

These new IED's were Explosively Formed Penetrators (EFP's), imported from Iran, that were able to pierce American and British armored vehicles. Admiral William Fallon, who was about to take over as the commander in chief of the U.S. Central Command, stated in Congressional testimony that the new IED's could penetrate armored Humvees.

Secretary of Defense Robert Gates went one step further and described the weapon's capability in even more dramatic terms, telling reporters that the improved IED "can take out an Abrams tank."[69] He also observed that serial numbers and markings on projectile fragments from the IED's provided the United States with evidence that the weapons were indeed of Iranian origin.[70] As tens of thousands of these IED's came to be used in Iraq yearly, they began to change the overall situation on the battlefield to the detriment of the U.S.-led coalition.[71]

Indeed, American combat deaths from IED's shot up as more advanced weaponry arrived from Iran. For most of 2004, there were twelve to twenty U.S. fatalities a month from IED's; by 2006, monthly fatalities from IED's reached as many as seventy-two.[72] In fact, these roadside bombs were quickly becoming the main source of American combat fatalities. In December 2006, for example, 63 percent of all American combat deaths could be attributed to IED's. A few months later, the U.S. Military Command in Baghdad concluded that more than 170 American soldiers had been killed in Iraq by Iranian-supplied roadside bombs with armor-piercing technology.[73] Far from being just a tactical device for terrorist operations, the Iranian-supplied IED's were having a strategic impact on the U.S. war effort.

The most effective smuggling network for getting the Iranian IED's across the border into Iraq was run by Abu Mustafa al-Sheibani, who had been a commander in the Iranian-supported Badr Corps.[74] The Iranians did not start this operation in 2005. A captured Iraqi intelligence document dated July 11, 2001—roughly two years prior to the U.S. invasion of Iraq—described a shipment of these weapons to Badr Corps operatives in Iraq.[75] Apparently, on September 9, 2002, Iran's Supreme Leader Ayatollah Ali Khamenei summoned the Supreme National Security Council to meet and decide on a plan for Iranian penetration of Iraq.[76] Clearly the Iranians were creating for themselves new military options for a future insurgency in Iraq, regardless of how U.S. policy on Iraq evolved.

Missed Opportunities?

Iran's intervention in Iraq raised a fundamental question of whether a second opportunity for a rapprochement between Iran and the West was missed. The first opportunity, as noted earlier, was in the case of Afghanistan in the aftermath of September 11. Flynt Leverett, who had served on the National Security Council, told the PBS program, *Frontline*: "Iranian diplomats have said privately to me that they made a fundamental calculation that 9/11 was, in its way, an opportunity, an opening for Iran...that it would prompt the United States to reconsider its own views of the Islamic Republic of Iran."[77]

But whatever *overt* help Iran provided the United States, there was a whole *covert* Iranian effort to help al-Qaeda. For that reason, on the very same PBS program, Deputy Secretary of State Richard Armitage rejected the notion that Iran helped the West against the Taliban but then got Bush's "Axis of Evil" speech as payback, resulting in Washington missing an opportunity for reconciliation and diplomatic engagement. Arimitage stated:

> We asked some things of them further, such as some of the Taliban and, more specifically, Al Qaeda pitched up in Iran and we asked them to turn these folks over. And for reasons not understood by me, they refused even though our information, we felt, was quite good that these folks did exist in Iran.[78]

The Afghanistan story repeated itself in Iraq. Through British Foreign Secretary Jack Straw, President Khatami signaled a willingness to work together with the United States prior to the fall of Saddam Hussein. Then came the Guldimann fax with its offer of a grand bargain with Washington and a diplomatic roadmap for reconciliation. Even if the fax was not authorized, it might be have been interpreted back in 2003 as an indicator by some U.S. analysts that the United States and Iran actually had shared interests. Just as they both sought the overthrow of the Taliban regime, both wanted to see Saddam Hussein's government eliminated.

Indeed, this idea that there was a strategic convergence in Iranian and American interests continued to capture the imagination of many serious policymakers in the years that followed, despite the mounting American losses in Iraq which were the direct result of Iranian weaponry. The most influential analysis of this sort was the *Iraq Study Group Report* that was based on the work of a high-level bipartisan commission chaired by former Secretary of

State James Baker and Lee Hamilton, who for years had served as chairman of the Committee on Foreign Affairs of the House of Representatives. The study group was created by Congress out of a sense that prevailed in March 2006 that the United States needed to re-consider its overall strategy in Iraq and chart an alternative way forward.

In its report, the Iraq Study Group recommended that the United States "engage directly with Iran and Syria in order to try to obtain their commitment to constructive policies toward Iraq and other regional issues."[79] Acknowledging "engaging Iran is problematic," the report nonetheless observed that "the United States and Iran cooperated in Afghanistan, and both sides should explore whether this model can be replicated in the case of Iraq."[80]

It seemed that the Iraq Study Group was looking to the "Six-Plus Two" talks on Afghanistan as their model by suggesting that all the states bordering Iraq, including Iran, as well as other key Middle Eastern countries like Egypt, should form an *Iraq International Support Group* along with the United States and the EU. The authors of the report explicitly assumed that there was a basis for western cooperation with Iran since "Iran's interests would not be served by a failure of U.S. policy in Iraq," especially if that failure "led to chaos and the territorial disintegration of the Iraqi state." There was a hope expressed in the report's analysis that just as the United States and Iran discovered their joint interests in Afghanistan, they would also find common ground on Iraq.

But were the two situations really comparable? Afghanistan under the Taliban was an extremist Sunni-majority state. It had an oppressed Shiite minority, which Iran aided, but maintained only intermittent involvement in its protection. During the "Six-Plus Two" talks in the 1990s, Iran had a definite interest in containing the Taliban threat and bringing the war in Afghanistan to an end.

In contrast, post-Saddam Iraq was a country with a Shiite majority towards which Iran harbored strong territorial ambitions, as was demonstrated during the Iran-Iraq War. Iraq had been one of the principal target states for the export of the Islamic Revolution. The Shiite holy cities of pilgrimage, Najaf and Karbala, were in Iraq, not in Afghanistan; after the fall of Saddam Hussein there were reports that nearly 10,000 Iranians were coming into Iraq daily, mainly to visit the Shiite holy cities.[81] No less than the Supreme Leader Ali Khamenei openly expressed Iranian aspirations toward Iraq back in the 1980s when he was serving as president of the Islamic Republic.

> The future of Iraq should be an Islamic and popular one. The policy of *velayat-e faqih* will be Iraq's future policy, and the leader of the Islamic nation is Imam Khomeini. There is no difference between the two nations of Iran and Iraq in accepting the Imam as the leader, and following the Imam and his line. Government and state officials are limited to international borders, but the Imam is not limited by geographic frontiers.[82]

According to the doctrine of *velayat-e faqih*, Khamenei in 2003, as the ruling jurisprudent who succeeded Khomeini, would be the ultimate ruler of both countries by his own analysis. His title fit this role. Khamenei called himself "Supreme Leader of Muslims" and not just "Supreme Leader of Iran."[83] Moreover, Iran's interest in dominating Iraq had not declined, especially given the fact that it was now a realistic possibility, since Saddam Hussein's regime had been overthrown. This was not the case back in the 1980s when Khamenei stated Iran's long-term goals.

Was it really true, as the report argued, that "Iran's interests would not be served by failure of U.S. policy in Iraq that led to chaos and the territorial disintegration of the Iraqi state?" First, a U.S. failure did not necessarily have to lead to Iraq's disintegration, as the Iraq Study Group suggested. There were other possibilities that could arise as well. Over the years, Iran had invested in Iraqi Kurds and in the Iraqi Sunnis; there was no reason for Iran to assume that if U.S. forces left Iraq, and Iran emerged as the main power, that these communities would secede and form their own separate states.

Second, Iran had its own interests in seeing the U.S. war effort fail, and it did not make an effort to hide them. This was pointed out by the former Iranian president Hashemi Rafsanjani, who still held the powerful position of head of the Expediency Council. In a Friday sermon he delivered at Tehran University on April 9, 2004, he declared:

> The present situation in Iraq represents a threat as well as an opportunity...it is a threat because the wounded American beast can take enraged actions, but it is also an opportunity to teach this beast a lesson so it won't attack another country.[84]

In short, from Rafsanjani's perspective, the more the United States and its coalition partners bled in Iraq, the more secure Iran would be from the threat of a western military attack, which would become increasingly less likely. A U.S. failure in Iraq was clearly a paramount Iranian interest, all evidence of strategic convergence notwithstanding. Years later, the Director of the CIA, Michael V. Hayden, put it succinctly: "It is the policy of the Iranian government, approved at the highest levels of that government, to facilitate the killing of American and other coalition forces in Iraq. Period."[85]

Part 3:

Why Western Dialogue with Iran Failed

Chapter 8:

Where Did the West Go Wrong?

THE REPEATED FAILURES OF THE UNITED STATES and its western allies to productively engage with Iran has been a remarkably consistent feature of their collective diplomacy since the 1979 Islamic Revolution. In that sense, the disappointing results of Europe's nuclear diplomacy with Iran from 2003 through 2006 should not have come as a surprise. Iran never wanted to negotiate. Far from desiring to reach a *modus vivendi* with its neighbors, the Iranian leadership has actively sought to export its Islamic Revolution with the aim of bringing ever larger parts of the Middle East under its hegemony. There was no way that a regime with such ambitions was going to concede the development of nuclear weapons that were so integral to the achievement of its goals.

Looking back at Washington's past involvement with Iran, virtually every administration tried to open a channel of communication with Tehran but found it a daunting task. Iran confounded

President Jimmy Carter, whose administration hoped for a cooperative relationship with Ayatollah Khomeini, but ended up having to focus on getting diplomats freed. There were hostages at the U.S. Embassy for 444 days. The Reagan administration found itself mired in the Iran-Contra Affair. Both the Bush (41) and Clinton administrations engaged in a futile search for new Iranian moderates, but in the interim, Iran became a more formidable foe as it built up its non-conventional capabilities. Its defiance of the West only seemed to grow.

If there is a core error that repeated itself over the years, it was the tendency to underestimate the true hostile intentions of Iran's revolutionary regime. Few accurately depicted its real aims. The Iranians themselves brilliantly exploited this western flaw, beginning with the entourage of Ayatollah Khomeini while he was in exile in France, who fed reporters stories that he had no intention to rule, and was concerned with human rights. They managed to obfuscate their ambitions throughout the 1980s as well. The European Union's senior body, the European Council, endorsed the idea of a "critical dialogue" with Iran back in 1992, which allowed European officials to express their mild reservations about aspects of Iranian behavior while promoting European trade with Iran. Despite this effort at bridging the gap, Europe was struck with repeated Iranian-sponsored terrorist attacks.

This dynamic of western officials misreading Iran and Iranian officials manipulating them is the heart of Tehran's success in repeatedly defying the United States and its allies. To understand how this happened, it is necessary to look back not only on the diplomatic assumptions prevailing in Washington or London, but also to delve into the techniques of persuasion adopted by the Iranians, as well. There were four factors that worked to the benefit of the Iranians in their repeated diplomatic encounters with the West since 1979, that to this day will influence the outcome of any attempted engagement with Tehran.

Underestimating the Depth of Hostility of the Iranian Regime

With each significant encounter it became apparent that successive U.S. administrations have totally misread Iran's revolutionary leadership, underestimating the deep enmity of the Iranian regime and its uncompromising commitment to its confrontational revolutionary ideology. It was the U.S. ambassador to the UN, Andrew Young, who best exemplified this tendency at the start of the relationship when he called Ayatollah Khomeini "some kind of saint."[1] Before his return to Iran in 1978, the U.S. ambassador to Iran, William H. Sullivan, reported to Washington that he expected Khomeini to assume a "Ghandi-like" role.[2]

However, Khomeini was not a benign religious figure, uninterested in political power, though his robes and turban were deceptive to western eyes. Khomeini had been closely associated with Shiite Islamic extremists since the late 1940s, like the "Fedayeen Islam," whose network of "holy killers" engaged in repeated attempts at political assassination—including attacks on three Iranian prime ministers.[3] One of his early works, *Kashf al-Asrar* ("the Revealing of Secrets"), published in 1944, served as a bible for the violent Fedayeen.[4] Khomeini had many of his Iranian supporters, including his son, trained in military camps run by Palestinian Liberation Organization (PLO) during the 1970s in Lebanon, prior to his arrival in Tehran where he took power.

Looking back on his rise to power, the former head of the CIA, Admiral Stansfield Turner, admitted: "We did not understand who Khomeini was and the support his movement had."[5] Khomeini had not been seeking to peacefully rid Iran of what his supporters viewed as the dictatorial government of the Shah. He was planning for a war, initially to oust the Shah and his government. But he also had wider revolutionary aims. Khomeini determined in early 1970 that jihad was part of a "universal movement" of all Muslims seeking to establish Islamic government everywhere in place of tyrannical regimes.[6] This idea appeared in *Islamic Government*, his lectures-turned-manifesto on Islamic theocracy. The principles of his work are embedded in the constitution of the Iranian regime; in the preamble, the "ideological mission" of the armed forces is said to be "to extend the sovereignty of God's law throughout the world."[7]

Amid repeated struggles between Iran and the West, U.S. and other western leaders tried to rationalize the motivation behind Tehran's bellicose behavior. In a post-Cold War world, in which struggles over worldview seemed to be over, governmental analysts had a difficult time understanding an ideologically driven state like the Islamic Republic. As a result, there was a common tendency among analysts to re-define Iran's political motivations in more easily understandable terms by imposing familiar concepts or templates on completely unfamiliar terrain.

Many diplomats bought into the idea that at the core of the Iranian-American conflict was the culpability of the West in ousting Iran's prime minister, Mohammad Mosaddeq, using the CIA in 1953. Mosaddeq had been nationalizing Iran's oil fields and endangering the interests of multinational oil companies. In turn, his downfall set the stage for the return of the Shah from exile, who was warmly embraced by Washington. This perspective tends to reduce the crisis of relations between Tehran and Washington to a Third World challenge to the imperial control of the western powers and an Iranian interest in obtaining complete control over its own natural resources.

Yet, while the fall of Mosaddeq was a defining political event for an entire generation of Iranians and caused strong anti-American resentment for many years in Iran (which Khomeini exploited), it is generally forgotten that many of Iran's leading clerics in 1953, who also served as Khomeini's mentors—like Ayatollah Abol-Qassem Husseini Kashani and Ayatollah Mohammad Hussein Borujerdi—actually backed the return of the Shah and the elimination of the secular Mosaddeq.[8] Years later, in 1981, the official organ of the Islamic Revolutionary Guards Corps, *Payam-e Enghelab*, explained that Mosaddeq had been an enemy since he and his supporters were "agents of the SAVAK (the Iranian domestic intelligence agency), Israel and the United States."[9] In any event, without Mosaddeq's own failure to hold together his internal support base, it is doubtful that the CIA's activities alone could have had any real effect in Tehran.

By accepting at face value the repeated Iranian declarations about the direct responsibility of the West for Mosaddeq's fall, thereby making the West into the scapegoat for Iran's hostile attitudes, analysts in Washington and European capitals were diverted from looking into the real source of friction between the two sides after 1979: Iran's aggressive revolutionary ideology and ambitions for dominating the Middle East, especially its oil-producing areas.

Key figures in the Carter administration bought into the argument and believed that if the United States would accept an international commission under the United Nations to investigate Washington's past role in Iran, then U.S.-Iranian relations would improve, setting the stage for the return of the American hostages seized by Khomeini's supporters from the U.S. Embassy in Tehran. This proposal indeed rose during the backchannel negotiations between Iran and the Carter administration over their release.

The same thinking underpinned the policy of the Clinton administration, when Secretary of State Madeleine Albright apologized in a public address in Washington on March 17, 2000, for America's involvement in the removal of Mosaddeq. She openly admitted: "In 1953, the United States played a significant role in orchestrating the overthrow of Iran's popular Prime Minister, Mohammad Mosaddeq." While the Carter team was willing to consider the idea of the international investigative commission, unlike the Clinton administration, it utterly refused to issue any apology.

In contrast, Secretary Albright apparently believed that times had changed and an American apology for the events of 1953 was essential for fostering a U.S.-Iranian rapprochement in the 1990s. In the end, the apology didn't work at all, for Tehran simply denounced Albright's gesture. But belief in the importance of the American apology had made an impact, nonetheless, and solidified the idea of U.S. culpability by placing a completely unnecessary onus for Iran's past actions on U.S. foreign policy. With the blame for tensions between the two countries focused on the United States, policy makers and diplomats were hesitant to hold the Iranian regime responsible for their actions, which Iran certainly perceived and exploited.

This trend was facilitated by another line of policy. During the Clinton years, when seemingly pragmatic politicians like President Mohammad Khatami arose in Iran, despite often being touted as men with whom the United States could do business, they were never empowered to fundamentally shift the policy of Iran away from Khomeini's radical roots. Incongruously, it was during Khatami's time in office that the Iranian nuclear program made some its most important advances under the direction of Iran's Supreme Leader, Ali Khamenei.

In attempts to negotiate with Iran, western analysts failed to understand that since the Islamic Revolution in 1979, Iran's clerical leadership has had its own powerful ambitions that best explain its international behavior. When Germany's former foreign minister, Joschka Fischer, looked back on the EU-3's nuclear talks with Iran between 2003 and 2006, he specifically cited "regional hegemonic aspirations" among the reasons why the Europeans failed to freeze Iran's nuclear program.[10] The dominant conflict in the Middle East, he concluded two years later, was the impending confrontation with Iran for "regional hegemony."[11] Iran was not just an injured party seeking to have its historical grievances addressed; it was an aggressive power seeking to establish its supremacy across one of the world's most turbulent regions.

Iran's Historical Use of Diplomatic Deception

The second reason Iran has been able to confound the West during each encounter revolves around different understandings of the diplomatic dance. Iranian negotiating strategy has been based on a long historical tradition that plays by very different rules than western diplomacy. As in a game of chess, Iranian tactics took into account not just the next move in a diplomatic struggle, but also several moves ahead.

These tactics have been most prevalent in the Iranian clerical leadership's use of the Shiite doctrine of *taqiya*, which historically allowed Shiite Muslims to deceive their Sunni adversaries in order to survive in the mostly Sunni Muslim world. The word *taqiya* is a derivative of the Arabic root word *waqa*, which means to shield or to guard. It clearly evolved as a tactic for protecting the Shiite community from external dangers.

Taqiya has most succinctly been described by Saudi analyst Dr. Wahid Hashim as a "major characteristic" of Shiite ideology involving a decision to "show an intention but yet [harbor] a different intention."[12]

As an Iranian diplomatic strategy, it gained official backing with the rise of the radical Shiite regime in 1979. Ayatollah Khomeini himself described the purpose of *taqiya* as the "preservation of Islam and the Shi'i school"[13] in *Islamic Government*. As he elaborated, "If someone wishes to speak about Islamic government, he must observe the principle of *taqiya*."[14]

Diplomats and political analysts who have come up against *taqiya* in different decades and political realities have described it in remarkably similar terms. Sir Denis Wright, Britain's ambassador to Iran in the 1970s, once remarked: "The Iranians are a people who say the opposite of what they think and do the opposite of what they say."[15] Giandomenico Picco, a brilliant Italian diplomat in the UN secretariat, tried to summarize Iranian negotiating strategy from his experiences negotiating the release of western

hostages in Lebanon and with ending the Iran-Iraq War, comment-
ing, "The problem is that the verbal dexterity they display is a
mask to hide reality."[16]

Picco detailed in his memoirs how an Iranian envoy, Javad Larijani, responded to a draft text for a cease-fire in the Iran-Iraq War
during the mid-1980s: "What do you want me to do with this?
Sign it? Fine, I will do it. Remember, I am also a professor of
semantics. The interpretation of this text can be what it seems
today and also the opposite of it tomorrow."[17] Picco realized that
the Iranians would change their positions during negotiations
making it extremely difficult to pin them down. Ultimately, they
did not want to change their original negotiating position at all. As
a result, he found that Iranian diplomacy would often "revisit
what everyone thought was settled ground."[18] But they skillfully
hid this intention. Under such conditions, every time the Europeans thought they had a real breakthrough in their nuclear negotiations with Iran, Iranian diplomats had managed to hide the fact
that they had made no concession at all.

Picco was not the only western diplomat who gained this impression. Warren Christopher served as Deputy Secretary of State in the
Carter administration (and Secretary of State in Clinton's first
term); in 1979 he negotiated with the Iranians the release of American hostages from the U.S. Embassy in Tehran. In his experience,
the Iranians negotiated very differently than the Chinese. For example, Christopher wrote that he always knew what China's Foreign
Minister, Qian Qichan, really wanted and "that if an agreement
was reached, its terms would be carried out."[19] In contrast, his
experience with the Iranians was entirely different: "The negotiating style is likely to resemble that of a Middle Eastern marketplace,
with outlandish demands, feints at abandoning the process and
haggling over minor details up to the very last moment. Christopher
added that the Iranians could disavow something to which they
already had agreed.[20] There was an enormous gap between what
the Iranians stated and what was ultimately concluded.

Some western diplomats did not always respond diplomatically to Iran's use of deception, delay, and denial. Jean-David Levitte was an experienced French diplomat, having been France's ambassador to both Washington and the UN, besides serving directly as a diplomatic advisor to two French presidents. During the EU-3 negotiations with Iran, he once quipped to the State Department's top arms control negotiator, John Bolton, as they discussed the Iranians' violations of their agreement with the Europeans: "I tell you having been Chirac's advisor on the Middle East for five years, the Shiites lie all the time."[21] In the context of the discussion, Levitte probably did not intend to make an ethno-religious slur, but was clearly referring to the diplomatic techniques of the Islamic Republic and perhaps its Lebanese surrogate, Hizbullah, with which the French had many dealings.

As Hassan Rowhani infamously revealed, the purpose of negotiations for an Iranian diplomat may not be to resolve a crisis or reach an agreed outcome, but rather to outsmart and get the best of one's adversary. In accordance with Persian culture, an Iranian official might be extremely gracious and warm to his western guest, trying to avoid any possible offense, yet getting straight to the point, through an honest exchange of views, is an alien idea.

For example, linguistically, Iranians of all persuasions may use the Persian term *balie*, which can be translated as "yes," when confronted with a request for a favor, even in the diplomatic realm. But the real meaning of this term depends on the intonation of the speaker and it can many times be just a courteous response in order to avoid saying no.[22] By using this term, an Iranian diplomat is not engaged in lying, but rather in avoiding an uncomfortable embarrassment. While western diplomacy is based on precision and getting quickly to the "bottom line," Iranians do not put everything on the table, preferring instead to engage in prolonged discussions that require great patience.

In light of these unique linguistic and cultural traits, misinterpretation of Iranian intentions is very common. A senior Israeli official once asked the Iranian foreign minister if he could get an audience with the Shah and was told: *balie*. What he took as a definite "yes" was intended as no more than "perhaps." Time passed and then nothing happened. When, months later, the Shah finally actually met the official and was asked why it took so long to get the meeting after he was told *balie*, the Shah laughed that his guest did not understand the real meaning of his foreign minister's reply.

Israeli diplomats, who regard themselves as part of the western diplomatic tradition, would often share these frustrating experiences with their American and British colleagues. Most western diplomats try to be precise with their language in order to avoid misunderstanding, for good reason. Westerners frequently seek to build credibility and trust in order to set the stage for the difficult decisions both sides might have to make in a subsequent stage in their contacts. Candor is of great value.

Of course, it is possible to be cynical about western diplomacy as well. As seventeenth century British diplomat, Sir Henry Wotton, famously remarked, an ambassador is "an honest man sent to lie abroad for the good of his country."[23] Certainly, the British and the French engaged in duplicity in the Middle East in the contradictory commitments they gave after the First World War. But in modern times, the idea of the diplomat as a master liar has been utterly rejected by experienced American envoys to the Middle East, like Philip Habib, who elaborated on Wotton's dictum by accurately stating that "the most fundamental requirement of successful diplomacy is honesty."[24]

Diplomats may argue over misunderstandings they might have about what their leaders said to one another in a previous meeting. Alternatively, they might raise conflicting interpretations over legal language in an international treaty or a UN Security Council Resolution. The contents of a private diplomatic meeting might be leaked to the press in order to gain some advantage. The West also practices "constructive ambiguity" when actual agreement is difficult to reach. But systematic deception as an instrument of diplomacy has not been part of normal western practice.

In contrast, Iranian diplomatic strategy is based on a completely different logic of outright strategic deception. For the Iranian diplomat, language is not used to clarify but to intentionally confuse. Obviously, this posed a huge problem for western diplomats engaging with Iran whose expectations of the very purpose of diplomacy were so radically different. As an old Persian adage, known to experts on Iranian negotiating behavior says: "A lie which brings benefit is preferable to a truth which causes damage."[25]

If one party believes in building credibility by dealing above board with his counterparts and the other party uses deception and false pretense as part of his *modus operandi*, then diplomacy is bound to fail. When the West began their efforts with the Iranians under the false assumption that they followed the same diplomatic code, the results of engagement were disastrous. The Iranians and the West were simply playing the diplomatic game by very different sets of rules.

Iran Challenged the United States and the West with Impunity

As the years have passed and the West has continued to attempt diplomatic engagement with Iran rather than fully confronting their deceptive diplomacy, Tehran has had no incentive to change its approach. Factually, after the first U.S. hostage crisis was resolved in 1981, the Iranians did not hesitate to use their Lebanese surrogate, Hizbullah, to seize more western hostages, including Americans, in the years that followed. It is doubtful that the Iranians believed they could be deterred in any way from further action against the United States or its western allies, considering they viewed themselves as the victors in the first confrontation with Washington over the U.S. Embassy in Tehran.[26]

Khomeini's famous words after the U.S. Embassy in Tehran was initially seized were "The Americans can't do a damn thing."[27] While the United States amassed enormous air and naval power in the surrounding seas of the Persian Gulf and Arabian Sea years later, this slogan continued to be ubiquitous in demonstrations and in graffiti.

Iranian arrogance might have had other causes, as well. Despite murdering Americans around the world in 1983—at the Marine Barracks in Beirut—and again in 1996 at the Khobar Towers housing complex in Saudi Arabia—Iran never once paid a serious price for engaging in overt terrorism against the United States and other western countries.

The Europeans had a built-in reluctance to take even the most minimal actions against Iran, even in the area of international trade. After the Mykonos verdict in 2007, which directly tied the highest levels of the Iranian government to a terrorist attack on German soil, the European diplomatic break with Iran that ensued lasted a little over a month. Upon the election of Mohammad Khatami as Iran's new president, meetings between senior Iranians and Europeans were quickly resumed.

When it finally decided to act, Washington found it extremely difficult to recruit its western allies into a more confrontational posture against Iranian provocations—even if only further economic sanctions were involved. Europe's aversion to using harsh economic measures to check Iran stemmed from a philosophy unique to the twenty-first century. As Robert Cooper, a British diplomat who became one of Javier Solana's key representatives during the nuclear talks in 2003–2005, explained in 2002, Europeans live in a "postmodern system," in which security is no longer based on the threat of force but on "transparency, mutual openness, interdependence and mutual vulnerability."[28]

Cooper asked himself "What is the origin of this basic change in the state system?" His answer was simple: "The fundamental point is that the world's grown honest." In other words, states don't lie to each other any more. As he elaborated, "the basic fact is that Western European countries no longer want to fight one another."[29] As Chris Patten, the EU Commissioner for External Affairs, argued in 2002: "There is more to be said for trying to engage these societies into the international community than to cut them off."[30]

This belief in engagement and creating networks of interdependence had its roots in recent European history. The EU had succeeded in taking some of the most hostile interstate relations in Europe, like the Franco-German rivalry, and limiting them through the European Coal and Steel Community and then the European Economic Community. Increased trade appeared to preclude war. This had been Europe's great achievement, resulting in a conviction that it could be applied everywhere—and to Iran, as well.

But while these doctrines perhaps applied to EU politics over tariffs and agricultural subsidies, they had limits when dealing with states, like Iran, that were not part of this "postmodern system" and whose interest in engaging with the international community was limited to buying time to pursue their illegal nuclear programs. When this postmodern belief system confronted the violent revolutionary politics of Iran, the results only encouraged Tehran.

Europe was not the only party giving Iran the precious time it needed by averting a confrontation with the Iranian leadership. As the pivotal international body dealing with the Iranian nuclear program, the Vienna-based International Atomic Energy Agency (IAEA) had the power to refer the Iranian case to the UN Security Council.

However, while the IAEA was invaluable in gathering details from its inspectors about various Iranian nuclear plants, detailing violations of past agreements, and insisting on credible answers from the Iranian government about unresolved issues, the IAEA's director-general, Dr. Mohamed ElBaradei, was reluctant to reach a final conclusion that would trigger a vigorous international diplomatic response.

Beyond dragging his feet, ElBaradei was accused by U.S. diplomats and in the international media of deleting references to IAEA requests made to Iran to inspect the Parchin weapons complex, where some of the most devastating evidence of an Iranian nuclear military program was later found.[31] The IAEA may have had certain concerns, like losing whatever limited access it had for its inspectors, but regardless of ElBaradei's motivation, his organization should have been far more decisive in confronting Iran's violations of its treaty commitments in a timely manner.

In fact, ElBaradei appeared to have all the time in the world. In late 2004, he estimated that even with full Iranian cooperation, it would take at least two years to resolve the questions that he had posed. He told the *New York Times*: "We're not rushing," elaborating, "It takes time."[32] Time was exactly what the Iranians needed and what the IAEA was, apparently, more than willing to provide.

ElBaradei only started to draw conclusions about Iran's military motivation just before finishing his term of office at the IAEA; in an interview with the BBC in June 2009, he finally admitted: "It is my gut feeling that Iran would like to have the technology to enable it to have nuclear weapons, if it decided to do so."[33] Had ElBaradei made this statement three years earlier, much more could have been done to recruit key global allies to take more effective action against Iran.

The Power of Western Business Interests

The fourth reason why diplomatic engagement with Iran has proven to be problematic is the economic power of Iran as an oil and natural gas producer with enormous petro-dollar buying power. The tie that binds Iran to the West is business. Strong economic interests have always trumped effective action by the United States and its allies, especially in using economic sanctions. After the United States passed sanctions in Iran in 1987, U.S. oil companies were prohibited from importing Iranian oil for American consumers. However, they were still permitted to purchase Iranian oil for their overseas markets. Because of this carefully crafted regulation, by the early 1990s, U.S. oil companies were the largest customers for Iranian crude oil, despite the existence of sanctions.[34]

The United States used the Iran-Libya Sanctions Act of 1996 to try to increase economic pressures on Iran by preventing U.S. companies from developing Iran's oil and gas fields. Despite imposing sanctions on companies, irrespective of nationality, that invested more than $40 million annually in the oil or gas sector of Iran, a loophole in the sanctions legislation exempted foreign subsidiaries of U.S. companies run by non-U.S. nationals from the penalties, which several U.S. companies exploited.[35]

In March 2008, the UN Security Council warned the international community "to exercise vigilance" with regard to all international banking transactions through Iranian banks, especially Bank Saderat and Bank Melli. There was growing concern that these banks supported illicit Iranian nuclear activities. The U.S. Treasury had blacklisted Bank Saderat in September 2006. Yet, the Iranian banks were determined to preserve their access to the western financial system. Bank Melli even opened a New York-based front organization in the United States called the Assa Corporation. In December 2008, the United States moved to seize its assets and closed down its operations.[36]

Nevertheless, Bank Saderat continued to operate a British subsidiary in London, even though it had been proven that the branch had been used as a vehicle for moving tens of millions of dollars of Iranian money to terrorist organizations such as Hizbullah and Hamas. There were also Bank Saderat branches in other European states, including France, Germany, and Greece.[37] The Iranians succeeded in cutting holes in the network of international sanctions that had been promoted by both the United States and the UN.

One of the most blatant actions of a western bank on behalf of Iran was committed by Lloyds TSB Group in London. Lloyds apparently would receive large wire transfers from Iranian banks in London, like Bank Saderat and Bank Melli, and then "strip" the Iranian identity off them before transferring the funds to a third party. Bank Sepah, which is owned and controlled by Iran's Revolutionary Guards, was one of the banks involved in the Lloyds scheme.[38]

A U.S. Treasury official called Bank Sepah "the financial linchpin of Iran's missile procurement network."[39] Bank Sepah also had the distinction of being blacklisted by the UN Security Council in Resolution 1747 (adopted on March 24, 2007) as one of a number of "entities involved in nuclear or ballistic missile activities."

Lloyds admitted on January 9, 2009 that it had illegally transferred Iranian money by "stripping" the Iranian identity from huge wire transfers on behalf of Iranian banks between the years 2001 and 2004. It also had branches in Dubai and Tokyo that engaged in the same activity. As a result of its admission, Lloyds agreed to pay a fine of $350 million in a deferred prosecution agreement with New York District Attorney Robert Morgenthau. And Lloyds was not alone. Nine other European banks are also under investigation for helping Iran evade international and U.S. sanctions on its nuclear and missile programs.[40]

Continuing Confusion

The real dangers a nuclear Iran would pose are still not fully appreciated. Many assume that even if Iran crosses the nuclear threshold, its power could be deterred. Iran has successfully challenged the West by constructing a clandestine nuclear program from the late 1980s until 2002 and continuing to significantly advance its nuclear weapons program even after it was revealed. Iran has expertly used diplomatic obfuscation to hide its real hostile intent and was able to draw Europe and eventually the United States into years of fruitless negotiations, which it knew how to brilliantly exploit.

Iran could absorb the costs the West imposed on it for its hostile policies over the years. It used surrogate organizations, like Hizbullah, to operate against western targets with impunity. Indeed, in many cases, western leaders accepted the pretense that Iran was not directly involved in the attacks by its surrogates—whether in Beirut or in the Khobar Towers—in order to avoid any confrontation with Tehran. And because western diplomats too often wanted to believe that Iran was just like any other country, they interpreted Iranian intentions according to their own, with disastrous consequences for the safety of the region. Too often, Iranian diplomatic deception has been facilitated by western self-deception.

From the rise of Ayatollah Khomeini in 1979 until today, there has been a strong tendency in the West to either underestimate the regime's true hostility or consciously to play it down. This has variously expressed itself in refusals to accept how dangerously doctrinaire Ayatollah Khomeini was, unsubstantiated hopes in the pragmatism of Rafsanjani, and failures to acknowledge the truly destructive intent blatant in the language of Ahmadinejad.

It also expressed itself in the easily misinterpreted summaries of the U.S. National Intelligence Estimate from 2007 that announced to the world that Iran had halted its drive for nuclear weapons. The cumulative impact of these repeated instances of misreading or misrepresenting what Iran was up to only reinforced the inner conviction of the Iranian leadership that they could get away with whatever military challenge they planned.

Government officials are not the only group affecting the interpretation of Iran in the West. A number of influential commentators have assigned Iran the most benign of intentions. Roger Cohen, a leading op-ed columnist in the *New York Times*, has been regularly reassuring his readers about Iranian policy, with generalities like "pragmatism lies at the core of the revolution's survival."[41] *Time* ran a feature story in 2006 on Ayatollah Khamenei describing his "pragmatism" as well, and accepting at face value the argument of an unnamed Iranian official that "he makes decisions based on the national interest."[42] This type of analysis completely plays down the priority that Khamenei gave in the past to the ideological imperatives of the Islamic Revolution, in favor of what an observer would judge as the interests of the Iranian state.

In the British press, it was not uncommon to find commentators, like John Pilger in the *Guardian*, who extrapolated from the failure of the West to find weapons of mass destruction in Iraq and concluded that Iran was the same kind of dubious case.[43] Other arguments have been made to the same effect. In 2009, *Newsweek*'s international editor, Fareed Zakaria, suggested in a cover story that Iran is not actually building nuclear weapons, because Ayatollah Khomeini described them as "un-Islamic" and his successor, Khamenei, issued a *fatwa* calling them immoral.[44]

Zakaria's assertion was significant because he is one of the most respected voices on trends in U.S. foreign policy. But his approach to the Iranian nuclear program not only flew in the face of the substantial and detailed evidence about uranium enrichment activities and nuclear warhead design in Iran that has been substantiated by the IAEA, but it also contradicted the understanding of well-versed observers about what, in fact, happened with Khomeini's stand on nuclear weapons, once Iraq began using weapons of mass destruction during the Iran-Iraq War.[45]

The Iranians themselves have presented Khamenei's supposed fatwa against nuclear weapons as proof that they have no intention to build them. Iranian nuclear negotiator Sirus Naseri made this precise point in appearing before the IAEA Board of Governors in Iran's defense on August 10, 2005.[46] Nonetheless, a year earlier, in November 2004, an Iranian legistlator, Hojat al-Islam Taqi Rahbar, explained that Iran needed to be cautious on any ban of on nuclear weapons because it was located in a region of proliferators. He concluded that "there are no Sharia or legal restriction on having such [nuclear] weapons as a deterrent."[47] It was as though Khamenei's fatwa didn't exist.

Moreover, Iranian clerics themselves have argued that the Islamic ban on nuclear weapons is really "ambiguous." It has been pointed out that Khameini's supposed fatwa banning nuclear weapons was not even published by the Office of the Supreme Leader, which carefully updates the record of his religious edicts.[48] In any case, there are other voices, like Taqi Mesbah-e Yazdi, the spokesman of the powerful Ayatollah, who justify the development of nuclear weapons by Iran.[49]

Remarkably, seven years after Iran's clandestine nuclear program was unveiled, the idea is still advanced in serious circles that Iran only wants a civilian nuclear program. To understand the present challenges posed by Iran, a realistic assessment of its nuclear program is necessary. It is also essential to understand how Iran's drive for regional supremacy in the Middle East and South Asia has made it into the main state-sponsor of terrorism and subversion in the region around it. Finally, it is necessary to consider how these two aspects of Iranian policy will work together. Will a nuclear Iran provide a protective umbrella for international terrorism and create a security problem that the world has not yet witnessed?

Chapter 9:

Understanding Ahmadinejad and the Revolutionary Guards' Regime

Pᴿᴵᴼᴿ ᴛᴏ ʜᴵˢ ᴀᴘᴘᴏᴵɴᴛᴹᴱɴᴛ as Britain's ambassador to the UN in 2007, Sir John Sawers was one of the most experienced British diplomats in the Middle East. In 2005, he was Political Director in the British Foreign and Commonwealth Office, working on the Iranian nuclear file directly under Foreign Secretary Jack Straw. Before holding that position, he served as Prime Minister Tony Blair's special envoy to Baghdad, where he warned in 2003 that Iran was giving "unwelcome" support to Shiite insurgent groups in Iraq.[1] He had also been the British ambassador to Egypt.

In June 2009, he would receive yet another promotion in his impressive career, with his appointment as the chief of MI6— Britain's external intelligence agency. He was well acquainted with the Middle East as well as the problem of Iranian intervention in the affairs of post-Saddam Iraq. Most importantly, he was fully aware of the escalating fatalities among U.S. and British coalition soldiers from Iranian-supplied roadside bombs across Iraq.

As part of his work on Iran in 2005, Sawers held behind-the-scenes meetings with Iranian envoys who wanted to communicate directly with the British Government. "There were various Iranians who would come to London and suggest we had tea in some hotel or other," he recalled.[2] London was also an ideal place to signal messages for the United States as well, since Washington had no embassy in Tehran. It was the EU-3 who were negotiating with the Iranian leadership over the nuclear question, not the Bush administration. In late 2005, he had a meeting with a visiting Iranian envoy with a bold proposal he sought to test with one of Britain's most senior diplomats.

Sawers recalled the Iranian proposal as follows: "The Iranians wanted to be able to strike a deal whereby they stopped killing our forces in Iraq in return for them being allowed to carry on with their nuclear programme."[3] He put the Iranian offer in an even more blunt way: "We stop killing you in Iraq, undermining the political process there, you allow us to carry on with our nuclear programme without let or hindrance." It was shocking for several reasons. First, the Iranian envoy was for the first time admitting, albeit privately, that Iran was in fact behind the mounting deaths of coalition forces. U.S. intelligence teams did not have to examine shrapnel or look for Iranian markings on captured weapons anymore; an Iranian representative was voluntarily disclosing that the Iranians were involved in the Iraqi insurgency.

Secondly, the meeting demonstrated that Iran was seeking to obtain diplomatic leverage from the lethal weaponry that it was supplying. It was a kind of brinksmanship, for Iran tried to obtain a nuclear *quid pro quo* for giving up violence. Influence in Iraq had been of great importance to the Iranians even prior to the fall of Saddam Hussein. But they were now willing to give up one of the most important sources of their influence in Iraq for the sake of their nuclear program.

This was also extremely revealing. If Iran was seeking to complete its nuclear projects for civilian purposes, then sacrificing its role in Iraq seemed excessive on their part. The offer to pull back Iranian influence over the insurgency only made sense if Iran was using it to safeguard an interest of even greater importance like a nuclear weapons program, which they would have wanted to complete at all costs. The British did not accept the Iranian offer. Jack Straw called the offer "realpolitik," noting that "the Iranians wanted freedom on the nuclear dossier."[4]

Sawers's exchange with the Iranian envoy was disclosed by a BBC news show, and was quickly all over the British press. Tim Sebastian, the tough British interviewer from the BBC News program *Hardtalk,* asked Iran's ambassador to the UN, Javad Zarif, point blank: "You said we can make life easier for you in Iraq if you give Iran's nuclear program a pass—what sort of deal were you offering?"[5] After fumbling with his response, Zarif did not give a straight answer. He spoke about many members of that meeting denying the story, though there was only one Iranian present with Sawers. When pressed by Sebastian, Zarif would not deny the story himself and instead shifted the discussion to the "supportive role" Iran played in the past in Afghanistan and Iraq.

Regardless of what Zarif might have said, the Iranians had established through their proposal a definite link between their nuclear diplomacy and the security situation of coalition forces on the ground in Iraq. It was a two-way link, for what was also implied by the offer in London was that if the West came down hard on Iran with respect to its nuclear ambitions, then Tehran would retaliate against U.S. and British troops in Iraq.

In the following months there were mounting Iranian statements that were intended to remind the West of how Iran might retaliate against an actual U.S. strike on its nuclear facilities. As the Iranian Army Chief of Staff told Iran's Channel 2, "Knowing that our number one enemy is the criminal America, we focused on it. We identified its strengths and weaknesses." He then added: "We studied all the details of America's war in Iraq and Afghanistan," and he concluded that the Iranian armed forces had developed scenarios accordingly.[6]

Subsequently, the Revolutionary Guards Commander, Yahya Rahim Safavi, broadened the threat to all U.S. forces in the Middle East: "Assuming they attack Iran, their troops in their 33 bases are highly vulnerable." He specifically noted: "The Americans are stuck in the quagmire of Afghanistan and Iraq."[7] His commander for the Revolutionary Guards naval forces threatened all U.S. ships in the Persian Gulf: "American warships are heavy and easily sunk."

A further ominous development in this period provided Iran with the capability to actually strike at U.S. and European interests, well beyond the Middle East. It was disclosed that Iran was procuring weapons systems that could reach targets thousands of kilometers from its territory. In one of his last appearances as the head of Israeli military intelligence, Major General Aharon Zeevi (Farkash) testified in late 2005 in front of the Knesset Foreign Affairs and Defense Committee and reported that Iran had acquired twelve former Soviet cruise missiles, which it had just purchased from Ukraine. He added that the cruise missile in question had a range of 3,000 kilometers and could carry a nuclear warhead.[8]

Four months later, Zeevi's successor, Major General Amos Yadlin, made another astounding disclosure: the Iranians had purchased BM-25 surface-to-surface missiles from North Korea that were known to have a range of 2,500 kilometers.[9] The German newspaper *Bild* carried the same story in December 2005, but based its claim on German intelligence sources. The German report added that the Iranians wanted the North Koreans to extend the range of the BM-25 to 3,500 kilometers.[10] If all the Iranian leadership wanted to do was to destroy Israel, it would only need a 1,300 kilometer range missile, like the Shahab-3, that they successfully tested in 1998. By seeking to procure a whole new family of missile systems—ones with the capability to fly over

Israel to hit targets in Europe—Iran was demonstrating far more expansive aims. Significantly, both missile procurements occurred after an important change in the leadership of Iran.

The Rise of Ahmadinejad

Iran's increasingly confrontational stance with the West coincided with the surprise victory on June 24, 2005, of Mahmoud Ahmadinejad, the hard-line mayor of Tehran, in a runoff election for the Iranian presidency. His biography was considerably different than his most prominent predecessors. He had no clerical background. His formative years were during the Iran-Iraq War when he was attached for a brief period to an engineering unit of the Revolutionary Guards. (Later, he joined a Revolutionary Guards intelligence unit, although he was never technically one of their officers, since he was seconded to Revolutionary Guards from the popular Basij paramilitary.)[11] Details surrounding his exact combat background remain murky. Nevertheless, his name came to be connected with one of the most daring commando operations in the Iran-Iraq War when the Revolutionary Guards infiltrated over 100 miles inside Iraqi territory in 1987 to sabotage the Iraqi oil refineries in Kirkuk.[12]

During this period, Ahmadinejad established close ties with commanders in the Revolutionary Guards who would later become important political allies. Indeed, two decades later, Ahmadinejad would turn to his fellow veterans from the Revolutionary Guards to take up key positions in his government. He gave veterans from the 1980 Iran-Iraq war nine of twenty-one ministerial portfolios.[13] His Minister of Defense, Mostafa Mohammad Najjar had been a brigadier general in the Revolutionary Guards, while his Minister of Foreign Affairs, Manouchehr Mottaki, had served as a liaison officer between the Revolutionary Guards and the Iranian Foreign Ministry. Finally, he replaced Hassan Rowhani as the Secretary to the Supreme

National Security Council and chief nuclear negotiator with Ali Larijani, who also came out of the Revolutionary Guards.

Ahmadinejad swept the provincial governors who had been appointed by Rafsanjani and Khatami in Iran's thirty provinces from power, replacing them with Revolutionary Guard officers and other officials who came out of the Iranian security services. A former prosecutor-general of the Islamic Republic called this massive entry of the Revolutionary Guards into the Iranian political world nothing less than a "military takeover." Ahmadinejad's support of the Revolutionary Guards was very much a reciprocal relationship—he gave them important appointments, and they fully backed him politically.

In fact, during the 2005 campaign, the Revolutionary Guard command and its Basij militia functioned like party activists in a western presidential race: they turned out the vote, acted as election monitors, and even got into the business of buying votes.[14] After his victory, the commander of the Revolutionary Guards, Yahya Rahim Safavi, commented: "President-elect Ahmadinejad is a son of the Islamic Revolutionary Guard." He then added: "It is our duty to make sure that he succeeds."[15]

For his part, Ahmadinejad interpreted his election mandate as an expression of the people's desire to see "a revival of the Islamic Revolution's ideals." He believed his rise to power marked a turning point for Iranian history because, in his words: "A new Islamic revolution had arisen."[16] Most revolutions eventually lose their zeal; however, he felt that he was reversing that trend. For that reason one analyst called Ahmadinejad's victory the "Second Islamic Revolution."[17]

Understating Ahmadinejad's Intentions

Ahmadinejad quickly became known for his fiery rhetoric, especially his declaration at a conference in Tehran on October 26, 2005, that "Israel must be wiped off the map."[18] His remarks engendered an enormous international debate about whether he really was calling for the outright destruction of Israel. The debate had broader implications, for if indeed he was planning Israel's physical elimination, then that would put a whole new light on Iran's nuclear program, which would have to be taken far more seriously than it had in the past.

However, if Ahmadinejad had been mistranslated or misunderstood, then it might even be possible to entertain a policy of diplomatic engagement with Iran, his rhetoric notwithstanding. Skeptics of the accuracy of the translation of Ahmadinejad's words had another concern: they thought that the West might seize upon his language to justify a military strike against Iran's nuclear facilities. In short, there were powerful political forces interested in understating the enmity that Ahamadinejad was expressing, and they spread their analysis throughout the mass media and even in some governmental circles.

The campaign to give Ahmadinejad the benefit of the doubt about his rhetoric began with Professor Juan Cole of the University of Michigan, who argued that there had been a mistranslation: "Ahmadinejad did not say he was going to wipe Israel off the map because no such idiom exists in Persian."[19] Cole was partially correct, but that didn't change the import of what Ahmadinejad was proposing. Though the *New York Times* did not translate Ahmadinejad literally, choosing the phrase that Israel "must be wiped off the map," a literal word-for-word translation was not any better, reading: "Our dear Imam ordered that this Jerusalem-occupying regime must be erased from the page of time."[20]

Cole also focused on the fact that Ahmadinejad did not refer to "Israel" by name, but instead called it the "Jerusalem-occupying regime." He explained that Ahmadinejad only hoped the regime in Israel would collapse, which was a far cry from a nuclear holocaust. Similarly, a British commentator in *The Guardian*, Jonathan Steele, suggested: "He was not making a military threat," but rather was calling only for "an end to the occupation of Jerusalem at some point in the future."[21]

These were not theoretical differences of translation being debated solely in the academic world. In 2007, when the U.S. House of Representatives debated a bill condemning Ahmadinejad's language as nothing less than incitement to genocide, Representatives Dennis Kucinich (D-Ohio) and Ron Paul (R-Texas) had strong reservations. Kucinich demanded that alternative translations of Ahmadinejad's words be introduced into the Congressional Record. Both congressmen voted against the bill, which was adopted by a massive bi-partisan majority of 411 to 2.

Thus, only a small minority in the House of Representatives bought into the argument that Ahmadinejad had been misrepresented. However unjustified, the seeds of doubt about the veracity of the translation of Ahmadinejad's intentions were sown, and manifested in subtle ways beyond the House debate. Noticeably, the House bill was never reported out of the Senate Foreign Relations Committee for a vote on the Senate floor.

Did Ahmadinejad's defenders have a case? The fact that Ahmadinejad called Israel "the Jerusalem-occupying regime" did not reduce the severity of what he was saying. Since the Islamic Republic of Iran does not formally recognize the State of Israel, Ahmadinejad chose a euphemism rather than explicitly mentioning Israel by name. In order to remove any doubt about Ahmadenejad's intention, on his own website—www.president.ir—where his speech was reported in 2005, the editors put in the Persian word *Esraiil* (Israel) for clarification.

Two years later, an Iranian website hung a banner on the front of a building in Tehran belonging to the Revolutionary Guards' Basij militia. The banner paraphrased Ahmadinejad, but used the word "Israel" explicitly—both in English and in Farsi: "Israel should be wiped off the face of the world."

It is difficult to wipe a country off the map or off the face of the world without wiping out the people who live there.[22]

Significantly, Ahmadinejad was not the only Iranian leader to use this language. Many other members of the Iranian establishment picked up this theme of destroying Israel. Some times they were even more explicit than Ahmadinejad, adding de-humanizing language on a par with threats against minority populations in the past. In Rwanda, Hutu propaganda against the Tutsi tribe prior to genocide described them as "cockroaches." In Germany, Nazis depicted the Jews as parasites and locusts.

In February 2008, General Mohammad-Ali Jafari, commander of the Revolutionary Guards, spoke about "the destruction of the cancerous microbe Israel."[23] His predecessor, General Safavi, spoke about "the death of this unclean regime."[24] Mohammad Ali Ramin, a close Ahmadinejad advisor, spoke in 2006, saying that it was said the Jews were a source of "such deadly diseases as the plague and typhus."[25] He explained that "the Jews are a very filthy people." On another occasion he noted: "By taking the Jews to the Muslim world, they [the West] have created a situation in which the Jews *will* be destroyed."[26]

When Ahmadinejad made his high profile comments in October 2005, he prefaced them with "Our dear Imam ordered." This was a reference to Ayatollah Khomeini, whom he would not have misquoted in a paraphrase of the founder of the Islamic Revolution's intentions for Israel.

Supreme Leader Ayatollah Ali Khamenei stated in 2001 that "the perpetual subject of Iran is the elimination of Israel from the region." At variance with the theory that these statements only referred to the peaceful elimination of the regime in Israel were images of the Shahab-3 missiles (paraded on trucks through Tehran) on September 22, 2003, broadcast on Iranian television for the world to see. Featured on the sides of the trucks carrying the missiles were banners which read: "Israel must be uprooted and wiped off [the pages of] history."[27]

By juxtaposing Iran's destructive vision with the weapons it needed to carry it out, Tehran made it clear that Israel's elimination was not a long-term historical process that was to result from its own internal socio-economic problems, but rather the consequence of military action that was to be taken by Iran itself, presumably through the use of ballistic missiles.

The Iranians continued to put statements of this sort on their missiles in the years that followed. This led Michael Axworthy, who served as the Head of the Iran Section of the British Foreign Office in 1998–2000, to observe that as Ahmadinejad's formulations about Israel had indeed been used by Iranians in the past, there should not have been any controversy about their translation.

> The formula had been used by Khomeini and others, and had been translated by representatives of the Iranian regime as "wiped off the map." Some of the dispute that has arisen over what exactly Ahmadinejad meant by it has been rather bogus. When the slogan appeared draped over missiles in military parades the meaning was pretty clear.[28]

The primary difference between the sentiments expressed by Khamenei in 2001 and Ahmadinejad in 2005 was the world climate. Ahmadinejad's address was delivered after the stunning revelations of Iran's illicit nuclear program in 2002, at the height of the nuclear crisis between Iran and the West. This provided an entirely new context for his threatening remarks.

Another aspect of Ahmadinejad's October 2005 address was largely skipped over due to the focus on his call to destroy Israel. His speech also dealt with the threat to Islam of the "world oppressor." He asserted that the entire Islamic world had been "withdrawing for the past 300 years" in the face of the infidel nations. He was alluding to Iran's era of power under the Safavid Empire, which ruled over territory as far as Central Asia and the Persian Gulf until the encroachments of the Russians to the North and the British to the South. He then explained his vision of the future.

Many who were disappointed in the struggle between the Islamic world and the infidels have tried to spread the blame. They say it is not possible to have a world without the United States and Zionism. But you know *this is a possible goal* and slogan (emphasis added).[29]

Ahmadinejad was essentially telling his audience that the United States could also be eliminated in the future—not just Israel. In subsequent statements, he kept up the theme, saying, "The Iranian nation will not give up until the corrupt leadership in the world has been obliterated."[30] Several years later, he articulated what had clearly become part of his worldview when he announced, "Today, the time for the fall of the satanic power of the United States has come and the countdown to the annihilation of the emperor of power and wealth has started."[31] Yet the Iranian leader's deep hostility to America has been ignored or understated, which downplays the very real threat its efforts to become a nuclear capability has created.

Ahmadinejad's Adoption of Apocalyptic Ideologies

Besides the escalation of Ahmadinjad's anti-western incendiary rhetoric, the second feature of his presidency that has received enormous attention has been his repeated references to the imminent return of the Twelfth or Hidden Imam. In Twelver Shiite tradition, Muhammad ibn Hasan was the twelfth descendent of the Prophet Muhammad's son-in-law, Ali ibn Abi Talib. He was born in 868, but at the age of six, he vanished and was expected to reveal himself as the Mahdi (literally, the "Rightly Guided One") at the end of days before the Day of Judgment, when a new era of divine justice will prevail, and Shiite Islam will be recognized as the true global faith. The Mahdi is also called by other names, like Imam al-Zaman, sometimes translated as the "Lord of the Age."

For a time in the tenth century, Shiites believed they could be in contact with him through intermediaries, but even this connection was severed in 941.

Ahmadinejad made the re-appearance of the Twelfth Imam as the Mahdi into a hallmark of his presidency. He declared in an address to the Iranian nation shortly after his 2005 election victory: "Our revolution's main mission is to pave the way for the re-appearance of the Mahdi."[32] What he meant was that government policy should seek to hasten his return.[33] In September, he sponsored in Tehran the first annual International Conference of Mahdism Doctrine.[34] He required his cabinet members to sign a symbolic pledge of allegiance to the Twelfth Imam.[35] And in the years that followed, he invoked the Mahdi's name at special historical events for Iran, like the launch of the first Iranian satellite into orbit on an Iranian rocket.

Ahmadinejad has even made visits to the Jamkaran Mosque, which was built on the basis of a tradition that the Hidden Imam re-appeared in 984 and ordered its construction; it has been a site of pilgrimage for those anticipating his arrival and who make requests to him by dropping petitions into the Jamkaran well. Shiite traditions dictate that the Mahdi will emerge at the site by coming out of the Jamkaran well. Despite his government's economic struggles with unemployment at 30 percent, Ahmadnejad allocated $20 million in 2005 to expand the mosque complex at Jamkaran, and further funds for commemorating the Mahdi's birthday.

Ahmadinejad took his beliefs abroad, as well. In his debut before the UN General Assembly on September 17, 2005, Ahmadinejad ended his address with a clear reference to the Mahdi:

From the beginning of time, humanity has longed for the day when justice, peace, equality and compassion envelop the world. All of us can contribute to the establishment of such a world. When that day comes, the ultimate promise of all Divine religions will be fulfilled with the emergence of a perfect human being who is heir to all prophets and pious men. He will lead the world to justice and absolute peace. O mighty Lord, I pray to you to hasten the emergence of your last repository, the promised one, that perfect and pure human being, the one that will fill this world with justice and peace.[36]

Upon his return to Iran, Ahmadinejad visited Qom, the religious center of Shiite learning, and shared with the ayatollahs with whom he met that a "halo-like light" enveloped him during his UN address. He told them that someone in the audience told him that the halo formed around him as he began to speak and remained with him until he finished. He confided to the religious leaders: "I felt it myself too." He then explained: "I felt all of a sudden the atmosphere changed, and for 27-28 minutes none of the leaders blinked." The importance of what had happened according to Ahmadinejad was as follows: "They were astonished, as if a hand held them there and made them sit. It had opened their eyes and ears for the message of the Islamic Republic."[37]

Ahmadinejad's beliefs about the Mahdi's arrival are critical for two reasons. One, this is not an event for some day in the distant future; it is imminent. It was reported in November 2006 that Ahmadinejad told a visiting foreign minister from an unnamed Islamic country that the current crisis in Iran "presaged the coming of the Hidden Imam, who would appear within two years."[38] Presumably he was referring to the Iranian nuclear crisis with the West. On another occasion he said that it was his mission to hand over Iran to the Mahdi at the end of his presidency.[39] He completely rejected the view of his critics, who said that the arrival of the Mahdi was a matter for the distant future: "It is very bad to say that the imam will not emerge for another few hundred years; who are you to say that?"[40]

Second, under conditions of global conflict and even chaos, the Mahdi's arrival can be brought forward.[41] For example, in a meeting with French Foreign Minister Philippe Douste-Blazy and two other EU foreign ministers in New York on September 15, 2005, Ahmadinejad shifted the focus of their conversation unexpectedly and asked the European diplomats: "Do you know why we should wish for chaos at any price?" He then answered his own rhetorical question: "Because after chaos, we can see the greatness of Allah."[42] Given this belief structure, the more confrontational Iran becomes in its relations with the West, the more its religious objective of bringing about the Mahdi's arrival is served.

Belief in a Messiah is part of the religious doctrine of the other monotheistic faiths, as well. Traditionally, Shiites have not been messianic enthusiasts to the extent of Ahmadinejad and his followers, preferring to pursue a more quietist approach to their religion in which they are not trying to manipulate the timing of the end of days.[43] In fact, Shiism's mainstream leaders have voiced serious reservations about Mahdism. The same can be said for parts of the Iranian establishment. Former President Ali Akbar Rafsanjani attacked the rising interest in the arrival of the Mahdi when it appeared it was becoming more popular under Ahmadinjead: "The affairs of a country and nation cannot be run on the basis of a claim made by someone that the Lord of the Age is pleased. No one has met the Lord of the Age and we haven't heard him. So how can such a claim be made?"[44]

It is the combination of these two features of his worldview that have very disturbing implications. According to Shiite apocalyptic thought, after the Hidden Imam returns, the world will be enveloped by war and plague. Mehdi Khaliji, an Iranian Shiite scholar who was trained in the Iranian religious seminaries of Qom, has noted that there are apocalyptic *hadiths* (received Shiite traditions) that the Mahdi will not return unless one-third of the world population is killed and another third die.[45] But Ahmadinejad and his followers believe man can actively create the conditions for the Mahdi's arrival in the here and now, rather than at

The Founder: Ayatollah Ruhollah Khomeini (1902–1989) launched the Islamic Revolution in 1979, overthrowing the Shah of Iran and establishing the Islamic Republic. Here he is pictured in May 1988. (AP Photo/Sayaad)

The Successor: Ayatollah Ali Khamenei (b. 1939) succeeded Khomeini as Iran's Supreme Leader. His website did not call him Supreme Leader of Iran, but rather "Supreme Leader of Muslims." He promoted Iran's drive for regional hegemony and its nuclear program. (AP Photo/Vahid Salemi)

Exporting the Revolution–1: The Iranians established Lebanese Hizbullah in 1982, but Tehran launched other branches across the Middle East. In Saudi Arabia, Hizbullah al-Hijaz struck on June 29, 1996, at the Khobar Towers which housed U.S. servicemen based at the King Abdul Aziz Air Base. Nineteen U.S. servicemen were killed. In 1983, 241 servicemen were killed by Hizbullah in Beirut when the Marine barracks were bombed—by a direct order from Tehran. (AP Photo/U.S. Navy)

Exporting the Revolution–2: Bahrain has an overwhelming Shiite majority and a Sunni-minority government. It is also the headquarters of the U.S. Navy's Fifth Fleet. In 1995, Bahraini officials argued that Bahraini Hizbullah was seeking to overthrow their pro-American government with the assistance of Iranian intelligence. Pictured are anti-American Bahraini protestors, holding up a picture of Lebanese Hizbullah leader, Sheikh Hasan Nasrallah in January 2008. (AP Photo/Hasan Jamali)

Exporting the Revolution–3: Masked terrorist from the Jerusalem Battalions of Palestinian Islamic Jihad during training in Gaza City. Palestinian Islamic Jihad and Hamas are Iranian-funded organizations, engaged in suicide bombing and rocket attacks against Israeli civilians. Hamas operatives from the Gaza Strip regularly underwent military training outside of Tehran with the Revolutionary Guards. (AP Photo/Hatem Moussa)

Recovered from cache
September 15, 2005
Diwaniyah

Size correlation | 15 Sep 05, Diwaniyah

20 Jan 06, Baghdad

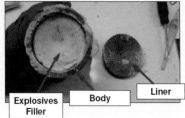

Recovered from emplaced EFP
arrays on January 20, 2006 in
Baghdad

Explosives Filler | Body | Liner

Iran Infiltrates Iraq–1: Pictured are armor-piercing "explosively formed penetrators" (EFPs) used as roadside bombs in Iraq. The U.S. military argued in 2007 that Iran supplied these EFPs to Shiite militias in Iraq and that they killed more than 170 American servicemen. (AP Photo/U.S. military)

Iran Infiltrates Iraq–2: Brig. Gen. Kevin J. Bergner, the U.S. military spokesman, explains in Baghdad how Iran was employing Lebanese Hizbullah to arm Shiite militias in Iraq. He also disclosed that the Quds Force of Iran's Revolutionary Guards were assisting Shiite militias in operations against U.S. forces, like in the case of Karbala where five U.S. servicemen were killed. (AP Photo/Wathiq Khuzaie, Pool)

Iran in South America–1: Iranian President Mahmoud Ahmadinejad expanded the Iranian presence across South America in the backyard of the United States. He traded reciprocal visits with Venezuelan President Hugo Chavez, who is pictured here with Ahmadinejad at a petrochemical plant near the Persian Gulf. Venezuela hosted a branch of Hizbullah and permitted Iranian missionaries to spread Shiite Islam to its Indian population. (AP Photo/Hasan Sarbakhshian)

Iran in South America–2: Bolivia's President Evo Morales, left, is pictured with President Mahmoud Ahmadinejad on a balcony at the presidential palace in La Paz. (AP Photo/Juan Karita)

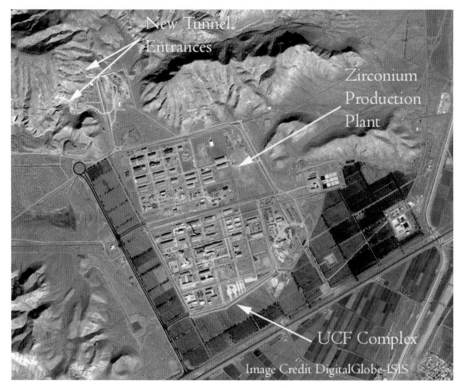

The Iranian Nuclear File–1: Satellite image of the Iranian Uranium Conversion Facility (UCF) at Isfahan. The UCF was built for converting processed uranium ore known as "yellowcake" into uranium hexafluoride (UF_6), which subsequently serves as the feedstock for the gas centrifuges that are located at the Natanz Uranium Enrichment Facility. Western observers took note that the Iranians were constructing special tunnels in order to hide their nuclear work. (AP Photo/Digital Globe)

The Iranian Nuclear File–2: Two members of the EU-3, French Foreign Minister Dominique de Villepin (right) and British Foreign Secretary Jack Straw (left), stand with Iran's Hassan Rowhani after their meeting on November 11, 2003. Rowhani revealed in 2006 that he negotiated with the Europeans in order to buy time and complete the Isfahan facility. (AP Photo/Thierry Charlier)

The Iranian Nuclear File–3: President Mahmoud Ahmadinejad is pictured here walking through a hall at the Natanz Uranium Enrichment Facility. On either side of him are gas centrifuges which receive UF_6 gas and produce enriched uranium. International inspectors claim Iran has only produced low-enriched uranium for civilian use, but could further enrich this stock to produce weapons-grade uranium, as well.

(AP Photo/Iranian President's Office)

The Revolutionary Guards: The Commander of the Revolutionary Guards is General Mohommad Ali Jafari, who was named to his post by Ayatollah Ali Khamenei, his commander-in-chief. The Revolutionary Guards have increased their power in recent years within the Iranian economy and in the Iranian Parliament. Ahmadinejad appointed ex-Revolutionary Guards to more than half of the members of his cabinet. The Revolutionary Guards control Iran's missile forces and the development of its nuclear weapons program.   (AP Photo/ISNA, Mehdi Ghasemi)

The Thirst for Freedom: Hundreds of thousands of Iranian protestors poured into Azadi (Freedom) Square in Tehran in rejection of the results of the June 12, 2009 presidential election which they felt had been rigged. Violent clashes between demonstrators and Iranian security forces across many cities produced the greatest domestic unrest in Iran since the February 1979 Islamic Revolution. (AP Photo/Ben Curtis)

some distant date at the end of time. What is unclear is whether creating the pre-conditions for his appearance includes instigating violent scenarios that have been traditionally reserved for the period after he arrives.

Where did Ahmadinejad obtain this world-view and how prevalent was it among the Iranian elites? While Mahdism was not promoted by Khomeini at the start of the Islamic Revolution, it seemed to have been given a boost during the Iran-Iraq War, among officers serving with the Revolutionary Guards. References that the Mahdi would help Iran win the war became common. Iranian state media carried stories of soldiers who claimed to have seen the Mahdi on a white horse leading them into battle.

Khomeini's government used belief in the Mahdi to motivate hundreds of thousands of volunteers who were part of the Revolutionary Guards' Basij militia. It even hired professional actors to play the role of the Mahdi on the front lines; they would wear a white shroud and ride a white horse while blessing the troops. This technique helped boost morale and provide young recruits with the motivation to become martyrs in human wave attacks against the Iraqi Army.[46]

High-ranking members of the Revolutionary Guards continued to believe in the coming of the Mahdi, even after the end of the Iran-Iraq War. General Mohammad Ali Jafari, who replaced General Safavi as commander of the Revolutionary Guards, told his fellow officers from the Revolutionary Guards in January 2008 that: "Our Imam did not limit the movement of the Islamic Revolution to this country, but drew greater horizons. Our duty is to prepare the way for an Islamic world government and the rule of the Lord of the Time [the Hidden Imam]."[47]

Given this background, the prevalence of Mahdism and apocalyptic religious beliefs among Ahmadinejad's allies in the Revolutionary Guards makes sense. Their control of Iran's most sensitive weapons systems, like its ballistic missiles forces, and especially its nuclear program, however, might be cause for concern if they do, in fact, believe it is their destiny to hasten the return of the Mahdi by inciting world chaos.[48] It has been observed that there is a faction among its mid-ranking commanders who regard themselves as "soldiers of the Mahdi."[49]

Ahmadinejad's Mahdism is no mere superstitious tradition carried over from his time with the Revolutionary Guards. During his student days in the late 1970s, he was linked with a secretive Islamist movement known as the Hojatieh Society.[50] Founded in 1954, its twofold mission was to fight the Bahai faith and pave the way for the appearance of the Mahdi. It did not accept Khomeini's doctrine of *velayat-e faqih*, the rule of the jurisprudent, since the arrival of the Mahdi make a cleric to represent him in the interim unnecessary.

Khomeini cracked down on the movement in 1983, but it had already gained adherents among significant Iranian elites, including two future foreign ministers of the Islamic Republic: Kamal Kharrazi, who served under President Khatami, and Ali Akbar Velayeti, who would continue to exercise influence as the diplomatic advisor to Supreme Leader Ayatollah Ali Khamenei.[51] At the time the Hojatieh was banned, two ministers of the Iranian government were dismissed because of their association with the movement.[52] Moreover, the purge of Hojjatieh members led to the dismissal of eight of the provincial governors in the Islamic Republic. Yet, despite the moves against the Hojatieh, it continued to have influence on certain sectors of the Iranian government and on key individuals who would take on important positions in the Islamic Republic in the years to come.

When Ahmadinejad came into power, one of the few high-level officials from the previous Khatami government he did not seek to replace was Gholam Reza Aghazadeh, the head of Iranian Atomic Energy Organization. Aghazadeh is rumored also to be a Hojatieh member.[53] The Hojatieh was organized through secret societies and under different organizational names, so the extent of its membership is difficult to discern. Nevertheless, there are indications that the Hojatieh has penetrated some of the most sensitive positions in the Iranian political establishment.

Regardless of the level of support in the Islamic Republic for Ahmadinejad's advance of Mahdism in public discourse, Iranian officials noted the renewed political activity of the Hojatieh even before the 2005 presidential elections. President Khatami's spokesman said openly in early 2003 that there were Hojatieh Society members who were infiltrating the Iranian government.[54] His minister of the interior went so far as to say that the Hojatieh represented "a clear and present danger for national security."[55]

Ahmadinejad's Mahdism had been advanced and supported by those who served as his religious mentors, particularly Ayatollah Mohammad Taqi Mesbah-e Yazdi, who attributed Ahmadinejad's victory in the presidential elections to the will of the Mahdi.[56] Like his predecessors, after he won the elections, Ahmadinejad headed for the city of Qom to meet with Iran's top clerics. Yet before sitting with the grand ayatollahs, it was noticeable that he went to consult first with Ayatollah Mesbah-e Yazdi, where the two had a high-profile exchange in a large conference room that was well attended. Moreover, Ahmadinejad's confidential advisor, Mojtabi Samarah Hashemi, is also known to be very close to Mesbah-e Yazdi. Therefore, his views are particularly important to consider.

In 2005, Mesbah-e Yazdi's monthly publication argued that the Koran "calls on believers to wage war against unbelievers and prepare the way for the advent of the Mahdi and conquering the world."[57] He has been quoted making statements that extol violence more generally: "We must wipe away the shameful stain whereby some people imagine that violence has no place in Islam."[58] One of his disciples, Mohsen Gharavian, gave a lecture at the religious seminaries in Qom providing the religious justification for actually using nuclear weapons, according to Islamic Law. The reformist Internet daily, *Rooz*, noted that it was the first time any of the top religious leaders in Iran had given explicit authorization for the use of nuclear weapons. It was the first public policy change to come out of "the Mesbah Yazdi group."[59]

Mesbah-e Yazdi's own lectures repeatedly stressed the theme of hastening the coming of the Mahdi. He spoke at an event in October 2006, marking the Mahdi's birthday. Among the actions that he considered to be the "noblest duty" were those that "weaken the control of the oppressive and tyrannical regimes over the oppressed"—which was a new religious justification of the export of the Iranian revolution. He let his audience understand that these actions can hasten "the return of the Hidden Imam." He continued: "If we wish to expedite the Mahdi's coming, we must remove any obstacles."[60] In the same address, he stressed that the "greatest obligation of those awaiting the appearance of the Mahdi is fighting heresy and *global arrogance*" (emphasis added). (Global arrogance is a euphemism, used by Ahmadinejad as well, for the West as a whole, but primarily the United States.[61])

Mesbah-e Yazdi is portrayed by his opponents as an isolated figure whose impact on past Iranian political life was very limited. However, he seems to have slowly built up a network of supporters and allies from his teaching position at the Haqqani School in Qom, where graduates attended before entering top positions in the Revolutionary Guards, the Ministry of Intelligence and Security, as well as in the Iranian Judiciary.[62]

Indeed, the Deputy Chief of Staff of the Revolutionary Guards, Brigadier General Mohammad Baqer Zolqadr, was a Haqqani graduate.[63] Moreover, three Haqqani graduates became Ministers of Intelligence and Security: the infamous Ali Fallahian (from the Mykonos and AMIA attacks), Ali Younesi, and Gholam Hossein Mohseni-Ejehei.[64] The latter, an Ahmadinejad appointment, was believed to have a Hojatieh background, as well.[65] The belief in the imminent arrival of the Mahdi made many inroads into Ahmadinejad's government.

Mesbah-e Yazdi also had influential allies like the Iranian professor, Ahmad Fardid, who, while a specialist in German philosophy, subsequently became a devoted supporter of Mahdism as well as an advocate of neo-Nazi anti-Semitic theories.[66] He may be one of the contributors to Ahmadinejad's outspoken anti-Semitism. As in the case of Mesbah-e Yazdi, Fardid's students were appointed to top positions in Iranian press and cultural institutions.[67] Fardid also served as a lecturer in the Political Bureau of the Revolutionary Guards, whose mission was to ideologically inculcate its elite personnel.[68]

There were other important religious authorities with whom Ahmadinejad met, who took strong positions advocating the study of Mahdism. One of Iran's leading hard-line clerics who supported speculation about the Mahdi was Grand Ayatollah Nouri-Hamedani from Qom. He explicitly asserted in one of his sermons that one of the pre-conditions for the Mahdi's appearance is the killing of the Jews: "One should fight the Jews and vanquish them so that conditions for the advent of the Hidden Imam can be met."[69] This might help explain how in Ahmadinejad's circles, the preoccupation with the arrival of the Mahdi and the destruction of Israel appeared at times to be mutually supportive.

Ahmadinejad's focus on the arrival of the Hidden Imam, or Mahdi, was not threatened by the Supreme Leader Ayatollah Ali Khamenei. Prior to Khamenei's entry into politics, he received his religious education not in Qom, but rather in Mashhad, where it is not uncommon to find clerics who claimed to be in direct contact with the Hidden Imam. Indeed, the founder of the Hojatieh, Sheikh Mahmoud Halabi, came out of the Mashhad seminary. Khamenei thus would not find Mahdism alien in any way. Reportedly, he told former Spanish Prime Minister Jose Maria Aznar back in 2004, before Ahmadinejad's election, that the Islamic Republic was waiting for the return of the Hidden Imam, at which time he expected the destruction of Israel and the United States.[70] Khamenei described Mesbah-e Yazdi as "one of the leading scholars of Islam."[71]

A revealing exchange between Khamenei and Ahmadinejad disclosed what were the real potential sources of tension between them. Khamenei mocked Ahmadinejad's observation that he would only serve as president for two years until the arrival of the "Lord of the Age." Ahmadinejad retorted that while the Supreme Leader thinks that he appoints the Iranian president, in fact, it was the "Lord of the Age" who made the appointment.[72] To the extent that Khamenei would have problems with Ahmadinejad, they would emanate from their potential political rivalry, for the Iranian president's Revolutionary Guards regime has progressively become an increasingly stronger center of power that could pose a challenge in the future to the clerics, especially if an alternative cleric to Khamenei were chosen to lead them.

How does Mahdism affect the nuclear issue? The Iranian internet daily *Rooz* tried to analyze the link between the two subjects: "Some of those close to Ahmadinejad, who frequently speak [of the need] to prepare the ground for the Mahdi's return, explicitly link the [fate of] the Iranian nuclear dossier to this need."[73] The article described how in private meetings, these associates of the Iranian president stressed that Iran's resistance to global pressure on the nuclear front was one of the ways to prepare the ground for the era of the Mahdi. The question of whether Iran's nuclear capabilities would help bring about the Mahdi's arrival or be used in the violent era which he would usher in is somewhat academic, since in Ahmadinejad's view, the Mahdi is to join this world imminently, and not at some distant date at the end of history. This has introduced an enormous irrational factor into the Iranian nuclear equation.

Nuclear Negotiations with Ahmadinejad

Precisely at the time Ahmadinejad had launched a "Second Islamic Revolution" and made clear his extremely hard line policies, the Bush administration decided to reverse its policy on Iran with a new diplomatic initiative towards Tehran. Part of the backdrop of this decision had been the escalation of Iranian-sponsored attacks on coalition forces in Iraq. On May 31, 2006, Secretary of State Condoleezza Rice said:

> We are agreed with our European partners on the essential elements of a package containing both benefits if Iran makes the right choice and costs if it does not. As soon as Iran fully and verifiably suspends its enrichment and reprocessing activities, the United States will come to the table with our EU colleagues and meet with Iran's representatives.[74]

The Bush administration was offering to engage with Iran, perhaps with the hope that the shift in U.S. policy would modify Iran's hardening stance on nuclear negotiations as well as its militant behavior across the Middle East. Still, the timing of the shift in Bush's policy was puzzling. Right after Ahmadinejad put together his hard-line government, Iran unilaterally removed IAEA seals on its nuclear equipment and began converting refined uranium yellowcake into UF_6 feedstock for its centrifuge enrichment plant. It appeared that the entire EU-3 diplomatic process with Iran had collapsed. Moreover, while Iran was building up its nuclear capabilities, Ahmadinejad and his regime were openly making declarations of outright hostile intent towards its neighbors, especially Israel.

The idea for engaging Iran at this point in time came from Secretary of State Condoleezza Rice, who carefully sounded out President Bush on her idea in early 2006 before pushing through the new policy.[75] The only sensible explanation for her initiative was that she was pursuing a dual-track approach with Iran. While working through the UN Security Council, the United States would go ahead and advance an escalating series of tough resolutions on Iran that would isolate Tehran and contain the threat of more severe action if the Iranians did not comply. At the same time, the United States would offer Iran a way of escaping the diplomatic noose that the UN Security Council was creating by re-engaging diplomatically with the EU-3 along with the United States, backed by the Russians and the Chinese.

Moreover, if diplomacy had failed in the past because the Iranians felt that concessions to the Europeans were a waste of time because of their limited global stature, that was about to change. With Rice's new format, Iran would no longer be negotiating with the EU-3 alone, as it had from 2003 through 2005, but with a more powerful P5 plus one: the permanent five members of the UN Security Council (Britain, France, China, Russia, and particularly the United States), as well as Germany.

The involvement of the Security Council began on March 29, 2006, when it issued a Presidential Statement on Iran. Within the Security Council there are a number of actions that can be taken before it actually adopts a resolution on a given matter: the convening of the Security Council to put an item on its agenda, a press release by the rotating president of the Security Council, and a Presidential Statement by the president of the Security Council based on an agreed text by its members.

The Security Council was already at the third step and expressed its hope that Iran would suspend its nuclear program. Four months passed, and Iran did not comply with the statement. The Security Council was left with little choice but to move to a full-blown resolution on July 31, 2006, when it adopted Resolution 1696.

Theoretically, the Iranians should have been extremely concerned. The resolution referred to the IAEA Director General's report, earlier in the year, which stated there were "outstanding issues and concerns on Iran's nuclear programme, *including topics which could have a military nuclear dimension*" (emphasis added). Additionally, the resolution noted that the IAEA was "unable to make progress in its efforts to provide assurances about the absence of undeclared nuclear material and activities in Iran." It noted with "serious concern" Iran's decision "to resume enrichment-related activities." The resolution requested that the Director General of the IAEA report to the Security Council by August 31 whether Iran suspended all its nuclear activities mentioned in the resolution, coming into compliance with its international obligations.[76]

The charges of the Security Council were extremely serious. They appeared to be backed by an implicit threat, since the resolution was adopted under Chapter VII of the UN Charter, which dealt specifically with "threats to the peace, breaches of the peace, and acts of aggression."[77] The inclusion of Chapter VII made the resolution binding international law. All the major resolutions adopted regarding Iraq back in 1990 and 1991, prior to the Gulf War, were Chapter VII resolutions and had served as the diplomatic backdrop of the internationally sanctioned use of force against Saddam Hussein.

Unfortunately, Resolution 1696 did not really have the teeth implied by the reference to Chapter VII. Russia wanted to make Iran's suspension of enrichment a legally binding obligation only by means of the resolution. It did not want to get into sanctions or even hint about the use of force in the event that Iran did not comply.[78] As a result, the resolution specifically stipulated that it was adopted under Article 40 of Chapter VII, adding that the Security Council reserved the right in the future to move to Article 41, by which the UN could impose economic sanctions, if Iran did not comply. These distinctions turned out to be critical. For example, the resolution did not mention Article 42, which contained the threat of moving to military force.

After the adoption of Resolution 1696, Russia's UN ambassador, Vitaly Churkin, spelled out the importance of these legal references:

By acting under Article 40 of the Charter, the council had rendered mandatory suspension of all uranium-enrichment activities. If Iran did not comply, members had expressed the intention to take appropriate action under Article 41. *It was crucial to note that, it followed from the resolution, any additional measures that could be required to implement the resolution ruled out the use of military force.*"[79] (emphasis added)

The Bush administration had repeatedly stated that with respect to Iran, "all options are on the table,"[80] by which it implied the threat of the use of force to move the West's nuclear diplomacy with Iran along. According to Churkin, the UN Security Council essentially removed that very threat from the table and precluded any American military option. Undoubtedly, the Russians shared their interpretation of Resolution 1696 with their Iranian allies, thereby undercutting the pressure on Iran to halt its nuclear program that should have emanated from the formal involvement of the Security Council. If the UN track was supposed to create pressures so that the negotiating track of the P-5 plus one would yield results, the watered down message that come out of the Security Council weakened the entire effort. Western diplomatic strategy against Iran had been badly impaired.

This became evident from the parallel negotiating process of the EU-3, which were still maintaining their contacts with Tehran, pending an American final decision to join the talks. The EU-3 formally presented a new incentives package to Iran on June 6, 2006. This time the incentives included a provision that the United States would join the talks with Iran. Nonetheless, the European-Iranian talks looked like they were going nowhere, especially when the Iranian side made clear that Tehran would not suspend enrichment again, as it had for a short time between 2003 and 2004, under the Tehran and Paris Agreements.

In a narrower private meeting, the EU foreign policy chief, Javier Solana, offered Iran's chief negotiator Ali Larijani a new western concession: allowing the Iranians centrifuges for research purposes.[81] This activity had been prohibited under the 2004 Paris Agreement between Iran and the EU-3. Back in 2004, Iranian Foreign Minister Kamal Kharrazi tried at the last minute to modify the Paris Agreement by obtaining this very concession from British

Foreign Secretary Jack Straw, who turned Kharrazi down. The British had been firm on this point after consulting their own nuclear authorities about its military implications.

Now Solana was dismantling an important stipulation from the EU-3's own signed agreement with Iran. The Iranians undoubtedly understood that the international environment was somehow shifting in their favor. Rice summarized the western approach to Iran in July 2006: "If the Iranians want to respond positively, I would hope that they would do so through the channel that is established between the six and the government of Iran, and that is Mr. Solana." But she added: "There is also a path ahead to the Security Council on which we are now launched."[82] She left the choice to Iran of deciding whether to go down a path of punitive sanctions or negotiations with the West.

How would Iran respond to the new proposals it received? The EU-3 gave Iran a June 22 deadline, just ahead of the formal adoption of UN Security Council Resolution 1696 in July. A day before the deadline, Ahmadinejad said that the EU-3 would get their answer on August 22, and not any earlier.[83] Ultimately, Iran's position on nuclear negotiations was a decision of the Supreme Leader Ayatollah Ali Khamenei. But through Iran's Supreme Council for National Security, where Larijani sat as its secretary, others were allowed to voice their views, as well. When the western proposals were set forward, apparently Larijani supported the idea of going forward with them as a basis for negotiations. However, Ahmadinjead opposed the western proposals.

The Iranians decided to obfuscate their true position in July—it was neither no or yes. Like his predecessors, Larijani seemed to be playing for time: "We should have more time—be patient and try to negotiate."[84] Nonetheless, a month later it appeared that the parties were prepared to take a half step forward. Privately, Larijani and Solana agreed to a plan they hoped would orchestrate a new round of negotiations in New York during September at the opening of the UN General Assembly. The formula they were pursuing was based on the idea that Iran would temporarily suspend enrichment, and the West would suspend sanctions.

The key to making their plan work was that they would make these concessions at the same time. Rice's deputy, Nick Burns, summarized the diplomatic choreography that was involved. Larijani would come to the Waldorf Astoria Hotel in New York and meet with the P-5 European foreign ministers as well as with the Russian and Chinese foreign ministers. He would accept the proposed basis of negotiations that had been worked out ahead of time with Solana. At that point, Secretary of State Condoleezza Rice would enter the room and have dinner with the Iranian negotiator along with the Europeans.[85] This way, the Bush administration would finally be diplomatically engaging with Iran.

The August 31, 2006, report from the International Atomic Energy Agency, mandated by Resolution 1696, was not reassuring. Iran was continuing to test its centrifuges for uranium enrichment at its Natanz Pilot Fuel Enrichment Plant, even though it had been put on notice by the Security Council. As recently as August 24—a week before the IAEA report—it fed UF_6 gas into a 164-machine cascade of centrifuges.[86]

During the summer months, Iran had enriched uranium "to various levels of U-235," though in June it had declared it had enriched only to a level of 5 percent U-235. This was not weapons-grade uranium that required close to 90 percent enrichment, but the leap from low-grade enriched uranium to high-grade enriched uranium was not very great. When IAEA monitors sought to see the much larger full-scale Fuel Enrichment Plant at Natanz, which was still under construction, Iran refused to grant them access. The IAEA informed the Security Council that Iran had not suspended its enrichment activities and was not acting in accordance with the Additional Protocol that it had signed with the IAEA in 2003. In short, it was defying the Security Council.

Despite the IAEA's findings, the diplomatic option with Iran still remained in play. The Bush administration feverishly prepared for the New York meeting between Rice and Larijani. At the last minute, it received word that Iran planned to provide Larijani a huge entourage of 300 officials. They would need visas into the United States, which would require the United States to process them through the weekend before the meeting, using the Swiss Embassy in Tehran as an intermediary.

American diplomats worked throughout the weekend; Iran was not to be given an excuse for cancelling what was being viewed as an historic meeting. But when the Iranian aircraft finally landed in New York, Larijani was not on board. Instead, Ahmadinejad descended from the aircraft. The Iranian president had apparently nixed Larijani's diplomatic moves. Indeed, the following year, Ahmadinejad replaced Larijani with Saeed Jalili, a close political ally who had served as Deputy Foreign Minister for European and American Affairs. It was in the foreign ministry where he worked closely with Mojtabi Samareh Hashemi, another Ahmadinejad confidante who, as noted earlier, was a student of Ayatollah Mesbah-e Yazdi.[87] Whether the new Secretary of Iran's Supreme National Security Council and chief UN negotiator actually subscribed to the same Mahdist doctrines was difficult to establish. But it was clear that he came from the same circles as Ahmadinejad, Samareh, and the new hard-liners that dominated the Iranian regime and its nuclear policies.

Iran had plainly violated the August 31 deadline imposed by the UN Security Council. It had also failed to exploit the negotiating track with Secretary Rice and the P-5 in New York, the following month. Ahmadinejad remained defiant of the United States and its western allies. He soon announced that Iran was planning to install 60,000 centrifuges in its Natanz nuclear enrichment facility. But the reaction in the UN Security Council was not as forceful as it should have been. Though it moved for the first time on December 23, 2006, to formally impose sanctions on Iran through the adoption Resolution 1737, it was ultimately a watered-down document.

For example, it could have imposed a travel ban on those involved in the Iranian nuclear program. Indeed, it listed in a special annex the individuals and entities engaged in Iran's ballistic missile and nuclear programs, specifying that the commander of the Revolutionary Guards, Major General Yahya Rahim Safavi, was involved in both. Instead, however, it only called on states to "exercise vigilance" if people listed in the annex entered the territories of UN member states. Like Resolution 1696, it based itself not on Chapter VII as a whole, but only on Article 41 of Chapter VII, thereby leaving out the threat to use force, if necessary, that appeared in Article 42.

Iran utterly rejected the new UN resolution, calling it invalid and even illegal. Upbeat about the Security Council's action, French Foreign Minister Philippe Douste-Blazy said that the resolution gave Iran a clear choice of cooperating with the international community or facing increased isolation.[88] Undersecretary of State Nick Burns called the resolution "a powerful message to Iran."[89] Tehran did not seem impressed. By its response in New York, Iran implied it did not care about the threat of being isolated. Even more worrisome was its response with even more escalatory moves on the ground as it stepped up its involvement in the Iraq War. Whether the United States and its western allies would develop a more effective strategy to cope with this challenge than they managed to craft in New York would remain to be seen.

Who Controls the Revolutionary Guards' Quds Force?

While the diplomatic option at the United Nations faltered, evidence of Iranian complicity with the Iraqi insurgency only grew. Iran had not been intimidated by the actions of the UN Security Council; it seemed almost emboldened. In December 2006, U.S. forces in Iraq captured Brigadier General Mohsen Shirazi and Colonel Abu Ahmad Davari, two senior officers in the Quds

Force, the special unit of the Revolutionary Guards that engaged in subversion beyond Iran's borders.[90] Shirazi was the third highest-ranking officer in the Quds Force and certainly the highest-ranking officer in the Iranian armed forces that was ever captured by the United States.[91]

The United States had intelligence about the presence of more senior Iranians in Iraq. A U.S. raid on an Iranian liaison office in the Iraqi Kurdish city of Irbil sought to capture General Minojahar Frouzanda, the Revolutionary Guards' Chief of Intelligence, and Mohammed Jafari, the deputy secretary of Iran's Supreme National Security Council. The two Iranians escaped before being captured, but U.S. forces managed to take five junior-level officers belonging to the Quds Force prisoner in Irbil.[92]

The Quds Force involvement was escalating beyond the supply of Iranian weaponry. It had trained "secret cells" belonging to Moqtada al-Sadr's Mahdi Army that orchestrated an attack on U.S. forces in Karbala on January 20, 2007, killing five Americans. One was killed at the start of the raid while the other four were captured and then shot to death. The presence of senior Iranian officers in Iraq during late 2006 and early 2007 raised the question of whether Iran was now more openly entering the Iraq War on the side of the insurgent forces.

The Bush administration appeared to be speaking in two different voices on the Quds Force's involvement. White House Press Secretary Tony Snow directly linked the Quds Force operations in Iraq to Iran's Supreme Leader, Ayatollah Ali Khamenei, and to "senior government leadership" in Iran. Snow's position was backed up by at least three U.S. intelligence analysts. At the same time, President Bush reflected the view of the Chairman of the Joint Chiefs of Staff that the United States lacked the specific intelligence to prove Quds Forces operations in Iraq had been approved by the Iranian leadership.[93]

Bush himself stated on February 14, 2007: "We also know that the Quds Force is part of the Iranian government....What we don't know is whether or not the head leaders of Iran ordered the Quds Force to do what they did."[94] He plainly stated that "the Quds force is a part of the Iranian government." But then Bush added: "Whether Ahmadinejad ordered the Quds force to do this, I don't know."[95]

Major media outlets also began to convey the position that Quds Force operations in Iraq may have been conducted without the authority of Iran's top leadership. On February 17, 2007, Scott Shane wrote in the *New York Times* that the Quds Force may have conducted a rogue operation. *Newsweek* presented a charitable explanation of the Quds Force presence in Iraq, asserting that the Iranian force was there to help the Iraqi government in its relations with the Shiite militias. CNN's Christiane Amanpour compared the Quds Force in Iraq to cultural or educational attaches in Iranian embassies.[96]

General David Petraeus, the senior U.S. commander in Iraq in 2007, listened to the internal American debate and said he was "mystified."[97] As far as he was concerned, Iran's Supreme Leader, Ayatollah Ali Khamenei "can't not know" about the involvement of the Quds Force in Iraq. He explained that what the Quds Force was doing in Iraq was a "massive operation." It was also extensive in one other respect: the Quds Force was helping the Sunni insurgents as well. Indeed, he explained that one of the Sunni insurgent leaders was recently in Tehran itself. U.S. forces would subsequently substantiate Petraeus's contention when they captured a Quds Force officer in the Northern Iraqi city of Sulaymaniyah, where there was no Shiite presence. He was involved in trafficking Explosively Formed Penetrators (EFP) for roadside bombs, which were being used at the time in areas controlled by Sunni insurgents.[98]

Petraeus also laid out how the command and control of the Quds Force worked to support his argument about Iran's direct responsibility for what was happening. Its commander, Brigadier General Qassem Suleimani, reported directly to Khamenei—and not to Ahmadinejad. Sulaimani apparently sought to promote operations that would wear out U.S. forces in Iraq and keep them engaged in Iraq, at the same time.[99] The Quds Force was so ubiquitous in Iraq, as Petraeus later noted, even Iran's envoy to Baghdad, Hassan Kazemi-Qomi, was a former Quds Force member.[100] Considering the scale of the Quds Force intervention in Iraq, the chances that it was running a rogue operation looked increasingly remote.

U.S. forces in Iraq continued to disclose information that eventually put this debate to rest. Brigadier General Kevin J. Bergner, who was the military spokesman, gave a press briefing in Baghdad on July 2, 2007. He explained that the "secret cells" operating out of Moqtada al-Sadr's Mahdi Army were armed, financed, and directed by Iran's Quds Force. He left little doubt that the Iranian government knew what the Quds Forces was doing. Bergner stated that U.S. intelligence indicated that "the senior leadership in Iran is aware of this activity."[101]

The Iraqi Shiite cells, moreover, were trained inside Iran by the Quds Force with the help of Lebanese Hizbullah. On a separate occasion, Petraeus focused on the Hizbullah dimension. He explained that "Lebanese Hizbullah Department 2800" was a specialized organization that had been established "to support the training, arming, funding, and in some cases, direction of militia extremists by the Iranian Republican Guards Corps' Quds Force."[102]

Bergner provided details to reporters that could also substantiate this argument. The United States had captured Ali Musa Daqduq in Iraq, a Lebanese citizen who commanded a special operations unit within Hizbullah. Since 2005, he had worked with the Quds Force to take groups of twenty to sixty Iraqi Shiites for training at three military camps near Tehran. Hizbullah operatives were extremely useful for the Quds Force. They had expertise in setting up secret military networks from their experience in Lebanon. And on the practical side, the Lebanese Shiites spoke Arabic and could communicate easily with the Iraqi Shiites; in contrast, the majority of Iranians involved in training only spoke Farsi.

Under interrogation, Daqduq and two other Iraqi Shiites stated that the senior leadership of the Quds Force supported the planning of the Karbala attack against U.S. forces in January 2007 that left five Americans dead. A captured 22-page document on the Karbala raid detailed how the Quds Force itself provided reconnaissance for the operation with information about the movements of American soldiers; Bergner told how the Quds Force had developed detailed information "regarding our soldiers' activities, shift changes, and defenses." Most importantly, he added that "this information was shared with the attackers."

There were other signs of Iranian escalation in Iraq at the time. Mortar and rocket teams that were trained in Iran launched high-trajectory weaponry at the Green Zone in Baghdad, where the United States and other international bodies had their headquarters. Major General Joseph Fil, who commanded coalition forces in Baghdad, admitted in June 2007 that "much of the indirect fire that we receive especially in that which is pointed at the International Zone, the Green Zone, is in fact Iranian."[103] He further elaborated, "When we check the tail fins of the mortars, when we find the rockets—and frequently we're able to find them preemptively, before they actually launch... there's no doubt that they're coming out of Iran."

Iranian brinksmanship with the West seemed to intensify. In southern Iraq, a team of fifteen British Marines were on a routine mission inspecting Iraqi territorial waters in the Shatt al-Arab waterway, when six naval craft belonging to the Revolutionary Guards intercepted them and took them hostage. It was not the first time British sailors had been captured by the Iranians; a similar instance occurred in 2004, when Iran captured eight sailors for three days claiming they had entered Iranian waters.

In this case, however, London was certain that their crew had not drifted into Iranian territorial waters, making this incident look like a deliberate provocation. The British Marines were eventually released. Ahmadinejad made the announcement at the end of a ceremony at which he pinned medals on the Revolutionary Guards who had seized them. But his appearance at the ceremony was misleading, since the Revolutionary Guards formally answer to Khameini, not to Ahmadinejad, despite all the political networks he had developed linking his presidency to their power in Iran.

The debate over whether the Iranian government itself had authorized the activities of the Quds Force in Iraq was odd. If U.S. Navy Seals were engaged in special operations, would anyone have any doubt that their use had been approved through the U.S. chain of command? It was as though a new standard of proof was being demanded from the U.S. intelligence establishment before Iranian culpability could be established. The United States would have to produce the signed orders by the Iranian political echelon to the Quds Forces or an electronic intercept of a telephone conversation. Moreover, of all the units of the Iranian armed forces, the command and control of the Quds Force was probably one of the tightest. Its commander reported directly to the Supreme Leader, Ayatollah Ali Khamenei, and did not have to restrict himself by first going to the Revolutionary Guards' commander.

The probable explanation for the doubt that was expressed over whether the Quds Force was operating under orders was political. If President Bush acknowledged that the Quds Force had been ordered by the Iranian government to conduct operations in Iraq that led to the killing of Americans, then he would have no choice but to retaliate even if his response led to open conflict with Iran. The Chairman of the Joint Chiefs of Staff, General Peter Pace, carefully offered an analysis that came close to accusing Iran without crossing this line; he said that Iran was "complicit" in the provision of weapons designed to kill U.S. forces.[104] He also issued a warning: "We will do all we need to do defend our troops in Iraq by going after the entire network, regardless of where those people come from."[105]

On the diplomatic level, the United States left the door open for diplomatic engagement in early 2007. Secretary of State Condoleezza Rice offered to meet her Iranian counterpart "anytime, anywhere" to discuss every facet of U.S.-Iranian relations. Starting on March 10, 2007, the United States actually engaged Iranian diplomats about stabilizing the situation in Iraq. Regular bilateral meetings between the U.S. ambassador to Iraq, Ryan Crocker, and the Iranian ambassador to Iraq, Hassan Kazemi Qomi, started on May 28. The readiness of the United States to sit down with the Iranians did not appear to ameliorate the Iranian-supported attacks on the ground that the Coalition military command was describing at the same time in mid-2007.

The repeated talk of how the United States would engage Iran and persuade it to drop its nuclear programs was losing credibility in light of Iran's continued defiance of the UN Security Council. For example, Undersecretary of State Burns held a press conference at the Waldorf-Astoria a year after Larijani failed to arrive for talks with the Bush administration at the opening of the UN General Assembly. Burns was asked: "Mr. Secretary, why is that a good idea to have Solana engage with Larijani again, given that past discussions have yielded nothing in the directions of suspension."[106]

Burns did not have a good answer. All he could say in response was: "Because we are dedicated to a peaceful diplomatic solution. That is the great desire of the United States and, I can say, of the other countries of the P5, that we want to try to achieve a negotiated solution. If you're serious about that—and we are—then you have to have engage in direct discussions." He sounded like an official who was better at articulating his faith in the diplomatic process than at clarifying the strategy that was needed to make it work: "We can't give up on diplomacy. We've decided not to give up on diplomacy."[107] Burns was an extremely experienced diplomat. It was just that the West as a whole, and not just Burns, did not have any good answers for dealing with Iran's drive for nuclear weapons. And all its past efforts to block Iran were simply failing.

Chapter 10:

The Iranian Octopus: Tehran's Subversion Across the Middle East

BAHRAIN IS A SMALL, INDEPENDENT Arab kingdom, roughly 665 square kilometers in size, located on an archipelago in the Persian Gulf that is strategically located right next to the oil-rich Eastern Province of Saudi Arabia. Ruled by the al-Khalifa family, who are Sunni Muslims, 70 percent of its population is Shiite. They have long been the object of Iranian efforts to incite an armed revolt and the emergence of a pro-Iranian regime through a Bahraini branch of Hizbullah. In 2007, important Iranian political figures renewed old territorial claims to the archipelago that had been last voiced by the Shah at the time of Bahrain's independence from Britain in 1971. Like Iraq, Bahrain has increasingly appeared to be a target for Iranian expansionism.

Hossein Shariatmadari, the powerful editor of the Iranian daily *Kayhan* and unofficial spokesman for the Supreme Leader Ayatollah Ali Khamenei, wrote on July 9, 2007, that "Bahrain is part of Iran's soil."[1] He added that "the principal demand of the Bahraini people today is to return this province, which was separated from Iran, to its mother, Islamic Iran."[2]

Shariatmadari's postion on Bahrain was backed up several days later by officials belonging to the Basij, the paramilitary militia of the Revolutionary Guards, in interviews they gave to Kayhan.[3] Days after that, an Iranian member of parliament who also sat on its National Security and Foreign Policy Committee released a statement that should have worried not only Bahrain but all its Arab neighbors. He reminded the Arab states as a whole that "most of them were once part of Iranian soil, when [Iran] stretched from Egypt to Syria."[4]

Finally, on February 10, 2009, Ali Akbar Nateq-Nouri, who was an advisor to Khamenei and his hand-picked choice for president of Iran in 1997, voiced again the Iranian claim to Bahrain, describing it as Iran's "14th province" in the past.[5] During a speech on the 30th anniversary of the Islamic Revolution, he reminded his listeners of the history of Bahrain, noting that "one of our provinces was taken from us."[6] For the Arab Gulf states, Iran's rhetoric had to be reminiscent of Iraqi declarations that Kuwait was to become Iraq's 19th province at the beginning of the Gulf War in 1990.

Given this background, probably no other country is as sensitive to every nuance of Iranian hegemonic ambitions as Bahrain. It was noteworthy when Bahrain's former chief of staff, General Khalifa ibn Ahmad, voiced his view of Iran in a high-profile interview in the London-based Arabic daily al-Hayat on May 16, 2008. Though retired, he was still a member of Bahrain's royal family. Looking at what was happening across the Arab world, he compared Iran to "an octopus," whose tentacles were reaching everywhere in the Middle East, since it was "rummaging around in Iraq, Kuwait, Lebanon, Gaza, and Bahrain."[7] He was clearly suggesting that Iran was behind much of the destabilization of the Middle East.

The Bahraini general's comments had a local context as well. In late October 2007, Bahrain itself was struck yet again by violent rioting from militant elements of its Shiite population that sought to topple the al-Khalifa government. Two years earlier, large Shiite crowds marched in Manama, Bahrain's capital, while shouting their support for Ayatollah Ali Khamenei.[8] Back in the 1990s, Bahraini representatives presented evidence in Washington of the involvement of the Quds Force in an attempted coup. With the headquarters of the U.S. Fifth Fleet located in Bahrain since 1995, any Iranian-sponsored coup that led to the eviction of the U.S. Navy would have enormous strategic implications. It would represent a major blow to the entire American naval presence in the Persian Gulf, degrading the West's ability to defend the oil-producing areas that were located there, and leave the entire area completely open to Iran's domination.

The perception of Iran's growing encroachment was widespread in many Arab countries. Responding to the Hamas takeover in the Gaza Strip in mid-2007, and the deepening ties between Hamas and the Iranian leadership, Egyptian President Hosni Mubarak once quipped that a new situation had emerged with "Egypt in practice having a border with Iran."[9] As Iran sought to spread Shiism in the Arab world, Mubarak openly questioned whether Sunni Muslim states could ever trust their Shiite minorities, which he said were ultimately loyal to Iran—and not to the countries in which they lived.[10]

Some Sudanese feared the spread of Iranian influence in their country as well. One Sudanese writer described how Iran had turned its embassy in Khartoum into a center for spreading Shiism in Sudan: "We should be aware of the Shiite octopus in Sudan, before it is too late—otherwise, the day will come when we see tanks of the Sudanese Hizbullah racing through the streets of Khartoum."[11]

The editor-in-chief of the Kuwaiti daily *al-Siyassa*, Ahmad al-Jarallah, bluntly wrote in 2007: "The entire Arab world is in danger" from Iran's policies. He warned that "Iran is trying to extend its aggressive policies to all the Gulf countries and to Egypt."[12]

In Yemen, on the western side of the Arabian Peninsula, President Ali Abdullah Saleh's ruling General People's Congress Party accused Iran of supporting an armed insurgency in 2004—known as the al-Houthi Rebellion—by Yemen's Zaydi Shiites (who differ from Iranian Shiites over the succession of the Fifth Imam in 713—they chose Zayd al-Baqir over his brother Muhammad and are hence called "fivers" or Zaydis).[13] Despite their doctrinal differences, mainstream Twelver Shiites have demonstrated some degree of protectiveness to the Yemeni adherents of Fiver Shiism from threats from the Sunni majority.[14] Yemeni officials have asserted that during the 1980s, Yemeni Shiites underwent training in Iran during the rule of Ayatollah Khomeini, and prepared themselves to eventually launch a rebellion against the state.[15]

According to Abu al-Hareth Muhammad al-Oufi, a former field commander of al-Qaeda in the Arabian Peninsula, the al-Houthi rebels in Yemen were working with both al-Qaeda and Iranian intelligence.[16] Muhammad Al-Oufi was released from Guantanamo Bay in November 2007 and took part in a Saudi rehabilitation program before returning to al-Qaeda in Yemen. After turning himself in to Saudi authorities in February 2009, he revealed that his units were conducting surveillance operations in Saudi Arabia in order to strike at its oil installations.[17] Thus, by creating local alliances in Yemen's insurgency war, Iran was able to extend its influence to Saudi Arabia's south and pose a threat to its petroleum resources from both sides of the Arabian peninsula.

Jordan's King Abdullah had been concerned about the Iranian threat for years. In 2004, he warned in the *Washington Post* of a new Shiite crescent that was encircling the Arab world, beginning in Iran, running through Iraq to Syria, whose Alawite leadership was recognized as truly Muslim only by Lebanese Shiite clerics in the 1970s—but never by Sunni religious leaders.[18] (The Alawites were an offshoot of Shiism who incorporated elements of Christianity and pre-Islamic religious practices in their faith; they amounted to less than 20 percent of the Syrian population, but the ruling Assad family and many senior Syrian officers are Alawites.) The end point for Abdullah's Shiite crescent was Lebanon, where the Shiites make up at least 35 percent of the population and benefit from having their own powerful militia, Hizbullah.

One of Jordan's leading newspapers wrote in January 2007 about a conspiracy to spread Shiism across the Middle East and South Asia, from Egypt to India.[19] Indeed, concern over the spread of Iranian influence even reached the far western end of the Arab world. In early March 2009, Morocco severed its diplomatic relations with Iran, charging that Tehran was using the Iranian Embassy in Rabat to spread Shiism.[20] Iran's ascendancy and determination to become the hegemonic power in the region elevated the fears of Middle Eastern leaders from North Africa to the Persian Gulf.

Iran Deepens Its Role in Lebanon: The 2006 Second Lebanon War

The growth of Iranian power in Lebanon dates back to the early 1980s with the establishment of pro-Iranian Shiite militias, who eventually became Hizbullah, backed by a contingent of Revolutionary Guards deployed from Iran. When Israel Defense Forces unilaterally withdrew on May 24, 2000, from its previously declared security zone in Southern Lebanon, the scale of the Iranian presence fundamentally changed.

Iran had always maintained strong relations with Syria, which reinforced its power in Lebanon. For years, Iranian aircraft would fly into Damascus International Airport and unload large amounts of weapons into trucks, which were transported across the Syrian border to Hizbullah bases in Lebanon's Bekaa Valley.

However, Iran's power massively increased after the death of Syrian president Hafez al-Assad in 2000 and the succession of his son, Bashar al-Assad. Syria was pulled closer into the Iranian orbit, even taking on the attributes of an Iranian satellite.

Tehran invested heavily in all aspects of the Syrian economy, particularly in the energy sector.[21] More importantly, Iran provided increasing military assistance to Syria and financed some of its weapons purchases from Russia. There were far greater numbers of Iranian military personnel actually stationed in Syria under Bashar Assad than in the days of his father, Hafez al-Assad. Steadily, Tehran built up the groundwork to convert Syria into a platform for projecting its power and influence.

As former Syrian Vice President Abd al-Halim Khaddam disclosed as recently as January 2009, "Iran is involved in the very heart of the regime—in its security agencies, in its military forces, in its economic [institutions], and in its mosques."[22] Khaddam quipped that "the Mufti of Syria is like an Iranian preacher." There has been increasing talk of Iranian attempts at seeking the "Shi'ization" of eastern Syria.[23] As one Arab analyst concluded: "Tehran is exporting Khomeini's Islamic Revolution to the Arab world with force—and the gateway for export is Arab Syria."[24] Growing Syrian dependence on Iran helped set the stage for creating a military axis for building up the military power of Hizbullah.

The Israeli withdrawal from Lebanese territory theoretically removed Hizbullah's reason for continuing the war with Israel. A UN team consisting of representatives of UN Secretary-General Kofi Annan had carefully inspected the line of Israel's withdrawal and verified that Israel was no longer sitting in Lebanese territory. The whole argument for justifying Hizbullah's war against Israel—liberating Lebanese soil from the Israeli army—was expected to collapse, whether it was made externally to the international community or internally to the Lebanese people.

However, the Iranians had a deep interest in continuing to fight Israel—which they instigated from their increased position of power in Syria. Therefore, Hizbullah came up with a new *causus belli*—Israel's continuing presence in the Shebaa Farms, a small piece of territory approximately 24 square miles in area within the

Golan Heights, which was contested since 1967 between Israel and Syria, but which Hizbullah now claimed was really Lebanese territory given to Lebanon by Syria in 1951.[25] There was no proof that such a transfer of territory had in fact occurred at that time; according to a report issued by Secretary-General Annan, Lebanese Army maps from before 1967 showed the Shebaa Farms to have been Syrian territory.[26] The Syrian Census of 1960 showed the Shebaa Farms to have been part of Syria, as well.[27]

Nonetheless, Hizbullah had very tangible interests motivating them to make this argument. Back in 1989, when the Lebanese Civil War came to an end with the Saudi-sponsored Taif Accord, all the Lebanese militias were supposed to disarm. Only Hizbullah refused, arguing that it needed its weapons in order "to resist the Israeli occupation." Thus, Hizbullah needed the grievance of the Shebaa Farms in order to fend off demands for it to dismantle its militia, so that it could retain its arms and remain a powerful military force that could dominate Lebanon internally. And if Hizbullah could make the case that it needed its weapons, then Iran could retain its influence through Hizbullah upon Lebanese affairs.

While the Lebanese Government formally backed the new Hizbullah demand, other Lebanese leaders like Walid Jumblatt, who was a Lebanese Druze, rejected the argument that the area of the Shebaa Farms was ever Lebanese. An Arab commentator in the London-based Arabic daily *al-Hayat* frankly admitted that most Lebanese had never heard of the Shebaa Farms question before Hizbullah raised it.[28] He called the demand to re-draw Lebanon's boundaries with the Shebaa Farms an effort to construct "Persian Borders," which were being sought by Hizbullah in order to keep open a window for Revolutionary Iran to insert itself in the region.

The point was that there was no serious reason for the conflict between Lebanon and Israel to continue, given the weakness of Hizbullah's claim, unless a third party like Iran had a direct interest in sustaining a dispute with Israel as a pretext for future escalation.

For example, it was clear that Iran wanted to convert Lebanon into a launching pad for its rocket forces against Israel. Beginning in 2001 (after the Israeli withdrawal), Iran transferred massive numbers of rockets to Hizbullah in Lebanon that could strike deep into Israel, well beyond the reach of the standard 12-mile range Katyusha rocket that Hizbullah had deployed for many years. These new rockets included 25-mile range Fajr-3 rockets and 45-mile range Fajr-5 rockets.[29] In the narrow geography of the Middle East, these upgraded ranges fundamentally altered the impact of this weaponry. In a later transfer, Iranians also supplied the Zalzal rocket, whose range reached between 125 and 150 miles. A member of Hizbullah's political bureau boasted in 2001 that with these new weapons, "2.5 million Israelis are now in range of our missiles."[30]

There was some analogy between what Iran was doing with Lebanon and what the Soviet Union did in Cuba back in 1962, during the Cold War. At that time, Moscow was only developing its intercontinental range missiles, which were not fully reliable, so it sought to deploy its more reliable intermediate range missiles next to the southern United States as a stopgap measure.

In 1998, Iran had focused on Shahab-3 missiles that could hit Israel from Iranian territory; by sending thousands of missiles to Lebanon in 2001, it had a ready-to-use force deployed right next to Northern Israel. Given the admission of a former Hizbullah secretary-general that the organization was in fact "an integral part of the Iranian intelligence apparatus," the new rocket forces in the hands of Hizbullah were essentially in the hands of Iran itself.[31] Certainly, were Israel to even consider pre-emptively striking any part of Iran's nuclear weapons infrastructure, it would have to expect Iran to use the Hizbullah rocket force in retaliation. Iran had always viewed the export of its revolution to Lebanon through its Shiite community as a paramount interest.

Thus from 2000 through 2006, the Israeli-Lebanese border remained tense as Hizbullah, serving Iran, kept alive the conflict with Israel. Hizbullah kidnapped three Israeli soldiers from the Israeli side of the security fence in the area of the Shebaa Farms on October 7, 2000, only five months after the Israeli withdrawal from Lebanon. Less than two years later, on March 12, 2002, Palestinian terrorists, acting for Hizbullah, penetrated Israeli territory in the area of the town of Shlomi, killing five Israeli citizens and one Israeli officer. Hizbullah sought again to kidnap Israeli soldiers along the border on November 21, 2005, using rocket fire against Israeli towns like Kiryat Shmona and Nahariya. Hizbullah rocket fire against Israeli towns and villages continued the following year in May 2006.[32]

When the Second Lebanon War began on July 12, 2006, the Israeli-Lebanese front had not been quiet. The incident that sparked the war was a Hizbullah attack on Israeli territory which killed three Israeli soldiers on patrol and led to the kidnapping of two others. Within hours, a total of eight Israeli soldiers had been killed, including members of a force sent into southern Lebanon to rescue their kidnapped colleagues. Hizbullah unleashed rocket forces with a barrage that covered much of Northern Israel.

The day after the kidnapping, the Israeli Air Force went after Hizbullah's Iranian-supplied Fajr rocket forces, destroying fifty-nine stationary launchers in thirty-four minutes.[33] Hizbullah thought that the locations of its Iranian-supplied rocket forces were a secret, but after the Israeli air strike, up to two-thirds of its strategic force was destroyed.[34] Later, Israel attacked the Zalzal rockets, as well. But for much of the war that followed, Hizbullah was still able to fire more than 200 short-range Katyusha rockets a day at Israeli civilian targets.[35] Formally, the Second Lebanon War pitted Israel against Hizbullah, but the Israeli defense establishment saw it as a war between Israel and Iran.

What motivation did Iran have to launch a war against Israel in July 2006? Reportedly, Ali Larijani, Iran's chief nuclear negotiator and also the secretary of Iran's Supreme National Security Council, visited Damascus the very day the war broke out on July 12.

At the time, Iran was facing international pressures concerning its continuing nuclear enrichment program. Ahmadinejad had agreed to give the EU-3 an answer by August 22 concerning their latest package of proposals to Iran which sought to reestablish a suspension of all enrichment and reprocessing activities. There was also a second deadline of August 31, by which the IAEA had to report to the UN Security Council if Iran had indeed complied with Resolution 1696 and halted its nuclear activities accordingly.

Certainly, an Israeli-Hizbullah crisis over Lebanon could provide a needed diversion of international attention from Iran back to the Arab-Israeli conflict and a respite for Iranian diplomacy. Iran had used escalation in Iraq to serve its negotiating interests on the nuclear issue. In fact, it was reported that Larijani threatened the West in January 2006 that if Iran was pushed too hard on the nuclear question, it could not rule out "dragging the region into war."[36]

Iran acted suspiciously weeks later, as though it had something to hide. For when Larijani came back to Damascus on July 27, as the Second Lebanon War raged on, the Iranian Foreign Ministry tried to deny his visit, even though it had been reported by several Iranian news agencies.[37] The news reports indicated that Larijani met there with Hizbullah's secretary-general, Hassan Nasrallah. Iran may have wanted to get all the benefits of the crisis along the Israeli-Lebanese border without being assigned any responsibility for its outbreak.

Whether Iran only wanted a controlled crisis—and not a full-scale war that prematurely disclosed its rocket capabilities—is difficult to establish. Regardless of the level of conflict it sought, the Second Lebanon War demonstrated that Iran had the power to destabilize a part of the Middle East that was hundreds of miles from its borders. Moreover, it was prepared to use this influence to serve its national interests.

The Second Lebanon War unveiled how Iran had worked steadily to build up Hizbullah's military capabilities in the preceding years.

It turned out that Iran had trained many Hizbullah operatives in Lebanon at facilities in the Bekaa Valley in the east. It also brought hundreds of operatives to Iran for training by the Quds Force; interrogations of captured Hizbullah members revealed that they trained at the Imam Ali Camp in Tehran and at the Bahonar Camp, near Karaj.[38] The Quds Force was also integrated into Hizbullah's command structure during the war and armed it more like an Iranian division rather than like a pure terrorist organization.[39]

Hizbullah did not win the Second Lebanon War. As noted earlier, the Israeli Air Force succeeded in destroying a large portion of its stock of long-range rockets at the outset of the conflict. It also demolished Hizbullah's headquarters in Beirut. But Hizbullah itself was not destroyed by Israel's operation and still managed to launch short-range rockets into Northern Israel, especially at the port city of Haifa, until the end of the war. By embedding their short-range rockets in densely populated areas, Hizbullah limited the Israeli Air Force's freedom of action to use airpower to suppress the remaining rocket-fire. They effectively turned the Lebanese people into human shields. Because Hizbullah was not crushed and still could operate at the war's end, its leaders claimed victory against Israel.

Clearly, Iran's influence in Lebanon did not diminish because of the war. Tehran replaced all of the weaponry that Hizbullah lost and in fact greatly expanded its pre-war arsenal—all in defiance of UN Security Council Resolution 1701, which prohibited such weapons supplies. The UN secretary-general reported that he had received information from Israeli sources that by early 2008, Hizbullah had 10,000 long-range rockets and another 20,000 short-range rockets at its disposal.[40] Israel's defense minister, Ehud Barak, told the Knesset's Foreign Affairs and Defense Committee that Hizbullah possessed "three times as many rockets as it did prior to the Second Lebanon War."[41]

For Iran, the Second Lebanon war was as much a war against the United States as it was against Israel. By early 2008, Hizbullah could flex its military muscles in the heart of Beirut, intimidating the pro-American government of Prime Minister Fouad Siniora and its supporters who led the 2005 "Cedar Revolution" against the Syrian presence in Lebanon. Hizbullah pulled back from the Lebanese capital after overrunning it, but it managed to get Siniora to grant it new veto powers within the Lebanese government. In short, Iran's influence over Lebanese decision-making by means of Hizbullah had been enhanced.

Iran's direct control in Lebanon also grew. In the aftermath of the 2008 assassination in Damascus of Hizbullah's head of overseas operations, Imad Mughniyeh, Iran deployed Revolutionary Guard and intelligence officers to take direct command over Hizbullah units and operations, so that the organization became even more integrated into the Iranian Armed Forces.[42] There was even a report that Brigadier General Qassem Suleimani, the commander of the Quds Force, visited Southern Lebanon toward the end of 2008.[43] Undoubtedly, the Second Lebanon War strengthened all aspects of Iran's grip on Lebanon.

Iran's Beachhead in the Gaza Strip

When Israel unilaterally withdrew the last of its military and civilian presence from the Gaza Strip in 2005, it expected that a more stable situation would emerge in its south. After all, the Palestinians' ongoing political grievance that Israel occupied part of the territory that was slated to become a Palestinian state had been addressed. And while Israel was within its rights under UN Security Council Resolution 242 to retain parts of the Gaza Strip for what the resolution called "secure boundaries," it decided to leave every square inch of Gaza territory to remove any pretext for the Palestinian organizations to threaten Israel from the Gaza Strip.

Critics of the withdrawal pointed specifically to the dangers entailed by leaving what the Israel Defense Forces had code-named the Philadelphia Route—a hundred meter-wide strip of land on the border between Southern Gaza and Egyptian Sinai. Hamas and other Palestinian organizations had erected tunnels under the Philadelphia Route for smuggling weapons. With Israel out of the Philadelphia Route, and no longer taking measures against the tunnels, the quality and quantities of weapons going into the Gaza Strip would undoubtedly increase.

In January 2006, several months after Israel's Gaza pullout, the Palestinian Authority held parliamentary elections in the West Bank and the Gaza Strip, and surprisingly Fatah, the party of the late PLO leader Yasser Arafat, was defeated. Instead, Hamas won the election. Hamas was essentially the Palestinian branch of the Muslim Brotherhood, and as a Sunni Muslim organization, it traditionally benefitted from the support of Sunni Arab states, especially Saudi Arabia. In recent years, however, it decided to draw closer to Iran.

Indeed, in the struggle between Fatah and Hamas in the Gaza Strip, during a massive Fatah demonstration on January 6, 2007, the Hamas were openly decried with the crowd chanting "Shia, Shia, Shia" because of their close association with Iran.[44] A tense power-sharing arrangement emerged by which Fatah controlled the Palestinian Authority presidency through Mahmoud Abbas (Abu Mazen), and Hamas dominated the Palestinian government as well as the Parliament.

The rise of the Hamas government opened new opportunities for Iran's policy of de-stabilization. There was a clear escalation in attacks against Israel, rather than the more peaceful outcome that had been expected. Hamas and its allied organizations had been using domestically produced Qassam rockets against Israeli civilian targets since 2001, but in relatively small numbers. In all of 2005, there had been 179 rocket attacks. But in 2006, in the year following Israel's pullout and the Hamas election victory, the number of attacks shot up to 946—an increase of 500 percent.[45]

Moreover, rather than employ just the domestically-produced Qassam with a limited range of six miles, Hamas began using imported Katyusha rockets with double the range that could hit larger Israeli cities. In 2006, the Israeli city of Ashkelon, with over 100,000 residents, was hit for the first time with Katyusha rockets. In the meantime, right before the start of Second Lebanon War, Hamas launched a Hizbullah-style operation by entering Israeli territory and kidnapping an Israeli soldier, Gilad Shalit, whom it held hostage.

Iran only deepened its influence in Gaza in subsequent years. Hamas operatives left the Gaza Strip with regularity to go to Egypt and then to Syria, and finally to Iran for training. Israeli forces found evidence of Iranian influence when they learned that Hamas was manufacturing its own explosively formed projectiles (EFP), not unlike those that were being used in Iraq.[46] A senior Israeli officer reported that Iranians were coming into Gaza in order to inspect the situation and to hold training exercises.[47]

Hamas tightened its grip on Gaza eighteen months after the Palestinian elections that brought it to power. In June 2007, it launched a violent takeover of the Gaza Strip, ending its power sharing arrangements with the Palestinian Authority and Fatah. According to Tawfik Tirawi, the head of Palestinian Authority intelligence, the Hamas coup in Gaza "was coordinated with Iran which provided training and weapons and was informed of every step."[48] Egypt's Foreign Ministry also pinned the blame for the Hamas takeover on Tehran.[49]

Through indirect contacts and intense Egyptian mediation, Israel and Hamas reached a temporary truce, called in Arabic a *tahdiya*, that went into effect on June 19, 2008. Iran exploited the time of the *tahdiya* to export more potent weaponry to the Gaza Strip. Even longer-range Katyusha rockets entered at this time, which brought into range for the first time the Israeli port city of Ashdod as well as Israel's largest city in the south, Beersheba. By November 2008, Hamas launched a new abduction operation, which the Israeli Defense Forces succeeded in thwarting, but a severe escalation between the parties followed. Hamas had no

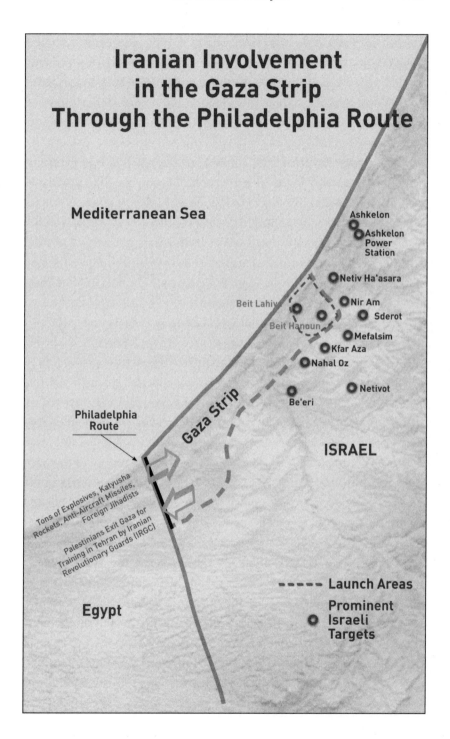

Iranian Involvement in the Gaza Strip Through the Philadelphia Route

Mediterranean Sea

Ashkelon

Ashkelon Power Station

Netiv Ha'asara

Beit Lahiy

Nir Am

Sderot

Beit Hanoun

Mefalsim

Kfar Aza

Nahal Oz

Netivot

Be'eri

Gaza Strip

Philadelphia Route

ISRAEL

Tons of Explosives, Katyusha Rockets, Anti-Aircraft Missiles, Foreign Jihadists

Palestinians Exit Gaza for Training in Tehran by Iranian Revolutionary Guards (IRGC)

Egypt

- - - - - Launch Areas

⊙ Prominent Israeli Targets

interest in extending the *tahdiya*, as Egypt suggested. Khaled Mashaal, its Damascus-based leader, announced that the *tahdiya* would end on December 19. Within days, Hamas rocket and mortar fire on Israel escalated. In response, the Israel Defense Forces launched its Gaza campaign, known as Operation Cast Lead, on December 27, 2008.

Egypt understood that the collapse of the *tahdiya* had been the interest of Iran and its local surrogates, Hamas and Hizbullah. It was difficult to imagine that Hamas would undertake such a bold move like unilaterally ending its *tahdiya* with Israel without making sure that it had the backing of its Iranian patrons. A senior Palestinian Authority official argued that Iranian Foreign Minister Manouchehr Mottaki told Hamas leaders in Damascus that they should resume the "resistance" against Israel and keep Egypt out of any internal Palestinian dialogue between Hamas and Fatah.[50]

Tehran's role was not lost on Cairo. Egypt's foreign minister, Ahmed Aboul Gheit plainly told Egypt's Orbit satellite channel that Hamas, Hizbullah, and Iran had worked together to provoke the conflict in Gaza in order to serve Tehran's agenda: "[They tried] to turn the region to confrontation in the interest of Iran, which is trying to escape Western pressure . . . on the nuclear file."[51]

The Iranian role in the Gaza War looked like a replay of the Second Lebanon War in that the Iranians were diverting international attention away from their nuclear challenge with the West. Moreover, in both cases, the Iranians had an interest in the destabilization of the situation in order to increase the dependence of their local allies. Should Hizbullah or Hamas need more support, it would present Iran with an opportunity to enlarge its presence in the Arab world—either in Lebanon or in the Gaza Strip.

Aboul Gheit's analysis gained more validity when the Iranian role at the end of the Gaza War is also considered. Egypt was again the central player trying to work out a new cease-fire in January 2009. But while Egyptian diplomacy was seeking to end the conflict during talks with Hamas in Cairo, Ali Larijani, in his capacity as Speaker of the Iranian Parliament, and Saeed Jalili, the secretary of the Supreme National Security Council, arrived in Damascus on an urgent mission to persuade Hamas to reject any truce.[52] Iran's role in promoting Middle Eastern instability became even more clear with the activities of its two envoys.

The Gaza War did not end Iran's involvement in its Gaza beach-head. During the war, the Israeli Air Force had pounded the tun-nels underneath the Philadelphia Route. But the tunnel system was eventually re-built. Iran sought new ways of bringing in even more threatening weaponry in early 2009. It delivered weapons by sea to its African ally, Sudan, dispatching truck convoys from there to cross into Egypt and eventually to eastern Sinai.

Western news agencies reported that Israeli air strikes destroyed several convoys with Iranian arms in Sudan before they reached Egypt. Reportedly, one such convoy contained Fajr-3 rockets used by Hizbullah in Lebanon. Had they been deployed by Hamas, they would have enabled the organization to strike at Tel Aviv from the Gaza Strip.[53]

In the meantime, Iran's influence on Hamas decision-making seemed only to have grown. Iranian Revolutionary Guards partic-ipated in an investigation of Hamas' poor military performance during the Gaza War, when Hamas avoided direct confrontations with the Israel Defense Forces and caused only limited Israeli casu-alties. As a result, Iran insisted on the removal of two Hamas brigade commanders in the Gaza Strip: Bassam Issa and Imat Aakel.[54] Iran was clearly micromanaging the Hamas forces as though they were their own.

The Formation of Regional Coalition against Iran and Its Dismantlement

The United States saw Iran behind the escalation that was spreading across the Middle East in 2006. Assistant Secretary of State David Welch, who was the senior official in the State Department dealing with the Middle East, said that he saw an Iranian "hand" in all the crises in Lebanon, Gaza, and Iraq.[55] He noted that the Hizbullah attack on Israel that sparked the Second Lebanon War had been planned, according to the testimony of Hizbullah itself. Their intention, in his view, was "to escalate and widen the battleground."

Iran was clearly posing serious problems for most of the Arab states of the region, and not just for Israel. During the Second Lebanon War, while Egypt, Jordan, and Saudi Arabia were leery about the Hizbullah campaign, President Hosni Mubarak held a joint press conference with Jordan's King Abdullah in Cairo, in which both leaders criticized Israel but then turned their attention to Hizbullah: "We condemn the irresponsible escalatory acts that have the potential of leading the region into a dangerous situation."[56]

Saudi Arabia's foreign minister, Prince Saud al-Faisal, was even more explicit during an Arab summit at the outbreak of the war, describing Hizbullah's attack as "unexpected, dishonorable and irresponsible."[57] The Saudi Press Agency issued an official statement at the beginning of the conflict that was unusually strong:

> The Kingdom would like to clearly announce that a difference should be drawn between legitimate resistance and miscalculated adventures carried out by elements inside the state and those behind them without consultation with the legitimate authority in their state and without consultations or coordination with Arab countries.[58]

The Arab leaders' motivations emanated from their concern that Iran was trying to use Hizbullah's war against Israel to infiltrate the Arab world in order to widen support for the Islamic Revolution, which had received a new lease on life under the leadership of Iranian president Mahmoud Ahmadinejad.

Indeed, speaking on Hizbullah's al-Manar Television on December 28, 2008, a day after the Gaza War began, Hassan Nasrallah, the Hizbullah Secretary General, openly accused the Arab regimes, and above all Egypt, of collaborating with Israel. He urged Egyptian officers to rebel against their government's policies.[59] He called on the Egyptian masses to storm and open up the Rafah crossing between Egypt and the Gaza Strip. Nasrallah was instigating a revolt, for he declared: "Let the Egyptian people go out into the street in their millions." He then rhetorically asked: "Can the Egyptian police arrest millions of Egyptians?"

Iran and its Hizbullah allies had important local allies who could act upon Nasrallah's message. The Egyptian government's largest opposition, the Muslim Brotherhood, fully backed the Iranian-sponsored war. Its Supreme Guide, Muhammad Mahdi Akif, called for the mobilization of 10,000 volunteers to support Hizbullah. Appearing on the Qatari-based Arabic network, al-Jazeera, Akif attacked the wartime behavior of Mubarak's government as disgraceful.[60]

In the past, the Muslim Brotherhood, which was a Sunni fundamentalist organization, kept Shiite Iran at arm's length. Only the Palestinian branch of the Muslim Brotherhood, Hamas, had built up strategic ties with Tehran. Elsewhere, many remembered that in 1982, Ayatollah Khomeini did not lift a finger when his Syrian allies slaughtered Muslim Brotherhood members in Hama, Syria, where an estimated 20,000 Sunni Muslims were killed by the Syrian Army. But the sympathies of the Muslim Brotherhood in Egypt were changing. The Jordanian branch of the Muslim Brotherhood was also supportive of Hizbullah's military efforts. Iran had acquired an important instrument with which it could threaten the internal stability of its Arab rivals.

However, in Saudi Arabia, the situation was very different. Its religious establishment was clearly against Hizbullah and Iran. For example, Sheikh Abdullah bin Jabreen, who once served on the Saudi government's *fatwa* committee, explained what should be the proper policy towards the Second Lebanon War from the standpoint of the *Sharia* (Islamic Law) in a statement entitled "The Sharia Position on What Is Going On." He declared that it was

unlawful to support or pray for Hizbullah. With regard to the Shiites more generally, he said: "Our advice to the Sunnis is to
denounce them and shun those who join them to show their hostility to Islam and to the Muslims."[61] Sheikh Safar al-Hawali, one of
Saudi Arabia's most radical Wahhabi clerics, renamed Hizbullah—
which literally means "Party of Allah—to "Party of the Devil."[62]
And in late 2006, one of its most influential clerics, Sheikh Abdul
Rahman al-Barrak, issued a *fatwa* that the Shiites were "in truth
polytheist infidels."[63]

The Iranians retorted to the Saudi statements through their
press; an editorial in *Jomhouri-ye Eslami*, which was closely
linked to Iran's clerical leadership, condemned "the reactionary
Arab leaders...and the fatwa's issued by the Arab reaction."[64]
Iranian policy was undermining the interests of the Arab states,
and for the Saudis, their rivalry had a clear ideological dimension.
The calls for an anti-Iranian alliance grew among the Gulf states,
especially in Saudi Arabia, while the awareness of the dangers of
a nuclear Iran deepened. Indeed, Tariq Alhomayed, the editor-in-
chief of the London-based, Saudi-owned newspaper *al-Sharq
Awsat*, would write a year later that "Iran's pursuit of nuclear
weapons is a serious threat to our region, not Israel."[65] But the
prospects for the Arab states' successful containment of Iran were
about to change.

The Regional Consequences of the U.S. National Intelligence Estimate on Iran

National Intelligence Estimates (NIE) are supposed to be "the
most authoritative written judgments" of the U.S. Intelligence
Community. They are prepared at the request of U.S. policymakers and Congressional leaders by the National Intelligence Council. They take into account the views of most of the agencies that
make up the U.S. Intelligence Community. The U.S. government
had issued NIE's on Iran before, but the November 2007 report

entitled "Iran: Nuclear Intentions and Capabilities" would have enormous significance for all the Middle Eastern countries who were concerned with Iran's growing power.

Understandably, the coordination of the views of multiple agencies is a very complex process, and trying to distill a joint position on national security challenges can lead to awkward phraseology. Theoretically, the authors of an NIE should focus on producing a report which most accurately summarizes their joint assessment. But the language they decide upon can easily have unintended—or perhaps intended—side effects, if it is made public. More than any previous report, the 2007 NIE on Iran had profound diplomatic consequences, for parts of it were declassified and released to the public.

It may well be that the declassified version was prepared and released to prevent the longer, classified report from being leaked from the U.S. Congress.[66] But because it dealt with one of the most sensitive and politically explosive intelligence questions—whether Iran was in fact seeking nuclear weapons—every word and punctuation mark it contained would be carefully scrutinized, by every media outlet and intelligence agency in the world.

The declassified NIE made public in early December 2007 was a short nine-page report with none of the nuances of its classified version. Three pages contained its "Key Judgments," but many who read it stopped at its first sentence: "We judge with high confidence that in fall 2003, Tehran halted its nuclear weapons program."[67] The sentence was footnoted with an explanation: "For purposes of this Estimate, by 'nuclear weapons program' we mean Iran's nuclear weapons design and weaponization work and covert uranium conversion-related work." The footnote then added: "We do not mean Iran's declared civil work related to uranium conversion and enrichment."

In other words, the NIE had a narrow definition of the Iranian nuclear weapons program that focused mostly on its weaponization work and covert conversion effort. The definition excluded

Iran's massive uranium enrichment project at Natanz, which it was continually expanding, and which could easily have military applications. It did not clarify how far the Iranians progressed with their weaponization work before they halted it in 2003 for an unknown time period. There would be a huge difference between their completing 90 percent of their work before stopping or only finishing 20 percent. Did Iran have one month or two years of work left? It was not clear from the language of the report.

The NIE made two other important statements that were often ignored in subsequent analyses. It established "with high confidence" that in fact Iranian military entities had been developing nuclear weapons under government direction prior to 2003, and that "Iranian entities" were continuing to develop "a range of technical capabilities that could be applied to producing nuclear weapons." And regardless of whatever part of the Iranian nuclear program was suspended in 2003, the NIE admitted that the U.S. intelligence community had only "moderate confidence" that it knew for certain Tehran had not started up these programs again.

Even though the NIE specifically concluded that the freeze on components of the Iranian nuclear program lasted several years, the authors of the report had to admit that there were dissenting opinions on this point inside the intelligence community—due to "intelligence gaps."[68] Finally, the U.S. intelligence officials admitted that it was possible that the information about the Iranian suspension could have been a deception, though they did not consider it likely.[69]

So what was the upshot of the NIE's complex language? The best summary of the NIE's bottom line came from Deputy Secretary of State John D. Negroponte, who had previously served as the Director of National Intelligence. In his new capacity, it was his job to present the NIE to the international community, and in doing so he reached the following conclusions:

We are having some success in clarifying what the NIE actually means. And what it does mean is that we have information that at some time back in 2003, Iran stopped its activity in the area of designing a warhead. That's what they stopped doing. But building a nuclear weapon involves three distinct activities. One is to acquire the fissile material, and as you know that activity continues in Iran. They are continuing their work on enriching uranium. Another is to develop a delivery system. And of course the Iranians are working hard on the acquisition and development of missile technology, and they already have a lot of missiles. And thirdly, of course, the actual warhead. So it's only the work on the warhead that stopped, and we don't even have absolute certainty that activity has not resumed.[70]

In short, looking at all the elements of the NIE together, it was a stretch to say that the Iranian nuclear weapons program had come to a complete halt.

Nonetheless, the impression most people in the world gained was not that only a part of the Iranian nuclear program was frozen, but that the entire nuclear weapons effort had been halted. The *New York Times* ran a headline on December 3, 2007 declaring: "U.S. Says Iran Ended Atomic Arms Work."[71] The *Boston Globe* announced in its December 4, 2007 headline: "U.S. Finds No Iran Bomb Program."[72]

The careful qualifications that typically appear in an intelligence document inevitably disappear in bold newspaper headlines that yet have as much power to mold public opinion as the substance of the article that follows. The NIE had a similar impact on the electronic media. The opening few lines of the NIE were enough to pull the plug on the global diplomatic effort to press Iran to halt its uranium enrichment program and its work on plutonium reprocessing.

While in the past, America's European allies were reluctant partners in many anti-Iranian initiatives, they indicated that they did not accept the general impression that was emerging of the NIE's findings. Britain's *Daily Telegraph* reported the reaction coming out of the British intelligence services with a headline that had a very different tone from what was coming out on the other side of the Atlantic: "Britain: Iran 'Hoodwinked' CIA Over Nuclear Plans."[73] The article that followed stated that Britain's intelligence chiefs had "grave doubts that Iran...mothballed its nuclear weapons program."[74]

French President Nicolas Sarkozy and German Chancellor Angela Merkel also came forward after the release of the NIE and stated that Iran still remained a danger.[75] Despite the NIE's findings, they insisted that pressure had to be maintained on Tehran over its nuclear program. A former head of Israeli military intelligence, Major General Aharon Zeevi Farkash also expressed ongoing concern with the Iranian nuclear program despite the NIE. He admitted that Iran halted parts of its nuclear program in 2003, but not because they had a change of heart.[76]

Any suspension of nuclear activities, in his view, was temporary, and came about because the Iranians had been caught red-handed in 2002, when their clandestine nuclear program was first revealed by the Iranian opposition. Consequently, the Iranians closed down and dismantled their nuclear facility at Lavizan, which specialized in weaponization, and apparently they moved the work to another site, where it was resumed. He suspected that the weaponization effort was renewed by January 2005.

Moreover, during the period that the program was shut down, Iran continued with the development of its ballistic missile force, which made absolutely no sense if it planned to stick to firing conventional warheads, alone.[77] It also conducted missile exercises, which showed that its missile forces were aiming at two targets: Tel Aviv, Israel's largest commercial center, and Riyadh, the capital of Saudi Arabia.[78] Despite the NIE, the states of the Middle East certainly had reason to be concerned about what the Iranians were up to. But the way the NIE's conclusions were presented and ultimately reported, it looked like Washington had intentionally decided to underestimate—and in effect underplay—the magnitude of the Iranian threat.

Thus the significance of the NIE went well beyond the world of intelligence experts. It became a diplomatic document that helped dissipate the global pressures that were building on Iran. The Bush administration's critics were pleased that the NIE essentially undercut any talk of a U.S. military option against the Iranian nuclear program. But it also undercut most non-military alternative courses of action, including tighter international sanctions. Russia and Iran very quickly reached an agreement on completing the necessary preparations for the Bushehr civilian reactor. The Chinese also went ahead with a new $2.3 billion agreement on investment in the Iranian energy sector, which previously Beijing had been reluctant to conclude, out of deference to western policy.[79]

The consequences of the NIE for the diplomacy of the Middle East were profound. For two years, Saudi Arabia had actively sought to build a bloc of countries to stem the expansion of Iranian influence in the Middle East. After the publication of the NIE, this effort collapsed.[80]

Among the Arab Gulf states, Bahrain and the United Arab Emirates have been the most directly intimidated countries by the Iranian threat. Iranian spokesmen keep talking about Bahrain as Iranian territory and Iran still occupies three UAE islands. Saudi Arabia was targeted by the Iranian Air Force during the Iran-Iraq War and recently by Iranian-supported terrorist attacks by Hizbullah and even al-Qaeda. Iranian aircraft also threatened Kuwait's oil trade during the 1980s. Certainly four of the six Arab Gulf states had a great deal of common ground when it came to the Iranian threat.

Qatar was the most reluctant of the Gulf countries to adopt the anti-Iranian line. It had concerns about the fact that it had to share its maritime natural gas fields in the Persian Gulf with Iran, so it chose an approach that accommodated Iran. After the NIE, this nuanced Qatari policy became a sharp break from the other Sunni Arab states. During December 2007, when Qatar hosted the summit meeting of the six Arab Gulf states, in the framework of the Gulf Cooperation Council (GCC), the Qataris decided to invite President Mahmoud Ahmadinejad of Iran to attend, without consulting with any of the other leaders.

The other Gulf states acquiesced to the Qatari move; in fact, Saudi Arabia invited Ahmadinejad to the Hajj ceremonies in Mecca. Their deep reservations from the Iranian presence at the GCC summit were expressed largely through newspapermen who were close to the ruling families.[81] Saudi columnists wrote about Iran's "octopus-like expansion" in the Arab world, or that the Arab states were now subject to "Persian colonialism."[82]

The Gulf Arab leaders were increasingly concerned that in the aftermath of the NIE, the United States and Iran would intensify their political negotiations in the context of a new policy of engagement and new agreements would be reached between them, enshrining Iran's regional power status at the expense of the Arab Gulf states.[83]

Despite all the talk that followed the summit about a possible rapprochement between Iran and the Arab Sunni states, their relations soon deteriorated. Iranian newspaper attacks against Arab leaders intensified, with calls to topple the Egyptian and Saudi regimes, in particular. Again it was the editor of *Kayhan*, Hossein Shariatmadari, who was the spokesman for the Supreme Leader, Ayatollah Ali Khamenei, who established the tone. He wrote an editorial on December 2, 2008, that essentially called for murdering President Mubarak of Egypt: "The absence of [Sadat's assassin] the martyr Khaled Islambouli, God bless his soul, is sorely felt. Many more should follow his example."[84]

Qatar turned into an important strategic partner for Iran at this time, as its al-Jazeera satellite channel hammered the Arab leaders who were Iran's main rivals. For example, with the outbreak of the Gaza War at the end of 2008, al-Jazeera conducted a poll in Muslim countries showing that the Arab heads of state—and especially King Abdullah of Saudi Arabia—bore the greatest responsibility for the Gaza crisis.[85] Shariatmadari picked up on the al-Jazeera poll to slam the Arab leaders. Indeed, Iranian students protesting against Egypt in Tehran called for Mubarak's execution six days after Shariatmadari's editorial.[86]

As Iran moved closer to a nuclear weapons capability, it was clearly emerging as the primary military threat to the pragmatic pro-western Arab states. In fact, in April 2009, Egypt's public prosecutor ordered that forty-nine people be held in custody for plotting armed attacks in Egypt on behalf of Hizbullah. The statement he released did not detail what were the Hizbullah's targets, though it accused the organization of trying to spread Shiite ideology in Egypt.[87] Cairo's state-controlled media laid the blame for Hizbullah's presence at the feet of Iran. In a front-page editorial by the editor of *al-Goumhouria*, Muhammad Ali Ibrahim, Hizbullah's link to Tehran was stressed: "I say to you what every Egyptian knows, that you are an Iranian party."[88] Iran's war with the Sunni Arab states appears to be deepening.

Last Efforts at Nuclear Diplomacy

Despite the confusion created by the NIE, the United States and the permanent member states of the UN Security Council—as well as Germany—decided to try their hand at further nuclear diplomacy with Iran. Known collectively as the P-5-plus-1, they reworked their June 2006 proposal for broad-based negotiations with Tehran. Javier Solana took the latest incentives package to Tehran on June 13, 2008, and met with Foreign Minister Manouchehr Mottaki. One of the new components to the diplomatic package was the idea of a six-week "freeze-for-freeze," whereby Iran would suspend uranium enrichment and the UN would freeze sanctions.[89]

But beyond the Iranian reaction to these issues of substance, what was striking during the meeting was the way that Mottaki looked at the cover letter of the P-5-plus-1 proposal. It had the signatures of all the foreign ministers of the UN Security Council. The great powers of the world were collectively addressing Iran. The opening sentence of the letter moreover acknowledged Iran's special status as "one of the oldest civilizations in the world."[90] Mottaki's eyes became fixed when he came to the signature page of the proposal. The next to the last signature caught his attention: it was the signature of U.S. Secretary of State Condoleezza Rice. Mottaki then called in the Iranian television cameras to show the letter he had received.

Mottaki's behavior suggested how important it was for him that the United States was coming into the negotiations, even step-by-step. The EU-3, who led the contacts with Iran during the 2003–2005 period, had many times said to their American counterparts that if Washington were to sit at the negotiating table, then Iran might come around. In political life, Iranian diplomats were especially conscious of the status of their counterparts, always declining to deal with anyone they considered as having inferior power. Former British Foreign Secretary Jack Straw used to say that America was the "big cheese" that Iran wanted to engage with. With the United States a formal partner in the 2008 proposal, perhaps Iran might be more responsive than it had been in 2006.

Ahmadinejad, however, did not give much hope that this kind of analysis of Iranian behavior was correct. A day earlier he said in a televised speech that with respect to Iran the "West can't do anything." He singled out President Bush as a lame duck who failed to hurt Iran.[91] Upon receiving the new proposals, the Iranians indicated initially that they would be rejected since they call for a halt to their uranium enrichment activities. Yet a few weeks later, Mottaki again filled western diplomats with new optimism. He said Iran was "seriously and carefully examining" the proposals that

Solana had brought. He added: "We view the position taken by the five-plus-one as a constructive one."[92] And while rejecting the proposals in public, it took a more positive approach in private meetings with Solana. But what was the real Iranian position?

When Iran formally replied to the P-5-plus-1 in 2008, it offered to start comprehensive negotiations with Solana over the incentives package, but it insisted that it would not suspend uranium enrichment during the talks. Nevertheless, the P-5-plus-1 could not take no for an answer and persisted with their nuclear contacts with Tehran. There was one important change. In a major departure from past U.S. policy, the Bush administration decided to dispatch for the first time a senior U.S. envoy to the follow-up talks of the P-5-plus-1 in Geneva with Iran's chief nuclear negotiator, Saeed Jalili. U.S. Undersecretary of State William Burns joined the negotiations on July 18, 2008.

What caused the enhanced U.S. involvement? The Bush administration had been upbeat about the chances of reaching an understanding with Iran, despite all the negative signs coming from recent contacts between the P-5-plus-1 and Tehran. Reflecting the hopeful mood, the *Washington Post* carried a story on July 17, 2008, entitled "Iran and U.S. Signaling Chance of Deal."[93] It author, Glenn Kessler, reported that U.S. officials believed there were "increasing signs that Iran was open to negotiations and that international sanctions were having an impact." As a result, Secretary of State Rice pushed for Burns's attendance at the Geneva meeting.[94] On its part, the only clear signal Iran sent to the West before the talks was the test-firing of long-range missiles in the direction of the Persian Gulf the previous week.[95]

Unfortunately, the Bush team was completely wrong about there being any new Iranian flexibility. Indeed, the Iranians did their best to obfuscate their true position on the package during the upgraded negotiating session in Geneva. Solana summarized the situation accordingly: "We have not got a clear answer... [W]e didn't get an answer 'yes' or 'no' and we hope it will be given soon."[96]

Dragging out the negotiations with the West even further, Iran issued a formal letter of response that was finally delivered in early August. It asked for a "clear response" from the West to its "questions and ambiguities as well."[97] Tehran made no commitment to suspending uranium enrichment, and its position did not essentially change because of America's new involvement in the nuclear negotiations. Washington admitted that the Iranian response was unacceptable and as a result it sought to increase the severity of international sanctions on the Iranian regime.

The U.S. Treasury Department indeed took important measures against Iranian banks using the international finance system to pressure the Iranians on the nuclear issue. But ultimately, Iran ignored the repeated resolutions of the UN Security Council—including three resolutions calling for sanctions on Iran—as well as the repeated warnings of the foreign ministers of the P-5-plus-1.

Muhammad ElBaradei, the director-general of the IAEA, admitted the truth of what had happened as a result of years of active diplomacy with Iran over the nuclear question with which he was involved: "We haven't really moved one inch toward addressing the issues." He then concluded: "I think so far the policy has been a failure."[98] The West had seriously tried to engage Iran, but the results of this failed diplomacy had left the Middle East a far more dangerous region than it was before.

Chapter 11:

The Last Opportunity
to Stop Iran

Pᴿᴱˢᴵᴰᴱᴺᵀ Bᴬᴿᴬᶜᴷ Oᴮᴬᴹᴬ came into office on January 20, 2009, inheriting an extremely tough diplomatic legacy on Iran in every respect. At the beginning of the previous year, *The Economist*, the British newsweekly, ran an editorial that opened with the provocative question: "Has Iran Won?" It summarized what had essentially been a diplomatic debacle for the western alliance over the previous six years by asserting that "the ayatollahs have wriggled off the nuclear hook." It judged that Iran had run "diplomatic circles around America and its European allies."[1] Indeed, looking back at the diplomatic record of past nuclear talks, the prognosis for succeeding with a new approach to Iran did not look particularly good.

Nonetheless, while all western efforts at engaging Iran had failed from 2003 through 2008, the new Obama administration came into office with a renewed faith and optimism in the power of diplomatic engagement to dissuade Iran from crossing the nuclear threshold. Asked about Iran during his January 11, 2009, appearance on the ABC News Program *This Week*, Obama reiterated: "We are going to have to take a new approach." He added that it was his belief that "engagement is the place to start."[2]

In his inaugural address nine days later, while not singling out Iran, Obama stipulated that the extension of a diplomatic hand of the United States to an adversary required that he "unclench" his fist first. Though this sounded like an allusion to setting pre-conditions for diplomatic outreach, engagement was nonetheless the new guiding policy. Was there a chance that this time diplomacy might succeed?

During the 2008 presidential campaign, Obama had not altered the West's policy in respect to Iran obtaining nuclear weapons. He fully understood the implications of a nuclear Iran for the future of the Middle East, explaining in a high-profile interview on FOX Television: "It is unacceptable for Iran to possess a nuclear weapon. It would be a game changer, and I've said that repeatedly."[3] He did not elaborate about what the expression "game changer" meant, but it could be inferred that it would completely change the military landscape of the Middle East to the detriment of United States and western allied interests by causing a chain-reaction of Arab states from Egypt to Saudi Arabia to seek crash nuclear weapons programs in response.

Obama added one important element to his Iran strategy: "I've also said I would never take the military option off the table." What made his approach different was his removal of the pre-conditions the Bush administration had set for diplomacy to get started: no longer would Iran have to freeze its uranium enrichment program in order to get a meeting with a high-level U.S. envoy. The strategic goals of the United States thus remained unchanged, but the diplomatic tactics that the new administration was adopting were completely new.

Obama was not alone. There was a growing consensus among some of the best and the brightest foreign affairs experts in the

West about the need to renew western diplomacy with Iran despite the poor results from these efforts during previous six years. Five former U.S. secretaries of states appeared in a CNN debate in September 2008 entitled "A Nuclear Iran: Are Direct Talks the Answer?" All agreed with the proposition that the United States should engage directly with Iran without pre-conditions, meaning that they did not insist that Iran halt uranium enrichment and reprocessing programs as a price for getting the next U.S. administration to the negotiating table.

Important research institutes and study groups had reached the same conclusion over the previous four years. The Council on Foreign Relations released a report in 2004 concluding that "a political dialogue with Iran should not be deferred until such time as the deep differences over Iranian nuclear ambitions and its invidious involvement with regional conflicts have been resolved."[4] The report was chaired by President Carter's former national security advisor, Zbigniew Brzezinski and Robert Gates, who was later appointed to become the Secretary of Defense for President George W. Bush.

The Brzezinski-Gates report was tough on the nuclear question. It may have proposed diplomatic engagement, but it insisted that a future agreement between the West and Iran be based on "an Iranian commitment to permanently renounce uranium enrichment and other fuel-cycle capabilities." The report also called for the implementation of the more intrusive inspections of the Additional Protocol of the Nuclear Non-Proliferation Treaty—which Iran had signed but not ratified.

Two years later, The Iraq Study Group, chaired by former Secretary of State James Baker and former chairman of the committee on foreign affairs of the U.S. House of Representatives, Lee Hamilton, published its findings that proposed engagement with Iran.[5] It did not deal with the Iranian nuclear question, as such, but in the context of a diplomatic resolution of the Iraq War, it proposed that the "United States engage directly with Iran and

Syria in order to try to obtain constructive policies toward Iraq and other regional issues."

The Iraq Study Group assumed that Iran, like the United States, was not interested in the further de-stabilization of Iraq, suggesting that "Iran's interests would not be served by a failure of U.S. policy in Iraq that led to chaos and the disintegration of the Iraqi state." This was an extreme scenario, and did not consider a failure of U.S. policy that caused a premature American withdrawal, leaving Iraq under Iranian domination—which Tehran could not object to. On the nuclear issue, which was, for their purposes, secondary to addressing America's military position in Iraq, the report only suggested that it should continue to be dealt with by the UN Security Council and the P-5-plus-1 group.

In 2008, Chatham House—The Royal Institute for International Affairs—published the conclusions of a British study team chaired by Sir Richard Dalton, who had served as the British ambassador to Iran from 2002 through 2006. Its report admitted that Iran and the West were in a "nuclear deadlock."[6] It already assumed that the incoming Obama administration would upgrade bilateral contacts with Iran and did not articulate any reservation about Washington going forward with such a policy. In fact, it suggested that the United States start planning for "an eventual normalization of relations with Iran." But at the same time, it warned that "there is no consensus in Iran yet on how to respond and it is also unclear whether Iran will choose defiance or engagement."

In 2008, former President Jimmy Carter joined the chorus of former American officials calling for a new dialogue between the United States and Iran: "What we have to do is talk with them now and say to them we want to be friends." He added that he wanted the United States to resume all trade relations with Iran, and drop its policy of sanctions on the Islamic Republic.[7] The public buildup for engagement was widespread and crossed party lines within the United States On April 10, 2007, House Speaker Nancy

Pelosi (D-California) held a news conference in San Francisco at which she was asked if she would be ready to make an official trip to Iran; she immediately answered: "Speaking for myself, I would be ready to get on a plane tomorrow morning...it is important that we have a dialogue."[8]

A year later, Senator Richard Lugar (R-Indiana), the ranking member on the Senate Foreign Relations Committee, voiced a more nuanced position that appeared to give some support to Obama's policy of engagement: "But as Senator Obama has argued, isolating regimes, though sometimes necessary, rarely leads to a resolution of contentious issues."[9] Lugar then warned: "In some cases, refusing to talk can even be dangerous."

The hard question all advocates of engagement have to answer is why a new diplomatic initiative toward Iran now would cause Tehran to halt its nuclear program, when western engagement with Iran in the past has so utterly failed. During the engagement debate that developed in 2008, it became clear that officials had very different ideas about what the term meant and how it should influence future policies towards Tehran. For some commentators, diplomatic engagement meant a new U.S. commitment to working on the Iran issue multilaterally, especially through the United Nations, as opposed to what was often characterized as excessive unilateralism during the Bush administration.[10]

Others envisioned engagement as an alternative to the threat of the use of armed force, rather than seeing the threat of exercising military power as a complement to any diplomatic dialogue with Iran. Other factors were raised about what had to go into a new policy of engagement. For example, IAEA Secretary General Mohamed ElBaradei raised the idea that the Obama administration needed to "design an approach that was sensitive to Iran's pride."[11]There is no question that in the United States, the discourse about engagement was affected by a critique of the decision-making leading to the outbreak of the 2003 Iraq War and the internal American political debate it engendered.

Some of the key figures in the Obama administration had no illusions about the efficacy of an approach based solely on pure diplomatic outreach—absent the threat of coercive measures—when dealing with a state like Iran. In fact, Secretary of Defense Robert Gates did not put much stock in any diplomatic effort divorced from coercive measures achieved through economic sanctions; in fact, the latter was more promising than the former. He told FOX News Sunday on March 29, 2009: "I think, frankly, from my perspective the opportunity for success is probably more in economic sanctions in both places [North Korea and Iran] than it is in diplomacy."[12] He further explained, "If there is enough economic pressure placed on Iran, diplomacy can provide them with an open door though which they can walk if they choose to change their polices." In short, diplomatic engagement alone would not work.

For Dennis Ross, the Obama administration's point man on Iran, economic leverage alone was not going to make diplomacy work. He recalled that what caused Tehran to reach out to Washington in 2003, through the Swiss ambassador, according to the key figure on the Iranian side drafting the initiative, was "fear among the Iranian elite" after the United States crushed the army of Saddam Hussein.[13] By recalling the role of military pressure in determining past Iranian behavior, Ross was implicitly confirming it was important to keep all options on the table—including the military option—in order to make diplomacy work.

Further proof substantiated Ross's analysis. The 2007 U.S. National Intelligence Estimate (NIE), many of whose conclusions about the suspension of the Iranian nuclear weapons program had been subsequently discredited, nonetheless made an important point which dovetailed with Ross's opinion. The NIE suggested that "Iran halted the program in 2003 primarily in response to international pressure."[14] But what international pressure existed in 2003? The IAEA had not yet reached any sweeping conclusions; not a single UN Security Council resolution had yet been adopted on the Iranian nuclear program. There were no new international economic sanctions on Iran in 2003 as a result. The only pressure that existed emanated from the U.S.-led invasion of Iraq, and the fear that must have existed in Tehran at the time that Iran could be next.

In short, even an implicit threat of the use of force mattered to the Iranians and served as a powerful source of leverage for the United States and its allies. Clearly the architects of Obama's engagement policy were not about to forgo this pressure point on the regime in Tehran as they crafted the key elements of their initial policy.

A piece in an Iranian newspaper reinforced the idea that engagement and military power might work hand in glove for negotiating with Iran. The Iranian reformist newspaper *Aftab-e Yazd* published an interview on April 6, 2009, with the former head Iranian nuclear negotiator, Hassan Rowhani, in which he defended the agreements he reached with the EU-3 back in 2003 that led to a temporary suspension of the uranium enrichment program.[15] Rowhani reminded the interviewer that "America was near our borders and it occupied Iraq in the excuse of nuclear weapons." He then explained that there were anxieties at the time that Iran might face a "multilateral war against it." Given the pressures it faced in 2003, in the aftermath of the American victory against Saddam Hussein, Iran had little choice but to embrace the European call for engagement and accept a temporary suspension of uranium enrichment.

Did the new proposals for engagement, no matter how the term was defined, have any chance of success, given the glaring failure of past diplomatic efforts to stop the Iranian nuclear program? Almost all previous administrations tried to engage the Islamic Republic of Iran without success. The European "critical dialogue" with Tehran never produced a fundamental change in Iran's hostile international behavior. Nonetheless, there was one small opening for a last try with the Iranians. As British Foreign

Secretary Jack Straw once told Secretary of State Condoleezza Rice, so far as the Iranians were concerned, the Europeans who were involved in the EU-3 dialogue between 2003 and 2005 with Tehran were only "a sprat to catch a mackerel," as the United States was "the big fish."[16]

It was well known to Iran watchers that in Iranian political culture, rank and stature were particularly essential pre-conditions for determining whether two parties would seriously engage one another, let alone conclude any understandings between them. There was a chance that when placed across the table from the United States alone, Iran might behave differently than it did when it met a group of European states, even if the United States participated as a backseat partner, as was the case in the last years of the Bush administration. It was a long shot, but it appeared to be one that the Obama team was willing to try.

The direct involvement of the United States would have the effect of soothing the fears of the Iranian government, which was certain that Washington sought to topple the regime of the Islamic Republic. The Iranian leadership might have previously asked itself why it would make concessions to Europe, if the United States planned to pursue a policy of regime change. It appeared that President Obama sought to change this Iranian perception and address the mistrust of Iran toward the United States. In his March 20, 2009, videotaped remarks on the occasion of the Iranian festival, Nowruz, Obama specifically stated: "The United States wants the Islamic Republic of Iran to take its rightful place in the community of nations." The statement implied an acceptance of Iran's form of government in its current form. He signaled to Tehran that "in this season of new beginnings" the United States was prepared to open a new chapter in American-Iranian relations.[17]

If indeed the primary problem between the West and Iran emanated from Iranian leadership's fear of being a future target of regime change, then Obama's new policy could make a real difference. But if Iran's behavior resulted primarily from its own ideologically driven quest for regional supremacy in its Middle Eastern neighborhood and beyond, then the Islamic Republic would remain a strategic challenge no matter how much U.S. policy changed.

Even Obama voiced skepticism about whether engagement would ultimately bear fruit. He told *Newsweek* in May 2009: "Now will it work? We don't know. And I assure you, I'm not naïve about the difficulties of a process like this."[18] He tried to find other advantages that the United States might derive from engagement, nonetheless: "If it doesn't work, the fact we have tried will strengthen our position in mobilizing the international community, and Iran will have isolated itself, as opposed to a perception that it seeks to advance that somehow it's being victimized by a U.S. government that doesn't respect Iran's sovereignty."

Ahmadinejad did not give Obama much cause for any optimism. The Iranian president did not sound like a victim, but rather like someone who viewed himself as the leader of a nascent great power. While formally declaring that he welcomed the United States' call for dialogue with Iran, he bluntly warned Washington at the very same time:

We say to you today that you are in a position of weakness. Your hands are empty, and you can no longer promote your interests from a position of strength.[19]

It was as though Ahmadinejad wanted to say that the new willingness of America to reach out to Iran was a reflection of weakness, even though from a western diplomatic perspective it looked like a magnanimous act. His position on the nuclear issue also appeared to harden when he said that the "time of discussing the nuclear issue has come to an end."[20] Ultimately, the only way the administration could judge what stood behind Iran's difficult statements was to test Tehran diplomatically, with certain critical precautions that needed to be kept in mind in light of past efforts of negotiating with Tehran.

The Risks Entailed in Unlimited Engagement

Since 2006, Iranian nuclear negotiators had frankly admitted that they exploited periods of negotiation with the West in order to dissipate international pressures against them and to move forward in their clandestine nuclear programs. As Rowhani sketched the Iranian strategy in greater detail in 2009: "Our operation was to suspend Natanz (where the enrichment of UF_6 was to take place in centrifuges), but we continue[d] our activities in Isfahan (where the conversion of processed uranium ore to UF_6 gas was undertaken)."[21]

Rowhani described how feverishly the Iranians worked at the Isfahan uranium conversion plant during the period of their suspension agreement with the EU-3 on uranium enrichment: "We worked three shifts (per day) in 1382 (the Islamic year corresponding with 2003 and early 2004)." According to Rowhani, the deal with the EU-3 did not cover the production of centrifuges, only their operation: "We continued our production, because we had not enough centrifuges. We wanted more."

The nuclear situation in Iran had vastly changed since that time, for Tehran was much further along in 2009 in its uranium enrichment program than it was in 2003, when western diplomacy with Iran had been first initiated. For example, the February 19, 2009, quarterly report issued by the International Atomic Energy Agency disclosed that Iran had already produced 1,010 kilograms (2,227 pounds) of low enriched uranium.[22]

Iran already had 4,000 operating centrifuges, with another 1,600 centrifuges about to come online. In addition, Iran refused the IAEA inspectors access to its heavy water reactor construction site. Just three months later in June 2009, IAEA reported a further

30 percent increase in the size of Iran's stock of low-enriched uranium, which was now close to 3,000 pounds.[23] This growing stockpile of low enriched uranium had no civilian use; there still were no civilian reactors in use in Iran and when the Russian-built Bushehr reactor became fully functional, its fuel, according to agreements the Iranians made, was supposed to come from Moscow. That did not leave much imagination what Iranian uranium was really for.

While the United States and its allies formulated their new engagement policies, Iran's nuclear program was not static. Tehran was making serious progress and felt enormous confidence in its achievement. It was significantly boosting its supply of low-enriched uranium to new levels in a relatively short period of time. Its president did not sound like he was in any mood to compromise, but only sought to build on what Iran had gained through defiance. After deriding the past nuclear negotiations with the countries of the West and the demands made on Iran by them at the time, Ahmadinejad declared in April 2009 that now "nearly 7,000 centrifuges are spinning today at Natanz, mocking them."

Speaking in early March on CNN's *State of the Union*, the Chairman of the Joint Chiefs of Staff, Admiral Mike Mullen, concluded that Iran had enough low-enriched uranium, if enriched further to weapons grade fuel, to produce one nuclear weapon.[24] According to one calculation, all Iran needed to produce a single atomic bomb was about 700 kilograms (a little over 1,500 pounds) of low-enriched uranium, which, after further enrichment, could produce the minimal 20 kilograms (44 pounds) of high-enriched uranium needed for a weapon.[25] In mid-2009, Iran was already well beyond that point with nearly twice the minimal quantity that was needed. Applying Hassan Rowhani's type of diplomatic stalling under these new circumstances could have direct military implications for the Iranian armed forces and their acquisition of nuclear weapons.

The number of centrifuges Iran had set up speaks to their intentions. For Iran to produce 20 kilograms of weapons-grade uranium for one bomb, using just 3,000 centrifuges, would take only 30 days; once the Iranians have 6,000 centrifuges the time for further enrichment to weapons grade fuel for each bomb could be cut to 16 days. This number of days could be cut in half if Iran employed more advanced centrifuges in the future, which they have been developing.

In March 2009, looking at the timeline for manufacturing nuclear weapons, Mark Fitzpatrick, a former State Department proliferation expert, estimated in testimony before the Senate Foreign Relations Committee that Iran only needed several weeks to enrich its current stockpile of low-enriched uranium to weapons-grade uranium.[26] The very last phase of weapons production—converting the weapons-grade uranium into uranium metal and fashioning a warhead—would take another six months. In short, theoretically, Iran could be less than a year from its first nuclear-tipped missile.

However, the number of centrifuges that Iran could acquire and efficiently operate would ultimately affect the speed of the transition from a seemingly innocuous nuclear fuel to fuel for a nuclear warhead. It would also govern the quantities of weapons-grade uranium that would be produced—and ultimately the size of a future Iranian nuclear arsenal. Disturbingly, the leap from low-enriched uranium, which is purportedly for civilian use, to high-enriched uranium, that is essential for an atomic bomb, is not very great, and could be shortened even further.

Moreover, Iran actually declared back in 2006 that its goal was to build a uranium enrichment facility with 56,000 centrifuges.[27] Whether all 56,000 centrifuges would work optimally and be used for producing high-enriched uranium cannot be determined. But once this facility is completed, it would give Tehran the capability to produce nuclear fuel for a dozen or more atomic bombs every month. In any case, Iran is at a point that if it froze its nuclear enrichment facilities just to their current level, and did not put more centrifuges on line, it still could produce enough fuel for the production of several atomic bombs per year.

Another factor that is impossible to calculate is other unknown components of Iran's nuclear program that it has not disclosed to the West. Brigadier General Michael Herzog was a senior aide to Israel's Minister of Defense and addressed this concern in an address in Washington in 2005:

> The fundamental question is whether Iran is running a parallel, clandestine nuclear program in addition to its openly declared program. Although definitive evidence is lacking, most western intelligence agencies believe that Iran has such a program.[28]

Reportedly, the classified sections of the 2007 U.S. National Intelligence Estimate detailed Iranian efforts to enrich uranium covertly at sites other than the well-known Natanz facility.[29] Moroever, the Iranians themselves also dropped hints about such secret facilities. The newspaper *Kayhan*, which was close to Supreme Leader Ayatollah Ali Khamenei, provocatively reminded its readers: "The intelligence that the West currently has on Iran's nuclear program is limited to the sites accessible to IAEA inspectors, and more than that they do not know."[30]

Given Iran's record of blatantly deceiving western nuclear negotiators in the past, any U.S. engagement of Iran would have to take this troubling history into account. Undoubtedly, Iran still has an interest in playing for time, dragging out new nuclear talks in order to further expand the scope of its nuclear program, at the very same time. If the West does not put a clear time limit on its efforts to renew engagement with Iran, then it could be expected that Tehran would again adopt Rowhani's approach of exploiting nuclear negotiations as a cover for further nuclear work.

President Obama seemed to be aware of this problem when he first spoke about a time limit for his policy engagement. In a joint appearance with Israeli Prime Minister Benjamin Netanyahu, Obama told reporters: "We're not going to have talks forever." He then added that the Iranian-American talks he envisioned would begin right after the June 12 Iranian presidential elections. He raised the idea that "we should have a fairly good sense by the end of the year as to whether they are moving in the right direction." At that point, Obama did not suggest that he would shut down Iran's dialogue with the West. He only promised that at that point in time, he would order a "reassessment" of his engagement policy.

Tehran's Military Preparations Continue—The Iranian Octopus Reaches the Western Hemisphere

In the meantime, Iran continues to create for itself military options for any eventuality in the future. While Iran has invested in all branches of its armed forces since the end of the Iran-Iraq War, it does not possess a strong conventional army, in terms of front-line aircraft or top-of-the-line tanks. Instead, Iran has directed much of its military spending to its missile and non-conventional forces, its naval capacity to wreak havoc in the Persian Gulf, and its networks for global subversion, like Hizbullah. It has geared up for what specialists call asymmetrical warfare—defeating a technologically superior army with the natural strengths it has built over time.

In the Middle East, the Iranian mode of operation was to gradually increase its military capacity through surrogates for future contingencies, by building positions of strength along the borders of its adversaries. Iran followed that strategy in Iraq, even before the U.S. invasion in 2003, by backing multiple Shiite organizations that it financed, trained, and supplied. Along Israel's northern and southern borders, over the years it put an infrastructure in place of rocket forces using terrorist groups like Hizbullah and Hamas. It built up a presence in Sudan, to the south of Egypt, from where it could provide support for terrorist operations against the government of President Hosni Mubarak.

There were also growing signs that it sought to recruit anti-government groups in Yemen in order to create a staging area for threats to Saudi Arabia's oil infrastructure. Years could pass before these Iranian efforts came fully to light, when this military capacity was used as a pressure point against adversaries to serve the interests of the Iranian state. In the meantime, all this investment provided Iran with options for the future.

Iran has been working through operatives of Hizbullah in North America for some time, but in many cases they have been captured by U.S. and Canadian authorities. In Charlotte, North Carolina, there was a Hizbullah cell that was involved in an illegal interstate cigarette smuggling scheme used for purposes of fundraising. The cell also had an operational military side: they reported to a senior Hizbullah commander in South Beirut, named Sheikh Abbas Haraki.[31]

There was also a Canadian leg to the Charlotte group, which reported to a Hizbullah officer who was close to Iranian intelligence. They also procured night-vision goggles, GPS systems, and other equipment with military applications for Hizbullah. The previous head of the Canadian cell, Muhammad Dbouk, trained in the camps of the Revolutionary Guards in Iran before his arrival in Canada. He subsequently worked with Hizbullah's al-Manar satellite network to provide surveillance of potential targets in Lebanon. Notably, in April 2009, a New York City businessman was sentenced in a U.S. Federal Court for providing services for al-Manar.[32]

Whether they worked in the United States or Canada, Hizbullah operatives, who seemed to confine their activities to fundraising, education, or media outreach, could easily cross over and become involved on the operational military side. Hizbullah often provided military training to operatives who dealt with financing or other aspects of local logistics. Apparently, the FBI had an informant who claimed that Muhammad Hammoud, who was a leader of the Charlotte Hizbullah cell, was prepared to undertake such military assignments upon receiving orders from Lebanon.[33]

The newest front Iran seems determined to develop is to the south of the United States in Latin America. Since the election of Mahmoud Ahmadinejad in 2005, there has been a discernable increase in Iranian activities across South America. Ahmadinejad himself met with the presidents of Venezuela, Nicaragua, Bolivia, and Ecuador between 2006 and 2009—in some cases on repeated occasions. On January 27, 2009, Secretary of Defense Robert Gates sounded the alarm about what Iran was doing in Washington's backyard:

> I'm concerned about the level of, frankly subversive activity that the Iranians are carrying on in a number of places in Latin America, particularly in South America and Central America. They're opening a lot of offices and a lot of fronts, behind which they interfere in what is going on in some of these countries. To be honest, I'm more concerned about Iranian meddling in the region than I am the Russians.[34]

The U.S. armed forces also took note of Iran's entry into the Western Hemisphere. Normally the issue of Iran was covered by the commander of the U.S. Central Command (CENTCOM), General David Petraeus, whose area of responsibility covered Egypt, the Arabian Peninsula, Iraq, Iran, and eastward to Pakistan. Suddenly, the commander of the U.S. Southern Command (SOUTHCOM), Admiral James G. Stavridis, whose area of responsibility was primarily Latin American, was needed to provide a new perspective on how close the Iranian threat had come to the backyard of the United States.

Testifying before the Senate Armed Services Committee, Stavridis warned that there had been "an increase in a wide level of activity by the Iranian government" over the last five years.[35] Iran opened six new embassies in Latin America and enlarged its Islamic proselytizing activities throughout the region.[36] During the previous year, Stavridis noted the "connectivity between narcoterrorism and Islamic radical terrorism" in South America, which he said "could be disastrous for this region."[37]

In fact, in October 2008, authorities in Colombia broke up a drug and money-laundering ring that included three suspects who had been shipping funds to Hizbullah.[38] The ring's operations extended to Venezuela, Panama, and Guatamala. Colombia had been a target for many years of Iranian influence. For example, as recently as 1999, Iran offered to fund the construction of a suspicious meat-packing plant in the Colombian village of San Vincente that had previously served as the headquarters of the Revolutionary Armed Forces of Colombia, known by its Spanish acronym— FARC. It would have been a windowless facility that would receive regular deliveries, containing everything from narcotics to weapons. U.S. officials blocked the Iranian grant, fearing that the plant would be used as a cover for illicit operations. There was a concern that FARC would develop close operational ties with Hizbullah and Iran, given their presence in nearby countries like Venezuela.[39]

Indeed, Venezuela was becoming a country of particular concern. President Hugo Chavez personally helped broker Ahmadinejad's relations with a number of South American leaders. Chavez offered his personal aircraft to the Iranian president to fly him from Venezuela to Bolivia in 2007 to meet President Evo Morales and to build up Tehran's ties with La Paz. Weekly flights of IranAir from Tehran to Caracas began the same year. Hizbullah was well-placed to build up a presence in Venezuela. Its island of Margarita had a Hizbullah presence even before Chavez came to power.[40] Moreover, in June 2008, the U.S. Treasury Department identified two Venezuelan residents and one Venezuelan diplomat, named

Ghazi Nasr al-Din, as supporters of terrorism because of their close work with Hizbullah.[41]

There were other forms of Iranian penetration in Venezuela and the rest of Latin America, some longer-term, including an effort to send Shiite missionaries to South American Indian tribes. Several thousand members of the Wayuu tribe who lived in the border area between Venezuela and Colombia had converted to Shiite Islam in as a result of Iranian proselytizing.[42] A former Iranian ambassador to Mexico, Mohammad Hassan Qadiri-Abyaneh, characterized Latin America as "fertile ground" for the spread of Shiite Islam.[43] Whether seeking to spread its religion or a militant network to support eventual operations, Iran was carving out for itself a definite position of influence throughout the area.

Noting many of these developments, Dennis Blair, the director of U.S. National Intelligence, expressed the concerns of the American intelligence community that "Chavez's growing ties to Iran coupled with Venezuela's lax financial laws and border controls, with widespread corruption have created a permissive environment for Hizballah to exploit."[44] An internal Israeli foreign ministry document, which was obtained by the Associated Press, revealed an additional concern about Iran's ties with Chavez and his local allies: both Venezuela and Bolivia were supplying Iran with uranium.[45] Moreover, Venezuela was serving as an important platform for Iran's broader regional goals in Latin America, which Ahmadinejad even mapped out.

In January 2008, Ahmadinejad invited the ambassadors from Cuba, Brazil, Mexico, Uruguay, Colombia, Nicaragua, Ecuador, and Bolivia to Tehran, calling for an expansion of Iran's ties with these countries.[46] Indeed, the new Iranian embassies across Latin America that Tehran has pursued could provide an important instrument for the expansion of Iranian influence and a potential infrastructure for terrorism.

Throughout most of the world, Iran exploited its embassies in order to station abroad officers of the Revolutionary Guards or the Ministry of Intelligence and Security. In early May 2009, Secretary of State Hillary Clinton described the growing political and economic penetration of Latin America as "quite disturbing." When she turned to Iran's new embassy in Nicaragua, she confirmed concerns about its ultimate use: "The Iranians are building a huge embassy in Managua—and you can only imagine what that's for."[47]

In fact, according to Michael Braun, who had served until recently as the Chief of Operations at the U.S. Drug Enforcement Administration (DEA), members of the Quds Force of the Revolutionary Guards were now appearing in Latin America. He believed they were directing Hizbullah's criminal enterprises in the region. He suggested that in Mexico Hizbullah was using the same smuggling routes as the drug cartels in order to penetrate the southern borders of the United States. He also believed that they were working together.[48]

There had already been cases of Hizbullah elements trying to move into the United States from Mexico. A resident of Tijuana, Salim Boughader Mucharrafille, smuggled 200 Lebanese into the United States, including Hizbullah sympathizers, until he was arrested in December 2002. There were other smuggling rings working with Hizbullah-affiliated illegal immigrants that continued to operate in the area of the California-Mexico border.[49]

This was a growing source of concern for U.S. specialists on the terrorist threat to America. Robert Grenier, the former head of the CIA's Counterterrorism Center, warned in 2007, while speaking in Mexico, that the United States was concerned that Hizbullah—or Hamas—would seek to set up operations on Mexican soil in order to infiltrate America's porous southern border and carry out future terrorist attacks.[50]

There were some disturbing signs that Iran was starting to carve out a position of influence for itself in Mexico in recent years. For example, in July 2008, the Mexican newspaper, *El Universal*, reported that a U.S. Drug Enforcement Agency (DEA) document contained information that two Mexican drug cartels had been sending snipers to Iran for training with the Revolutionary Guards since 2005.[51] The training included the use of bazookas and rocket launchers. There was no independent confirmation by the DEA of the Mexican report, but it confirmed what many U.S. officials had feared: the link between the South American narcotics trade and Middle Eastern terrorism.

The presence of Hizbullah in South America's tri-border area between Brazil, Paraguay, and Argentina was not new. It dates back to the early 1990s and its attacks on Israeli and Jewish targets in Buenos Aires, like the 1994 AMIA bombing. In the last several years, the U.S. Treasury had identified activists in the tri-border area, like Sobhi Fayad, who served as a liaison between Iranian embassies and local Hizbullah associates.[52] Fayad had received military training in Lebanon and Iran.[53] He had other close associates in the tri-border area like Assad Ahmad Barakat, a naturalized Paraguayan of Lebanese origin, who lived in Brazil and moved millions of dollars for Hizbullah while serving as a regional operative for the organization.[54]

But there were increasing signs of Hizbullah and Iranian activity in the northern parts of South America, as well, which was inching forward to the southern border of the United States. Iran had succeeded in putting in place an infrastructure of terrorist operatives and support facilities which it could exploit against the United States right from its Latin American backyard, should Tehran to decide to take up such a course of action. The threat emanating from this Iranian presence and especially from its operational arm, Hizbullah, was not lost on officials in Washington.

Indeed, the former Secretary of Homeland Security, Michael Chertoff, concluded that while al-Qaeda was the "most serious immediate threat" to the United States, it was not the "most serious long-term threat."[55] He reserved that category for Hizbullah. Chertoff warned that it was Hizbullah that had developed capabilities that al-Qaeda "can only dream of." And he added that while Hizbullah had not carried out attacks in the United States itself, "it has developed a presence in the Western Hemisphere, specifically in South America."

The Risks Posed by a Nuclear Iran

Any future western policies towards Iran must be based on a realistic assessment of the risks emanating from Iran crossing the nuclear threshold. Over the last fifteen years, the Iranians have been investing heavily in their ballistic missile programs, acquiring capabilities to strike well beyond the Middle East into the heart of Europe. Certainly, Washington has monitored the growth of the Iranian missile program very carefully.

For example, Lieutenant General Henry Oberling, chief of the U.S. missile defense program, predicted in 2007 that Iranian missiles could threaten North America by 2015.[56] It was well known that a civilian space-launch vehicle that could put a satellite in orbit could provide Iran in the future with inter-continental range capabilities to reach the eastern seaboard of the United States. Western analysts were concerned that Iran could replace the satellite with a different payload—like a nuclear warhead. These concerns materialized when Iran managed to put its first domestically made satellite—called *Omid* (or "hope" in Farsi)—into earth orbit on February 3, 2009.

But despite these capabilities, direct missile attacks against the United States and its NATO allies are not the most likely scenario for how Iran would pose a threat in the coming years, given the way the Iranian armed forces—and the Revolutionary Guards, in particular—have stressed asymmetric warfare and covert operations in confrontation with the West.[57] In fact, noting the technological advantage of the West, Mohammad Ali Jafari, the commander of the Revolutionary Guards, stressed in 2007 that "asymmetrical warfare" was the basis of Iran's "strategy for dealing with the considerable capabilities of the enemy."[58] Two years earlier, when he headed the Revolutionary Guards' ground forces command, he spoke about Iran's "excellent deterrence capabilities outside its [own borders]... if necessary," he explained, "it will use them."[59]

Tehran clearly had the instruments for global reach, but its preference was to use acts of subversion, like terrorism, that it has employed successfully since the early 1980s in dealing with the military power of the West. Using suicide-bombing attacks, Iran forced the United States and its European allies out of Lebanon in 1983–84; by taking western hostages in Lebanon, it sought to change the policies of states, like France, towards the Iran-Iraq War. Striking Argentina, it sought to retaliate for the cessation of nuclear cooperation.

By supplying arms and training to insurgents in Iraq and Afghanistan, in recent years, it has sought to bog down the United States and its allies in long and difficult wars, thereby preventing the emergence of strong, stable, pro-western allies along its western and eastern borders. Iran has also tried for years to intimidate the Arab states of the Persian Gulf by using terrorism. Through Hamas and Hizbullah, Iran has tried to prevent too close an alignment with Washington while undermining any stable peace settlement between the Arab world and Israel. In 1941, when Japan wanted to push the United States out of the western Pacific, it attacked the U.S. Naval headquarters at Pearl Harbor with aircraft using symmetric warfare. Today, if Iran wanted to push the United States out of the Persian Gulf, it would not use its limited airpower, but it might seek to ignite a Shiite rebellion in Bahrain and order acts of subversion against its Sunni government that hosts the headquarters of the U.S. Fifth Fleet.

The question of what will happen with a nuclear-armed Iran depends on a more fundamental issue: will Iran be a *status quo* power, interested in fostering stability along its borders, or will Iran continue to be a *revolutionary* power, seeking to export the Islamic Revolution and to lead the war of radical Islam against the West.

As of 2009, it appears that Iran remains committed to the latter policy and the concomitant destabilization of the Middle East and South Asia. This was reconfirmed in 2008 by the commander of the Revolutionary Guards himself, General Mohammad Ali Jafari, who told his fellow officers: "Our revolution has not ended."[60] He added: "Our Imam did not limit the movement of the Islamic Revolution to this country, but drew greater horizons."

It had to be recalled that Iran's internal reform movements, which might have sought a *modus vivendi* with the West, have been quashed. The main power centers of Iran—centers that will determine its future direction—remain the Supreme Leader Ayatollah Ali Khamenei, the Revolutionary Guards (whose internal grip on Iran's economy and politics has only grown in recent years), and President Mahmoud Ahmadinejad, who has the support of both.

Nonetheless, there has been some speculation in western capitals that Iranian and western interests might begin to coincide on Afghanistan, and to a lesser extent on Iraq. Certainly, it was a paramount western interest to make sure that Afghanistan did not become a sanctuary for global terrorism again. Yet some of the trend lines in 2009 were troubling. The reconstitution of the Taliban's military power in Afghanistan, along with its rise in Pakistan, has been advancing.

At the same time, these developments were re-creating the political conditions that existed briefly right after September 11, when Tehran quietly seemed to support the U.S.–led war effort to topple the Taliban regime and create a new government to replace it. What undermined a U.S.-Iranian rapprochement at the time was the fact that Iran also opened itself up to elements of al-Qaeda that sought a new sanctuary. It also played a double game with the Taliban—seeking their overthrow using the West, while offering them support to fight the West at the very same time.

In 2006, former U.S. ambassador to Afghanistan, Peter Thomsen, explained the logic of Iranian behavior in those years, saying,

"A weakened Afghan state lessens the likelihood it can become a U.S. ally against Iran."[61] Indeed in 2007, NATO commanders noted an escalating flow of Iranian weapons into Afghanistan, including armor-piercing roadside bombs; Iranian arms shipments were repeatedly intercepted, showing that it was not a sporadic effort.[62] Yet might this Iranian behavior change under the conditions of 2009? Afghanistan looked like an important test case for evaluating whether Iran was about to alter its past tendency to intervene in the internal affairs of its neighbors.

In early 2009, the prospects for a fundamental shift in Iranian behavior still did not look particularly good. General David Petraeus, as commander of the U.S. Central Command, only noted on January 8, 2009, that "there are ... common interests between Afghanistan, the coalition, and Iran, but there are also conflicting interests, needless to say."[63] He cautiously raised the possibility that Iran might be part of a regional strategy for Afghanistan "at some point."[64]

But Iran was not yet there. The *Sunday Times* in Britain reported on March 1, 2009, that Iran was supplying the Taliban with shoulder-held SA-14 surface-to-air missiles which threatened NATO helicopters.[65] Counter-measures designed for more primitive shoulder-held missiles were ineffective against them. Indeed, Iraqi insurgents who had fired an SA-14 downed a British Lynx helicopter in May 2006, killing five British servicemen.[66]

Appearing before the Senate Armed Services Committee on March 10, 2009, Lieutenant General Michael D. Maples, who was the Director of the Defense Intelligence Agency (DIA), did not differ from implications of newspaper reports about Iran; he summarized the DIA's understanding of Iranian policy in 2009 toward the wars in Afghanistan and Iraq when he said:

Iran assesses that its use of terrorism provide benefits with few costs and risks. Iran continues to provide lethal aid to Iraqi Shi'a militants and Afghan insurgents while simultaneously providing weapons, training and money to Lebanese Hizballah, its strategic partner.[67]

In short, Iran remained a revolutionary regime in 2009. It could make tactical retreats if it felt international pressure, pulling back many of its Quds Force units from Iraq, when their network had been uncovered. The tentacles of what had been called in Bahrain the "Octopus" of Iranian subversion still had the ability to reach into a half-dozen or more Middle Eastern states through both Shiite and Sunni organizations that identified with its mission like Hizbullah, Hamas, and even some of the various branches of the Muslim Brotherhood.

What will happen when a state supporting terrorism, like Iran, crosses the nuclear threshold is analytically new territory. There are no precedents to guide a policymaker having to confront this scenario. Nonetheless, once Iran is equipped with nuclear weapons, there are certain developments that can be anticipated. First, it is certain that many of the terrorist organizations that have been operating with Iranian assistance will feel emboldened and will likely escalate many of their operations. Historically, Hizbullah tried to protect its Iranian sponsors, frequently using the names of front organizations that were neither connected to the Hizbullah leadership nor with Tehran.

There was good reason for this caution. The war that the United States and its allies launched against the Taliban in Afghanistan in the aftermath of September 11 demonstrated that a state providing sanctuary and support for international terrorist operations could come under western attack. In 1998, that principle had also been demonstrated when the Clinton administration launched a cruise missile attack on Afghanistan and Sudan. But what would have happened if the Taliban had possessed nuclear weapons and long-range missile delivery systems back in 2001? Would there not be a debate over the wisdom of western retaliation against a nuclear Taliban state?

Thus a nuclear Iran would pose a challenge of a far greater magnitude to the United States and its allies than the Taliban state did eight years ago. As a result, Iranian surrogates across the Middle East are likely to feel that they can operate with impunity, risking little for their Iranian backers in Tehran. And the Iranian leadership, which at times felt it needed to keep these groups on a short leash, is likely to be less sensitive to the political implications of their operations.

Where might this newly found freedom of action be felt? As discussed earlier, since 2006, Iranian spokesmen have ratcheted up their rhetoric against the legitimacy of the Sunni Arab regimes in the Arab world—especially Egypt and Saudi Arabia. Undoubtedly, the first to feel the heat from a nuclear Iran will be these Middle Eastern states. Egypt's Muslim Brotherhood opposition has declared its solidarity with Iran against the positions of the Egyptian government already.

In 2003, al-Qaeda attacked Riyadh with triple suicide bombings, which were ultimately linked to al-Qaeda commanders in Iran, under Tehran's protection. Hizbullah's Saudi branch, known as Hizbullah al-Hijaz, struck at Khobar Towers in 1996. Its natural area of operations is Saudi Arabia's Eastern Province, where both the Saudi oilfields and Saudi Arabia's Shiite minority are concentrated, from which Saudi Hizbullah derived its operatives. Attacks in this area would not only intimidate the Saudi leadership, it would be the quickest way to jack up the price of oil, which has always been an Iranian interest.

Along Israel's borders, a nuclear Iran would undoubtedly embolden Iranian surrogates like Hizbullah and Hamas to use greater military force without fearing Israeli military retaliation. Indeed, Iran might seek to extend its deterrent power to cover these groups, which would make them more prone to take risks and make their terrorist operations—and Israel's self-defense response—into a hairline trigger for a wider regional war.

A more regionally active Hamas would also pose a direct threat to the security of Jordan. In April 2006, Jordanian intelligence uncovered a Hamas cell, which smuggled weaponry from Syria to use against Jordanian installations.[68] Such activities against pro-western allies, like Jordan, would undoubtedly become more frequent in a Middle East under the growing influence of a nuclear Iran and its local surrogates.

The cardinal question that is often asked about a nuclear Iran is whether it would transfer any nuclear capabilities to Middle Eastern terror groups that it generally supports. It has been the conventional wisdom of security experts that states will not transfer weapons of mass destruction to other states; part of the crisis in Sino-Soviet relations during the early Cold War emanated from Moscow's refusal to deliver its nuclear technology to Beijing. The technology for producing nuclear weapons has historically been regarded as the "crown jewels" of a country's national power. It was axiomatic that this capability is shared with no one.

But this rule of behavior of the early nuclear powers has broken down. It was a Pakistani scientist, A. Q. Khan, who supplied centrifuge designs for Iran's uranium enrichment effort, with the full knowledge of the Pakistani defense establishment. North Korea provided much of the technology for Syria's clandestine nuclear reactor at Deir al-Zur, along the Euphrates River, that was destroyed by the Israeli Air Force on September 6, 2007, according to non-Israeli sources. According to U.S. intelligence briefings, the Syrian reactor was strikingly similar to North Korea's Yongbyon reactor, which produced plutonium for Pyongyang's nuclear weapons program.[69] The Syrians were working on a gas-cooled, graphite-moderated reactor, which only had been built by the North Koreans during the last thirty-five years.

If North Korea provided nuclear technology to Syria, why could it not help Iran's nuclear program as well? Indeed, Siegfried S. Hecker, a former director of the Los Alamos National Laboratory who visited North Korea, warned that Pyongyang could easily produce and ship plutonium oxide powder to Iran.[70] Ten to twenty kilograms of plutonium in the hands of Iran, he explained, "would catapult it into nuclear-weapon status." While North Korea froze its plutonium production program in 1994 under its "Agreed Framework" with the Clinton administration, it resumed production in 2003. There are widely varying estimates of its unmonitored plutonium stocks which would allow it to export certain quantities without getting easily caught.[71]

The transfer of plutonium or any sensitive nuclear technology from Iran to Hizbullah is a distinct possibility. Hizbullah is demonstrably part of the Iranian defense establishment, so Iran providing it with any weapons of mass destruction is like supplying itself. In this sense, Hizbullah is not a non-state actor, like al-Qaeda which, acting in its own self-interest, has sought to obtain weapons of mass destruction in the past.

Indeed, bureaucratically, within the Iranian security establishment, nuclear weapons development and global terrorism are both the responsibility of the Revolutionary Guards. In recent years, Iran has shown little reluctance to supply Hizbullah with its latest state-of-the-art conventional weaponry from C-802 anti-ship cruise missiles to 150-mile range Zalzal rockets. The barriers preventing the transfer of the most sophisticated Iranian weaponry have been steadily dropping.

But would Iran go this far with a nuclear device of any kind? The 1983 attack Iran launched against the U.S. Marine Barracks in Beirut was considered, at the time, to be the largest non-nuclear blast ever ignited. Iran has pushed the envelope with its use of conventional explosives. What would be more likely than Hizbullah resorting to a nuclear explosive device would be the use of a "dirty bomb" which spreads radioactive material with a conventional blast. Chechen terrorists actually tried to employ a "dirty bomb" in Moscow during 1995.[72] In 2008, Colombia's defense ministry recovered 66 pounds of uranium that it alleged FARC planned to use for a "dirty bomb."[73] As history has shown, ideologically divergent terrorist organizations have come to imitate each other's operational techniques over time.

For Iran, terrorism is all about intimidation for the purpose of achieving the goals of the Islamic Revolution—like evicting the United States from the Middle East and thereby facilitating Iran's emergence as the dominant power of the area. And many of Hizbullah's potential operatives are already positioned near their targets in the West, whether in the heart of western Europe, South America, or possibly in the United States itself.

What might cause the Iranian leadership to add any non-conventional capability to the arsenal of Hizbullah or its front organizations? Certainly one factor will be its calculus of what type of response it might face. The very fact that Iran itself might cross the nuclear threshold in the future, and the West, at the end of the day, might acquiesce to a nuclear armed Iran—after declaring for years that such a possibility was unacceptable—might well lead more activist elements in Iran's military hierarchy to risk

IRANIAN SUPPORT FOR GLOBAL ISLAMIST MILITANCY
SELECTED CASES

IRAN

Shiite Muslim Groups				Sunni Muslim Groups			
Funding, Training, Weapons				Funding, Training, Weapons			
Hizbullah (Lebanon)	Hizbullah al-Hijaz (Saudi Arabia)	Hizbullah (Bahrain)	Mahdi Army (Iraq)	Hamas (Gaza Strip, Syria, Lebanon)	Taliban (Afghanistan)	GIA (Algeria)	SDA (Bosnia)

Sunni Muslim Groups

Sanctuary

al-Qaeda

nuclear brinksmanship using Hizbullah terrorists under their direct control.[74] The threat of nuclear terrorism from some front organization, over which Iran could plausibly argue it only had "spiritual" influence, would be safer to use than a missile attack launched from Iranian territory.

Can a nuclear Iran be effectively deterred from engaging in nuclear brinksmanship in the future, just like the U.S.S.R. was deterred during the Cold War? This is an area where there is an extreme amount of uncertainty. Iran made the Shiite ethos about the martyrdom of the Third Imam, Hussein ibn Ali, into a military doctrine that extolled suicide bomber attacks. During the Iran-Iraq War, it used the ethos of martyrdom again for large human wave attacks against the well-equipped Iraqi Army. While the leaders of the Iranian regime may not want to lose their own lives in a military exchange with the West, they have not demonstrated many reservations about sacrificing hundreds of thousands of their own people.

It is not surprising that professionals in the U.S. foreign policy establishment have doubted the efficacy of deterrence in the case of Iran. For example, Dennis Ross, President Obama's point man on Iran, wrote in 2006 in the *Washington Post*: "As for those who think that the nuclear deterrent rules that governed relations between the United States and the Soviet Union during the Cold War will also apply in a nuclear Middle East: Don't be so confident."[75]

Ross did not focus on Shiite martyrdom but rather on the apocalyptic theories of President Mahmoud Ahmadinejad: "With an Iranian president who sees himself as an instrument for accelerating the coming of the 12th Imam—which is preceded in the mythology by the equivalent Armageddon—one should not take comfort in thinking that Iran will act responsibly." No one looking at this issue is suggesting that Iranians will not respond to the threat of retaliation. The serious question is how reliable this calculus of deterrence will be with the present Iranian leadership.

But Ahmadinejad is not the only problem; the belief in the imminent arrival of the Mahdi, while controversial inside Iran, nonetheless has a following among many of the elites of the Iranian regime, and especially among the Revolutionary Guards. It is difficult to evaluate how widely these ideas have penetrated those close to the top of its command structure who would undoubtedly have input into decision-making in sensitive nuclear decisions. The challenge this poses for deterrence only becomes more severe if Iran, while denying support for covert terrorist networks, falls back on *taqiya*, the religiously sanctioned practice of deception advocated by Ayatollah Khomeini, in depicting their true connection with terrorism.[76]

The present Iranian leadership hopes to change no less than the shape of the current world order with its acquisition of nuclear weapons. Unfortunately, the Iranians are right in their assessment that the emergence of a nuclear Iran has global implications beyond the Middle East. It will set off a chain reaction in the region of nuclear proliferation undermining the efforts of the world community since the late 1960s to prevent such an eventuality. It will embolden Iranian behavior towards U.S. allies in the area of the oil-rich Persian Gulf, pushing the price of oil much higher and undermining the recovery of western economies.

A nuclear Iran could also lead to an escalation of attacks against Israel by Iran's main surrogates on its borders, Hizbullah and Hamas, increasing the chances of a new Arab-Israeli War erupting and washing away any nascent peace arrangements between Israel and more pragmatic parts of the Palestinian leadership. Israel, itself, will have to make some hard judgments given Iran's growing nuclear and missile capabilities and the declared intentions of most of the Iranian leadership—and not just Ahmadinejad—to see "Israel wiped off the map."

In the meantime, Iran's networks across the Arab world will be emboldened and put many of the current Sunni Arab regimes at increased risk. Presently, they are seeking western intervention to stop what they see as a resurrection of the Persian Empire, spread with the fervor of a second Islamic Revolution and a revival of Shiite Islam.

Whether Egypt, Jordan, and Saudi Arabia would join forces with the West to contain a nuclear Iran or acquiesce to its leadership and join the bandwagon behind the new Islamic power will depend as much on the strength and conviction of the United States and its allies as on the skills of Tehran's envoys. It became popular in western foreign policy circles "to link" the question of an Arab coalition with Iran to progress on Israeli-Palestinian diplomacy, but Saudi Arabia clearly would not want to make the defense of its massive Ras Tanura oil terminal in the Persian Gulf contingent upon whether Israel and the Palestinians reach the sort of agreement that has alluded them for nearly two decades, since negotiations were first launched at the 1991 Madrid Peace conference.

The critical factor in halting Iran will be western leadership of a bloc of countries that are already threatened by Tehran's growing power, but are still waiting to see whether the United States will take any action. Western diplomacy failed to halt Iran's drive for nuclear weapons in the last decade. Whether it can contain the consequences of this legacy remains an open question.

Can Iran Still Be Stopped?

Iran has succeeded in outmaneuvering the West with its nuclear weapons program because of its own skillful diplomacy and the systematic mishandling of the Iranian file by western governments. Since the Islamic Revolution in 1979, the intentions of the Iranian leadership have been misread—and even worse—misrepresented to democratic publics. But even while it is late to halt Iran's drive for nuclear weapons, it is not too late to prevent their becoming a nuclear power. While Iran has developed its main areas of international strength through its backing of international terrorism and its development of weapons of mass destruction, it still has many areas of weakness that can be exploited, before it becomes a hostile threat with nuclear capabilities.

Unquestionably, the Iranian economy is a main area of vulnerability in Iranian leadership. Even in 2003–2006, in a period of relatively high oil prices, Iran's annual growth rate was dropping from 7.1 percent in 2003 to 4.3 percent in 2006; the growth rate continued to drop thereafter. Iran needs massive foreign investment to maintain the current level of production in its oil fields. Yet foreign direct investment in Iran has been sharply scaled back.[77]

And regardless of the level of its oil production, over half the Iranian government's revenue comes from oil exports. This presents an extremely difficult challenge for Tehran, when the price of oil declined nearly 70 percent between 2008 and 2009. Moreover, Iranian state spending had been increasing as the price of oil has been declining, with much of this increase going to state subsidies, like the subsidy on gasoline. The Iranians are extremely vulnerable to the price of oil; assuming they could find sufficient markets for their oil, they cannot just boost production so easily to make up for falling oil prices. The West still has enormous economic leverage over Iran, should it decide to use it.

But the most immediate area of Iranian economic vulnerability is unquestionably its dependence on imported gasoline, given its inadequate refinery capacity to produce gasoline from its own crude oil. Estimates vary as to the extent of Iranian foreign dependence, but it is estimated to be as much as 40 percent of its gasoline consumption, though it may have dipped to 25–30 percent since 2007.[78]

One problem with economic sanctions, however, is they are notoriously slow in their political impact, particularly if they are not sufficiently severe. UN sanctions against Iraq from 1991 to 2003 were insufficient to get Saddam Hussein to fulfill UN Security Council resolutions about his past weapons programs. The divestment campaign to get U.S. companies to stop investing in

South Africa in the 1980s also took more than a decade to have any considerable effect.

But denying Iran the ability to import refined petroleum products could have a far quicker impact on the Iranian leadership. It would likely force the regime to ration gasoline. When gasoline rationing was tried by the Iranian government in 2007, there were violent riots in response. Recognizing this vulnerability, the U.S. Congress has begun to act. In April 2009, Evan Bayh (D-Indiana) and Jon Kyl (R-Arizona) introduced a bill entitled the "Iran Refined Petroleum Sanctions Act" which sought to encourage foreign governments and companies to cease "all exports of refined petroleum products to Iran." It was referred to the Committee on Banking, Housing, and Urban Affairs and had sixty-four cosponsors by July 7, 2009.

Factually, Iran has been relying on five international corporations for its gasoline supplies: Vitol (Switzerland/Netherlands), Trafigura (Switzerland/Netherlands), Reliance Industries (India), Glencore (Switzerland), and Total (France).[79] An international effort must be made to force these companies to choose whether they want to sell gasoline to Iran or trade with the United States and the major industrial powers of the world.

In March 2009, a bipartisan group of members from the House of Representatives called on the U.S. Energy Department to reconsider a contract with Vitol to supply crude oil to the U.S. Strategic Petroleum Reserve.[80] They were concerned with Vitol's guilty plea to charges of grand larceny in connection with kickbacks paid to Iraq as part of the UN "oil-for-food" program. But these measures could also be taken in response to Vitol's role in supplying gasoline to Iran.

During the October 7, 2008, Presidential Debate, then-Presidential Candidate Barack Obama actually proposed that "Iran right now imports gasoline, even though it's an oil-producer, because its oil infrastructure has broken down...if we can prevent them from importing the gasoline they need and the refined petroleum products, that starts changing their cost-benefit analysis."[81] Senator John McCain made the same point four months earlier. Consensus at the time was that if sanctions against Iran are to be employed again, they will have to be extremely severe sanctions if they are to have a timely effect. The West may only have months to act in 2010. It cannot assume that it has the time to undertake a new sanctions policy that might take years.

Congressional bills sanctioning countries selling refined oil products—including gasoline—to Iran essentially provide President Obama with the authority to take the very tough measures that are needed to squeeze or even cripple the Iranian economy, if his engagement policy fails. Were the West able to additionally forgo Iranian oil, for a period of time, then this added pressure on the Iranian state budget, with its enormous outlays for subsidies, would help further bring the Iranian economy to a halt, forcing the government to negotiate for their needs. All the while such economic pressures are being applied, the United States and its allies must keep the military option on the table in order to persuade Iran to change its policies and arrest its nuclear work.

As the United States pursues a new diplomatic course with Iran, the gravest immediate danger to western security as a whole comes from a scenario in which a new P-5-plus-1 agreement with Iran is reached that leaves them with the capacity to acquire a military nuclear capability quickly if they so chose. For example, if the West decides that Iran can legally retain a large stockpile of low-enriched uranium (that it could easily enrich into weapons-grade uranium in a matter of weeks), then Iran will already be a nuclear power, with a very rapid breakout capability. In order to undermine the security of the Middle East and the world as a whole, Iran does not actually need to openly test its nuclear weapons, like North Korea did. It only has to get close to the nuclear threshold, with a sufficient stockpile of uranium, to profit from the resulting world fear of an imminent Iranian nuclear breakout.

In his June 4, 2009, speech at Cairo University, which was addressed to the Muslim world as a whole, President Obama touched on the Iranian nuclear program.[82] After reminding the Iranian leadership of his engagement strategy by stating "we are willing to move forward without preconditions," Obama bluntly said that "it is clear to all concerned that when it comes to nuclear weapons, we have reached a decisive point." He did not say what would happen next, but he did stress that Iran, like "any nation," had "the right to access peaceful nuclear power" if it complied with its commitments to the Nuclear Non-Proliferation Treaty. In short, that meant that an Iranian civilian nuclear program was acceptable as long as it did not become a military nuclear program.

But what Obama's idea means practically is not yet entirely clear. The P-5-plus-1 had proposed years earlier, as part of an incentives package, to provide Iran with light-water reactors, which U.S. officials believed to be more proliferation-proof (though this is unproven, as critics point out). Was this the same proposal? Or was the administration considering other options? One idea that President Obama is reportedly considering is the establishment of an international fuel bank that would supply low-enriched uranium for countries with civilian nuclear reactors, so that they would not enrich uranium by themselves and develop the capacity the produce highly-enriched uranium for weapons, as well.[83] Given Iran's determination to acquire nuclear weapons, it seems doubtful that this option would be workable with the regime presently in control in Tehran.

Other ideas are also under consideration. On June 11, 2009, Senator John Kerry, the Chairman of the Senate Foreign Relations Committee, told the *Financial Times* in an interview that Iran had a right to enrich its own uranium. This represented a sharp break not only from the Bush administration, but also from successive resolutions of the UN Security Council, which had called on Iran to suspend enrichment. Was Kerry speaking for himself or floating a trial balloon for how the administration might permit Iran to produce low-enriched uranium for a civilian program, with some safeguards in place to prevent the production of high-enriched uranium to fuel nuclear weapons?[84] Technically it is possible to install more IAEA cameras at Iranian facilities and increase the frequency of the inspections by its monitoring teams, but if Iran has covert enrichment plants, as has been suggested, then such arrangements could be easily evaded.

In any case, the international community has already been tested with this scenario in the case of North Korea, where safeguards were put in place to prevent the production of weapons-grade plutonium for nuclear bombs from the used fuel rods at the Yongbyon reactor, which was supposed to be for civilian purposes. In December 2002 the North Korean government removed the seals from the reactor's spent fuel rods and began to reprocess them in order to produce additional plutonium. It expelled the inspectors of the IAEA and announced its withdrawal from the Nuclear Non-Proliferation Treaty.[85]

Within four years, on October 8, 2006, North Korea conducted its first nuclear test. And although another nuclear accord was soon announced on February 13, 2007, North Korea easily broke out of its constraints and conducted its second underground nuclear test on May 25, 2009. There were reports that Pyongyang invited Iranian nuclear scientists to North Korea to study the nuclear tests.[86] The two countries have been closely collaborating in missile and nuclear technology for at least twenty years.[87]

Regardless of the scientific data they shared, the Iranians carefully watched how North Korea broke out of its international commitments and created a nuclear *fait accompli*. Although a harsh UN Security Council Resolution was adopted after the first North Korean nuclear test, within a few weeks, the western powers were back at the negotiating table and any stern measures that had been taken were ultimately of a limited duration.

The North Korean case is a warning about what could happen with Iran if an accord is reached with the Islamic Republic that leaves Tehran on the nuclear threshold with the capability to easily violate whatever agreement is reached. It cannot be assumed that the IAEA would automatically detect the diversion of Iranian low-enriched uranium for further enrichment to weapons-grade fuel.[88] Indeed, during the 2003–2005 period, the Iranians successfully delayed IAEA inspections multiple times in order to remove potentially suspicious materials from sites that were to be inspected.

In the event the world was pre-occupied with another crisis, elsewhere, Tehran's ability to defy the West would be facilitated. This is precisely what happened with North Korea's withdrawal from the Agreed Framework in 2002 when the United States was focused on Iraq. Over the last seven years, Iran has adeptly demonstrated that it can manipulate the international situation to protect its nuclear program. Prior to 2002, it systematically and successfully deceived the world with its clandestine nuclear program. Given its record, it is highly likely that it will try to deceive the world yet again. A nuclear Iran can still be averted with concerted allied action, but in safeguarding the security of the West, correct diplomatic choices are no less important than the military superiority that the United States and its allies still possess—for now.

Chapter 12:

Iranian Elections and New Western Options

WITHIN HOURS OF THE CLOSING of the polling booths, the Iranian government announced that Mahmoud Ahmadinejad won the June 12, 2009, presidential elections by a landslide, with 62.63 percent of the vote. The official Islamic Republic News Agency characterized his electoral victory in a communiqué as the "revival of the revolution." It also stated that Iran would utilize its power to prepare for "the return of the Master of Time"—a clear reference to the arrival of the Hidden Imam as the Mahdi and the beginning of the end of days, according to Shiite Islamic tradition.[1] Despite the efforts of the Iranian government to present the results in an authoritative manner, the whole election was perceived as fraudulent by many Iranian citizens, sparking the worst anti-government rioting in Tehran and cities throughout Iran since the 1979 Islamic Revolution.

The elections did not really touch on the nuclear issue. The lead challenger, former Prime Minister Mir Hossein Moussavi, was historically a strong supporter of Iran's nuclear aspirations during his time in office, as was his key ally, former Iranian President Hashemi Rafsanjani. According to Iran's former head nuclear negotiator, Hassan Rowhani, in 2005 Moussavi took part in a special meeting of decision makers, led by the Supreme Leader Ali Khamenei, that renewed uranium conversion work at Isfahan, in violation of Iran's 2004 agreements with the EU-3.[2]

From the perspective of the West, Moussavi has other problematic partners, as well. His representative to the electoral oversight board was none other than the infamous Ali Akbar Mohtashemi, the fiercely anti-American former Iranian ambassador to Syria, who founded Hizbullah[3] and was directly involved in the 1983 attacks on the U.S. Marine Barracks and French military headquarters in Beirut that killed 241 servicemen and 58 French paratroopers.[4] The elections looked like a struggle among tainted figures within the Iranian establishment rather than an effort to topple and replace the main power centers of the establishment. Moussavi was by no means a challenge to the current regime, for it is defined by a third figure who loomed well above the candidates for the presidency.

The moment that the Supreme Leader Ayatollah Ali Khamenei injected himself into the controversy, he became part of the problem for many in the masses in the streets. Instead of waiting for the publication of the official results of the election, he released a statement hailing Ahmadinejad's "historic victory."[5] And while it was the responsibility of Iran's Guardian Council to validate the results of the election by June 24, he endorsed the election of Ahmadinejad in a Friday sermon on June 19, at Tehran University, where he also threatened that there would be "bloodshed and chaos"[6] if the demonstrations continued.

When protestors shouted "Death to the Dictator," they could have been referring to Khamenei, who placed himself in the forefront of the struggle between the demonstrators and the regime. He raised the stakes of what was involved. What started as a dispute over the results of the Iranian presidential elections quickly evolved into wider question over the very legitimacy of the Islamic Republic, which he ultimately represents. The waves of demonstrators that filled central Tehran—and other Iranian population centers—came to express frustrations with the entire system of government in Iran and not just the electoral loss of Moussavi.

The discontent of the Iranian people with their regime has been building up for a long period of time, although it has not always been visible to western observers. Back in 1994, there were anti-regime riots in the city of Qazvin, northwest of Tehran, where the Revolutionary Guards refused to carry out orders to use force against the local population.[7] As a result, in 2007 the Revolutionary Guards brought the Basij under their direct command and used them increasingly for domestic disturbances, as they were the most ideologically committed forces to the Islamic Revolution. From the perspective of those in the ruling regime, their reliability was going to be needed as the regime anticipated dealing with increasing internal instability in the future.

That state of affairs was becoming more evident across Iran. Besides famous student riots in 1999, there was the case in which armed Iranian Kurdish rebels attacked a Revolutionary Guards outpost in September 2005.[8] In 2006, Ahmadinejad's minister of intelligence and security warned of the threat of a "velvet revolution" in Iran or a "colored revolution," an implicit reference to Ukraine's "Orange Revolution" in 2004.[9] Indeed, trade unionists organized strikes in 2007 and 2008 which were put down by Iran's security services.[10]

The Iranian leadership has been preparing for the new domestic challenge. Just after his appointment as the commander of the Revolutionary Guards, Mohammad Ali Jafari stated on September 29, 2007, that the "main responsibility" of his forces at present would be to counter "internal threats."[11] The leaders of the Iranian security establishment knew that they were going to have to face the pent-up rage of parts of their public in the period ahead.

The democratic challenge to the Islamic Republic is also evident beyond its borders. Iran's most successful case of exporting the Islamic Revolution was Hizbullah's grip on the Lebanese state. Many predicted that Hizbullah's coalition would win the June 7, 2009, parliamentary elections, taking away control of the Lebanese government from what was known as the U.S.-backed "March 14 bloc." Surprisingly, Hizbullah was defeated and the "March 14 bloc," led by the Sunni leader Saad Hariri, held on to power. The Lebanese elections were a blow to Iran and showed many in the Middle East that the tide was not necessarily in its favor. As the editor of the London-based Saudi daily *al-Sharq al-Awsat* concluded: "The significance of this victory lies in the fact that it is practically a declaration that the Iranian project in Lebanon and the Arab world has failed."[12]

Could Washington seize upon Iran's defeat in Lebanon and really turn the tide against Tehran? Events following the Iranian elections placed President Obama, who had hoped to diplomatically engage with the Iranian government, in a tough spot. Khamenei explicitly sharpened the choices that Washington had to make. In his June 19 sermon, he misquoted Obama as calling for more demonstrations by saying that he "expected the people of Iran to take to the streets." Then Khamenei disclosed that he actually had received a letter from the administration, which sought "to express their respect for the Islamic Republic and for re-establishment of ties."[13] He wanted to know which represented the true U.S. policy, asking: "Which of these remarks are we supposed to believe?"[14]

What Khamenei wanted to hear was whether the Obama administration wanted engagement with the present Iranian establishment or if it wanted to align itself with those who sought its overthrow. In answering this question, Washington would have to take into account its multiple interests. Most governments prefer not to be forced into situations in which they have to make hard choices between two stark alternatives. But events in Iran are requiring President Obama to make a call regarding the best course of action for halting Iran's drive for nuclear weapons: weakening the Iranian government or engaging with it diplomatically.

Initially, Obama was glued to his engagement policy. In his first public comments after the election results were announced, he reiterated that the United States would "continue to pursue a tough, direct dialogue" with Iran.[15] Obama remained absolutely neutral on developments in Iran in the following days as well by declaring: "It's important to understand that although there is some ferment taking place in Iran, that the difference between Ahmadinejad and Moussavi in terms of their actual policies may not be as great as advertised."[16] Yet the protestors seemed to want more from America; many held up signs at Iranian demonstrations in English.

By June 23, Obama's tone began to change, and he spoke openly that he was "appalled and outraged by the threats, beatings, and imprisonments"[17] that were transpiring in Iran. The weekend before his speech, the world had been shocked by a video clip showing the last moments of a young Iranian woman named Neda Agha Soltan, who had been shot in the streets by Iranian security forces. Clashes continued between Iranian protestors and the Iranian security forces during the following week, but for the most part the large demonstrations with hundreds of thousands of participants had largely petered out.

The Iranian nuclear question was still in the background for many of those who monitored what was happening in the streets of Tehran and other cities. Beginning June 22, 2009, the world received a stark reminder of Iran's intentions during three days of air exercises over the Persian Gulf and the Gulf of Oman. Besides testing its capabilities in low-flying flights, Iran sought to exercise aerial refueling for reaching ranges of more than 3,000 kilometers (1,800 miles) with its air force.[18] It also tested the performance of its reconnaissance aircraft.[19] The Iranians flew well past the Strait of Hormuz, the vital choke point through which much of the world's energy supplies flows.

Many of Iran's combat aircraft were from the 1970s, from the time of the Shah, and were no longer in service elsewhere in the world. Additionally, should Iran need to reach targets that were 900 miles away, it would likely use its missile forces. But the exercise called to mind how Iran saw how far its future regional influence should reach, despite its ongoing internal disorders. It also underlined that while Iran appeared to be mired with domestic challenges, it nonetheless still seeks to build up its military power and regional influence across the Middle East.

Halting Iran's drive to obtain nuclear weapons remains an imperative for the international community. It will take some time before the full implications of Iran's domestic troubles in June 2009 are clarified. It may be that, sensitive to being perceived as a weaker power, the Iranian regime will feel a greater need to demonstrably throw its weight around and engage in riskier levels of brinksmanship than before. The regime may also seek to accelerate its nuclear program in the belief that it can strengthen its internal position by casting itself as having made Iran into a nuclear power. But developments could also move in a very different direction, after the people of Iran have been mobilized to struggle for their freedom on a scale that has not been seen in the thirty-year history of the Islamic Republic.

The debate over what the West should do with the Iranian nuclear program has up until now involved very few alternatives: 1) accept Iran as a nuclear power that will be contained by deterrence; 2) engage with Iran diplomatically to negotiate and encourage limitations on its nuclear program; or 3) use military force to pre-empt Iran's construction of nuclear weapons by destroying selective parts of its nuclear infrastructure. Prior to the June elections, it appeared that Washington preferred the second option (which required employing the threat to use the third option), but was beginning to acclimate to the idea of having to settle with accepting Iran as a nuclear power that hopefully can be contained by deterrence. The previous chapters demonstrated how dangerous such a course of action would be, given the revolutionary ideology of the Iranian leadership.

However, the massive demonstrations in Iran in the aftermath of the June presidential elections have created a fourth option: encouraging the Iranian people in their drive for political freedom. The protest movement in Iran is no longer over the narrow issue of a fixed election, alone. The people who filled the streets of Tehran question the very legitimacy of the Islamic Republic, as a whole. The last thing the West should do is take diplomatic initiatives that grant the Iranian regime the recognition—and legitimacy—it might seek, after brutalizing its own people. Such a step would undercut the hopes of the Iranian people, who seek to be rid of the current regime. It would also undercut the cause of spreading freedom against authoritarian rule worldwide.

If the West has a choice between negotiating yet again with the regime in Tehran or undercutting it further, it should clearly seek to promote a process that leads to its collapse and replacement. Engagement was tried in the past and doesn't work. Using enhanced sanctions to achieve limited agreements with the Islamic Republic, which actually halted aspects of the nuclear program, would be important, but experience has demonstrated that they would not be reliable in the long-term. However, a freedom agenda for Iran has never been seriously tried, except for the limited legislation in the United States for covert operations in the 1990s that was never fully implemented. Presently, "regime change" administered from without is unnecessary—as long as it is happening from within.

It should still be stressed that changing the regime in Iran is not a process that can be achieved overnight. In the meantime, the centrifuges at Natanz will continue spinning, increasing the inventory of enriched uranium that the Iranian armed forces will eventually have for their future weapons. Iran has declared its hostile intent towards it neighbors and beyond—in word and deed.

The goal of "wiping Israel off the map" is not just the personal position of Ahmadinejad. It was stated by no less than the Supreme

Leader Ayatollah Ali Khamenei in December of 2000.[20] Mohammad Ali Jafari, commander of the Revolutionary Guards, wrote in
February of 2008: "In the near future, we will witness the destruction of the cancerous microbe Israel by the strong capable hands of
the nation of Hizbullah."[21] Both Khamenei and Jafari are likely to
serve as central figures in the command and control of Iranian
nuclear weapons in the future.

As has been shown, Ahmadinejad's obsession with the imminent arrival of the Mahdi and the "end of days" is shared by many
at the leadership level in Iran. In 2004, Spanish Prime Minister
Jose Maria Aznar revealed that Ayatollah Ali Khamenei himself
told him in 2001 that the Islamic Republic was waiting for the
return of the Hidden Imam and expected the destruction of Israel
and the United States.[22] While the Iranian leader explicitly spoke
about "setting Israel on fire,"[23] his statements were clearly
directed against America, as well. Moreover, the growing range of
the Iranian missile forces towards Europe—well past Israel—is
probably the best indicator that Iran is becoming a global threat
rather than a danger to the countries of the Middle East alone.

In the meantime, Iran has put a global terrorist network in place
using Hizbullah, with arms reaching into the Western Hemisphere
as well. Hizbullah's presence has received the attention of American law enforcement agencies who prepare for terrorist attacks on
the United States, such as September 11. The New York Police
Department's Deputy Commissioner for Counterterrorism,
Richard Falkenrath, stated in June of 2009 that at present, Hizbullah has not decided to attack America. Nevertheless, he warned:
"But our assessment is, if they ever change their minds, they have
the capacity to inflict terrible damage on the United States, and I
worry about that a lot."[24] What would happen to these calculations, should Hizbullah benefit from an Iranian nuclear umbrella,
needs to be carefully considered.

If the West fails to halt the Iranian nuclear program, and if in the
period ahead, Tehran takes steps that bring it closer to a nuclear

military capability, all states affected by the imminent rise of nuclear Iran will have to consider what measures they must take in their own self-defense. But should the people of Iran decide to overturn the leadership of the Islamic Republic, it would undoubtedly provide the best long-term solution for addressing the nuclear threat.

Could a new post-revolutionary Iranian regime with a nuclear program be trusted? Any assessment of a threat from a country like Iran has to look at both the intentions of the ruling regime and its capabilities. Since the advent of the Islamic Republic in 1979, Iran has sought to export its revolution and carry out acts of subversion against it neighbors. In many cases this Iranian role has been ideologically driven by the regime's hard-core supporters. But it also has helped the Iranian leadership, whose legitimacy has eroded, to divert public attention away from its own failures. A legitimate Iranian government which was democratically-elected would have a very different calculus.

There should be no illusions about a post-revolutionary Iran. It would still seek to be a great power in the Middle East region. The Shah of Iran saw his country that way and therefore used his country's oil earnings to procure state of the art weaponry, from AWACS aerial control aircraft to F-14 fighters. He saw Iran as protecting the free flow of oil to the West, once the British announced they would no longer act in that capacity in 1968. He also promoted the Iranian nuclear program, envisioning a network of nuclear power plants for his country, but he might have had military ambitions as well. Iranians recall their imperial past, and that is not likely to change.

But if a new Iranian government accepted the status quo in the Middle East and stopped seeking to overthrow the governments of its neighbors, then the security of the entire region would be substantially enhanced. And if it halted the export of its radical ideology and subversion to Europe, South America, Southeast Asia, and West Africa, then a change of regime in Tehran could have a global impact. An Iran with none of the revolutionary ideology of the present regime would presumably be more willing to accept monitoring mechanisms for its nuclear program, rather than constantly trying, as the present regime in Tehran does, to undercut it with a policy of diversion, deception and recalcitrance.

Until recently, the appearance of Iranian nuclear weapons on the world stage in the near-future appeared to be a *fait accompli*. The West may get another chance to halt the Iranian program if it understands what policies have universally failed to work and correctly exploits the new possibilities that are now being presented.

Acknowledgements

As EVERY AUTHOR KNOWS, THE SUPPORT he receives from the people immediately around him can make all the difference between an idea that never gets completed and a final published work. For that reason, I owe my greatest debt to my family, especially to my wife Ofra and my children, Yael and Ariel, for their devotion and patience, throughout the process of researching and writing this book.

This book would never have even been started without the support of a number of key individuals. I owe special thanks to Zak Gertler for encouraging me to undertake this project on Iran years ago, well before it became a serious possibility. Allen Roth recognized the importance of this topic at this point in time and besides reading my earliest drafts, he also gave me important strategic advice all through my preparation of the manuscript. Steven Schneier and his team helped me all though this entire project.

There are a number of people to whom I am indebted for their valuable input on this project. Brig. General (res.) Dr. Shimon Shapira, whose book in Hebrew, *Hizbullah Between Iran and Lebanon* served as an invaluable treasure chest on the history of Hizbullah. He was a constant source of information and analysis during the last year. Lt. Col. (res.) Michael Segall provided timely analyses of current developments inside Iran along with the entire team at Terrorgence, who translated Farsi documents for this project.

Ambassador Uri Lubrani, formerly ambassador to Iran, Coordinator of Israel Government Activities in Lebanon, and adviser to the Minister of Defense on Iranian affairs, read the manuscript and gave detailed comments. Isaac Barzilai also gave me his valuable time. Ephraim Asculai of the Institute for National Security Studies at Tel Aviv University commented on specific chapters having to do with the Iranian nuclear program and the operations of the IAEA. Yehuda Yaakov shared his research on the international nuclear crisis with Iran. I owe a special thanks to Mark Dubowitz, the executive director of the Foundation for Defense of Democracies, for sharing with me his organization's work on Iranian dependence on refined petroleum products. Finally, Roman Ortiz shared with me his insights on Iranian influence in South America, and his own country of Colombia.

I am also indebted to Chaya Herskovic, the Director-General of the Jerusalem Center for making available materials that it had accumulated in the last number of years for the production of this book. I also wish to add my appreciation to Dan Diker, who took the time to read some of the last chapters and to provide his important insights and help.

I would also like to express my special appreciation to Amir Taheri, who took time to meet me in London to discuss the latest trends in Iran, especially in the recent period.

Rachel Elrom assisted me with my research materials and with everything that had to do with computer work on this book.

Adam Shay provided invaluable assistance. Studio Rami & Jaki in Jerusalem generously shared their graphic talents in producing several of the maps in this book.

My agent Richard Pine, at Inkwell Management, gave me critical advice right from the start of this project.

This book was made possible by the dedication of the entire team at Regnery Publishing beginning with Marji Ross, who approached me with the idea of an Iran project. Harry Crocker provided timely interventions to keep the book on track. Anneke Green's hard work made it possible to make this text accessible to the widest possible audience. She provided true editing skills, by challenging every assertion that was not sufficiently proven and insisting that more evidence be marshaled to make a point.

APPENDIX

1. The EU-Iran Agreement of 21 October 2003
   (The Tehran Declaration) and the EU-Iran Agreement of 15 November 2004 (The Paris Agreement)

2. Proposal to Iran (P-5-plus-1)

The EU–Iran agreement of 21 October 2003 (the Tehran Declaration)

1. Upon the invitation of the Government of the Islamic Republic of Iran the Foreign Ministers of Britain, France and Germany paid a visit to Tehran on October 21, 2003.

The Iranian authorities and the ministers, following extensive consultations, agreed on measures aimed at the settlement of all outstanding IAEA . . . issues with regards to the Iranian nuclear programme and at enhancing confidence for peaceful cooperation in the nuclear field.

2. The Iranian authorities reaffirmed that nuclear weapons have no place in Iran's defence doctrine and that its nuclear programme and activities have been exclusively in the peaceful domain. They reiterated Iran's commitment to the nuclear non-proliferation regime and informed the ministers that:

a. The Iranian Government has decided to engage in full co-operation with the IAEA to address and resolve through full transparency all requirements and outstanding issues of the Agency and clarify and correct any possible failures and deficiencies within the IAEA.

b. To promote confidence with a view to removing existing barriers for co-operation in the nuclear field:

i. having received the necessary clarifications, the Iranian Government has decided to sign the IAEA Additional Protocol and commence ratification procedures. As a confirmation of its good intentions the Iranian Government will continue to co-operate with the Agency in accordance with the Protocol in advance of its ratification.

ii. while Iran has a right within the nuclear non-proliferation regime to develop nuclear energy for peaceful purposes it has decided voluntarily to suspend all uranium enrichment and reprocessing activities as defined by the IAEA.

Dialogue

3. The Foreign Ministers of Britain, France and Germany welcomed the decisions of the Iranian Government and informed the Iranian authorities that:

a. Their governments recognise the right of Iran to enjoy peaceful use of nuclear energy in accordance with the nuclear Non-Proliferation Treaty.

b. In their view the Additional Protocol is in no way intended to undermine the sovereignty, national dignity or national security of its State Parties.

c. In their view full implementation of Iran's decisions, confirmed by the IAEA's Director General, should enable the immediate situation to be resolved by the IAEA Board.

d. The three governments believe that this will open the way to a dialogue on a basis for longer term co-operation which will provide all parties with satisfactory assurances relating to Iran's nuclear power generation programme. Once international concerns, including those of the three governments, are fully resolved Iran could expect easier access to modern technology and supplies in a range of areas.

e. They will co-operate with Iran to promote security and stability in the region including the establishment of a zone free from weapons of mass destruction in the Middle East in accordance with the objectives of the United Nations.

―――――

Source: 'Statement by the Iranian Government and visiting EU foreign ministers', Tehran, 21 Oct. 2003, URL <http://www.iaea.org/NewsCenter/Focus/Iaea Iran/statement_iran21102003.shtml>.

The EU–Iran agreement of 15 November 2004 (the Paris Agreement

The Government of the Islamic Republic of Iran and the Governments of France, Germany and the United Kingdom, with the support of the High Representative of the European Union (E3/EU), reaffirm the commitments in the Tehran Agreed Statement of 21 October 2003 and have decided to move forward, building on that agreement.

The E3/EU and Iran reaffirm their commitment to the NPT.

The E3/EU recognise Iran's rights under the NPT exercised in conformity with its obligations under the Treaty, without discrimination.

Iran reaffirms that, in accordance with Article II of the NPT, it does not and will not seek to acquire nuclear weapons. It commits itself to full cooperation and transparency with the IAEA. Iran will continue implementing volun-

tarily the Additional Protocol pending ratification.

To build further confidence, Iran has decided, on a voluntary basis, to continue and extend its suspension to include all enrichment related and reprocessing activities, and specifically: the manufacture and import of gas centrifuges and their components; the assembly, installation, testing or operation of gas centrifuges; work to undertake any plutonium separation, or to construct or operate any plutonium separation installation; and all tests or production at any uranium conversion installation. The IAEA will be notified of this suspension and invited to verify and monitor it. The suspension will be implemented in time for the IAEA to confirm before the November Board that it has been put into effect. The suspension will be sustained while negotiations proceed on a mutually acceptable agreement on long-term arrangements.

The E3/EU recognize that this suspension is a voluntary confidence building measure and not a legal obligation.

Sustaining the suspension, while negotiations on a long-term agreement are under way, will be essential for the continuation of the overall process. In the context of this suspension, the E3/EU and Iran have agreed to begin negotiations, with a view to reaching a mutually acceptable agreement on long term arrangements. The agreement will provide objective guarantees that Iran's nuclear programme is exclusively for peaceful purposes. It will equally provide firm guarantees on nuclear, technological and economic cooperation and firm commitments on security issues.

A steering committee will meet to

launch these negotiations in the first half of December 2004 and will set up working groups on political and security issues, technology and cooperation, and nuclear issues. The steering committee shall meet again within three months to receive progress reports from the working groups and to move ahead with projects and/or measures that can be implemented in advance of an overall agreement.

In the context of the present agreement and noting the progress that has been made in resolving outstanding issues, the E3/EU will henceforth support the Director General reporting to the IAEA Board as he considers appropriate in the framework of the implementation of Iran's Safeguards Agreement and Additional Protocol.

The E3/EU will support the IAEA Director General inviting Iran to join the Expert Group on Multilateral Approaches to the Nuclear Fuel Cycle.

Once suspension has been verified, the negotiations with the EU on a Trade and Cooperation Agreement will resume. The E3/EU will actively support the opening of Iranian accession negotiations at the WTO.

Irrespective of progress on the nuclear issue, the E3/EU and Iran confirm their determination to combat terrorism, including the activities of Al Qa'ida and other terrorist groups such as the MeK. They also confirm their continued support for the political process in Iraq aimed at establishing a constitutionally elected Government.

the agreement signed in Paris on 15 November 2004', IAEA document INFCIRC/637, 26 Nov. 2004, URL <http: // www. iaea. org /Publications/ Documents/ Infcircs / 2004 / infcirc637. pdf>.

Source: IAEA, 'Communication dated 26 November 2004 received from the permanent representatives of France, Germany, the Islamic Republic of Iran and the United Kingdom concerning

Proposal to Iran

by

**China, France, Germany, the Russian Federation,
the United Kingdom, the United States of America
and the European Union**

**Presented to the Iranian authorities
on 14 June 2008
Teheran**

پیشنهاد به ایران

از سوی

چین، فرانسه، آلمان، فدراسیون روسیه
بریتانیا، ایالات متحده ی آمریکا
و
اتحادیه ی اروپا

ارایه شده به مقامات ایرانی
در تاریخ 14 ژوئن 2008
(25 خرداد 1387)
در تهران

HE Manuchehr Mottaki
Minister of Foreign Affairs of the Islamic Republic of Iran
Tehran

12 June 2008

Sir,

Iran is one of the oldest civilisations in the world. Its people are justifiably proud of their history, culture and heritage. It sits at a geographical crossroads. It has vast natural resources and great economic potential, which its people should be reaping to the full.

But in recent years, Iran's relationship with the international community has been overshadowed by growing tension and mistrust, since there remains a lack of confidence in Iran's nuclear programme. We have supported the IAEA's efforts to address this with Iran but successive IAEA reports have concluded that it is not able to provide credible assurances about the absence of undeclared nuclear material and activities in Iran. Two years ago, the IAEA referred the matter to the UN Security Council, which has now passed four Resolutions calling on Iran to comply with its obligations.

We, the Foreign Ministers of China, France, Germany, Russia, the United Kingdom and the United States of America, joined in this endeavour by the European Union High Representative for the Common Foreign and Security Policy, are convinced that it is possible to change the present state of affairs. We hope that Iran's leaders share the same ambition.

In June 2006, we set out an ambitious proposal for a broad-based negotiation. We offered to work with Iran on a modern nuclear energy programme, with a guaranteed fuel supply. We were also prepared to discuss political and economic issues, as well as issues regarding regional security. These proposals were carefully considered and designed to address Iran's essential interests and those of the international community.

Today, bearing in mind the provisions of UN Security Council resolution 1803, we restate our offer to address constructively these important concerns and interests.

Our proposals are attached to this letter. Iran is, of course, free to suggest its own proposals. Formal negotiations can start as soon as Iran's enrichment-related and reprocessing activities are suspended. We want to be clear that we recognise Iran's rights under the international treaties to which it is a signatory. We fully understand the importance of a guaranteed fuel supply for a civil nuclear programme. We have supported the Bushehr facility. But with rights come responsibilities, in particular to restore the confidence of the international community in Iran's programme. We are ready to work with Iran in order to find a way to address Iran's needs and the international community's concerns, and reiterate that once the confidence of the international community in the exclusively peaceful nature of your nuclear programme is restored, it will be treated in the same manner as that of any Non-Nuclear Weapon State party to the Non-Proliferation Treaty.

We ask you to consider this letter and our proposals carefully and hope for an early response. The proposals we have made offer substantial opportunities for political, security and economic benefits to Iran and the region. There is a sovereign choice for Iran to make. We hope that you will respond positively; this will increase stability and enhance prosperity for all our people.

c.c:
Saeed Jalili
Secretary of the National Security Council of the Islamic Republic of Iran

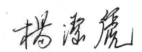

HE Mr Yang Jiechi
Minister of Foreign Affairs of the People's Republic of China

HE Dr Bernard Kouchner
Minister of Foreign and European Affairs of the French Republic

HE Dr Frank-Walter Steinmeier
Deputy Federal Chancellor and Federal Minister of Foreign Affairs of the
Federal Republic of Germany

HE Mr Sergei Viktorovich Lavrov
Minister of Foreign Affairs of the Russian Federation

HE Mr David Miliband
Secretary of State for Foreign and Commonwealth Affairs of the
United Kingdom of Great Britain and Northern Ireland

HE Dr Condoleezza Rice
Secretary of State of the United States of America

HE Dr Javier Solana
High Representative for the Common Foreign and Security Policy/
Secretary-General of the Council of the European Union

Possible Areas of Cooperation with Iran

In order to seek a comprehensive, long-term and proper solution of the Iranian nuclear issue consistent with relevant UN Security Council resolutions and building further upon the proposal presented to Iran in June 2006, which remains on the table, the elements below are proposed as topics for negotiations between China, France, Germany, Iran, Russia, the United Kingdom, and the United States, joined by the High Representative of the European Union, as long as Iran verifiably suspends its enrichment-related and reprocessing activities, pursuant to OP 15 and OP 19(a) of UNSCR 1803. In the perspective of such negotiations, we also expect Iran to heed the requirements of the UNSC and the IAEA. For their part, China, France, Germany, Russia, the United Kingdom, the United States and the European Union High Representative state their readiness:

to recognize Iran's right to develop research, production and use of nuclear energy for peaceful purposes in conformity with its NPT obligations;
to treat Iran's nuclear programme in the same manner as that of any Non-nuclear Weapon State Party to the NPT once international confidence in the exclusively peaceful nature of Iran's nuclear programme is restored.

Nuclear Energy

-       Reaffirmation of Iran's right to nuclear energy for exclusively peaceful purposes in conformity with its obligations under the NPT.
-       Provision of technological and financial assistance necessary for Iran's peaceful use of nuclear energy, support for the resumption of technical cooperation projects in Iran by the IAEA.
-       Support for construction of LWR based on state-of-the-art technology.
-       Support for R&D in nuclear energy as international confidence is gradually restored.
-       Provision of legally binding nuclear fuel supply guarantees.
-       Cooperation with regard to management of spent fuel and radioactive waste.

Political

-       Improving the six countries' and the EU's relations with Iran and building up mutual trust.
-       Encouragement of direct contact and dialogue with Iran.
-       Support Iran in playing an important and constructive role in international affairs.
-       Promotion of dialogue and cooperation on non-proliferation, regional security and stabilisation issues.
-       Work with Iran and others in the region to encourage confidence-building measures and regional security.
-       Establishment of appropriate consultation and co-operation mechanisms.
-       Support for a conference on regional security issues.
-       Reaffirmation that a solution to the Iranian nuclear issue would contribute to non-proliferation efforts and to realizing the objective of a Middle East free of weapons of mass destruction, including their means of delivery.
-       Reaffirmation of the obligation under the UN Charter to refrain in their international relations from the threat or use of force against the territorial integrity or political independence of any state or in any other manner inconsistent with the Charter of the United Nations.

- Cooperation on Afghanistan, including on intensified cooperation in the fight against drug trafficking, support for programmes on the return of Afghan refugees to Afghanistan; cooperation on reconstruction of Afghanistan; cooperation on guarding the Iran-Afghan border.

Economic

Steps towards the normalization of trade and economic relations, such as improving Iran's access to the international economy, markets and capital through practical support for full integration into international structures, including the World Trade Organization, and to create the framework for increased direct investment in Iran and trade with Iran.

Energy Partnership

Steps towards the normalization of cooperation with Iran in the area of energy: establishment of a long-term and wide-ranging strategic energy partnership between Iran and the European Union and other willing partners, with concrete and practical applications/measures.

Agriculture

- Support for agricultural development in Iran.
- Facilitation of Iran's complete self-sufficiency in food through cooperation in modern technology.

Environment, Infrastructure

- Civilian Projects in the field of environmental protection, infrastructure, science and technology, and high-tech:
= Development of transport infrastructure, including international transport corridors.
= Support for modernisation of Iran's telecommunication infrastructure, including by possible removal of relevant export restrictions.

Civil Aviation

Civil aviation cooperation, including the possible removal of restrictions on manufacturers exporting aircraft to Iran:

= enabling Iran to renew its civil aviation fleet;
= assisting Iran to ensure that Iranian aircraft meet international safety standards.

Economic, social and human development/humanitarian issues

- Provide, as necessary, assistance to Iran's economic and social development and humanitarian need.
- Cooperation/technical support in education in areas of benefit to Iran:
= Supporting Iranians to take courses, placements or degrees in areas such as civil engineering, agriculture and environmental studies;
= Supporting partnerships between Higher Education Institutions e.g. public health, rural livelihoods, joint scientific projects, public administration, history and philosophy.

-       Cooperation in the field of development of effective emergency response capabilities (e.g. seismology, earth quake research, disaster control etc.).
-       Cooperation within the framework of a "dialogue among civilizations".

Implementation mechanism

-       Constitution of joint monitoring groups for the implementation of a future agreement.

Notes

INTRODUCTION

1. Yossi Melman, "IAEA: Ahmadnejad Election Rival Launched Iran Nuclear Program," *Haaretz,* June 12, 2009.

2. Ibid.

3. Dilip Hiro, *Iran Under the Ayatollahs* (London: Routledge & Kegan Paul, 1985), 198–99.

4. Michael Slackman and Alan Cowell, "Top Clerical Council in Iran Rejects Plea to Annul Vote," *New York Times,* June 24, 2009.

5. Amir Taheri, *The Persian Night: Iran Under the Khomeinist Revolution* (New York: Encounter Books, 2009), 318. Detailed election numbers are available in Anoushiravan Ehteshami and Mahjoob Zweiri, *Iran and the Rise of the Neoconservatives: The Politics of Tehran's Silent Revolution* (London: I.B. Taurus, 2007), 167.

6. Ali M. Ansari, *Iran Under Ahmadinejad: The Politics of Confrontation* (London: International Institute for Strategic Studies, 2007), 36.

7. Ali Alfoneh, "The Revolutionary Guards' Role in Iranian Politics," *Middle East Quarterly,* Fall 2008.

8. Amir Taheri, "Iran's Clarifying Election," *Wall Street Journal,* June 16, 2009.

9. "Profile: Iran's Revolutionary Guards," BBC, October 26, 2007.

10. Ali Alfoneh, "Iran's Parliamentary Elections and the Revolutionary Guards' Creeping Coup d'Etat," *Middle Eastern Outlook,* No. 2, February 2008.

11. Raz Zimmt, "Has the Status of Iranian Clerics Been Eroded," *Iran-Pulse,* Center for Iranian Studies, Tel Aviv University, No. 24, September 22, 2008.

12. Mehdi Khalaji, "Khamenei's Coup," *Washington Post,* June 15, 2009.

13. Amir Taheri, *The Persian Night,* 339–40.

14. "Assembly of Experts Expresses Strong Support for Leader's Guidelines," *Tehran Times,* June 21, 2009.

15. The White House, "Videotaped Remarks by the President in Celebration of the Nowruz," March 20, 2009.

16. Helen Cooper and Mark Landler, "Obama Pressured to Strike a Firmer Tone," *New York Times*, June 17, 2009.

17. Jeff Zeleny and Helene Cooper, "Obama Warns Against Direct Involvement by U.S. in Iran," *New York Times*, June 16, 2009.

18. Helen Cooper and Mark Landler, Op. Cit.

19. "GOP Lawmakers Press Obama to Take Tougher Stance on Iran," FOX News, June 21, 2009.

CHAPTER 1

1. Elaine Sciolino, "Showdown at U.N.? Iran Seems Calm," *New York Times*, March 14, 2006.

2. Ibid.

3. Alireza Jafarzadeh, "The Islamic Revolutionary Guards Corps Use Universities for Research to Build the Bomb," statement to National Press Club, Washington, D.C., March 20, 2006.

4. Therese Delpech, *Iran and the Bomb: The Abdication of International Responsibility* (New York: Columbia University Press, 2007), 113.

5. Con Coughlin, "Defiant Iran Begins Nuclear Production for 'Five Bombs,'" *The Daily Telegraph*, September 13, 2004.

6. Mustafa al-Labbad, "Character and Mechanism of the Iranian Institutions Holding the Nuclear Decision: From the Khatemi-Rouhani to Ahmadinejad-Larijani Eras," *Dar al-Hayat*, October 10, 2007.

7. Therese Delpech, *Iran and the Bomb*, 9.

8. Shahram Chubin, *Iran's Nuclear Ambitions* (Washington: Carnegie Endowment for International Peace, 2006), 25.

9. Therese Delpech, *Iran and the Bomb*, 9.

10. Shmuel Bar, Rachel Machtiger, and Shmuel Bachar, *Iranian Nuclear Decision Making Under Ahmadinejad* (Herzliya: The Interdisciplinary Center, Lauder School of Government, Diplomacy and Strategy, Institute for Policy and Strategy, 2008), 19–20.

11. Philip Sherwell, "How We Duped the West, by Iran's Nuclear Negotiator," *The Daily Telegraph*, April 3, 2006.

12. Ibid.

13. "Chief Iranian Nuclear Affairs Negotiator Hosein Musavian: The Negotiations with Europe Bought Us Time to Complete the Esfahan UCF Project and the Work on the Centrifuges in Natanz," MEMRI, Special Dispatch No. 957, August 12, 2005.

14. Therese Delpech, *Iran and the Bomb*, 129.

15. Michael Rubin, "Diplomacy By Itself Won't Work With Iran," *Investor's Business Daily*, February 13, 2009, reproduced by *Middle East Forum*, February, 14, 2009.

16. Michael Rubin, "Obama or McCain, Iran's Stance Won't Change," *The Australian*, October 3, 2008.

17. "Diplomacy Must be Used to Lessen Pressure on Iran: Scholar," *Tehran Times*, March 3, 2009.

18. "Vision of the Islamic Republic of Iran," Network 2, Tehran, in Persian, November 8, 2006.

19. Ibid.

20. Shahram Chubin, *Iran's Nuclear Ambitions*, 80.

21. These observations about Rowhani's approach to his talks with the EU largely correspond to the findings of an un-named American scholar on Iran, who spent years in the country and wrote a text *Dealing with the Iranian Government; The Importance of Understanding Iranian Culture*, February, 2008.

CHAPTER 2

1. Transcript of Interview with Iranian President Mohammad Khatami, CNN, January 7, 1998.

2. David Blow, *Shah Abbas: The Ruthless King Who Became an Iranian Legend* (London: I.B. Taurus, 2009) pp. 65-129.

3. Patrick Clawson and Michael Rubin, *Eternal Iran: Continuity and Chaos* (New York: Palgrave Macmillan, 2005), 30.

4. Bob Woodward, *The War Within: A Secret White House History, 2006-2008* (New York: Simon & Schuster, 2008), 347. The U.S. official that Woodward mentions was David Satterfield.

5. Anoushiravan Ehteshami and Mahjoob Zweiri, *Iran and the Rise of the Neoconservatives* (London: I.B. Taurus, 2007), 143.

6. Ray Takeyh, *Hidden Iran: Paradox and Power in the Islamic Republic* (New York: Henry Hold and Company, 2006), 61.

7. Amir Taheri is the source of this famous Khomeini quote whose veracity was contested by Shaul Bakhash and Andrew Sullivan. Taheri has countered saying that the quote can be found in several editions of Khomeini's collected speeches like *Messages and Speeches of Imam Khomeini* (Tehran: Nur Research and Publication Institute, 1981). In subsequent editions, Taheri explains the quotation in question was removed, as Iran tried to mobilize nationalistic sentiment during the Iran-Iraq War. For the details on this debate, see Norman Podhoretz, "A Response to Andrew Sullivan," *Commentary Magazine—Contentions*, November 19, 2007.

8. There is something of debate over when Hizbullah was actually founded. Augustus Richard Norton argues that Hizbullah did not exist as "a coherent organization" until the mid-1980s. See Augustus Richard Norton, *Hezbollah* (Princeton, NJ: Princeton University Press, 2007). While acknowledging that the formal public launch of Hizbullah was in 1985, the Deputy Secretary-General of Hizbullah, Naim Qassem, has explained that it existed previously, but it engaged in "secret resistance activity" and had no interaction with the media or the political realm. He traces the beginning of Hizbullah to 1982, when the Iranians' Islamic Revolutionary Guards Corps set up training camps in the Bekaa Valley, which served many members of Hizbullah's early leadership. See: *Hizbullah: The Story from Within* (London: Saqi, 2005), 66–67, 98.

9. United States District Court for the District of Columbia, "Deborah D. Peterson and Joseph and Marie Boulous versus the Islamic Republic of Iran," March 17–18, 2003. The Iranian ambassador to Syria was Ali Akbar Mohtashemi. Martin Kramer points out that Mohtashemi was instrumental in the founding of Hizbullah in 1982, when he helped establish its first governing council of which he was a member. See: Martin Kramer, "Hizbullah in Lebanon," *The Oxford Encyclopedia of the Modern Islamic World* (New York: Oxford University Press, Volume 2, 1995), 130–33. For a description of Mohtashami's role as the "godfather" of Hizbullah, see: Manal Lutfi, "The Making of Hezbollah," *al-Sharq al-Awsat*, May 18, 2008.

The former Iran specialist on President Carter's National Security Council, Gary Sick, provides a different interpretation of the Iranian relationship to terrorist attacks in Lebanon, but his view is difficult to substantiate: "Iran cultivated the image and avoided direct criticism of guerrilla actions, often leaving the impression of closer association with these groups and their operations than may have been justified. This sometimes backfired. Iran was occasionally embarrassed—and its interests damaged—by acts of violence over which it probably had little or no influence." See: Gary Sick, *All Fall Down: America's Tragic Encounter with Iran* (Lincoln, NE: iUniverse.com, Inc, 2001), xxix–xxx.

10. Kenneth M. Pollack, *The Persian Puzzle: The Conflict Between Iran and America* (New York: Random House, 2004), 209.

11. Matthias Küntzel, "Ahmadinejad's Demons," *The New Republic*, April 24, 2006.

12. Farhad Khosrokhavar, *Suicide Bombers: Allah's New Martyrs* (London: Pluto Press, 2005), 76.

13. Barry Rubin, *Paved with Good Intentions: The American Experience and Iran* (New York; Penguin Books, 1981), 303.

14. Interview: Hossein Shariatmadari, "Showdown with Iran," *PBS Frontline*, October 23, 2007.

15. Manoucher Ganji, *Defying the Iranian Revolution: From a Minister to the Shah to a Leader of Resistance* (Westport, CT: Praeger Books, 2002), 82–83.

16. Karim Sadjadpour, *Reading Khamenei: The World View of Iran's Most Powerful Leader* (Washington, D.C.: Carnegie Endowment for International Peace, 2008), 22.

17. Islamic Republic News Agency, December 14, 2001. Cited in Michael Rubin, "Can Iran Be Trusted?" *Middle Eastern Outlook*, September 2006, American Enterprise Institute.

18. Kenneth M. Pollack, *The Persian Puzzle*, 281.

19. Louis J. Freeh, *My FBI: Bringing Down the Mafia, Investigating Bill Clinton, and Fighting the War on Terror* (New York: St. Martin's Griffin, 2005), 29.

20. Ibid.

21. Ibid., 17.

22. Hizbullah set up a terrorist cell in Singapore in 1995 and hoped to attack U.S. and Israeli targets on the island. The cell also planned to launch explosive boats against U.S. and Israeli ships passing through the Singapore Straits. In March 1992, Iranian intelligence and Hizbullah bombed the Israeli Embassy in Buenos Aires killing 29; two years later they bombed the AMIA Jewish community building in Buenos Aires, killing 85 and wounding

hundreds. See: Intelligence and Terrorism Information Center and the Center for Special Studies, *Hezbollah (Part 1): Profile of the Lebanese Shiite Terrorist Organization of Global Reach Sponsored by Iran and Supported by Syria* (Tel Aviv: Intelligence and Terrorism Information Center, June 2003), 67–70, 82.

23. J. B. Kelly, *Arabia, the Gulf and the West* (New York; Basic Books, 1980), 87.

24. Douglas Jehl, "U.S. Says It's Worried about Iranian Military Buildup in the Gulf," *The New York Times*, March 23, 1995.

25. Kenneth M. Pollack, *The Persian Puzzle*, 358.

26. Mehdi Khaliji, *Apocalyptic Politics: On the Rationality of Iranian Policy* (Washington: The Washington Institute for Near East Policy, 2008), 26.

27. "Paper: French FM in Memoir—Ahmadinejad Tells European FMs in 2005 Meeting, 'After the Chaos We Can See the Greatness of Allah,'" The MEMRI Blog, February 2, 2007 (Source: *al-Sharq al-Awsat*, London, February 2, 2007).

28. Y. Mansdorf and A. Savyon, "Escalation in the Positions of Iranian President Mahmoud Ahmadinejad—A Special Report" MEMRI Inquiry and Analysis Series—No. 389, September 17, 2007.

29. Joby Warrick, "U.S. Cites Big Gains Against Al-Qaeda," *Washington Post*, May 30, 2008.

30. Rebecca Anna Stohl, "French President: Nuclear Iran Is Totally Unacceptable," *Jerusalem Post*, June 23, 2008.

CHAPTER 3

1. Comment by David Albright, president of the Institute for Science and International Security, William Broad, "Nuclear Weapons in Iran: Plowshare or Sword?" Nuclear Age Peace Foundation, May 25, 2004.

2. Kenneth M. Pollack, *The Persian Puzzle: The Conflict Between Iran and America* (New York: Random House, 2004), 361.

3. Greg Bruno, Iran's Nuclear Program, Backgrounder, Council on Foreign Relations, September 4, 2008.

4. John Bolton, *Surrender Is Not an Option: Defending America at the United Nations and Abroad* (New York: Threshold Editions, 2007), 316.

5. Lee Kass, "Iran's Space Program: The Next Genie in a Bottle?" *The Middle East Review of International Affairs,* Vol. 10, Number 3 (September

2006). Dinshaw Mistry, "European Missile Defense: Assessing Iran's ICBM Capabilities," *Arms Control Today,* October 2007.

6. "Iranians Test RD-214 Engine in Russian Transfer Deal," *Military Space*, April 28, 1997.

7. Kenneth Timmerman, *Countdown to Crisis: The Coming Nuclear Showdown with Iran* (New York: Three Rivers Press, 2006), 239.

8. U.S. Senate, Committee on Foreign Relations, *Iran: Where We Are Today* (Washington: U.S. Government Printing Office, May 4, 2009), 5–6. David E. Sanger, *The Inheritance: The World Obama Confronts and the Challenges to American Power* (New York: Harmony Books, 2009), 65.

9. Ibid., 74.

10. Ibid., 92.

11. International Atomic Energy Agency, Board of Governors, "Implementation of the NPT Safeguards Agreement in the Islamic Republic of Iran," GOV/2003/75, November 10, 2003, p. 10.

12. Steven R. Ward, *Immortal: A Military History of Iran and Its Armed Forces* (Washington: Georgetown University Press, 2009), 320.

13. Laurent Zecchini, "Iran Document Shows Tehran Pursued a Military Program," *Le Monde*, March 28, 2008. Translated from French by NCR-Iran.org.

14. Ibid., 136.

15. Amir Taheri, "Turban or Hat: In Iran, That's the Question," *Arab News*, November 9, 2004.

16. Anton La Guardia, "'Tehran Jack' Gets Confrontational," *Daily Telegraph*, March 14, 2006.

17. International Atomic Energy Agency, "Statement by the Iranian Government and Visiting EU Foreign Ministers," October 21, 2003 and International Atomic Energy Agency, Board of Governors, "Implementation of the NPT Safeguards Agreement in the Islamic Republic of Iran," Report by the Director General, February 24, 2004.

18. "Solana: Iran 'Honest' So Far in Nuclear Dealings," AFP, November 17, 2003.

19. John Bolton, *Surrender Is Not an Option*, 140.

20. Pierre Goldschmidt and George Perkovich, "Correcting Iran's Nuclear Disinformation," *Proliferation Analysis*, Carnegie Endowment, March 27, 2007.

21. Steven R. Weissman, "U.S. and Europe Are at Odds, Again, This Time Over Iran," *The New York Times*, December 12, 2004.

22. Ibid.

23. William J. Broad, David E. Sanger, and Elaine Sciolino, "Arms Inspectors Said to Seek Access to Iran Sites," *The New York Times*, December 2, 2004.

24. John Bolton, *Surrender Is Not an Option*, 157.

25. Ibid.

26. Therese Delpech, *Iran and the Bomb*, 90–91.

27. William Broad and Elaine Sciolino, "Iranians Retain Plutonium Plan in Nuclear Deal," *The New York Times*, November 24, 2004.

28. "Iran Constructing the 40 MW Heavy Water Reactor at Arak Despite Calls Not To Do So by the European Union and the IAEA Board of Governors," Institute for Science and International Security, March 4, 2005.

29. Alissa Rubin, "U.S. Warns Iran on Nuclear Issue," *Los Angeles Times*, June 17, 2005.

30. Paul Kerr, "U.S. Offer Fails to End EU-Iran Impasse," *Arms Control Today*, April 2005. The proposals to Iran for a light-water reactor instead of the heavy-water reactor at Arak continued in 2006. See Steven R. Weisman, "Light-Water Reactor in EU Plan for Iran," *The New York Times*, May 17, 2006.

31. Robert Einhorn, "Iran's Heavy-Water Reactor: A Plutonium Bomb Factory," Arms Control Association, November 9, 2006; available online at: www.armscontrol.org.

32. Ibid.

33. Both the EU-3 August 5, 2005 proposal and the Iranian Reply are available at The Acronym Institute for Disarmament Diplomacy, www.acronym.org.uk; full text available at: http://www.acronym.org.uk/textonly/docs/0508/doc03.htm.

34. "Interview with Philippe Douste-Blazy, French Minister of Foreign Affairs," *Paris Match*, August 18, 2005.

35. Anoushiravan Ehtehshami and Mahjoob Zweiri, *Iran and the Rise of the Neoconservatives*, 142.

36. Paul Kerr, "News Analysis: Behind Iran's Diplomatic Behavior," Arms Control Association; available online at: www.armscontrol.org.

37. "Implementation of the NPT Safeguards Agreement in the Islamic Republic of Iran," Report by the Director General, International Atomic Energy Agency, GOV/2006/15, February 27, 2006.

38. Yehuda Yaakov, *The Implementation of Coercive Diplomacy in the International Nuclear Crisis with Iran, 2003-2004*, Masters Thesis, University of Haifa, July, 2008. See footnote 75.

39. "Implementation of the NPT Safeguards Agreement in the Islamic Republic of Iran," Report by the Director General, International Atomic Energy Agency, GOV/2006/27, April 28, 2006.

40. "Europe: 'Our Discussions with Iran Have Reached an Impasse,'" *Middle East Quarterly*, Spring 2006, pp.65–66.

41. Ibid.

42. Glenn Kesssler, *The Confidante: Condoleezza Rice and the Creation of the Bush Legacy* (New York: St. Martin's Press, 2007), 203.

43. Nazila Fathi, "Iran Snubs Europe's Nuclear Plan," *The New York Times*, May 18, 2006.

44. Joschka Fischer, "The Case for Bargaining with Iran," *Washington Post*, May 20, 2006.

45. Ibid.

46. Elaine Sciolino, "U.S. and Europe Draft U.N. Resolution on Iran," *The New York Times*, May 2, 2006.

47. Y. Mansdorf, "Editor of Kayan: 'A Country that Has...Uranium Enrichment Is Only One Step Away from Producing Nuclear Weapons'" *MEMRI, Inquiry and Analysis*—No. 342, April 13, 2007.

CHAPTER 4

1.Amir Taheri, *The Spirit of Allah: Khomeini & The Islamic Revolution* (Bethesda, MD: Adler& Adler, 1985), 27.

2. Nikki R. Keddie, *Modern Iran: Roots and Results of Revolution* (New Haven, CT: Yales University Press, 2006), 225.

3. Michael Ledeen and William Lewis, *Debacle: The American Failure in Iran* (New York: Alfred A. Knopf, 1981), 130.

4. Ofra Seliktar, *Failing the Crystal Ball Test: The Carter Administration and the Fundamentalist Revolution in Iran* (Westport: Praeger Publishers, 2000), 121.

5. "The Vision of Ruhollah Khomeini," *Washington Post*, January 5, 1979.

6. Hamid Algar, trans. *Islam and Revolution: Writings and Declarations of Imam Khomeini* (Mizan Press, 1981), 115.

7. Ibid., 116.

8. Gary Sick, *All Fall Down: America's Tragic Encounter with Iran* (Lincoln, NE: Author's Guild, 1986), 162.

9. Ibid.

10. Michael Ledeen and William Lewis, *Debacle*, 130.

11. Ibid.

12. Ofira Seliktar, *Failing the Crystal Ball Test*, 92.

13. Warren Brown, "CIA Didn't Forsee 'National Revolution' in Iran, Chief Says," *Washington Post*, February 9, 1979.

14. Zbigniew Brzezinski, *Power and Principle: Memoirs of the National Security Advisor* (New York: Farrar, Straus, and Giroux, 1983), 355.

15. Charles Kurzman, *The Unthinkable Revolution in Iran* (Cambridge: Harvard University Press, 2004), 13.

16. General Robert E. Huyser, *Mission to Tehran* (New York: Harper&Row, 1986), 31–32.

17. Ibid.

18. Ofira Seliktar, *Failing the Crystal Ball Test*, 116.

19. William Sullivan, *Mission to Iran* (New York: W.W. Norton & Company, 1981), 201–203.

20. Zbigniew Brzezinski, *Power and Principle*, 368.

21. Memorandum of Conversation, Shahpour Bakhtiar, Iran Party Leader and Member of Executive Board of the National Front, John D. Stempel, Political Officer, W. Gregory Perett, Political Officer. October 22, 1978. See: www.espionage_den01.pdf.

22. General Robert E. Huyser, *Mission to Tehran*, 24.

23. Jimmy Carter, *Keeping Faith: Memoirs of a President* (New York: Bantam Books, 1983), 443.

24. Amir Taheri, *The Spirit of Allah*, 225–26.

25. Shaul Bakhash, *The Reign of the Ayatollahs: Iran and the Islamic Revolution* (New York: Basic Books, 1984), 48.

26. Jonathan C. Randal, "Exile Leader Shifts View on U.S.-Iran Ties," *Washington Post*, January 2, 1979.

27. Amir Taheri, *The Spirit of Allah*, 227–28.

28. Michael Ledeen and William Lewis, *Debacle*, 190.

29. Gary Sick, *All Fall Down*, 163.

30. Amir Taheri, *The Spirit of Allah*, 229.

31. Ibid., 239.

32. Ofira Seliktar, *Failing the Crystal Ball Test*, 132.

33. U.S. Department of State, From: SECSTATE WASHDC To: AMEM-BASSY TEHRAN, "Further Report of Richard Cottam," January 7, 1979. See: www.espionage_den01.pdf.

34. Barry Rubin, *Paved With Good Intentions: The American Experience and Iran* (Middlesex: Penguin Books, 1980), 208; and Ofira Seliktar, *Failing the Crystal Ball Test*, 133.

35. Michael Rubin, "The U.S. vs. Iran: One Side is Playing for Real, the Other Only for Time," *The Wall Street Journal*, September 20, 2006.

36. Michael Rubin, "Getting Religion Wrong: Three Decades of Misreporting Iran and Iraq," *Middle East Forum*, October, 2008.

37. Gary Sick, *All Fall Down*, 195.

38. Amir Taheri, *The Spirit of Allah*, 128; Shaul Bakhash, *The Reign of the Ayatollahs*, 110.

39. Between February 1989 and June 1981 close to 1,500 people were executed. Shaul Bakhash, *The Reign of the Ayatollahs*, 111.

40. Manouchehr Ganji, *Defying the Iranian Revolution: from a Minister to the Shah to a Leader of the Resistance* (Westport, CT: Praeger Publications, 2002), 1–3, 79.

41. Nikki R. Keddie, *Modern Iran*, 250.

42. Kenneth Pollack, *The Persian Puzzle*, 150.

43. Nikki R. Keddie, *Modern Iran*, 245.

44. Kenneth Pollack, *The Persian Puzzle*, 151–52.

45. William Sullivan, *Mission to Iran*, 257–62.

46. Ibid., 264.

47. Ibid., 265.

48. Bernard D. Nossiter, "Ex-Envoy to Iran Tells of His Frustrations," *New York Times*, June 22, 1980.

49. Amir Taheri, *The Spirit of Allah*, 107.

50. Ervand Abrahamian, *Iran between Two Revolutions* (Princeton, NJ: Princeton University Press, 1982), 475.

51. Amir Taheri, *The Spirit of Allah*, 166.

52. Ibid., 250.

53. Shaul Bakhash, *The Reign of the Ayatollahs*, 63.

54. Amir Taheri, *The Spirit of Allah*, 279.

55. For the Carter administration's efforts to argue for PLO involvement in the peace process see: William B. Quandt, *Camp David: Peacemaking and Politics* (Washington, D.C.: The Brookings Institution, 1986), 46.

56. Embassy of the United States of America, Letter to L. Paul Bremmer, September 2, 1979. See: www.espionage_den01.pdf .

57. Henry Precht, letter to the Hon. L. Bruce Laingen, September 13, 1979.

58. "Comments By the French Ambassador Raoul Delaye," Memorandum for the Files, US Embassy, Tehran. Ocotber 25, 1979. Digital National Security Archive.

59. "Moderation: Does It Have a Chance?" Confidential Cable, Tehran, US Embassy, October 26, 1979. Digital National Security Archive.

60. Gary Sick, *All Fall Down*, 223.

61. Michael Ledeen and William Lewis, *Debacle*, 225.

62. "Secretary's Meeting with Foreign Minister Yazdi," Secret, Cable State, October 4, 1979, National Security Archive.

63. Ibid.

64. Ibid.

65. Michael A. Ledeen, *The Iranian Time Bomb: The Mullah Zealots' Quest for Destruction* (New York: St. Martin's Press, 2007), 148.

66. James Bill, *The Eagle and the Lion: The Tragedy of American-Iranian Relations* (New Haven, CT: Yale University Press, 1988), 294.

67. Jimmy Carter, *Keeping Faith*, 455.

68. Mark Bowden, *Guests of the Ayatollah: The First Battle in America's War with Militant Islam* (New York: Grove Press, 2006), 12.

69. Dilip Hiro, *Iran Under the Ayatollahs* (London: Routledge, 1987), 134.

70. Ibid., 615.

71. Elton L. Daniel, *The History of Iran* (Westport, CT: Greenwood Press, 2001), 191.

72. Kenneth Katzman, *The Warriors of Islam: Iran's Revolutionary Guard* (Boulder: Westview Press, 1993), 36.

73. *Iranian Hostage Crisis: Government Declassified Documents*, Core Federal Information CD-ROM.

74. Mark Bowden, *Guests of the Ayatollah*, 173.

75. Kenneth Katzman, *The Warriors of Islam*, 37.

76. Robin Wright, *Sacred Rage: The Wrath of Radical Islam* (New York: Touchstone, 1985), 87.

77. "Iranian Who Met McFarlane Is Tied to Takeover of U.S. Embassy," Reuters, November 28, 1996.

78. Media Analysis, Iran, From: JTF/J-2 To: SFOD/S-2, February 1980. *Iranian Hostage Crisis: Government Declassified Documents*, Core Federal Information CD-ROM.

79. Ibid.

80. Cyrus Vance, *Hard Choices: Critical Years in America's Foreign Policy* (New York: Simon and Schuster, 1983), 380.

81. Gary Sick, *All Fall Down*, 253.

82. Ibid.

83. Michael Rubin, "Can Iran Be Trusted?" *AEI Middle Eastern Outlook*, September 1, 2006.

84. Kenneth Pollack, *The Persian Puzzle*, 153.

85. Amir Taheri, "It All Started in Tehran," *Arab News*, October 30, 2004.

86. Baqer Moin, *Khomeini: Life of the Ayatollah* (London: I.B. Tauris, 1999), 227.

87. Cyrus Vance, *Hard Choices*, 376.

88. Kenneth Pollack, *The Persian Puzzle*, 164.

89. Eric Pace, "P.L.O. Aides Say Group Is in Iran, But U.S. Official Expresses Doubt," *The New York Times*, November 8, 1979.

90. Cyrus Vance, *Hard Choices*, 383.

91. Gary Sick, *All Fall Down*, 292.

92. Ibid., 242.

93. Ibid., 292.

94. "Key Players Recall Iranian Hostage Crisis," *National Public Radio*, January 20, 2006.

CHAPTER 5

1. Colonel Timothy J. Geraghty, U.S. Marine Corps (Retired) "25 Years Later: We Came in Peace," *Proceedings Magazine*, U.S. Naval Institute, October 2008, Volume 134/10/1, 268.

2. MEMORANDUM OPINION, Peterson v. Islamic Republic of Iran, U.S. District Court for the District of Columbia, 2003.

3. Colonel Timothy J. Geraghty, "25 Years Later: We Came in Peace."

4. Douglas Brinkley, ed. *The Reagan Diaries* (New York: Harper Collins, 2007), 190.

5. Caspar Weinberger, *Fighting for Peace: Seven Critical Years in the Pentagon* (New York: Warner Books, 1991), 161.

6. Douglas Brinkley, ed. *The Reagan Diaries*, 198.

7. Interview: Caspar Weinberger, "Target America," PBS Frontline.

8. Ibid.

9. Robert C. McFarlane, "From Beirut to 9/11," *The New York Times*, October 23, 2008.

10. Caspar Weinberger, *Fighting for Peace,* 162.

11. MEMORANDUM OPINION, Peterson, Op. Cit.

12. Shimon Shapira, *Hizbullah Between Iran and Lebanon* (Tel Aviv: Hakibbutz Hameuchad, 2006), 166.

13. Ibid.

14. Colonel Timothy J. Geraghty, "25 Years Later: We Came in Peace."

15. Shimon Shapira, *Hizbullah Between Iran and Lebanon*, 123.

16. Robert Baer, *See No Evil: The True Story of a Ground Soldier in the CIA's War on Terrorism* (New York: Crown Books, 2002), 67.

17. MEMORANDUM OPINION, Peterson, Op. Cit.

18. Eric Pace, "Car Bombing Has Become Favored Tactic of Terrorists in the Middle East," *The New York Times*, September 21, 1984.

19. Ibid.

20. Kenneth Pollack, *The Persian Puzzle: The Conflict Between Iran and America* (New York: Random House, 2004), 198.

21. Martin Kramer, "Hizbullah in Lebanon," *The Oxford Encyclopedia of the Modern Islamic World* (Oxford: Oxford University Press, 1995) Vol. 2, 130–33.

22. Martin Kramer, *Arab Awakening & Islamic Revival* (New Brunswick: Transaction Publishers, 1996), 213.

23. Shimon Shapira, *Hizbullah Between Iran and Lebanon*, 106.

24. Roschanack Shaery-Eisenlohr, *Shi'ite Lebanon: Transnational Religion and the Making of National Identities* (New York; Columbia University Press, 2008), 104.

25. Robert Baer, *The Devil We Know: Dealing with the New Iranian Superpower* (New York: Crown Books, 2008), 75.

26. Naim Qassem, *Hizbullah: the Story from Within* (London: Saqi Books, 2005), 78.

27. Magnus Ranstorp, *Hizb'Allah in Lebanon: The Politics of the Western Hostage Crisis* (London: Palgrave, 1997), 69–70.

28. "In an Interview to an Iranian TV Channel, Sheikh Naim Qassem Stresses that Hezbollah's Policy of Terrorist Operations Against Israel (Including Suicide Bombings and Rocket Fire) Requires Jurisprudent Permission of the Iranian Leadership." Intelligence and Terrorism Information Center at the Israel Intelligence Heritage & Commemoration Center (IICC), April 29, 2007.

29. "Interview to an Iranian TV Channel, Sheikh Naim Qassem..." Op. Cit.

30. Shimon Shapira, *Hizbullah Between Iran and Lebanon*, 162.

31. Interview with Brig. General (ret.) Dr. Shimon Shapira, October 24, 2008.

32. Martin Kramer, "Imad Who?" Middle East Strategy at Harvard, February 14, 2008.

33. Central Intelligence Agency, Directorate of Intelligence, "Lebanon: The Hizb Allah," September 27, 1984. Available at www.cia.gov.

34. Interview, Robert Baer. PBS *Frontline*, Tehran and Terror, March 22, 2002. www.pbs.org/wgbh/pages/frontine/shows/tehran/interviews/baer.html.

35. Baer, *See No Evil*, 92.

36. Sick, pp. xxix-xxx.

37. Augustus Richard Norton, *Hezbollah* (Princeton: Princeton University Press, 2007), 44, 73.

38. Ali Nouri Zadeh, "Tehran and Hezbollah's Secret History," al-Sharq al-Awsat, May 8, 2006.
Zadeh paraphrases Mohtashemi's statements to Sharq, an Iranian newspaper.

39. Ibid.

40. "Former Hizbullah Sec-Gen: Hizbullah Is an Integral Part of Iranian Intelligence," MEMRI, Special Dispatch—No. 1431, January 19, 2007.

41. "Interview to an Iranian TV Channel, Sheikh Naim Qassem Stresses that Hezbollah's Policy of Terrorist Operations Against Israel" op. cit.

42. Olivier Guitta, "France and Hizbullah: The End of the Affair," U.S.-Europe Analysis Series, The Brookings Institution, November 2005.

43. Kenneth Pollack, *The Persian Puzzle*, 209.

44. Nathan Thrall, "How the Reagan Administration Taught Iran the Wrong Lesson," *MERIA Journal*, Vol. 11, No. 4, December 2007, p. 16.

45. Ibid.

46. Hezbollah: Profile of the Lebanese Shiite Terrorist Organization of Global Reach Sponsored by Iran and Supported by Syria, (Tel Aviv: Intelligence and Terrorism Information Center at the Center for Special Studies [C.S.S.]) June, 2003. p. 78.

47. Olivier Guitta, Op. Cit.

48. Kenneth Pollack, *The Persian Puzzle*, 210.

49. George P. Shultz, *Turmoil and Triumph: My Years as Secretary of State* (New York: Scribners, 1993), 662.

50. Ibid., 667.

51. Nathan Thrall, Op. Cit. The presence of Moughniyeh's fingerprints is reported by Baer, *The Devil We Know*, 80.

52. Manouchehr Ganji, *Defying the Iranian Revolution*, 88.

53. Central Intelligence Agency, Directorate of Intelligence, "Middle East Terrorism: The Threat and Possible US Responses," February 15, 1985. See www.cia.gov, Freedom of Information Act Electronic Reading Room. Full text available at: http://www.foia.cia.gov/browse_docs.asp.

54. United States Court of Appeals for the District of Columbia Circuit, *Final Report of the Independent Counsel for Iran/Contra Matters, Volume 1: Investigations and Prosecutions Lawrence E. Walsh, Independent Counsel* (Washington D.C.: August 4, 1993), See Part I, The Underlying Facts.

55. Nathan Thrall, Op. cit. The draft directive was not adopted and was hotly contested by the Department of State and the Department of Defense. See David Rothkopf, Running the World: The Inside Story of the National Security Council and the Architects of American Power (New York: Public Affairs, 2005), 243.

56. Weinberger, 363.

57. Central Intelligence Agency, Directorate of Intelligence, "Iran: The Struggle to Define and Control Foreign Policy," May 1985.

58. Fouad Ajami, "The Opening to Iran: Part Burden, Part Responsibility," *The New York Times*, November 16, 1986.

59. CIA Profile of Ghorbanifar, July, 25, 1984. Digital National Security Archive. See also, Tim Weiner, *Legacy of Ashes: The History of the CIA* (New York: Doubleday, 2007) p.307

60. Ed Magnuson, "Double-Dealing Over Iran," *Time*, February 2, 1987.

61. Lawrence E. Walsh, *Firewall: The Iran-Contra Conspiracy and Cover-Up* (New York: W.W. Norton& Company, 1997), 38.

62. Tim Weiner, *Legacy of Ashes*, 402.

63. United States Court of Appeals for the District of Columbia Circuit, *Final Report*, Op. Cit.

64. Lawrence E. Walsh, *Firewall*, 39.

65. David Rosenbaum, "Iran-Contra Hearings: Regan Testifies Reagan Felt Iran 'Snookered' Him," *The New York Times*, July 31, 1987.

66. Fox Butterfied, "Arms for Hostages—Plain and Simple," *The New York Times*, November 27, 1988.

67. Central Intelligence Agency, "Iran: Enhanced Terrorist Capabilities and Expanding Target Selection . . ." April, 1992.

68. Don Oberdorfer, "Iran Paid for Release of the Hostages; Tehran Gave Captors Up to $2 Million for Each," *Washington Post*, January 12, 1992.

69. Ibid.

70. "DCI Testimony Before the House Appropriations Committee," December 8, 1986 (Secret, December 7, 1986), Digital National Security Archive.

71. Ibid.

72. Magnus Ranstorp, *Hizb'Allah in Lebanon*, 164.

73. John H. Cushman, Jr. "Iran Sends Mixed Signals, Often on Purpose," *The New York Times*, August 23, 1987.

74. David Crist, "Iran's Small Boats Are a Big Problem," *The New York Times*, January 20, 2008.

75. Martin Kramer, "Islam's Enduring Feud," Itamar Rabinovich and Haim Shaked, eds. *Middle East Contemporary Survey*, Volume XI, 1987 (Boulder: Westview Press, 1989), 172–74.

76. Youssef Ibrahim, "Leading Hard-Line Politician is Elected to Iran's Parliament," *The New York Times*, December 19, 1989.

77. http://www.dia.mil/publicaffairs/Foia/panam103.pdf.

78. Giadomenico Picco, *Man Without a Gun: One Diplomat's Secret Struggle to Free the Hostages. Fight Terrorism, and End a War* (New York: Times Books, 1999) p. 110.

79. Ibid. p. 104.

80. Central Intelligence Agency, Directorate of Intelligence, "Redirecting Iranian Foreign Policy: Rafsanjani's Progress..."June 1, 1990; www.foia.cia. gov.

81. Ibid., 113.

82. Central Intelligence Agency, Memorandum for the Honorable Robert B. Oakley, Special Assistant to the President for National Security Affairs, "Iran and the US Hostages in Lebanon," August 1, 1988; www.foia.cia. gov.

83. "Iran Honors Hezbollah Commander," *PRESS* TV, December 25, 2008.

84. Robert Worth, "Hezbollah Shrine to Terrorist Suspect Enthralls Lebanese Children," *The New York Times*, September 2, 2008.

85. Augustus Richard Norton, *Hezbollah* (Princeton: Princeton University Press, 2007), 43.

86. Ronen Bergman, *The Secret War with Iran* (New York: Free Press, 2008), 106–8.

87. Giandomenico Picco, *Man Without a Gun*, 125.

88. Ibid., 118.

89. Central Intelligence Agency, "Iran: Enhanced Terrorist Capabilities..." April 1992. www.foia.cia.gov.

90. Central Intelligence Agency, "Iran: Patterns of Assassination..." October 1994; www.foia.cia.gov.

91. Ephraim Kam, *From Terror to Nuclear Bombs: The Significance of the Iranian Threat* (Tel Aviv: Ministry of Defense Publishing Jaffee Center for Strategic Studies, 2006), 253.

CHAPTER 6

1. Amir Taheri, "How Iran's Nuke Quest Began," *New York Post*, October 5, 2006.

2. Karl Vick, "Iran's Gray Area on Nuclear Arms," *Washington Post*, June 21, 2006.

3. Con Coughlin, *Khomeini's Ghost: The Iranian Revolution and the Rise of Militant Islam* (New York: Harper Collins, 2009), 225–26.

4. "Letter from Ayatollah Khomeini Regarding Weapons During the Iran-Iraq War," *Essential Documents*, Council on Foreign Relations, 2009.

5. Elaine Sciolino, "Report Says Iran Seeks Atomic Arms," *The New York Times*, October 31, 1991.

6. Anthony H. Cordesman, *Iran's Military Forces in Transition: Conventional Threats and Weapons of Mass Destruction* (New York: Praeger Publishers, 1999), 363.

7. Michael Rubin, "Can a Nuclear Iran Be Deterred?" *Middle Eastern Outlook*, November 5, 2008.

8. Steve Coll, "Iran Reportedly Trying to Buy Indian Reactor; Sale Would be Delhi's First Nuclear Export," *Washington Post*, November 15, 1991.

9. Steve Coll, "Iran's Extremists Seen Losing Power in Government," *Washington Post*, June 29, 1990.

10. Ibid.

11. Ibrahim Mahmoud Yaseen Alnahas, *Continuity and Change in the Revolutionary Iran Foreign Policy: The Role of International and Domestic Factors in Shaping the Iranian Foreign Policy, 1979-2006* (Morgantown: Dissertation Submitted to Eberly College of Arts and Sciences, 2007), 150.

12. Kenneth M. Pollack, *The Persian Puzzle: the Conflict Between Iran and America* (New York: Random House, 2004) 253.

13. Elaine Sciolino, "The World; After a Fresh Look, U.S. Decides to Still Steer Clear of Iran," *The New York Times*, June 7, 1992.

14. Elaine Sciolino, "Rafsanjani Sketches Vision of a Moderate, Modern Iran," *The New York Times*, April 19, 1992, p. 25.

15. Ibid.

16. Ibid.

17. Reuel Marc Gerecht, "The Mullah's Manhattan Project," *The Weekly Standard*, June 9, 2003.

18. Robert J. Einhorn, "Iran's Heavy-Water Reactor: A Plutonium Bomb Factory," Arms Control Association, Novmber 6, 2006. www.armscontol.org/print2548.

19. Ibid.

20. Ephraim Kam, *From Terror to Nuclear Bombs: The Significance of the Iranian Threat* (Tel Aviv: Ministry of Defense Publishing House/Jaffee Center for Strategic Studies, 2006), 67.

21. International Atomic Energy Agency, "Implementation of the NPT Safeguards Agreement in the Islamic Republic of Iran," Report by the Director General, GOV/2003/75, November 10, 2003, p. 4; Anthony Cordesman and Khalid R. Al-Rodham, Iranian Nuclear Weapons? The Uncertain Nature of Iran's Nuclear Programs (Washington: Center for Strategic and International Studies, 2006), 25.

22. Alireza Jafarzadeh, *The Iranian Threat: President Ahmadinejad and the Coming Nuclear Crisis* (New York: Palgrave Macmillan, 2007), 133–36.

23. Kenneth M. Pollack, *The Persian Puzzle: The Conflict Between Iran and America* (New York: Random House, 2004), 269.

24. Anthony Cordesman and Khalid R. Al-Rodham, *Iranian Nuclear Weapons?* Op. Cit., p. 25.

25. Muhammad Sahimi, Iran's Nuclear Program, Part II, www.payvand. com. Jafarzadeh, p. 136. Robert Einhorn of the US Department of State confirmed that China had provided the uranium conversion facility blueprints to the Iranians in Congressional hearings, see: Shirley A. Kan, *China and Proliferation of Weapons of Mass Destruction and Missiles: Policy Issues, Congressional Research Service*, The Library of Congress. February 26, 2003, p. 8.

26. Secretary of Defense William Perry revealed in April 1996, that the Chinese had sold the electronic isotope separation unit. See: Kan, Op. Cit.

27. William C. Potter, "Project Sapphire: U.S.-Kazakhstani Cooperation for Non-proliferation," John M. Shields and William C. Potter, U.S. and NIS Perspectives on the Nunn-Lugar Cooperative Threat Reduction Program (Cambridge: MIT Press, 1997), 346–47.

28. Strobe Talbott, *The Russia Hand* (New York: Random House, 2002), 158.

29. Steve Coll, "U.S. Halted Nuclear Bid by Iran; China, Argentina Agreed to Cancel Technology Transfers," *Washington Post*, November 17, 1992. See also: Robert Gates, Director, Central Intelligence Agency, "Testimony Before the House Armed Services Committee, Defense Policy Panel," March 27, 1992. *LexisNexis*.

30. "U.S. Nuclear Technology Tactics Vex Iran" (no author), *The New York Times*, November 18, 1991.

31. Elaine Sciolino, "Christopher Signals a Tougher U.S. Line Towards Iran," *The New York Times*, March 31, 1993.

32. Ibid.

33. Douglas Jehl, "U.S. Seeks Ways to Isolate Iran; Describes Leaders as Dangerous," *The New York Times*, May 27, 1993.

34. Martin Indyk, *Innocent Abroad: An Intimate Account of American Peace Diplomacy in the Middle East* (New York: Simon & Schuster, 2009) , 36.

35. Anthony Lake, "Confronting Backlash States," Foreign Affairs, March/April 1994, pp. 52-53.

36. Ibid., 53.

37. Ibid.

38. Martin Indyk, *Innocent Abroad*, 41.

39. Cited in Alnahas, p. 153. His data comes from Spot Crude Oil Prices, 1980-2003, at www.opec.org.

40. "Mixed Response from Europe on Ruling Linked to Killings," *New York Times*, April 30, 1997.

41. Pollack, p. 264

42. "Mixed Response from Europe on Ruling Linked to Killings," *The New York Times*, April 30, 1997.

43. Patrick Clawson, "What to Do About Iran?" *Middle East Quarterly*, December 1995, p. 1.

44. Ibid., 6.

45. Ibid., 3.

46. Peter Rudolph, "Managing Strategic Divergence: German-American Conflict Over Policy Towards Iran," in *The Iranian Dilemma: Challenges for German and American Foreign Policy*, (Washington: American Institute for Contemporary German Studies, The Johns Hopkins University, 1997), p. 6.

47. U.S. DEPARTMENT OF STATE, Office of the Spokesman, PRESS BRIEFING BY SECRETARY OF STATE WARREN CHRISTOPHER ON THE PRESIDENT'S EXECUTIVE ORDER ON IRAN, U.S. Department of State Monday, May 1, 1995.

48. Hooman Estelami, "A Study of Iran's Response to U.S. Economic Sanctions," *MERIA, Middle East Review of Internationals Affairs*, September 1999.

49. Hermann Franssen and Elaine Morton, "A Review of US Unilateral Sanctions Against Iran," *Middle East Economic Survey*, August 26, 2002.

50. "Doing Business With the Enemy," *Sixty Minutes*, CBS News, August 28, 2004.

51. Charles Lane, "Germany's New Ostpolitik: Changing Iran," *Foreign Affairs*, November/December 1995, pp. 79–80.

52. Ibid.

53. Ibid., 81.

54. Ibid.

55. For an excellent summary of the Mykonos attack and the legal process around it see: Iran Human Rights Documentation Center, *Murder at Mykonos: Anatomy of a Political Assassination*, March 2007.

56. "Mixed Response From Europe on Ruling Linking Iran to Killings," *The New York Times*, April 30, 1997.

57. Michael Rubin and Danielle Pletka, "Table Talk," *Wall Street Journal*, February 1, 2007.

58. Amir Taheri, *The Persian Night: Iran Under the Khomeinist Revolution* (New York: Encounter Books, 2009), 285.

59. Manouchehr Ganji, *Defying the Iranian Revolution: From a Minister to the Shah to a Leader of Resistance* (Westport: Praeger, 2002), 114–115.

60. Daniel Benjamin and Steven Simon, *The Age of Sacred Terror* (New York: Random House, 2002), 225.

61. Frhang Mehr, *A Colonial Legacy: The Dispute over the Islands of Abu Musa and the Greater and Smaller Tumbs* (Lanham: Univerity Press of America, 1997), 143. Cited in Ibrahim Mahmoud Yaseen Alnahas, pp. 168–69.

62. Douglas Jehl, "U.S. Says It's Worried about Iranian Military Buildup in the Gulf," *The New York Times*, March 23, 1995. See also "Abu Musa Island," Federation of American Scientists, Weapons of Mass Destruction Around the World.

63. Kenneth M. Pollack, *The Persian Puzzle: The Conflict Between Iran and America* (New York: Random House, 2004), 281.

64. Richard A. Clarke, *Against All Enemies: Inside America's War on Terror* (New York: Free Press, 2004), 112.

65. Ibid.

66. Ephraim Kam, *From Terror to Nuclear Bombs: The Significance of the Iranian Threat* (Tel Aviv: Ministry of Defense Publishing/Jaffee Center for Strategic Studies, 2006), 262.

67. Ganji, 136.

68. John R. Schindler, *Unholy Terror: Bosnia, Al-Qa'ida, and the Rise of Global Jihad* (St. Paul: Zenith Press, 2006), 137.

69. Ephraim Kam, *From Terror to Nuclear Bombs*, 261.

70. Gilles Kepel, *Jihad: The Trail of Political Islam* (Cambridge: Harvard University Press, 2002) See endnote 30, p. 423.

71. "Yugoslavia-Iran: Concern About Subversive Activity," April 28, 1983. www.cia.gov.

72. Schindler, 138-139.

73. Ibid.

74. Dr. Alberto Nisman provided an English translation of his Spanish language legal analysis to the author.

75. Ibid.

76. Ibid.

77. Alberto Nisman and Marcelo Martinez Burgos, "Report: Request for Arrests," English translation of Spanish report provided by Alberto Nisman to the author, 147–50.

78. Central Intelligence Agency, Directorate of Intelligence, "Hizballah: Expanding Terrorist Capabilities," July 21, 1991. www.cia.gov.

79. Laurence Louer, *Transnational Shia Politics: Religious and Political Networks in the Gulf* (New York: Columbia University Press, 2008), 210.

80. Richard A. Clarke, *Against All Enemies*, 113.

81. Ibid., 114.

82. Ibid., 118.

83. Michael Eisenstadt, "The Long Shadow of Khobar Towers: Dilemmas for the U.S. and Iran," Policy Watch, #144, October 8, 1999. The Washington Institute for Near East Policy.

84. Gary Sick, "Iran: Confronting Terrorism," *The Washington Quarterly*, Autumn, 2003, p. 88.

85. Jim Hoagland, "As Europe Looks 'South,' America Watches a Wider Screen," *International Herald Tribune*, March 6, 1997.

86. Kenneth Katzman, *Iran: Current Developments and U.S. Policy* (Washington: Congressional Research Service, January 2, 1997).

87. Nikki R. Keddie, *Modern Iran: Roots and Results of Revolution* (New Haven: Yale University Press, 2006), 269.

88. Ibid., 270.

89. Gary Sick, 89.

90. Martin Indyk, *Innocent Abroad*, 220.

91. Ibid., 219.

92. Ibid., 223.

93. Madeleine Albright, *Madam Secretary: A Memoir* (New York: Miramax Books, 2003), 321.

94. "Statement by the Secretary of State, Iran and Libya Sanctions ACT (ILSA): Decision in the South Pars Case," May 18, 1998.

95. "DCI Tenet, Testimony before the Senate Armed Services Committee," February 2, 1999. The CIA and the War on Terrorism, Public Statements on Potential Terrorist Use of Chemical, Biological, Radiological, and Nuclear (CBRN) Agents since July 1997. www.cia.gov.

96. "Memorandum: Hizballah Reactions to Khatami's Election," December 22, 1997. www.cia.gov.

97. For details on the presidential message to Khatami, see Indyk, pp. 224-225.

98. Elton L. Daniel, *The History of Iran* (Westport: Greenwood Press, 2001) 258. See also: Robert Fisk, "'They Are All Reformers Now, Even the Hangmen,'" *The Independent*, February 18, 2000.

99. This was the assessment of Akbar Ganji, a former Revolutionary Guard, who was a real reformer and paid the price for his positions by being imprisoned. See: Robin Wright, *Dreams and Shadows: The Future of the Middle East* (New York: Penguin Books, 2008), 276.

100. Ibrahim Mahmoud Yaseen Alnahas, *Continuity and Change in the Revolutionary Iran Foreign Policy*, 204.

101. Ibid., 207.

102. Ali Alfoneh, "The Revolutionary Guards' Role in Iranian Politics," *Middle East Quarterly*, Fall 2008.

103. Mehdi Khalaji, "Iran's Revolutionary Guards Corps, Inc." Policy Watch #1273, Washington Institute for Near East Policy, August 17, 2007.

104. Ibrahim Mahmoud Yaseen Alnahas, *Continuity and Change in the Revolutionary Iran Foreign Policy*, 209.

105. UN Security Council Resolution 1737, See Resolution Annex, December 23, 2006. www.un.org.

106. Anoushiravan Ehteshami & Mahjoob Zweiri, *Iran and the Rise of the Neoconservatives: The Politics of Tehran's Silent Revolution* (London: I.B. Taurus, 2007), 83–4.

107. Kenneth M. Pollack, *The Persian Puzzle*, xxvi.

108. Ibid., 339.

109. Barton Gellman, "Shift by Iran Fuels Debate Over Sanctions; While Urging Dialogue, Tehran Pursues New Arms," *Washington Post*, December 31, 1997.

110. Stuart D. Goldman, Kenneth Katzman, Robert D. Shuey, and Carl E. Behrens, *Russian Missile Technology and Nuclear Reactor Transfers to Iran* (Washington: Congressional Research Service, Library of Congress, July 29, 1998) 6.

111. Ibid.

112. Strobe Talbott, *The Russian Hand*, 265. Michael R. Gordon and Eric Schmitt, "Iran Nearly Got Alloy From Russians," *The New York Times*, April 25, 1998.

113. Michael R. Gordon and Eric Schmitt, "Iran Nearly Got Alloy From Russians."

114. The Honorable Robert Gallucci, "A United States View," in Joseph Cirincione, ed., *Repairing the Regime: Preventing the Spread of Weapons of Mass Destruction* (London: Routledge, 2000), 186.

115. Ibid., 188.

116. United States District Court for the District of Columbia, Estate of Michael Heiser, et al. Plaintiffs v. Islamic Republic of Iran, et. al. Defendants and Estate of Millard D. Campbell, et al. Plaintiffs, v. Islamic Republic of Iran, et al., Defendants. Filed December 22, 2006.

CHAPTER 7

1. Kenneth M. Pollack, *The Persian Puzzle: The Conflict Between Iran and America* (New York: Random House, 2004), 346.

2. Nazila Fathi, "A Nation Challenged: Tehran; Iran Softens Tone Against the United States," *The New York Times*, September 21, 2001.

3. Ibid. In public, President Khatami did make the public remark that "A tragedy must not be answered with another tragedy and innocent people in Afghanistan, or in any other place, must not be attacked or hurt." Supreme Leader Khamenei was more blunt in his pronouncements: "...Iran condemns any attack on Afghanistan that may lead to another human tragedy." See Nazila Fathi, Op Cit.

4. Ahmed Rashid, *Taliban: Militant Islam, Oil & Fundamentalism in Central Asia* (New Haven: Yale University Press, 2000), 74.

5. Ibid.

6. Ibid.

7. BBC, Nuclear Confrontation: Iran and the West, (February, 2009).

8. Kenneth M. Pollack, *The Persian Puzzle*, 346.

9. Hillary Mann, "U.S. Diplomacy with Iran: The Limits of Tactical Engagement," Statement to the Subcommittee on National Security and Foreign Affairs, Committee on Government Oversight and Reform, U.S. House of Representatives, November 7, 2007.

10. BBC, "Nuclear Confrontation," Op. Cit.

11. General Tommy Franks, *American Soldier* (New York: Regan Books, 2004), Lt. General Michael DeLong, *Inside Centcom: The Unvarnished Truth About the Wars in Afghanistan and Iraq* (Washington: Regnery Publishing, 2004).

12. Ibid.

13. Madeleine Albright, Madam Secretary: A Memoir (New York: Miramax Books, 2003), 325, See footnote 5.

14. Puneet Talwar, "Iran in the Balance," *Foreign Affairs*, July/August 2001, p. 66.

15. Bob Woodward, *Bush at War* (New York: Simon & Schuster, 2002), 298.

16. Rowan Scarborough, "Iran Underground Route Aids al Qaeda: Route Goes Through Lebanon, U.S. Says," *The Washington Times*, National Weekly Edition, April 8-14, 2002. Scarborough also quotes an April 2, 2002 statement by Secretary of Defense Donald H. Rumsfeld in which he says: "There is no question but that al Qaeda have moved into Iran and out of Iran to the south and dispersed to some other countries."

17. Michael Rubin, "Can Iran Be Trusted?" *Middle Eastern Outlook*, American Enterprise Institute, September 2006.

18. Cited in Patrick Clawson and Michael Rubin, *Eternal Iran: Continuity and Change* (New York: Palgrave Macmillan, 2005), 149.

19. Ronen Bergman, *Authority Given* (Tel Aviv: Yediot Books, 2002), 318.

20. Matthew Levitt, "New Arenas for Iranian-Sponsored Terrorism: The Arab-Israeli Heartland," Policy Watch #605, The Washington Institute for Near East Policy, February 22, 2002.

21. "Rafsanjani Says Mideast Nuclear Conflict Possible," Agence France Presse, December 14, 2001, Michael Rubin, "Iran and the Palestinian War Against Israel: Implications of the Karine-A Affair," Washington Institute for Near East Policy, February 26, 2002. The text used here comes from "Former Iranian President Rafsanjani on Using a Nuclear Bomb on Israel," *MEMRI*, Special Dispatch Series-No. 325. January 3, 2002.

22. Ibid.

23. George Gedda, "U.S. Says Iran Making Headway on Nuclear Weapons Program," *Associated Press*, February 11, 2002.

24. Kenneth M. Pollack, *The Persian Puzzle*, 351.

25. Ibid.

26. Barbara Slavin, *Bitter Friends, Bosom Enemies: Iran, the U.S., and the Twisted Path to Confrontation* (New York: St. Martin's Griffin, 2007), 200.

27. Kenneth M. Pollack, *The Persian Puzzle*, 352.

28. Two critical works on the Guldimann Fax are Steven J. Rosen, "Did Iran Offer a 'Grand Bargain' in 2003?" American Thinker, November 16, 2008 and Michael Rubin, "The "Guldimann Memorandum," *The Weekly Standard*, October 22, 2007. Slavin, Op. Cit. also deals extensively with the document.

29. Ibid.

30. Barbara Slavin, *Bitter Friends, Bosom Enemies*, 205.

31. Ibid.

32. Flynt Leverett, "The Gulf Between Us," *The New York Times*, January 24, 2006.

33. Ibid.

34. Glenn Kessler, "2003 Memo Says Iranian Leaders Backed Talks," *Washington Post*, February 14, 2007.

35. Nichlas D. Kristof, "Iran's Proposal for a 'Grand Bargain,'" *The New York Times*, April, 28, 2007.

36. Ibid.

37. Steven J. Rosen, "Did Iran Offer a 'Grand Bargain' in 2003?" Op Cit.

38. BBC, "Nuclear Confrontation: Iran and the West."

39. Ibid.

40. Ibid, See *Newsweek*, February 19, 2007.

41. Steven J. Rosen, "Did Iran Offer a 'Grand Bargain' in 2003?" Op Cit.

42. "Showdown with Iran," *PBS Frontline*, October 23, 2007.

43. Ibid.

44. "U.S. Worried About More al Qaeda Attacks," *CNN*, May 14, 2003.

45. "Saudis Suspect al-Qaida in Deadly Bombing in Riyadh," Voice of America, Novmber 10, 2003.

46. Douglas Jehl and Eric Schmitt, "Aftereffects: Havens; "U.S. Suggests a Qaeda Cell in Iran Directed Saudi Bombings," *The New York Times*, May 21, 2003.

47. Daniel Benjamin and Steven Simon, *The Age of Sacred Terror* (New York: Random House, 2002), 263–64.

48. *The 9/11 Commission Report; Final Report of the National Commission on Terrorist Attacks on the United States* (New York: W.W. Norton &Company, 2004), 240.

49. Rohan Gunaratna, *Inside al Qaeda: Global Network of Terror* (New York: Columbia University Press, 2002), 147.

50. The 9/11 Commission Report, Op. Cit.

51. Richard A. Clarke, *Against All Enemies*.

52. Peter Finn, "Al Qaeda Deputies Harbored by Iran; Pair Are Plotting Attacks, Sources Say," *Washington Post*, August 28, 2002.

53. Jean-Charles Brisard, *Zarqawi: The New Face of al-Qaeda* (New York: Other Press, 2005), 93.

54. Al-Mustaqbal (Beirut), October 5, 2004, cited in Eurasia Security Watch, No. 53, American Foreign Policy Council, Washington, D. C., October 7, 2004.

55. Dan Darling, "The Cicero Article," *The Weekly Standard*, November 10, 2004.

56. Jean-Charles Brisard, *Zarquwi*.

57. Peter Finn and Susan Schmidt, "Al Qaeda Is Trying to Open Iraq Front; Plot Said to Be Hatched in Iran Last February," *Washington Post*, September 7, 2003. Finn and Schmidt assert that the Sunni insurgency was planned from a safe house in Iran by Muhammmad Ibrahim Makawi, the military chief of al-Qaeda who is also known as Said Adel, and Abu Musab al-Zarqawi in February 2002, prior to the US-led invasion of Iraq.

58. U.S. Department of the Treasury, "Treasury Targets Al Qaida Operatives in Iran," Press Release, January 16, 2009.

59. Josh Meyer, "Some U.S. Officials Fear Iran Is Helping Al Qaeda," *Los Angeles Times*, March 21, 2006.

60. Rubin, Op. Cit.

61. Ibid.

62. Joseph Felter and Brian Fishman, *Iranian Strategy in Iraq: Politics and 'Other Means'* (West Point: Combatting Terrorism Center, 2008), 17–19.

63. Ibid., 17.

64. Edward Pound, "Special Report: The Iran Connection," *U.S. News & World Report*, November 14, 2004.

65. Rubin, Op. Cit. (Fleischer statement is from the American Presidency Project, University of California, Santa Barbara, www.presidency.ucsb.edu.

66. Rubin, Op Cit.

67. This summary of Iranian ties to Iraqi political organizations is derived from Joseph Felter and Brian Fishman, *Iranian Strategy in Iraq*, 22-25. See also: Kenneth Katzman, "Iran's Influence in Iraq," Congressional Research Service, June 13, 2006.

68. Mshari al-Zaydi, "An Insight to Iranian Influence in Iraq," al-Sharq al-Awsat, June 10, 2005.

69. Michael Gordon, "Deadliest Bomb in Iraq Is Made by Iran, U.S. Says," *The New York Times*, February 10, 2007.

70. Scott Conroy, "Gates: Iranian Weaponry Found in Iraq," CBS News/AP, February 9, 2007.

71. Rick Atkinson, "The Single Most Effective Weapon Against Our Deployed Forces," *Washington Post*, September 30, 2007. Atkinson reports that US military sources stated that 81,000 IED's had been used in the Iraq War through the date of his article. This required a major smuggling effort on the part of Iran.

72. Michael E. O'Hanlon and Jason H. Campbell, *Iraq Index: Tracking Variables of Reconstruction & Security in Post-Saddam Iraq* (Washington: The Brookings Institution, 2007), 18.

73. Steven Hurst, "Officials: Iran Behind Advanced, Lethal IED," *Associated Press*, February 11, 2007.

74. Joseph Felter and Brian Fishman, *Iranian Strategy in Iraq*, 38.

75. Ibid.

76. Michael Ware, "Inside Iran's Secret War for Iraq," *Time*, August 15, 2005.

77. "Showdown with Iran," *Frontline* October 23, 2007., See analysis interviews entitled "A 'Slap in the Face' from America," PBS.

78. Ibid.

79. James A. Baker, III and Lee H. Hamilton, Co-Chairs, *The Iraq Study Group Report* (New York: Vintage Books, 2006), 52.

80. Ibid.

81. Nimrod Raphaeli, "Iran's Stirrings in Iraq," *MEMRI* Inquiry and Analysis –No. 173, May, 5, 2004.

82. Shaul Bakhash, *The Reign of the Ayatollahs: Iran and the Islamic Revolution* (New York: Basic Books, 1984), 234.

83. Karim Sadjadpour, *Reading Khamenei: The World View of Iran's Most Powerful Leader* (Washington: Carnegie Endowment for International Peace, 2008), 22.

84. Nimrod Raphaeli, "Iran's Stirrings in Iraq," Op Cit.

85. Joby Warrick, "U.S. Cites Big Gains Against Al-Qaeda," *Washington Post*, May 30, 2008.

CHAPTER 8

1.Ofira Seliktar, *Failing the Crystal Ball Test: The Carter Administration and the Fundamentalist Revolution in Iran* (Westport: Praeger Publishers, 2000), 121.

2. Gary Sick, *All fall Down: America's Tragic Encounter with Iran* (Lincoln: Baninprint, 2001), 193.

3. Amir Taheri, *The Spirit of Allah: Khomeini and the Islamic Revolution* (Bethesda: Adler & Adler, 1986), 107; and Gholam Reza Afkhami, *The Life and Times of the Shah* (Berkley: University of California Press, 2009), 366.

4. Gholam Reza Afkhami, *The Life and Times of the Shah*, 368.

5. Tim Weiner, *Legacy of Ashes: The History of the CIA* (New York: Doubleday, 2007), 370.

6. Imam Khomeini, *Islam and Revolution* (North Haledon: Mizan Press, 1981), 108–9.

7. Shaul Bakhash, *The Reign of the Ayatollahs: Iran and the Islamic Revolution* (New York: Basic Books, 1984), 233.

8. Amir Tahcri, *The Spirit of Allah*, 110–11.

9. Ali Alfoneh, "The Revolutionary Guards' Role in Iranian Politics," *Middle East Quarterly*, Fall 2008.

10. Joschka Fischer, "The Case for Bargaining with Iran," *Washington Post*, May 20, 2006.

11. Joschka Fischer, "Is the Middle East State System About to Disintegrate?" *Daily Star* (Beirut), May 5, 2008.

12. "Iran on the Horizon: Iran and the Gulf," The Middle East Institute (Washington: Saudi-US Information Service), February 18, 2008.

13. Imam Khomeini, *Islam and Revolution* (North Haledon: Mizan Press, 1981), 144.

14. Imam Khomeini, *Islam and Revolution*, 34.

15. Shmuel Bar, "Iran: Cultural Values, Self Images and Negotiating Behavior," (Herzliya: Institute for Policy and Strategy, IDC Herzliya, 2004), iv.

16. Giandomenico Picco, *Man Without a Gun: One Diplomat's Secret Struggle to Free the Hostages, Fight Terrorism, and End a War* (New York: Times Books, 1999), 71.

17. Ibid., 67.

18. Ibid., 71.

19. Warren Christopher, "Welcome to the Bazaar," *New York Times*, June 13, 2006.

20. Warren Christopher, "Welcome to the Bazaar," *The New York Times*, June 13, 2006.

21. John Bolton, *Surrender Is Not an Option*, 149.

22. Shmuel Bar, "Iran: Cultural Values, Self Images and Negotiating Behavior," 35.

23. Dominic Head, ed. *The Cambridge Guide to Literature in English* (Cambridge: Cambridge University Press, 2006), 1226.

24. Phillip C. Habib Interview: Conversations with History: Institute of International Studies, University of California, Berkeley. May 14, 1982. http://globetrotter.berkley.edu/conversations/Habib/habib2.html.

25. Quoted by Shmuel Bar, "Iran: Cultural Values, Self Images and Negotiating Behavior," 34, see footnote 128.

26. Mark Bowden, *Guests of the Ayatollah* (New York: Grove Press, 2006), 596. Bowden quotes an Iranian negotiator who said as the hostages flew away: "We rubbed dirt in the nose of the world's greatest superpower."

27. Baqer Moin, *Khomeini: Life of the Ayatollah* (New York: Thomas Dunne Books, 1999), 227.

28. Robert Cooper, "The New Liberal Imperialism," *The Observer*, April 7, 2002.

29. Ibid.

30. Michael Rubin, "Iran Means What It Says," *Middle East Forum*, January 25, 2006.

31. John Bolton, *Surrender Is Not an Option*, 157.

32. William J. Broad, David E. Sanger, and Elaine Sciolino, "Arms Inspectors said to Seek Access to Iran Sites," *The New York Times*, December 2, 2004.

33. "Iran Would Like 'Nuclear Option,'" BBC News, June 17, 2009.

34. Hooman Estelami, "A Study of Iran's Response to U.S. Economic Sanctions," *MERIA, Middle East Review of Internationals Affairs*, September 1999.

35. "Doing Business With the Enemy," *Sixty Minutes*, CBS News, August 28, 2004.

36. Vikas Bajaj and John Eligon, "Iran Moved Billions Via U.S. Banks," *The New York Times*, January 10, 2009.

37. "London's Terror Bank," Review and Outlook, *Wall Street Journal*, August 21, 2008.

38. Ami Taheri, "Who Are Iran's Revolutionary Guards?" November 15, 2007.

39. "Tehran's Strip Club: How Lloyds Bank Helped Iran's Global Shopping Spree," *Wall Street Journal*, January 12, 2009.

40. Vikas Bajaj and John Eligon, "Iran Moved Billions via U.S. Banks," *New York Times*, Janurary 10, 2009. And Laura Italiano, "Brit Bank Slapped for Iran Loot Laundering," *New York Post*, January 10, 2009.

41. Roger Cohen, "Iran, Jews, and Pragmatism," *New York Times*, March 16, 2009.

42. With Reporting by Elaine Shannon, "Iran's Power in the Shadows," *Time*, June 25, 2006.

43. Emanuele Ottolenghi, *Under the Mushroom Cloud: Europe, Iran and the Bomb* (London; Profile Books, 2009), 31.

44. Fareed Zakaria, "They May Not Want the Bomb: And Other Unexpected Truths," *Newsweek*, June 1, 2009.

45. Dilip Hirro, for example, has noted that Khomeini changed his position on nuclear weapons when he was confronted with Saddam Hussein's use of weapons of mass destruction during the Iran-Iraq War; See: Dilip Hiro, "Why Iran Didn't Cross the Nuclear Weapons Road," *Yale Global Online*, December 11, 2007.

46. Anthony Cordesman and Adam Seitz, "Iranian Weapons of Mass Destruction: Doctrine, Policy and Command (Washington: Center for Strategic and International Studies), Janurary 12, 2009, p. 2.

47. Ibid.

48. Shmuel Bar, Rachel Machtiger, and Shmuel Bachar, "Iranian Nuclear Decision Making Under Ahmadinejad" (Herzliya: The Interdisciplinary Center, Lauder School of Government, Diplomacy, and Strategy, Institute for Policy and Strategy, 2008), 12.

49. Karl Vick, "Iran's Gray Area on Nuclear Arms," *Washington Post*, June 21, 2006.

CHAPTER 9

1. Rory McCarthy, "Iran Helping Religious Militias in Iraq, British Envoy Warns," *The Guardian*, June 4, 2003.

2. "Iran and the West: Nuclear Confrontation," BBC, February 2009.

3. "Iran and the West: Nuclear Confrontation," BBC, February 2009. The relevant portions of the BBC program for this analysis can also be found at Julian Borger, "Iran Offered to End Attacks on British Troops in Iraq, Claims Diplomat," *The Guardian*, February 20, 2009.

4. Ibid.

5. Ibid.

6. "Iranian Army Chief of Staff Reveals in Interview Preparations for Military Confrontation with U.S." *MEMRI*, Special Dispatch—No. 1156, May 4, 2006.

7. "Top Iranian Military Commanders: In Case of Attack on Iran, We'll Target U.S. Troops in Gulf," *MEMRI*, Special Dispatch—Number 1378, December 6, 2006.

8. Sheera Claire Frenkel, "Iran Obtained 12 Long-Range Missiles," *Jerusalem Post*, December 20, 2005.

9. "Israeli Intelligence Says Iran Has BM-25 Missiles: New Missiles Will Put Europe Within Firing Range," Associated Press, April 27, 2006.

10. Daveed Gartenstein-Ross, "Purchase of North Korean Missiles Extends Iran's Force Projection Capability," *The Counterterrorism Blog*, January 18, 2008.

11. Amir Taheri, *The Persian Night: Iran Under the Khomeinist Revolution* (New York: Encounter Books, 2009), 285.

12. Kasra Naji, *Ahmadinejad: The Secret History of Iran's Radical Leader* (Berkeley: University of California Press, 2008), 32.

13. Ali Alfoneh, "The Revolutionary Guards' Role in Iranian Politics," *Middle East Quarterly*, Fall, 2008.

14. Ali M. Ansari, *Iran Under Ahmadinejad: The Politics of Confrontation*, Adelphi Paper 393, (London: The International Institute for Strategic Studies with Routledge, 2007).

15. Amir Taheri, "Ahmadinejad: Muscular Style," *Arab News*, July 9, 2005.

16. Robin Wright, *Dreams and Shadows: The Future of the Middle East* (New York: Penguin Books, 2008), 317.

17. A. Savyon, "Iran's 'Second Islamic Revolution': Fulfilled by Election of Conservative President," *MEMRI* Inquiry and Analysis No. 229, June 28, 2005.

18. Nazila Fathi, "Wipe Israel 'off the map,' Iranian says," *The New York Times,* October 27, 2005; http://www.nytimes.com/2005/10/26/world/africa/26iht-iran.html.

19. Much of this section is based on the excellent monograph by Joshua Teitelbaum, *What Iranian Leaders Really Say About Doing Away with Israel: A Refutation of the Campaign to Excuse Ahmadinejad's Incitement to Genocide* (Jerusalem: Jerusalem Center for Public Affairs, 2008).

20. Ibid.

21. Ibid.

22. Ibid.

23. Ibid.

24. Joshua Teitelbaum, *What Iranian Leaders Really Say About Doing Away with Israel: A Refutation of the Campaign to Excuse Ahmadinejad's Incitement to Genocide* (Jerusalem: Jerusalem Center for Public Affairs, 2008).

25. "Iranian Presidential Advisor Mohammad Ali Ramin: 'The Resolution of the Holocaust Issue Will End in the Destruction of Israel,'" MEMRI, June 15, 2006; available online at: http://memri.net/bin/articles.cgi?Page=archives&Area=sd&ID=SP118606.

26. Jon Lee Anderson, "Can Iran Change?" *The New Yorker*, April 13, 2009.

27. Joshua Teitelbaum, "What Iranian Leaders Really Say about Doing Away with Israel," op cit.

28. Michael Axworthy, *A History of Iran: Empire of the Mind* (New York: Basic Books, 2008), 313. See endnote 11.

29. "Text of Mahmoud Ahmadinejad's Speech," *The New York Times*, October 26, 2005.

30. "Iran's Ahmadinejad Targets 'Corrupt World Leadership,'" *AFP*, April 10, 2008.

31. Amir Taheri, *The Persian Night: Iran Under the Khomeinist Revolution* (New York: Encounter Books, 2009), 309.

32. Kasra Naji, *Ahmadinejad*, 92.

33. Vali Nasr, *The Shia Revival: How Conflicts Within Islam Will Shape the Future* (New York: Norton, 2007), 134.

34. Mohebat Ahdiyyih, "Ahmadinejad and the Mahdi," *Middle East Quarterly*, Fall 2008.

35. Vali Nasr, *The Shia Revival*, 134.

36. Islamic Republic News Agency, September 17, 2005.

37. Kasra Naji, *Ahmadinejad*, 94–95.

38. A. Savyon and Y. Mansharof, "The Doctrine of Mahdism: In the Ideological and Political Philosphy of Mahmoud Ahmadinejad and Ayatollah Mesbah-e Yazdi," *MEMRI*, Inquiry and Analysis #357, May 2007.

39. Kasra Naji, *Ahmadinejad*, 93.

40. Nazila Fathi, "Iranian Clerics Tell the President to Leave the Theology to Them," *The New York Times*, May 20, 2008.

41. Mehdi Khalaji, *Apocalyptic Politics: On the Rationality of Iranian Policy* (Washington: Washington Institute for Near East Policy, 2008). Khalaji notes on page 26: "Certain Shiite traditions state that the Imam's return will come at a time of world chaos, and Ahmadinezad seems at times to promote chaos for that end."

42. "Paper: French FM in Memoir—Ahmadinejad Tells European FMs in 2005 Meeting, 'After the Chaos We Can See the Greatness of Allah,'" *The MEMRI Blog*, February 2, 2007 (Source: *al-Sharq al-Awsat*, London, February 2, 2007).

43. Ze'ev Maghen, "Occulation in Perpetuum: Shi'ite Messianism and the Policies of the Islamic Republic," *The Middle East Journal*, Spring, 2008.

44. Vision of the Islamic Republic of Iran, Network 2, November 1, 2008.

45. Mehdi Khalaji, "Apocalyptic Visions and Iran's Security Policy," Patrick Clawson and Michael Eisenstadt, eds. *Deterring the Ayatollahs: Complications in Applying Cold War Strategy to Iran* (Washington: The Washington Institute for Near East Policy, 2007), 32. See especially footnote 6.

46. Vali Nasr, *The Shia Revival*, 132; and Matthias Küntzel, "Ahmadinejad's Demons: A Child of the Revolution Takes Over," *The New Republic*, April 24, 2006.

47. Amir Taheri, *The Persian Night*, 209.

48. Mehdi Khalaji, *Apocalyptic Politics*, viii.

49. Mehdi Khalaji, "Apocalyptic Visions and Iran's Security Policy," Patrick Clawson and Michael Eisenstadt, eds. *Deterring the Ayatollahs: Complications in Applying Cold War Strategy to Iran* (Washington: The Washington Institute for Near East Policy,2007), 31.

50. Kasra Naji, *Ahmadinejad*, 15.

51. Ibid., 11.

52. Anoushiravan Ehteshami, *After Khomeini: The Iranian Second Republic* (London: Routledge, 1995), 8–9.

53. Amir Taheri, *The Persian Night*, 273.

54. Bill Samii, "Is the Hajjatieh Society Making a Comeback?" *Iran Report*, Radio Free Europe—Radio Liberty, Septmber 13, 2004.

55. Amir Taheri.

56. "Iran's Ayatollah Mohammad Taqi Mesbah-Yazdi; Mentor, Leader, Power Broker," *BBC Monitoring Service*, February 5, 2006. Ahdiyyih, Op. Cit.

57. Mohebat Ahdiyyih, "Ahmadinejad and the Mahdi," *Middle East Quarterly*, Fall 2008, pp. 27-36, http://www.meforum.org/1985/ahmadinejad-and-the-mahdi.

58. Kasra Naji, *Ahmadinejad*, 98.

59. "Reformist Iranian Internet Daily: A New Fatwa States that Religious Law Does Not Forbid Use of Nuclear Weapons," *MEMRI*, Special Dispatch—No. 1096, February 17, 2006.

60. Savyon and Mansharof, Op Cit.

61. Ibid.

62. "Iran's Ayatollah Mohammad Taqi Mesbah-Yazdi; Mentor, Leader, Power Broker," BBC Monitoring Middle East, February, 5, 2006.

63. Shmuel Bar, Rachel Machtiger, and Shmuel Bachar, *Iranian Nuclear Decision Making under Ahmadinejad* (Herzliya: Lauder School of Government, Diplomacy, and Strategy, 2008), 17.

64. Anoushiravan Ehteshami and Mahjoob Zweiri, *Iran and the Rise of the Neoconservatives: The Politics of Tehran's Silent Revolution* (London: I.B. Taurus, 2007), 183.

65. "Shi'ite Supremists Emerge from Iran's Shadows," *Asia Times*, September 9, 2005.

66. Abbas Milani, "Pious Populist," *Boston Review*, November/December 2007.

67. Kasra Naji, *Ahmadinejad*, 109.

68. Frederic Wehrey, Jerrold D. Green, Brian Nichiporuk, Alireza Nader, Lydia Hansell, Rasool Nafisi, and S. R. Bohandi, *The Rise of the Pasdaran:*

Assessing the Domestic Roles of Iran's Revolutionary Guards Corps (Santa Monica: RAND Corporation, 2009), 36.

69. "Ayatollah Nouri-Hamedani: 'Fight the Jews and Vanquish Them So As To Hasten the Coming of the Hidden Imam,'" *MEMRI*, Special Dispatch—No. 897, April 22, 2005.

70. Amir Taheri, *The Persian Night*, 310.

71. Kasra Naji. *Ahmadinehad*, 102.

72. Mohebat Ahadiyyih, "Ahmadinejad and the Mahdi," Op. Cit.

73. A. Savyon and Y. Mansharof, "The Doctrine of Mahdism," Op. Cit.

74. Secretary of State Condoleezza Rice Holds News Conference on Iran, CQ Transcripts Wire. Wednesday, May 31, 2006. Available at http://www.washingtonpost.com/wp-dyn/content/article/2006/05/31/AR2006053100937.html.

75. Glenn Kessler: *The Confidante: Condoleezza Rice and the Creation of the Bush Legacy* (New York: St. Martin's Press, 2007), 196.

76. UN Security Council, "Security Council Demands Iran Suspend Uranium Enrichment By 31 August, Or Face Possible Economic, Diplomatic Sanctions," 5500 Meeting (AM), news release, July 31, 2006.

77. Chapter VII: Action with Respect to Threats to the Peace, Breaches of the Peace, and Acts of Aggression, Article 39," June 26, 1945, Charter of the United Nations, Available at http://www.un.org/en/documents/charter/chapter7.shtml.

78. John Bolton, *Surrender if Not an Option: Defending America at the United Nations and Abroad* (New York: Threshold, 2007), 332.

79. "Security Council Demands Iran Suspend Uranium Enrichment by 31 August, or face Possible Economic, Diplomatic Sanctions," UN Security Council SC/8792, Department of Public Information.

80. "Bush: 'All options are on the table,' regarding Iran's nuclear aspirations," *USA Today*, August 13, 2005; available online at: http://www.usatoday.com/news/washington/2005-08-13-bush-iran-nuclear_x.htm.

81. "Iran and the West: Nuclear Confrontation," BBC, February 2009, Op. Cit.

82. Ali Akbar Dareini, "Iran Calls Western Incentives Acceptable," *Associated Press*, July 16, 2006.

83. John Bolton, *Surrender Is Not an Option*, 332.

84. Elaine Sciolino and Helene Cooper, "Rice is Disappointed by Iran's 'Incomplete' Response," *International Herald Tribune*, July 12, 2006.

85. "Iran and the West: Nuclear Confrontation," BBC, February 2009, Op. Cit.

86. Implementation of the NPT Safeguards Agreement in the Islamic Republic of Iran," *International Atomic Energy Agency*, August 31, 2006, GOV/2006/53.

87. Meir Javedanfar, "Another Major Victory for Messianics," *Jerusalem Post*, October 24, 2007.

88. "Iran Calls U.N. Resolution 'Invalid' and 'Illegal,' Vows to Continue Enriching Uranium," Associated Press, *International Herald Tribune*, December 23, 2006.

89. Under Secretary for Political Affairs R. Nicholas Burns and Afghanistan Foreign Minister Abdullah Abdullah, "Joint Statement: United States—Afghanistan Strategic Partnership." Loy Henderson Conference Room,Washington, DC. March 21, 2006. Available at http://statelists.state.gov/scripts/wa.exe?A2=ind0603c&L=dossdo&P=1064

90. "Using the Quds Force of the Revolutionary Guards as the Main Tool to Export the Revolution Beyond the Borders of Iran," Intelligence and Terrorism Information Center at the Israel Intelligence Heritage & Commemoration Center (IICC), April 2, 2007.

91. Robin Wright and Nancy Trejos, "Iranians Captured Inside Iraq," *Washington Post*, January 12, 2007.

92. Robin Wright, *Dreams and Shadows*, Op Cit., 334.

93. Dan Diker, "President Bush and the Qods Force Controversy; Lessons Learned," *Jerusalem Issue Briefs*, Institute for Contemporary Affairs, Jerusalem Center for Public Affairs, March 6, 2007.

94. Ibid.

95. "Who's Behind Iran's Death Squad?" *ABC News*, February 14, 2007.

96. Dan Diker, "President Bush and The Qods Force Controversy; Lessons Learned," Op. Cit.

97. Sean D. Naylor, "Iran Deeply Involved in Iraq, Petreaus Says," *Marine Corps News*, May 25, 2007.

98. Frederick W. Kagan, Kimberly Kagan, Danielle Pletka, *Iranian Influence in the Levant, Iraq, and Afghanistan* (Washington: American Enterprise Institute), 23.

99. Ibid., 21.

100. "General Petraeus Accuses Iran of Fueling Violence," Fox News, October 7, 2007.

101. John F. Burns and Michael Gordon, "U.S. Says Iran Helped Iraqis Kill Five G.I.'s," *The New York Times*, July 3, 2007.

102. http://www.defenselink.mil/pdfs/Petraeus-Testimony20070910.pdf See also Lt.-Gen. (ret.) Moshe Yaalon, "The Second Lebanon War: From Territory to Ideology," in Dan Diker, ed. *Iran's Race for Regional Supremacy: Strategic Implications for the Middle East* (Jerusalem; Jerusalem Center for Public Affairs, 2008), 31.

103. W. Kagan, Kimberly Kagan, Danielle Pletka, *Iranian Influence in the Levant, Iraq, and Afghanistan*, 29.

104. Robin Wright and Nancy Trejos, "Iranians Captured Inside Iraq," Op Cit.

105. Ibid.

106. U.S. Department of State, "Briefing After Secretary Rice's Meeting with the P-5 Plus Germany Plus EU," R. Nicholas Burns, Under Secretary of State for Political Affairs, September 28, 2007.

107. Ibid.

CHAPTER 10

1. Y. Y. Mansharof and I. Rapoport, "Tension in Iran-Bahrain Relations After *Kayhan* Editor Claims Bahrain Is Inseparable Part of Iran," *MEMRI*, No. 379, August 3, 2007.

2. Ibid.

3. Ibid.

4. Ibid.

5. "Leading Saudi Daily: Iran Was Once a Sunni Country," *MEMRI*, No. 2256, February 23, 2009.

6. Ibid.

7. "Former Bahrain Chief of Staff: 'Iran Is an Octopus That Stirs Trouble,'" *MEMRI* Special Dispatch, No. 1949, June 5, 2008.

8. Vali Nasr, *The Shia Revival*, 235.

9. Barak Ravid and Yoav Stern, "Mubarak: Gaza Tension Brings Iran Closer," *Haaretz*, March 26, 2008.

10. "Egyptian President Hosni Mubarak, 'Shiites Are Mostly Loyal to Iran Than to their Own Countries,'" *MEMRI* TV, April 8, 2006.

11. "Saudi and Sudanese Writers Warn of 'Shiite Octopus' Taking Over Sudan," *MEMRI*, Special Dispatch—No. 2079, October 12, 2008.

12. "Editor of Kuwaiti Daily: Arab Countries Must Join Forces to Counter Iranian Threat," *MEMRI*, Special Dispatch—No. 1651, July 12, 2007.

13. Andrew McGregor, "Shi'ite Insurgency in Yemen: Iranian Intervention or Mountain Revolt," The Jamestown Foundation, August 11, 2004.

14. Vali Nasr, *The Shia Revival*, 240.

15. International Crisis Group, "Yemen: Defusing the Saada Time Bomb" *Middle East Report*, Number 86, May 27, 2009.

16. Abul Rahman Shaheen, "Surrendered Militant Reveals Plots to Strike Oil Facilities," *Gulf News,* March 28, 2009.

17. Ibid. See also: Tariq Alhomayed, "Look Who's Defending Hezbollah," *al-Sharq al-Awsat*, April 14, 2009.

18. Robin Wright and Peter Baker, "Iraq, Jordan See Threat to Election From Iran," *Washington Post*, December 8, 2004.

19. Anthony Shadid, "Across Arab World, a Widening Rift: Sunni-Shiite Tension Called Region's 'Most Dangerous Problem,'" *Washington Post*, February 12, 2007.

20. "Morocco Severs Relations with Iran," ALJAZEERA.NET, March 7, 2009.

21. Frederick Kagan, Kimberly Kagan, and Danielle Pletka, *Iranian Influence in the Levant, Iraq, and Afghanistan* (Washington: American Enterprise Institute, 2008), 3–6.

22. "Syrian Opposition TV Accuses Syrian Regime of 'Shi'izing' Syria," *MEMRI*, Special Dispatch—No. 2197, January 20, 2009.

23. Ibid. See also, Jonathan Dahoah Halevy, "The Middle East in the Shadow of the Developing Conflict between the Sunnis and the Shiites," Jerusalem Center for Public Affairs, January 9, 2007.

24. Tariq Alhomayed, "Who Seeks to Hinder the Damascus Summit," *al-Sharq al-Awsat,* February 22, 2008.

25. Dr. Reuven Erlich, "Raising the Issue of the Sheba'a Farms in the Proposed American-French Security Council Draft Resolution for the Ending the Fighting: Background Information and Significance," Intelligence and Terrorism Information Center at the Center for Special Studies (C.S.S.), August 9, 2006.

26. Annan's report was issued on May 22, 2000. See, Israel Ministry of Foreign Affairs, "The Legal Status of the Shabaa Farms," April 8, 2002.

27. Dr. Reuven Erlich, "Raising the Issue of the Sheba'a Farms in the Proposed American-French Security Council Draft Resolution for the Ending the Fighting: Background Information and Significance," Op. Cit.

28. Hassan Haydar, "Persian Borders," *al-Hayat*, August 10, 2006.

29. Michael Gordon, "Militants Are Said to Amass Missiles in South Lebanon," *The New York Times*, September 27, 2002.

30. Gary C. Cambill, "Hezbollah's Strategic Rocket Arsenal," *Middle East Intelligence Bulletin*, November-December 2002. The Hizbullah quote came from AFP, May 28, 2008.

31. "Former Hizbullah Sec-Gen: Hizbullah Is an Integral Part of Iranian Intelligence," *MEMRI*, Special Dispatch—No. 1431, January 19, 2007.

32. These incidents are summarized by the official Israeli inquiry into the Second Lebanon War. See *Winnograd Commission Partial Report*, (Jerusalem: State of Israel, 2007), 41 and 42.

33. Amos Harel and Avi Issacharoff, *34 Days: Israel, Hezbollah, and the War in Lebanon* (New York: Palgrave Macmillan, 2008), 91.

34. Ibid.

35. Ze'ev Schiff, "Israel's War With Iran," *Foreign Affairs*, November/December 2006, 27.

36. "January 2006 Prediction by Arab Journalist Raghida Dergham: Iran and Syria Will Try to Use Hizbullah to Draw Israel Into a War" *MEMRI*, Special Dispatch—No. 1272, August 30, 2006.

37. "Iranian Regime Tries to Deny a Report About the July 27 Meeting in Damascus Between Iranian Supreme National Council Secretary Larijani and Hizbullah Leader Nasrallah," *MEMRI*, Special Dispatch—No. 1228, August 2, 2006.

38. "Using the Quds Force of the Revolutionary Guards as the Main Tool to Export the Revolution Beyond the Borders of Iran," Intelligence and Terrorism Information Center at the Israel Intelligence Heritage & Commemoration Center (IICC), April 2, 2007.

39. Ibid.

40. UN Security Council, "Report of the Secretary-General on the Implementation of Security Council Resolution 1701 (2006)," February 28, 2008.

41. Tova Lazaroff and Yaakov Katz, "Barak: IDF Ops Could Lead to War," *Jerusalem Post*, February 11, 2008.

42. Amos Harel, "Iran Assuming Mughniyeh Role inside Hezbollah," *Haaretz*, February 26, 2009.

43. "Senior Iranian Commander Leads Hezbollah Drill in Southern Lebanon," *Haaretz*/Channel 10, December 3, 2008.

44. Shmuel Bar (Project Leader), *When Green Meets Black: Relations Between a Shiite Patron and Its Sunni Protégé Organizations* (Herzliya: Lauder School of Government, 2008), 30.

45. Dore Gold, "Israel's War to Halt Palestinian Rocket Attacks," Jerusalem Issue Brief, Jerusalem Center for Public Affairs, March 3, 2008.

46. "Using the Quds Force," Op. Cit.

47. Maj.-Gen. Yoav Galant, "The Strategic Challenge of Gaza," Jerusalem Issue Brief, Jerusalem Center for Public Affairs, April 19, 2007.

48. Lt. Gen. (ret.) Moshe Yaalon, "Iran's Race for Regional Supremacy," in Dan Diker, ed. *Iran's Race for Regional Supremacy: Strategic Implications for the Middle East* (Jerusalem: Jerusalem Center for Public Affairs, 2008), 9. See also: "Iran 'Played Role' in Gaza Takeover," *al-Jazeera*, June 24, 2007.

49. Shmuel Bar, *When Green Meets Black*, 20.

50. The Palestinian official was al-Tayyeb Abd al-Rahim, the secretary-general of the Palestinian Authority Presidency. His comments were reported in *al-Hayat al-Jadida*, January 1, 2009. See: Y. Carmon, Y. Yehoshua, A. Savyon, and H. Migron, "And Escalating Regional Cold War—Part I: The 2009 Gaza War," MEMRI, Inquiry and Analysis—No. 492, February 2, 2009. Endnote 1.

51. "Egypt Attacks Iran and Allies in Arab World," *Reuters*, January 28, 2009.

52. Khaled Abu Toameh, "Iran Warns Hamas Not to Accept Truce," *Jerusalem Post*, January 12, 2009.

53. Alex Fishman, "Tehran Aims to Create Gaza Missile Base That Can Cover the Whole of Central Israel," Ynet, April, 2, 2009.

54. Avi Issacharoff, "Hamas Dismisses Commanders on Iran Order," *Haaretz*, June 5, 2009.

55. Robin Wright, "Options for the U.S. Limited as Mideast Crises Spread," *Washington Post*, July 13, 2006.

56. Amos Harel and Avi Issacharoff, *34 Days*, 103.

57. Ibid.

58. "Crisis in the Region: Who Is Responsible?" Saudi-US Relations Information Service, July 18, 2006.

59. "Hizbullah Secretary-General Nasrallah Urges Egyptian Officers to Rebel Against Their Regime's Policies," *MEMRI*, Special Dispatch—No. 2172, January 2, 2009.

60. Amr Hamzawy and Dina Bishara, *Islamist Movements in the Arab World and the 2006 Lebanon War* (Washington, D.C.: Carnegie Endowment for International Peace, 2006), 7.

61. For an excellent compellation of these statements see Daniel Pipes, "Saudis Condemn Hamas and Hizbullah," *Daniel Pipes Blog*, July 13, 2006—Updated, December 3, 2006.

62. Ibid.

63. "Revered Saudi Cleric Denounces Shi'ites as Infidels," *Reuters*, December 29, 2006.

64. Daniel Pipes, Op. Cit. The Iranian quote comes originally from *MEMRI*.

65. Tariq Alhomayed, "A Second Balfour Declaration?" *al-Sharq al-Awsat*, December 12, 2008.

66. David E. Sanger, *The Inheritance: The World Obama Confronts and the Challenges to American Power* (New York: Harmony Books, 2009), 5.

67. Office of the Director of National Intelligence, *Iran: Nuclear Intentions and Capabilities* (Washington: Director of National Intelligence, 2007).

68. Michael S. Goodman and Wyn Q. Bowen, "Behind Iran's Nuclear 'Halt,'" *Bulletin of the Atomic Scientists*, February 19, 2008.

69. John R. Bolton, "The Flaws in the Iran Report," *Reflections on the National Intelligence Estimate* (Washington: American Enterprise Institute, 2007).

70. Robert McMahon, ed. "Negroponte Says China Mostly 'In Sync' with U.S. on Iran," Council on Foreign Relations, February 4, 2008.

71. Mark Mazzetti, "U.S. Says Iran Ended Atomic Arms Work," *The New York Times*, December 3, 2007; available online at: http://www.nytimes.com/2007/12/03/world/middleeast/03cnd-iran.html

72. Bryan Bender and Farah Stockman, "US Finds No Iran Bomb Program," *The Boston Globe*, December 4, 2007; available online at: http://www.boston.com/news/world/articles/2007/12/04/us_finds_no_iran_bomb_program/.

73. Tim Shipman, Philip Sherwell and Carolynne Wheeler, "Britain: Iran 'Hoodwinked CIA Over Nuclear Plans," *Daily Telegraph*, December 10, 2007.

74. Ibid.

75. Katrin Bennhold, "Despite Report, France and Germany Keep Pressure on Iran," *The New York Times*, December 7, 2007.

76. Maj.-Gen. (ret.) Aharon Zeevi Farkash, Maj.-Gen. (ret.) Yaakov Amidror, Brig.-Gen. (ret.) Yossi Kuperwasser, "The U.S. National Intelligence Estimate on Iran and its Aftermath; A Roundtable of Israeli Experts," *Jerusalem Viewpoints*, Jerusalem Center for Public Affairs, March-April 2008.

77. Ibid.

78. Ibid.

79. Ibid.

80. Y. Yehoshua, I. Rapoport, Y. Mansharof, A. Savyon, and Y. Carmon, "The Collapse of the Saudi Sunni Bloc against Iran's Aspirations of Regional Hegemony in the Gulf," *MEMRI*, Inquiry and Analysis—No. 416, January 11, 2008.

81. Ibid.

82. Y. Carmon, Y. Yehoshua, A. Savyon, and H. Migron, "An Escalating Regional Cold War—Part I: The 2009 Gaza War," *MEMRI* Inquiry and Analysis—No. 492, February 2, 2009.

83. Y. Yehoshua, I. Rapoport, Y. Mansharof, A. Savyon, and Y. Carmon, Op. Cit.

84. Y. Mansharof, "Calls in Iran to Topple Egyptian, Saudi Regimes," *MEMRI*—Inquiry and Analysis—No. 479, December 12, 2008.

85. Ibid.

86. Ibid.

87. Ali Waked and Reuters, "Report: Hizbullah Cell in Egypt Smuggled Arms in Gaza," Ynetnews.com, April 9, 2009.

88. "Egypt State-Controlled Paper Denounces Hezbollah," *Reuters*, April, 12, 2009.

89. Julian Borger and Ewen MacAskill, Hopes for Peace Grow as Iran and US Hold First High-Level Talks for 30 Years,*The Guardian*, July 17, 2008.

90. UN P-5 + 1, Proposal to Iran by China, France, Germany, the Russian Federation, the United Kingdom, the United States of America and the European Union (Tehran: June 14, 2008).

91. "Iran Unmoved by Threats Over its Atomic Program," *The New York Times*, June 12, 2008.

92. Robin Wright, "Iran Appears to Warm To Diplomacy," *Washington Post,* July 2, 2008.

93. Glenn Kessler, "Iran and U.S. Signaling Chance of Deal," *The Washington Post*, July 17, 2008; available online at: http://www.washingtonpost.com/wp-dyn/content/article/2008/07/16/AR2008071600199.html.

94. Ibid.

95. Ibid.

96. "No Answer from Iran on Nuclear Proposals—Solana," Reuters, July 19, 2008.

97. Colum Lynch and Karen DeYoung, Iran Seeks Details on Nuclear Offer," *Washington Post*, August 16, 2008.

98. Borzou Daragahi, "Head of Nuclear Watchdog Calls Efforts Against Iran 'A Failure,'" *Los Angeles Times*, December 6, 2008.

CHAPTER 11

1. "Has Iran Won?" *The Economist*, January 31, 2008.

2. Brian Knowlton, "In Interview, Obama Talks of 'New Approach' to Iran," *The New York Times*, January 11, 2008.

3. "Interview Part 1: Obama Talks War on Terror, Iran and Pakistan," *The O'Reilly Factor*, FOX News, September 5, 2008.

4. Zbigniew Brzezinski and Robert M. Gates (Co-chairs), and Suzanne Maloney, Project Director, *Iran: Time for a New Approach* (New York: Council on Foreign Relations, 2004).

5. James A. Baker, III and Lee H. Hamilton (Co-chairs), *The Iraq Study Group: The Way Forward—A New Approach* (New York: Vintage Books, 2006).

6. Richard Dalton, ed. *Iran: Breaking the Nuclear Deadlock: A Chatham House Report* (London: Chatham House, 2008).

7. Joy Lo Dico, "Jimmy Carter Calls for US to Make Friends with Iran after 27 Years," *The Independent*, May 26, 2008.

8. Caral Marinucci, "Pelosi is Open to Iran Trip," *San Francisco Chronicle*, April 11, 2007.

9. Press Release of Senator Lugar, "Lugar Lays Out Foreign Policy Agenda for Next President," October 15, 2008; available online at: http://lugar.senate.gov.

10. For a useful breakdown of how the renewed interest in diplomacy, more generally, was being discussed in the United States see: Jakub Grygiel, "The Diplomacy Fallacy," *The American Interest*, May/June 2008.

11. "Obama Considering Iran Policy Shift," *Jerusalem Post*, April 14, 2009.

12. "CQ Transcript: Defense Secretary Gates on 'Fox News Sunday,'" March 29, 2009; available online at: www.cqpolitics.com.

13. Dennis Ross, "Iran: Talk Tough with Tehran," *Newsweek*, December 8, 2008.

14. U.S. Office of the Director of National Intelligence, *Iran: Nuclear Intentions and Capabilities*, November, 2007.

15. www.aftabnews.ir/vdcewz8v.jh8pvi9bbj.html, Translation by the Open Source Center, Director of National Intelligence.

16. BBC, "Iran and the West: Nuclear Confrontation," http://www.bbc.co.uk/programmes/b00hydcg.

17. President Barack Obama, "Videotaped Remarks By The President In Celebration Of Nowruz." The White House. March 20, 2009.

18. Jon Meacham, "A Highly Logical Approach" *Newsweek*, May 25, 2009.

19. "Ahmadinejad to West: You Are Weak, Your Hands Are Empty, And You Can't Force US to Do Anything," *MEMRI*, Special Dispatch—No. 2317, April 17, 2009.

20. See *Iran Early Bird*, April 17–19, 2009.

21. Tehran *Aftab-e Yazd* in Persian—reformist daily published in Tehran and Yazd; affiliated with the leftist Militant Clerics Society, translated by OSC (Open Source Center), U.S. Director of National Intelligence, http://www.aftabnews.ir/vdcewz8v.jh8pvi9bbj.html.

22. William Broad and David E. Sanger, "Iran Has More Enriched Uranium Than Thought," *The New York Times*, February 20, 2009. See also: International Atomic Energy Agency, "Implementation of the NPT Safeguards Agreement and Relevant Provisions of Security Council Resolutions 1737 (2006), 1747 (2007), 1803 (2008), and 1835 (2008) in the Islamic Republic of Iran," February 19, 2009.

23. Borzou Daragahi, "Iran Nuclear Program Advancing, U.N. Agency Says," *Los Angeles Times*, June 6, 2009.

24. Jay Solomon, "Adm. Mullen Says Iran Has Material for Bomb," *Wall Street Journal*, March 2, 2009.

25. Senators Daniel Coats and Charles Ross, Co-Chairs, Michael Makovsky, Project Director, *Meeting the Challenge: U.S. Policy Toward Iranian Nuclear Development* (Washington: The Bipartisan Policy Center, 2008), 40. The calculations of the amount of low-enriched uranium that would be needed to produce the minimally required amount of highly-enriched uranium for an atomic bomb come from a study commissioned by Greg Jones, "Iran's Centrifuge Enrichment Program as a Source of Fissile Material for Nuclear Weapons." This analysis also explains how increasing the number of centrifuges would shorten the production time for the manufacture of weapons-grade uranium, as explained in the paragraph that follows.

26. U. S. Senate, Committee on Foreign Relations, *Iran: Where We Are Today* (Washington: U.S. Government Printing Office, May 4, 2009), 2.

27. Statement by Mohammed Saedi, Deputy Head of Atomic Energy Agency of Iran, "ELBaradei: Times for Iran to Suspend Enrichment," VOA News, April 12, 2006.

28. Michael Herzog, "The Ticking Clock toward a Nuclear Iran," Policy Watch #997, May 26, 2005. The Washington Institute for Near East Policy.

29. David E. Sanger, *The Inheritance: The World Obama Confronts and the Challenges to American Power* (New York: Harmony Books, 2009), 6.

30. "Iranian Daily: 'The Intelligence That the West Currently Has on Iran's Nuclear Program Is Limited to the Sites Accessible to IAEA Inspectors—And More Than That They Do Not Know," *MEMRI*, Special Dispatch—No. 1727. September 27, 2007.

31. Matthew A. Levitt, "Iranian State Sponsorship of Terror: Threatening U.S. Security, Global Stability, and Regional Peace," Joint Hearing of the Committee of International Relations, Subcommittee on the Middle East and Central Asia, and the Subcommittee on International Terrorism and Non-proliferation, U.S. House of Representatives, February 16, 2005.

32. Benjamin Weiser, "S.I. Man Gets Prison Term for Aid to Hezbollah TV," *The New York Times*, April 23, 2009.

33. Tom Diaz and Barbara Newman, *Lightening Out of Lebanon: Hezbollah Terrorists on American Soil* (New York: Ballantine Books, 2005), 69.

34. "Iran Increases Its Political and Economic Presence in Latin America," Intelligence and Terrorism Information Center at the Israel Intelligence Heritage & Commemoration Center," April 8, 2009 (Hebrew Edition), 36.

35. Al Pessin, "US Military Commander Warns of Iran-Hezbollah Influence in Latin America," VOA News, March 17, 2009.

36. Ibid.

37. AFP, "U.S. fears 'Disastrous' Links in Latin America with Islamic Militants," January 16, 2008.

38. "Colombia Ties Drug Ring to Hezbollah," Reuters, October 22, 2008.

39. "U.S. Stops Iranian Project in Colombia," ABC News, February 6, 2002.

40. Diaz and Newman, 14, 127.

41. Chris Kraul and Sebastian Rotella, "Fears of a Hezbollah Presence in Venezuela," *Los Angeles Times*, August 27, 2008.

42. "Iran Increases Its Political and Economic Presence in Latin America," Intelligence and Terrorism Information Center at the Israel Intelligence Heritage & Commemoration Center," Op. Cit., 18.

43. Ibid.

44. Dennis C. Blair, Director of National Intelligence, *Annual Threat Assessment of the Intelligence Community for the Senate Select Committee on Intelligence*, February 12, 2009, p. 32.

45. Mark Lavie, "Israeli Document: Venezuela Sends Uranium to Iran," AP-*Washington Post*, May 25, 2009.

46. "Iran Increases Its Political and Economic Presence in Latin America," *Israel News*, April 19, 2009, p. 16.

47. Paul Richter, "Clinton Sees China, Iran Inroads in Latin America," *Los Angeles Times*, May 2, 2009.

48. Sara A. Carter, "Exclusive: Hezbollah Uses Mexican Drug Routes into U.S.," *Washington Times*, March 27, 2009.

49. Pauline Arrillaga and Olga R. Rodriguez, "The Terror-Immigration Connection," AP/ MSNBC, July 3, 2005.

50. Roee Nahmias, "Expert: Hamas, Hizbullah Cells May Be Active in Mexico," YNET, November 2, 2007.

51. "Iran Increases Its Political and Economic Presence in Latin America," *Israel News*, April 19, 2009, 34.

52. Matthew Levitt, "Hezbollah: Narco-Islamism," Middle East Strategy at Harvard, March 22, 2009.

53. Ibid.

54. Harris Whitbeck and Ingrid Arneson, "Sources: Terrorists Find Haven in South America," CNN, November 7, 2001.

55. Andrew Beatty, "Former US Security Chief Warns on Hezbollah," Agence France Presse, July 16, 2009.

56. "Iran Could Strike the U.S. by 2015, U.S. Official Says," FOX News, October 3, 2007.

57. Anthony Cordesman and Khalid R. Al-Rodhan, *Gulf Military Forces in an Era of Asymmetic Wars*, (New York: Praeger, 2006), 336

58. "New IRGC Commander: Asymmetrical Warfare IS Out Strategy for Dealing with Enemy's Considerable Capabilities," *MEMRI* Special Dispatch—No. 1716, September 19. 2007.

59. Ibid.

60. Amir Taheri, *The Persian Night: Iran Under the Khomeinist Revolution* (New York: Encounter Books, 2009), 209.

61. Greg Bruno, "Iran and the Future of Afghanistan," The Council on Foreign Relations, March 30, 2009.

62. Robin Wright, "Iranian Arms Destined for Taliban Seized in Afghanistan, Official Say," *Washington Post*, September 16, 2007.

63. Andrew Gray, "U.S., Iran share interests in Afghanistan: Petraeus," Reuters, January 8, 2009; available online at: http://www.reuters.com/article/topNews/idUSTRE5080A720090109.

64. Ibid.

65. Michael Smith, "Missile Threat to British Troops," *The Sunday Times*, March 1, 2009.

66. Ibid.

67. Lieutenant General Michael D. Maples, U.S. Army, Director, Defense Intelligence Agency, "Annual Threat Assessment," Statement before the Committee on Armed Services, United States Senate, March 10, 2009.

68. "Interrogated Hamas Operatives Say They Smuggled Weapons from Iraq into Jordan at the Order of Hamas Leaders in Syria," Intelligence and Terrorism Information Center at the Center for Special Studies (C.S.S.), May 5, 2006.

69. Peter Crail, "U.S. Shares Information on NK-Syrian Nuclear Ties," Arms Control Association, May 2008, www.armsconrol.org.

70. Siegfried S. Hecker and William Liou, "Dangerous Dealings: North Korea's Nuclear Capabilities and the Threat of Export to Iran," *Arms Control Today*, March 2007.

71. David Albright and Paul Brannan, "The North Korea Plutonium Stock, February 2007," Institute for Science and International Security, February 20, 2007.

72. Dr. Liam Fox MP, *Nuclear Terror: The Ultimate Threat* (London: 2007).

73. Chris Kraul, "Colombia Links Uranium to FARC Rebels," *Los Angeles Times*, March 27, 2008.

74. A similar scenario is considered in Gregory Giles, "Command-and-Control Challenges of an Iranian Nuclear Force," Patrick Clawson and Michael Eisenstadt, eds. *Deterring the Ayatollahs: Complications in Applying Cold War Strategy to Iran* (Washington: The Washington Institute for Near East Policy, 2007), 13. See also: Kori Schake and Judith S. Yaphe, *The Strategic Implications of a Nuclear-Armed Iran*, McNair Paper 64 (Washington: Institute for National Strategic Studies, National Defense University, 2007).

75. Dennis Ross, "A New Strategy on Iran," *Washington Post*, May 1, 2006.

76. See concluding chapter by Patrick Clawson and Michael Eisenstadt, in *Deterring the Ayatollahs*, 34.

77. Brig. Gen. (ret.) Yossi Kuperwasser, *Halting Iran's Nuclear Program: Iranian Vulnerabilities and western western Policy Options* (Jerusalem: Jerusalem Center for Public Affairs, 2007), 9.

78. Ed Morse and Michael Makovsky, "Over a Barrel," *The New Republic*, May 29, 2009.

79. Mark Dubowitz and Joshua D. Goodman, "Hit Iran Where it Hurts," *National Post*, April 16, 2009.

80. Daniel Goldstein, "U.S. Lawmakers Urge DOE Review of Vitol SPR Contract," *Platts*, March 2, 2009.

81. "Transcrpipt of second McCain, Obama debate," http://www.cnn.com/2008/POLITICS/10/07/presidential.debate.transcript/ (I am indebted to the Foundation for the Defense of Democracies for providing these quotes).

82. The White House, "Remarks by the President on a New Beginning," Cairo University, Cairo, Egypt, June 4, 2009.

83. Bryan Bender, "Obama Seeks Global Uranium Fuel Bank," *Boston Globe*, June 8, 2009.

84. Daniel Dombey, "Kerry Defends Tehran on Uranium," *Financial Times*, June 11, 2009.

85. "North Korea Expelling IAEA Inspectors," CNN, December 27, 2002. John Bolton, *Surrender Is Not an Option* (New York: Threshold Editions, 2007), 121.

86. Con Coughlin, "Iran 'Is Seeking N Korea's Nuclear Expertise,'" *Daily Telegraph*, April 17, 2007.

87. Bret Stephens, "The Axis of Evil, Again," *Wall Street Journal*, June 2, 2009.

88. David Albright and Jacqueline Shire with Paul Brannan and Andrea Scheel, *Nuclear Iran: Not Inevitable* (Washington: Institute for Science and International Security, 2009), 11.

CHAPTER 12

1. Amir Taheri, "Tehran's Re-Election Fixers Script a 'Landslide' for Hate," *New York Post*, June 14, 2009.

2. Shmuel Bar, Rachel Machtiger, and Shmuel Bachar, "Iranian Nuclear Decision Under Ahmadinjad," (Herzliya: The Interdisciplinary Center, Lauder school of Government, Diplomacy, and Strategy, Institue for Policy and Strategy, 2008), 11.

3. *Ilaph*, June 11, 2009, http://www.elaph.com/Web/Politics/2009/6/450266.htm

4. Jeff Stein, "Mousavi, Celebrated in Iranian Protests, Was the Butcher of Beirut," Spy Talk, *CQ Politics*, June 22, 2009.

5. Amir Taheri, Iran's Clarifying Election, *Wall Street Journal*, June 16, 2009.

6. Nazila Fathi, "Iran's Top Leader Dashes Hopes for a Compromise," *New York TImes*, June 19, 2009.

7. Steven R. Ward, *Immortal: A Military History of Iran and its Armed Forces*, (Washington, DC: Georgetown University Press, 2009), 307.

8. Amir Taheri, *The Persian Night: Iran Under the Khomeinist Revolution* (New York: Encounter Books, 2009), 346.

9. Safa Haeri, "Iranian Intelligence Ministry Warns Against 'Velvet Revolution,'" Iran Press Service, July 5, 2006.

10. Amir Taheri, *The Persian Night*, 336.

11. Golnaz Esfandiari, "Warnings Hint at a Greater IRGC Role in Muzzling Critics," *Radio Free Europe/Radio Liberty*, October 5, 2007.

12. "The Moderate Camp in the Arab World: Lebanon's Election Results Spell Iran's Defeat," *MEMRI* Special Dispatch—No. 2419, June 23, 2009.

13. Barbara Slavin, "Exclusive: U.S. Contacted Iran's Ayatollah Before Election," *Washington Times,* June 24, 2009.

14. Ibid.

15. Helene Cooper, "Bit by Careful Bit, Obama Toughens Stance on Iran," *New York Times*, June 25, 2009.

16. Jeff Zeleny and Helene Cooper, "Obama Warns Against Direct Involvement by U.S. in Iran," *New York Times*, June 16, 2009.

17. Jay Solomon, Jonathan Weisman, and Yochi J. Dreazen, "Obama Rips Iran in Tactical Shift," *Wall Street Journal*, June 24, 2009.

18. Barbara Starr, "Iranian Military Conducts 'Routine Aerial Exercises," CNN, June 23, 2009.

19. "Iran Carries Out Second Stage of Air Maneuver," *Tehran Times*, June 24, 2009.

20. Joshua Teitelbaum, *What Iranian Leaders Really Say About Doing Away With Israel: A Refutation of the Campaign to Excuse Ahamadinejad's Incitement to Genocide* (Jerusalem: Jerusalem Center for Public Affairs, 2008), 15.

21. Ibid., 17.

22. Amir Taheri, *The Persian Night*, 310. Yossi Verter, "Aznar: Khamenei Said in 2001 Iran Aimed 'To Set Israel Alight'" *Haaretz*, March 15, 2006.

23. Ibid.

24. Hilary Leila Krieger, "Hizbullah Could Hit US Harder than al-Qaida," *Jerusalem Post*, June 26, 2009.

Index

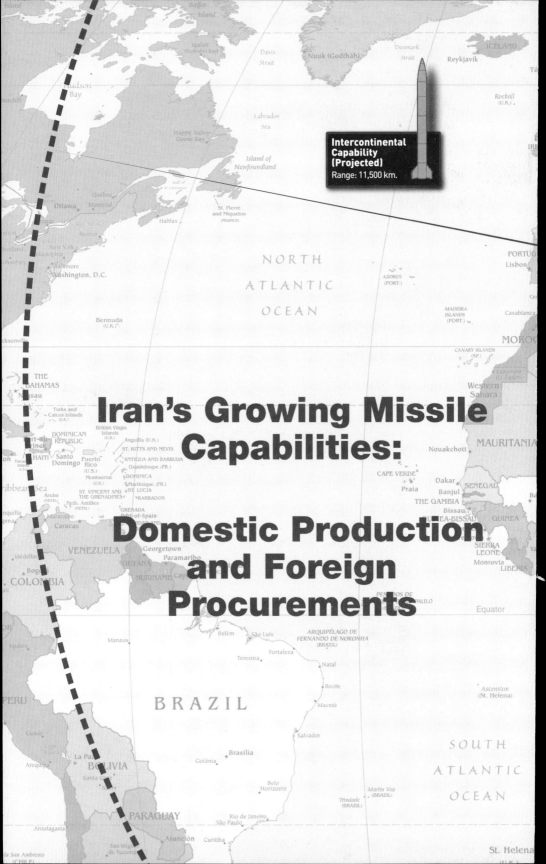

Intercontinental
Capability
(Projected)
Range: 11,500 km.

Iran's Growing Missile Capabilities:

Domestic Production and Foreign Procurements